Edward Luce is a graduate from Oxford University in Politics, Philosophy and Economics. He also completed postgraduate studies in newspaper journalism from City University London. He has worked for the *Financial Times* since 1995 with a one-year break to work in Washington, DC as the speechwriter to Larry Summers, the final US Treasury Secretary of the Clinton administration. He was the *FT*'s South Asia bureau chief based in New Delhi between 2001 and 2005 and is now based in Washington, DC as the *FT*'s Washington bureau chief.

'*In Spite of the Gods* is some way ahead of the game. Luce is a highly perceptive and intelligent writer and, unusually, he understands how India works' *Sunday Times*

'Without question the best book yet written on the New India: witty, clear and accessible yet minutely researched and confidently authoritative. Edward Luce has proved himself an affectionate and unusually perceptive observer of the Indian scene' William Dalrymple

'Not only fun to read, it is also a deeply insightful account of contemporary India. Based on the author's rare combination of intimacy and detachment, the book can serve, remarkably enough, both as a fine introduction for unacquainted outsiders and as a mature scrutiny that is bound to stimulate insiders' Professor Amartya Sen, winner of the Nobel Prize in Economics

'*In Spite of the Gods* is an exceptional book, and that's because its author is unusual: he's a foreigner who gets India' *Time*

'A wonderfully engaging portrait of India, written with that mixture of affection and exasperation people feel for something they love in spite of everything they know about it' *Sunday Telegraph*

'A brilliantly observant book' *The Times*

'Thoughtful and thorough . . . Luce is better placed than most to write this book [and] his combination of closeness and distance lends him objectivity and credibility' Soumya Bhattacharya, *Observer*

'A brilliant, bracingly uncondescending introduction to the new India in its many-layered modernity, written with perceptiveness, humour and real respect' *Scotsman*

'This socio-historical overview of India is immediately readable and consistently beguiling . . . *In Spite of the Gods* is an unalloyed treat, rich in information, stimulation and humour. Believe the blurb' *Irish Examiner*

'Luce delivers genuine insight and revealing observations, among the exhaustive facts, interviews and history' Rahul Verma, *Metro*

IN SPITE OF THE GODS

THE STRANGE RISE OF MODERN INDIA

EDWARD LUCE

ABACUS

ABACUS

First published in Great Britain in 2006 by Little, Brown
This paperback edition published in 2007 by Abacus
Reprinted 2007

A CIP catalogue record for this book
is available from the British Library.

ISBN 978-0-349-11874-1

Papers used by Abacus are natural, recyclable products made from
wood grown in sustainable forests and certified in accordance with
the rules of the Forest Stewardship Council.

Typeset in Goudy by M Rules
Printed and bound in Great Britain by
Clays Ltd, St Ives plc
Paper supplied by Hellefoss AS, Norway

Abacus
An imprint of
Little, Brown Book Group
Brettenham House
Lancaster Place
London WC2E 7EN

A Member of the Hachette Livre Group of Companies

www.littlebrown.co.uk

CONTENTS

PREFACE

This book is not about a love affair with the culture and antiquities of India. I have read too many paeans to India by foreigners to have any thoughts of adding to that extensive list. It is about the changing political economy and society of a country whose future will increasingly affect the rest of the world. When reporting on India for the *Financial Times* I usually adhered to the detached and impersonal style that journalists follow. But a book is different and much of what follows is in the first person. Some of what is contained in these pages is of a critical nature, occasionally very critical. It is hard to observe and chronicle the workings of India's political, economic and legal systems without sometimes feeling outrage at the squandering of life opportunities for the hundreds of millions of Indians who still live in poverty. Their opportunities are improving, albeit not rapidly enough – but improving nevertheless. It is hard, too, not to feel frustration with the large numbers of foreigners and Indians who are still wont to see India through a purely spiritual lens. A lot is written about American and French exceptionalism (neither of which sanctifies poverty, it should be added). A lot more could still be written on the Indian variety.

Yet without my deep affection for – and fascination by – India I would never have written this book. Over the years and in the most unexpected ways, India has taught me as much about humanity in general as it has about itself. Although occasionally mystifying, India has always opened its doors to me and other inquiring outsiders. With amazingly few exceptions, Indians have been unreservedly kind, open, hospitable and tolerant of the interrogations of an intrusive foreigner. Quite without meaning to do so, India has also taught me how inhospitable we in the west – and especially in Britain – can often be. I hope the reader will recognise that there is no contradiction between criticism and affection. That way the reader will more easily chime with the book's anticipation of India's rise to a much more significant global role in the first few decades of the twenty-first century.

In five years of travelling around India, observing events and interviewing people – four years as bureau chief for the *Financial Times* and one for this book – I can think of only a handful of occasions when I was denied access to somebody or to some information that I was seeking. Since I have interviewed many hundreds of Indians, some of them on many occasions, it would take a chapter simply to list them. So I will confine mention to a few people who have been consistently helpful, many of whom have become firm friends. With a few exceptions, I have omitted the names of politicians and businessmen, since availability to journalists is a normal part of their professional lives. I would like to express my profound thanks to: Shankar Acharya, Swami Agnivesh, Montek and Isher Ahluwalia, Mani Shankar Aiyar, M. J. Akbar, Sohail Akbar (and his delightful parents in Allahabad), Anil Ambani, Kanti Bajpai, Sanjaya Baru, Surjit Bhalla, Kiran Bhatty and Aslam Khan ('Karen and Islam'), Jagdish Bhagwati, Uday Bhaskar, Rahul Bedi, Farhan Bokhari, Michael and Jenny Carter, Ram Chandra ('Golu'), Vikram Chandra, Vijay Chautiawale, Ashok Chowgule, Stephen P. Cohen, Tarun Das, Nikhil Dey, Jean Dreze, Gordon Duguid, Verghese George, Sagarika Ghosh, Omkar Goswami, Dipankar and Mala Gupta, Shekhar Gupta, Swapan Das Gupta, David Housego, Tony Jesudasan, Prem Shankar Jha, Vijay Kelkar, Sunil Khilnani, Sudheendra Kulkarni, Hanif Lakdawala, Ram Madhav, Moni Malhoutra, Kamal M, Harsh Mander, Ashok

Mehta, Pratap Bhanu Mehta, Vinod Mehta, Murli Menon, Khozem Merchant and Malavika Sanghvi, Anjali Mody, Raja Mohan, Jayaprakash Narain, Sunita Narain, Kishan Negi, Nandan Nilekani, T. N. Ninan, Udit Raj, N. and Mariam Ram, Mahesh Rangarajan, Aruna Roy, Raman Roy, Rajdeep Sardesai, Navtej Sarna, Tesi Schaffer, Suhel Seth, Jyotirmaya Sharma, Ajai and Sonia Shukla, N. K. Singh, Mala and Tejbir Singh, Arun Singh, Ashley Tellis, Karan Thapar, Ashutosh Varshney and George Verghese.

I would like to underline my thanks to the following people who very kindly took the time to read this manuscript in full and correct errors of fact, judgement and grammar. These were Michael Arthur, Suman Bery, Ramachandra Guha, Andrew Davis and Jackie Shorey, and Krishna Guha. Throughout the process of writing and researching this book, the help, expertise and encouragement of Natasha Fairweather, my agent at A. P. Watt, was always indispensable. It was also a great pleasure and an intellectual stimulation to work with Tim Whiting and Steve Guise, my editors at Little, Brown in London and Kris Puopolo, my editor at Doubleday in New York. In addition, I would like to express my gratitude to the *Financial Times*, which, apart from allowing me a year's leave of absence to research and write this book, is the ideal employer for a foreign correspondent. No other newspaper permits its reporters such autonomy and latitude in pursuing their interests. The space it makes available for serious stories about India continues to mark it out from most other publications. Not once did the FT attempt to impose any preconceptions on what I wrote. Of very few other newspapers would this description consistently hold true.

My acknowledgements conclude with Aparna and Prahlad Basu, my parents-in-law, whose encouragement of my interest in India was equalled only by the insights and experience they were always ready to share. Aparna is a historian and was a professor at Delhi University for many years. Prahlad was – and is – a senior civil servant in New Delhi. Not many foreign correspondents (or sons-in-law) get this kind of assistance. I would also like to thank my own parents, Rose and Richard, who bear the heroic distinction of having read everything I have ever written, including – I subsequently found out – the diaries that I had clearly marked Do Not Read which I kept as a teenager. Their unquestioning support is one of the reasons I am doing what I want to do in life. This book is dedicated partly to them. The other half of the dedication is to Priya, my wife, whose patience with my eccentric behaviour during the course of this book snapped only once or twice, but whose love has always been unwavering. Although she does not agree with all of my views, discussing them with Priya has helped me to clarify and enrich them. She is my victim and occasionally my culprit. Priya is also in many ways a cause of this book.

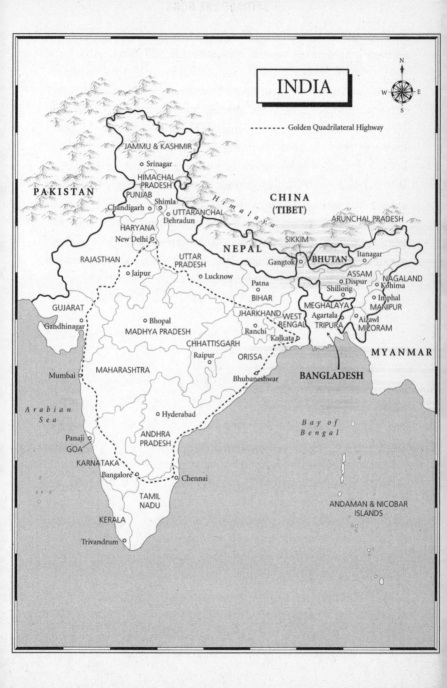

INTRODUCTION

To a western observer our civilisation appears as all metaphysics,
as to a deaf man piano playing appears to be mere movements of
fingers and no music.

Rabindranath Tagore, perhaps India's greatest poet, who
won the Nobel Prize for literature in 1913

I had been living in India more than four years when I met André,
a sixty-three-year-old Frenchman with a greying ponytail and a
passion for Vedantic philosophy. But it felt as though we had met
on many previous occasions. I was on a short visit to Auroville, a
town in south India founded in 1968 by Mira Alfassa, a nonage-
narian Frenchwoman whom everybody calls Mother. She had
named the town after Sri Aurobindo, one of India's most celebrated spiritual leaders, whose life's journey – from student years at
Cambridge to underground activism against British colonial rule
and finally incarnating as a teacher-savant in a charming corner of
peninsular India – merits a book or two in itself. Mother, André
told me, had 'departed her body' in 1973, twenty-three years after
Sri Aurobindo but, fortunately for the questing Frenchman, several months after he had arrived in Auroville.

Since André had moved to Auroville, the town – really an
extended ashram – had grown to include several thousand people,
most of whom, like the Frenchman, were westerners who had
come in search of the elixir of Indian philosophy. Most of them
accepted, like André, that India was special among nations. It
possessed a moral and spiritual force that was unique. India, he

said, was the key to the survival of the human race. I had come to find out what it was about India that gave rise to such faith. 'When you are living in the west, in Europe, you feel completely lost,' said André, who had welcomed me into his spacious white-washed home. We were sipping hibiscus juice. 'In the west you have to belong to society and follow a certain pattern. You are supposed to get a house, a career and the whole of life is oriented towards money. India is not like that. India is a unique country,' he emphasised, to the agreement of the others present. 'Without India, the world is doomed to the poverty of materialism.'

André was born during the Second World War and lived an unexceptional early life apart from an unpleasant stint as a soldier in Algeria during the insurgency against French rule. Then, one afternoon in Paris, he heard there was a conference on Auroville. Having already picked up a copy of the Bhagavad Gita, probably the most widely cited book in Hinduism, André already had some idea of what Indian philosophy might entail. Soon afterwards he left for India. Up to this stage André's account was straightfor-ward, but he had not explained what it was that drew him to the Gita or India in the first place. 'It seems to me obvious why – I do not see why anybody should have difficulty understanding it,' André said, although not unkindly. 'India has thousands and thousands of years of practice at harmonising differences and pen-etrating to the unity beyond. There is an essence to India that other countries do not have, which tells you that behind the diversity of life there is a spiritual reality called unity.' I must have seemed nonplussed, since André saw the need to elaborate. 'The human race today is in a global crisis that only India can solve by showing the way to super-consciousness, by explaining reincarna-tion and the unity of all things,' he said. 'No other country would accept Auroville. It would never survive in the west – they would turn it into a cult.'

Mother wanted Auroville to be much more than a cult. But it is hard to get beyond all the hagiographical accounts to a sense of what she was really like. She left behind a lifetime's worth of Delphic utterances. Born in Paris in 1878 to a Turkish father and an Egyptian mother, Mira Alfassa had as a child demonstrated a tendency to 'commune with nature'. She had also been able to leap great distances and could 'talk with fairies and beings from the world hidden behind ours'.[1] As a young woman, Mira embarked on a restless journey across different countries and many cultures in search of the key to understanding human existence. Finally, in 1916, she moved to India and met Sri Aurobindo, who provided her with the answers. Together they launched a new spiritual movement. Its objective was to teach people that India would be the vehicle that would move the human race to a higher consciousness. They called this 'supramentalism'. There were other such movements in India, and other Mother-type figures. But the Aurobindo ashram struck deeper roots.

Before meeting André, I had visited the Matrimandir (Mother Temple) – a vast elevated globe, about 150 feet in diameter and covered in petal-like golden discs. It was a peculiar sight that prompted thoughts of a spaceship that had been made in Hollywood but had somehow landed in the tropics. In the large clearing around the temple there must have been twenty or thirty people, spread out at polite distances from each other, doing an assortment of yogic stretches under a large banyan tree in the fading light of the day. Most of them were white. One or two might even have been from Los Angeles. Auroville's two or three thousand inhabitants, most of whom live in similar style to André, come from all over the world, as a brief glance at its telephone book makes clear – names from Russia, South Korea, Latin America, Japan and Europe were there in strength. My guide, Manob Tagore, a soft-spoken Bengali and one of the most delightful people one could hope to meet, told me there were fewer Indians than you might deduce from leafing through the directory, since many of the westerners had adopted Indian names. Manob told me that as a child he would be taken to see Mother. 'She always seemed very calm and that made me feel calm,' he said. 'That is what I most remember.'

André asked me to explain who I was and what I wanted to ask him. I said I was a British journalist who had lived in India for several years and that my wife, Priya, was Indian. I wanted to know why India exerted such a powerful spiritual pull on so many foreigners, since it had not had that effect on me. What I did not say was that I felt India had laboured too long under the burden of spiritual greatness that westerners have for centuries thrust upon it and which Indians had themselves got into the habit of picking up and sending back (with a cherry on top). Over the centuries, and particularly during the era of British colonial rule and its aftermath, many Indians endorsed in one form or another the view that India was a uniquely metaphysical civilisation. To most Indians this was certainly preferable as a self-image to the belittlement that was doled out by many, although not all, of India's colonial rulers. Lord Macaulay, who authored India's first national penal code, infamously wrote that the entire corpus of Indian philosophy and literature was not worth a single bookshelf of western writing. Even worse, but sadly not atypical, Winston Churchill said India 'was a beastly country with a beastly religion' and that it was 'no more a country than the Equator'.[2]

Conversely, and from an equally emphatic but more deeply rooted tradition, André Malraux, the French novelist, wrote: 'Remote from ourselves in dream and in time, India belongs to the Ancient Orient of our soul.'[3] Again not untypically, Arthur Schopenhauer, the German philosopher, said the Christian New Testament must have come from India since it had the gentlest civilisation known to mankind.[4] Given a choice between Macaulay and Malraux, or between Churchill and Schopenhauer, one would naturally choose Malraux and Schopenhauer. And although the west has also produced many balanced and scholarly assessments of India over the past 250 years, the view of most ordinary westerners has been tinged with either the dismissive or the romantic (as many still are). Much of India latched on to the romantic. Amartya Sen, India's Nobel prize-winning economist, wrote: 'The European exoticists' interpretations and praise found in India an army of appreciative listeners, who were particularly welcoming given their badly damaged self-confidence resulting from colonial domination.' Nor was such an approach confined to Europeans or to the distant past. On arriving at Harvard University in the late 1980s, Dr Sen found that every single book on India in the famous 'Harvard Coop' bookstore was kept in the section called 'Religions'.[5]

André would have approved of this. But the question I most wanted to ask him was whether his spiritual view of India was qualified by the existence of so much poverty in India. No visitor to India can fail to notice the juxtaposition of great human deprivation with its deeply religious culture. In India the sacred and the profane always seem to be linked. Some Indian philosophers have justified poverty as a consequence of the actions the poor committed in their past lives. The doctrine of reincarnation, it seems, makes it easier to overlook the squalor of the here and now. For some it even provides a moral underpinning to poverty. Did André not feel affected by the poverty he saw all around him? He looked at me with mild exasperation. 'India is an unbelievably wealthy country because India alone understands the futility of materialism,' he pronounced. He re-emphasised this point. He must have guessed what I was thinking. Nowadays in India there is also an increasingly visible cult of wealth. Half the country seems to be in pursuit of it. 'If India is now acquiring all the TV channels and the mobile phones and trappings of modern living, then it will not misuse them or become intoxicated,' he said. 'It does not worry me. This is India.'

What André put forward could not be dismissed as the eccentric musings of a hippie or the ravings of a cult follower. The

Frenchman, who had clearly engaged with the complexities of the Rig Veda, the Upanishads and much else besides in the multi-storeyed library of Hinduism, was not a hippie and did not – in the sense most westerners would understand it – belong to a 'cult', with its undertones of fanaticism, days of judgement and orgiastic misjudgements. Most Aurovillians, as they call themselves, neither drink alcohol nor smoke marijuana. Equally, they are not required to sign on to any defined set of beliefs or creed. What they would all agree on, and what large numbers of educated and uneducated Indians alike would also affirm, is the unique philosophical and moral importance of India to the future of the world.

Although Auroville is mostly populated by foreigners, its sentiments are common in contemporary India. By the same token, large chunks of what André said, particularly regarding India's other-worldliness, would pass uncontroversially at many a dinner party in Notting Hill, Montparnasse or Beverly Hills. In short, a spirit of romance continues to guide the perceptions both of outsiders and of many Indians themselves. Indeed, so deeply embedded is other-worldliness in our conventional images, symbols and vocabulary of India that those who consciously reject it are sometimes its unwitting promoters.

When we were leaving, André put his arm around me and said that in spite of my nationality he still liked me. Most British he disliked, he said apologetically, because of what they had done to India, for the fact that they always did things differently, like driving on the left and refusing to join the European Monetary Union, and because they always acted so superior. 'India will take the world to a higher plane,' he said. 'Everybody should understand that, even the British.'

Powerful new images have emerged of India in the last decade or so, fed mostly by its success in information technology and offshore call centres, the growing reach of Bollywood abroad – popularised in part by the increasing wealth and visibility of

Indian communities in the US, the UK and elsewhere – and by India's much-analysed nuclear weapons programme, which was first openly declared in 1998. In the same way that viewing India through a purely religious lens often distorts one's view of the country – and can lead to a basic misreading of what is happening – these new images can also mislead. India's economy is changing rapidly by previous standards. But the nature and scope of the changes are sometimes exaggerated. Indians themselves have got into a habit of counting their chickens before they are hatched. In recent years it has become commonplace in India to talk of the country as being on the verge of superpower status.

There is another way of viewing India that is perhaps more representative, and certainly more illuminating: through its deep-seated and dynamic culture of politics. In the late 1990s Rupert Murdoch visited India to explore launching satellite and cable joint-venture operations in the country's growing English-language market. After meeting all the government ministers in New Delhi, he flew to Mumbai, India's commercial capital, to meet Dhirubhai Ambani, the owner of Reliance Industries, India's largest private sector company. Ambani, who had a reputation as the shrewdest Indian businessmen of his generation, asked Murdoch who he had met in Delhi. Murdoch said he had seen the Prime Minister, the Finance Minister and others. 'Ah, you've met all the right people,' said Ambani, 'but if you want to get anywhere in India you must meet all the wrong people.'[6]

By this he meant the corrupt politicians (and probably their counterparts in the bureaucracy as well). In India if you are the wrong sort of person there is a reasonable chance you will end up in politics. But sometimes, perhaps a little less frequently, the right people do, too. While Bill Clinton kept reminding himself in the 1992 US presidential election that it was 'The economy, stupid', in India it is more a case of 'The politics, stupid'. Changes to India's economic and religious character cannot be fully grasped without an appreciation of its all-enveloping political culture and the role of the state.

My aim with this book is to provide an unsentimental evaluation of contemporary India against the backdrop of its widely expected ascent to great power status in the twenty-first century. The first chapter deals with the country's booming but peculiarly lopsided economy. I will then move on to an evaluation of India's ubiquitous state and its main political movements. An exploration of India's volatile relations with Pakistan and with its own Muslim minority is followed by an assessment of the country's triangular dance with the United States and China that will come to shape the world in the twenty-first century. Finally the book looks at India's experience of modernity and urbanisation, in which the country's religious values are proving versatile at reinventing themselves in contemporary form. I conclude by looking at the challenges India faces in sustaining its much-anticipated emergence over the coming years.

We start, in this introduction, by looking briefly at the enduring impact of the three most important figures of twentieth-century India: Mohandas K. Gandhi, Jawaharlal Nehru and Bhimrao Ambedkar. The continuing influence of these men on the country's character and direction arguably exceeds that of all of India's gods, software executives and nuclear scientists combined. Each of them wrestled with India's religious traditions. Two ultimately rejected them, whereas the third, Gandhi, harnessed the religious sensibilities of the masses to pursue the goal of Indian independence.

Three generations have passed since India gained freedom from British rule 'at the stroke of midnight' on 15 August 1947. Three generations have also passed since Gandhi, the spiritual and strategic leader of India's Congress Party-led freedom struggle, was assassinated en route to his evening prayers in New Delhi by Nathuram Godse, a right-wing Hindu fanatic, on 30 January 1948. Yet Gandhi, whose success in maintaining a mostly non-violent struggle against the British was an extraordinary feat of personal magnetism, continues both to divide Indians and to haunt their dreams. Great attention is still lavished on the transformative – and in some ways magical – effect that he had on ordinary people, in his capacity alone to bring the freedom struggle to the unlettered masses and to inspire their participation. It was Gandhi's ability to speak in the demotic that converted the freedom struggle from a club of London-educated lawyers in three-piece suits seeking 'English rule without the English' to a mass-based movement of all Indians.

Gandhi's role as a master of political strategy and tactics is well understood. However, less attention has been devoted to the influence of Gandhi's anti-materialist philosophy on India's development since 1947. In many ways this influence lingers on. Societies are like human beings: things that happen to them in their formative years tend to shape their decisions and character long after those events have lost their context. Yet if Gandhi returned to India today, he would be surprised by much of what he found. India in the early twenty-first century is an increasingly self-confident, materialistic and globalised place. In 1991 India sharply altered its economic course when it dismantled the tight system of controls and permits known as the 'Licence Raj' that it had adopted after independence. Since then, India has clearly been on the economic ascent, capturing an ever greater share of software markets in the United States and Europe and starting to develop a manufacturing sector that can compete in world markets. The country has also acquired the military trappings of an aspiring superpower: its elites openly debate when – not whether – India will develop intercontinental nuclear missiles. And its urban, English-speaking middle classes are soaking up consumer brand culture as if it were a new religion. If Gandhi had not been cremated, he would be turning in his grave.

At the same time, India today remains home to more than a

third of the world's chronically malnourished children (as defined by the United Nations), and has an average life expectancy and literacy rate that lag pitifully behind many other developing countries, most glaringly China. Roughly 750 million of India's 1.1 billion people continue to live in its 680,000 villages, almost half of which lack access to all-weather roads, and countless numbers of which are not in reach of effective primary healthcare centres or competent elementary schools. Almost half of India's women do not know how to read and write, and a large proportion of those who are technically literate can do little more than sign their name.

It is also a country where much of the elite continue to subscribe to Gandhi's belief – enunciated in the context of a freedom struggle that was seeking to broaden its appeal – that the village should remain the main building block of Indian society. Many others, including Nehru, India's first Prime Minister and Gandhi's protégé, argued against him. The debate continues today. India is slowly urbanising and it is hard to imagine what could stop the continuing expansion of its cities. But Gandhians continue to believe the village should occupy a holy place at the centre of Indian nationhood. Their influence continues to undermine attempts to provide better planning for the cities.

In a letter to Nehru, Gandhi wrote: 'I am convinced that if India is to attain true freedom, and through India the world also, then sooner or later the fact must be recognised that people will have to live in villages, not towns; in huts, not in palaces. Crores [tens of millions] of people will never be able to live in peace with each other in towns and palaces. They will then have no recourse but to resort to both violence and untruth.'[7] In *Hind Swaraj* (*Self-Rule for India*), Gandhi's most important book and probably the most widely cited today, he wrote: 'Remove his [the villager's] chronic poverty and his illiteracy and you have the finest specimen of what a cultural, cultivated free citizen should be . . . To observe morality is to attain mastery over our minds and passions. So doing, we know ourselves. If that definition be correct, then India, as so many writers have shown, has nothing to learn from anybody else.'

An element of Gandhi's cultural pride and some of his profound disdain for modernism should be seen in historical context as an effective tactical riposte to the insults that were often hurled at 'benighted India' by the colonialists, and as a way of raising the self-esteem of the masses. Gandhi was brilliantly equipped to do this. Born in the western Indian state of Gujarat, he qualified as a barrister in London in the 1890s. Before returning to India in 1913, he had already come to the world's attention in South Africa, where he had opposed the racial pass laws, and had suffered imprisonment in the process. It was there that he developed his strategy of non-violent civil disobedience that he was to use to such good effect in India.

But Gandhianism was not merely a tactic to bolster the freedom struggle. It was also a philosophy of how society should be organised and how people should live. It continues to influence the conscious and unconscious thoughts of much of India's intelligentsia today. To cite an enduring example: without an appreciation of Gandhi's impact on economic thinking, it is hard to explain why India has so badly disabled the ability of its textile sector to grow to a size more fitting with its potential. As any student of development knows, textile production has played a critical role in the industrialisation of most societies, from Britain in the eighteenth century to China in the twenty-first. Gandhi's legacy can be seen in India's continued tariff bias against synthetic fabrics in favour of cotton* (when the bulk of export demand is for the former), and in regulations that provide disincentives for textile companies to grow beyond 'cottage industry' size, which penalises commercial success and protects failure.

---

*Gandhi's use of the simple spinning wheel as a device to popularise knowledge of Britain's exploitative imperial tariff system served India's freedom struggle brilliantly. But, as Amartya Sen has pointed out, it made no sense as an economic policy after independence.

Some of these policies have been relaxed since India changed economic course in 1991, and many of those now resisting any further relaxation are doing so not on Gandhian grounds but because they represent vested interests that benefit from the status quo. But India's more dynamic competitors, notably China, do not have to wrestle with the legacy of someone who in many ways is a modern saint. It has been cited many times over the years but it is still well worth repeating what Sarojini Naidu, an Indian freedom fighter, once said of the Mahatma: 'It costs us a lot to keep Gandhiji in poverty.' That meter is still running. Yet there are important lessons from Gandhi about respect for the natural environment that India would do well to rediscover, as I shall argue later in the book.

Bhimrao Ambedkar is much less well known than Gandhi outside India. However, to millions of Indians he is an even more important figure. Ambedkar's bespectacled statues can be found in villages the length and breadth of this densely populated subcontinent. Unlike Gandhi, with whom he clashed repeatedly and often bitterly, he saw no contradiction between accepting modern science and technology and opposing imperial rule. But as the first recognised leader of the caste that was formerly known as 'the untouchables' and which is now called Dalit – meaning 'oppressed' or 'broken to pieces' – Ambedkar gave India's most marginalised human beings their first real hope of transcending their hereditary social condition.* He saw the caste system as India's greatest social evil, since it treated millions of people as sub-humans by the simple fact of their birth. The hope that he gave to Dalits may not yet have been redeemed in full measure or even substantially, to paraphrase the poetic address Nehru gave at independence. But there are enough among India's estimated 200 million Dalits who have tasted freedom and mobility since 1947

---

*Ambedkar rejected as patronising the name 'Harijan' – literally 'children of God' – that Gandhi used for the untouchables.

for it to be unimaginable they would retreat to the mindset of deference, acquiescence and even invisibility that had been required of them for so long.

Ambedkar, who was India's first untouchable to be educated abroad, undertaking his postgraduate studies at Columbia University in New York and then qualifying as a barrister in London in 1916, was also the principal author of India's 1950 constitution, which enshrines equality of individuals before the law and gives all adult Indians the right to vote, regardless of caste or any other identity. The blue-suited lawyer had the last laugh over his Gandhian opponents during the drafting process when he used his superior knowledge of the law to neutralise upper-caste Hindu demands. He succeeded in shifting several clauses – which, for example, called for the banning of cow slaughter, the prohibition of alcohol and the social primacy of the village – out of the 'Fundamental Rights' section of the constitution, which had legal teeth, and into the innocuous 'Directives Principles' section, which was a non-binding wishlist.

Ambedkar's view of the village stemmed from his own experience, in which the humiliations he suffered as a child, when barbers refused to cut his hair and wayside cafés denied him entrance, were only partially assuaged by the opportunities that an education in Bombay provided him. With apologies to Indian readers, many of whom will have memorised these words, this is what Ambedkar thought of the Indian village: 'The love of the intellectual Indian for the village community is of course infinite, if not pathetic . . . What is the village but a sink of localism, a den of ignorance, narrow mindedness and communalism?'*[8]

---

*Communalism in India is taken to mean allegiance to one's own ethnic group, rather than to society in general, usually in terms of religion but also caste. The normal western usage 'communal', common living or sharing, is not meant anywhere in this book.

Ambedkar, whose statue even today – in fact, especially today – can trigger a backlash wherever it is erected, described caste hierarchy as 'an ascending scale of hatred and a descending scale of contempt'. Megasthenes, the envoy of the Seleucid emperor to the court of Pataliputra, then India's leading power, in 300 BC observed of India's caste rules: 'No one is allowed to marry outside his caste or exercise any calling or art except his own.'[9] This held good for more than two thousand years, but it does not serve as an accurate description of India any more.

From Ambedkar's writings it is clear he hoped democracy would help dissolve the caste system. That has not happened, at least not in the way he would have hoped. Caste as political identity is alive and kicking in today's India, even if in the process it has been severed from its ritualistic and economic roots. Doubtless the Dalit lawyer would be horrified by some of the larceny and thinly disguised mafia rule that passes for lower-caste politics in much of India today, particularly in the densely populated and least advanced states of northern India. He would also be disappointed to observe that many of India's lower-caste parties today seek not to abolish caste but simply to improve their position vis-à-vis other castes, whether by agitating to raise their respective government job quotas or by building more monuments to their leaders and gods. Caste has not, as many had expected, given way to class in terms of political loyalties. As the joke goes, 'In India you do not cast your vote, you vote your caste.'

Nevertheless, hereditary occupation defined by caste has gradually been eroded. Urban Indians, and many even in the villages, are no longer forced to perform hereditary functions, although many still do out of necessity. For example, upper-caste Brahmins can be found in the leather trade, a previously taboo occupation; and Dalits cook food for people of other castes – again something that would have been unthinkable until recently. Caste intermarriage is also rising, although it is still extremely rare in the villages where more than two-thirds of Indians continue to reside. So it is tempting to believe that history is on Ambedkar's side.

Perhaps the largest ghost stalking today's India is that of Jawaharlal Nehru, whose legacy is as divisive as that of Gandhi or Ambedkar but whose role in shaping India's modern character, whether the state, democracy or civil society, exceeds that of the other two. As Prime Minister between 1947 and 1964 no other Indian leader, except his own daughter, Indira Gandhi, who held the job for fourteen years, has come close to Nehru's political longevity at the top. Several of the seemingly bewildering contradictions of today's India can be traced to Nehru. Although a strong believer in modernity, he towers over the closest thing India has to a feudal royal family, the Nehru–Gandhi dynasty.* In fact, he was the second of the dynasty since his father, Motilal Nehru, had been president of the Congress Party and one of its earliest members after it was founded in 1885.

After Gandhi was murdered, Nehru became India's foremost nationalist. Yet he only half-jokingly referred to himself as 'the last Englishman to rule India'. Educated at Harrow, one of Britain's most rarified public schools, and Cambridge University before qualifying as a barrister in London, Nehru and his father were typical of the Anglicised lawyers who dominated Congress before Gandhi dressed the party in homespun cotton. While in Paris on 'Vac' from Cambridge, Nehru wrote to his father about a Shakespearean drama that he had seen performed in French: 'I don't think the actors were quite sure whether it was a pantomime or a tragedy!'[10] Although he accepted Gandhi's logic of dressing and behaving like an Indian, Nehru never lost the demeanour of

---

*Indira married Feroze Gandhi, a philandering journalist from north India who was no relation to the Mahatma. Feroze, who died young from a heart attack, belonged to the Parsi community of Persian Zoroastrians. A more common Parsi surname is Daruwallah (seller of alcohol). One can but speculate whether a Nehru–Daruwallah dynasty would have been quite so successful.

an Edwardian gentleman. On the many occasions when he was arrested by the British and imprisoned, he would, as a rule, eat cornflakes, fried eggs, bacon and tomatoes, before submitting to his captors. Gandhi would have a drop of lime juice and some goat's milk.

But Nehru's Anglophilia stretched much further than his private tastes. As Prime Minister in 1947 he took the decision to retain the services of India's elite imperial civil servants, roughly half of whom were Indian. In an era when imperial collaborators in other newly independent colonies were being executed, sent to labour camps, fleeing into exile, or at the very least losing their jobs, Nehru was having them round to tea and reading their briefing papers. He even prevailed upon Lord Mountbatten, Britain's last viceroy of India, to remain for a year as the country's first head of state.*

The legacy of Nehru's Englishness – for want of a better word – is visible in every corner of early twenty-first-century India, in the little-altered system of district collectors, who continue to combine both executive and judicial sway over the country's sub-provincial units. This is a source of both strength and weakness for India. It is a strength because the Indian Administrative Service (IAS) provides a glue that helps to keep a mind-bogglingly heterogeneous country together. But it is a weakness because it is staffed by an unsackable elite, for whom democracy is something of a rival. The uneasy, at times bizarre relationship between the IAS and India's elected but often semi-educated provincial leaders is a recurrent theme in this book.

Nehru's Edwardian stamp is also visible in the continued cult of the omnipresent state, which he shared with many left-wing upper-class Englishmen of that era – notably the Fabians, who believed that socialism could be implemented peacefully through

---

*Nehru enjoyed an intimate friendship with Edwina Mountbatten, the viceroy's wife, which could have been an added incentive.

the state by a qualified class of 'Platonic' technocrats. That Nehru was more influenced by the Fabians than by the Russian Bolsheviks, Indians can be thankful. But Nehru's economic model, in which the state would lead the country's drive to industrialise at the expense of both consumption, which he saw as frivolous, and effective land reform, which he felt unable fully to accomplish in a democracy, lingers in spite of the decision to begin dismantling his notorious 'Licence Raj' in 1991.

There are still strong echoes today of the distaste Nehru felt for private business and the pursuit of money-making, although they have grown fainter since 1991. But as a Brahmin – who, in spite of his sincere aversion to the caste system, was still known as Pandit Nehru (an honorific indicating his caste origin) – traces of Nehru's personal complexities are easy to recognise in the attitudes of many modern upper-caste Indians. Nehru wrote disparagingly of 'bania civilisation' and said socialism would lead to the end of the 'acquisitive society'. Banias are petty traders and money-lenders who are much lower in the caste pecking order than Brahmins. Contemporary India has a deeply ambivalent view of money and money-making that owes much to Nehru.

But Nehru's most important legacy, and one which remains mostly intact, was his secularism and his strong disdain for communalism. He was a self-confessed atheist with an ill-concealed dislike of religiosity and all its ritual habits. This tendency, again common among upper-class Englishmen of his time, to distrust spiritual or theological fervour sometimes spilled over into frustration with Gandhi, at whose feet he figuratively and sometimes literally sat.

'Religion as practised in India,' Nehru wrote, 'has become the old man of the sea for us and it has not only broken our backs but stifled and almost killed all originality of thought or mind.' For the most part Nehru tolerated and even admired Gandhi's ability to speak in the language of the masses. But when the Mahatma talked of doing God's will, Nehru sometimes snapped: 'His

[Gandhi's] frequent references to God – God has made him do this, God even indicated the dates of that fast – were most irritating,' he wrote.[11]

To the despair of almost all Indians, including Nehru, the country was partitioned in 1947 to create a separate homeland for India's Muslims, sparking riots that killed up to a million people and triggering the movement of twelve million across the newly drawn borders. Nehru's insistence that Muslims be given equal rights in a secular, independent India earned him the undying hatred of right-wing Hindu revivalists. Unlike Gandhi, Nehru died peacefully in his bed. But his secular legacy has suffered repeated and partially successful assaults from a resurgent Hindu right wing since the mid-1980s. It is revealing that India's Hindu revivalist movement, whose political organisation, the Bharatiya Janata Party (India People's Party), headed the coalition government that took India into the twenty-first century, has co-opted the names and images of almost every national icon – including those of Gandhi and Ambedkar. But Nehru remains hate-figure-number-one to the Hindu right more than forty years after his death. The feeling was entirely mutual: 'It is said,' wrote Nehru, 'that there are 52 lakh [5.2 million] sadhus [wandering ascetics] and beggars in India. Possibly some of them are honest. But there is no doubt that most of them are completely useless people, who wish to dupe others and live on their earnings without working themselves.'[12] There is no estimate of how many sadhus India has today although the country's population has more than tripled since Nehru made that remark.

The title of this book, *In Spite of the Gods: The Strange Rise of Modern India*, is inspired to some extent by Nehru's contention that India's greatest strengths are not exclusively, or even necessarily, located in its religious traditions. India's advantages are found in its vibrant democracy, which has confounded expectations by not only surviving but entrenching itself deep within India's culture. They are also to be found in its traditions of pluralism, which have given the country hundreds of years of practice at managing social conflict without automatic resort to violence. It is true that the partition of the country along religious grounds and the subsequent aftershocks led to great bloodshed. But there is nothing in India's history that could approximate to the mass killing Europe has suffered. India's strengths are also to be found in its deep well of intellectual capital and technological prowess, which finally today is helping to propel the country towards a global role more befitting the country's size.

However, as the subtitle states, the character of India's rise is also strange, or unusual. That it is finally emerging as an important economic and political force on the world stage while remaining an intensely religious, spiritual and, in some ways, superstitious society is unusual by the standards of many countries. Likewise, the fact that India, alone among large nations, embraced full democracy before it had a sizeable middle class or anything close to majority literacy among its voters was unique at the time and remains so on this scale.

India's economy is now expanding rapidly without having gone through a broad-based industrial revolution – again, unusually so. The vast bulk of India's workforce remains in the villages. India's economic engine is powered not principally by its factories or by the manufacture of physical products but by its competitive service industries. This might gradually be correcting itself. But for the time being India's service sector has an economic weighting that gives it more in common with mature, developed economies, such as the United States or Britain.

India's rise is also unusual because of the volatile and sometimes harsh character of its politics. No other democracy has to operate with twenty-four-party coalitions. Deeply fragmented and often incoherent government is likely to be the norm in India for the foreseeable future. By most expectations, the corruption and administrative cynicism that are the result of this ought to be slowing India's development – and to some extent they are. And yet, much like Italy, where, so the joke goes, 'the economy grows at night, while the government is sleeping', India over the last twenty years has been expanding at a rate exceeded only by China.

Finally, India's rise is unusual because it is explicitly desired – and to some extent facilitated – by other countries, most notably the United States. Rightly or wrongly, many countries around the world fear the rise and growing military reach of China in the coming decades, and have concluded that India is the only country large and like-minded enough to act as a counterweight to its giant and growing neighbour across the Himalayas. India sometimes bristles at the suggestion that it should play such a role. Whether it likes it not – and in spite of appearances, India does enjoy the attention – its role as a potential counter-balance to China is a key element in the calculations of policy-makers in the west and elsewhere. Perhaps the most important Indian piece on the geopolitical chessboard is the country's expanding nuclear arsenal.

In India things happen when you least expect them. And vice versa. It is a constant source of both delight and frustration of living in India. I had requested an interview with Abdul A. P. J. Kalam, the President of India, about a vast engineering project to link up India's rivers. Opponents of the scheme (which, at the time of writing, had yet to get off the ground) called it 'Pharaonic'. Supporters said it would solve India's timeless drought and flood problems once and for all.

Kalam, whose presidential powers are strictly limited in India's Westminster-style parliamentary system, was a supporter of the project. I was looking forward to hearing his views. 'There is absolutely no possibility of an interview with the President – presidents of India don't give interviews,' his private secretary told me over the telephone. I felt crestfallen and was about to hang up when he continued: 'But the President would be very happy to invite you for a cup of tea and a little chit-chat.'

An engineer and scientist by profession, Kalam is known in India as the 'father of the nuclear missile', since he was in charge of the country's missile development programme for many years. He was also the head of India's defence research and development organisation when India first openly tested nuclear warheads in May 1998.* To the disquiet of some – but not many – in India, Kalam hailed the successful tests, which had been carried out underground in the deserts of Rajasthan in western India, with the following words: 'I heard the earth thundering below our feet and rising above us in terror. It was a beautiful sight.'

The three tests were greeted with street parties and ceremonial distribution of sweets around India, causing great disquiet in Washington and around the world. Pakistan followed suit a few days later, sparking even greater celebrations there. Since then, and in spite of attempts by India and Pakistan to 'normalise' relations and resolve their long-simmering dispute over the Himalayan state of Kashmir, the Indian subcontinent has frequently been labelled the 'most dangerous nuclear flashpoint in the world' – a phrase first used by President Clinton. It was only under the Bush administration, after 2001, that the US began to modify and ultimately change its judgement about India's nuclear status.

It is hard, in spite of the risks of accident or misunderstanding, for someone living in the region to imagine nuclear war taking place: not because of Pakistan, which is usually controlled by the army and views its nuclear arsenal as a genuine military tool; but because of India, which sees its nuclear deterrent as a purely hypothetical symbol that will win it recognition as a great power. 'Oh no, we don't talk about nuclear weapons,' said the diminutive septuagenarian President, with his trademark mop of hair. 'Would you like a biscuit?' I had quickly got bored of rivers, on which the President had said nothing startlingly new, and anyway, it was an

---

*India had already conducted an oxymoronic 'peaceful nuclear test' in 1974.

off-the-record conversation so what he said could not be put to much use. As a reporter I felt it would be remiss not to steer the conversation on to more fissile terrain. To no avail.

The next time I saw the President was at some distance at India's annual Republic Day Parade, which takes place on 26 January, the date in 1930 when Gandhi, Nehru and the other leading lights of Congress first unfurled the Indian tricolour flag in defiance of the British. Seventy-five years later I caught a glimpse of Abdul Kalam sitting in his presidential enclave with several visiting dignitaries observing the parade. A grand tableau of tanks, aeroplanes, artillery and nuclear-capable missiles was cruising down the broad, long avenue that links the presidential palace to the India Gate. 'And this', proclaimed a soupy voice over the Tannoy system, in a tone more suitable for a beauty pageant, 'is the Agni II class nuclear-capable missile which has a range of up to fifteen hundred kilometres.' I could not see the President's expression. But I imagine it was happy.

Indian nationalism has evolved considerably since Gandhi elevated non-violence and non-cooperation into a badge of identity for his emerging nation. Gandhi would surely not have been pleased to discover that India has nuclear weapons or that its missiles are named after ancient Hindu gods – for example, Agni is the Vedic god of fire. But in spite of this, today's India would not be unrecognisable to Gandhi. Nor would it be unrecognisable to Ambedkar or Nehru.

Although this book is not so rash as to predict the future, there are one or two things that can be suggested. Most Indians will remain proud of their nuclear status, since it proves they can accomplish technological feats without much help or encouragement from outside. In contrast, most of Pakistan's nuclear technology comes straight from China. It also puts India in the same league as the major powers, a misplaced vanity perhaps, but one that should not be confused with aggression. Unlike many other countries in the neighbourhood, India has no unfinished business, neither seeking nor claiming new territory. As the diplo-mats say, India is a status quo power.

To go a little further, India's emergence as a stronger economic and military power over the next generation is much likelier to add to, rather than subtract from, global stability. This, admittedly, strays close to prediction, an art form I would normally leave to André, Mother and others. But whatever India's vulnerabilities or faults, and this book grapples with some of the major ones, terri-torial expansion can almost certainly be removed from the checklist. As we have seen, spiritual expansion is quite another matter.

CHAPTER ONE

GLOBAL AND MEDIEVAL

India's schizophrenic economy

> Its stupendous population consists of farm laborers. India is one
> vast farm – one almost interminable stretch of fields with mud
> fences between. Think of the above facts: and consider what an
> incredible aggregate of poverty they place before you.
>
> Mark Twain, *Following the Equator*, 1897[1]

It took a long time. But finally, in the late 1990s, India started to
build roads which could get you from A to B at something better
than a canter. Until then, India's most significant highway was the
Grand Trunk Road that bisects the country from north to south.
Laid at various stages by the late medieval Mughal dynasty, then
upgraded and extended by the British in the nineteenth century
and popularised by Rudyard Kipling in his novel *Kim*, most of the
'GT Road', as it is known, got acquainted with asphalt only after
independence. But it is single lane and one can rarely exceed an
average speed of thirty miles an hour. So the relative novelty of
India's double-lane expressways still generates a buzz. By 2006,
India had all but completed the three-thousand-mile Golden
Quadrilateral expressway linking the country's four largest cities:
Delhi to Mumbai (formerly known as Bombay) to Chennai
(formerly known as Madras) to Kolkata (formerly known as

Calcutta)* and back to Delhi. Average speeds on the better stretches are close to sixty miles an hour.

For some, the expressways have heralded a modern era of speed, punctuality and hygienic roadside bathrooms. For others, they represent a brash intrusion on the more lackadaisical world they cut through. To me, the new expressways provide an intriguing juxtaposition of India's multi-speed economy. Curiosity – and an instinct of self-preservation – means I occasionally move into the slow lane. One of the best ways to observe India's galloping new economy is to count the number of car marques that whirr past you in the fast lane. You tend to lose count at thirty or forty. In the early 1990s, as India was starting to relax import and investment restrictions on foreign manufacturers, you would at best have counted six or seven makes of car. More than 90 per cent of the cars you saw would have been Ambassadors, the stately but desperately uncomfortable colonial-era vehicles which are still used by VIPs, and Marutis, the cramped family passenger car, still manufactured under a joint venture between Suzuki of Japan and the Indian government. Nowadays you have little time to register the tinted and reflective windows of Toyotas, Fiats, Hondas, Tatas, Fords, Volkswagens and Mercedes-Benz as they flash past.

But your speed is never quite what it should be. Coming far too frequently from the opposite direction, but on your side of the road, you encounter decrepit scooters, bicycles and even camel-drawn carts, whose drivers appear blissfully unfazed by the fact they are breaking all known rules of traffic and common sense. Once or twice, on the two-hundred-mile Delhi expressway to Jaipur, my journey has been brought to a halt by a herd of goats. Even without the local fauna, the absence of lane discipline means you are mostly on the edge of your seat.

But it is to the side of the expressways in the glaring billboards

*The earlier names of all three cities were associated with the era of British rule but were changed only in the 1990s.

advertising mobile phones, iPods and holiday villas and in the shiny gas stations with their air-conditioned mini-supermarkets, that India's schizophrenic economy reveals itself. Behind them, around them and beyond them is the unending vista of rural India, of yoked bullocks ploughing the fields in the same manner they have for three thousand years and the primitive brick kilns that dot the endless patchwork of fields of rice, wheat, pulses and oilseed. There are growing pockets of rural India that are mechanising and becoming more prosperous, but they are still islands. In this almost continuous contrast you observe the two most striking features of India's early twenty-first-century economy: its modern and booming service sector in a sea of indifferent farmland. It would be tempting, as you cruise happily towards your destination with a reasonable chance of being on time, to believe they are from different worlds. Along the way, you might also glimpse an occasional factory and an assembly plant or two for vehicles or washing machines, but evidence of manufacturing in India is far thinner on the ground than it is in neighbouring China.

By the time of independence, Nehru had already helped to forge a consensus in which the country would aim for complete economic self-sufficiency and the state would lead the effort by building up heavy industry, with an emphasis on steel plants and large dams. It has become fashionable since 1991 to write off Nehru as a hopeless idealist who tied the country up in socialist red tape for forty years. Much of the criticism is fair, since India failed to achieve the high economic growth rates that were seen at the time in Japan and later in South Korea, Taiwan, Thailand and Malaysia. But in the late 1940s and 1950s Nehru's economic strategy was perfectly in step with worldwide economic fashion.* It came with the blessings

---

*India's average growth rate of just 3.2 per cent between 1950 and 1980 was subsequently labelled the 'Hindu rate of growth' since it was barely higher than the country's population growth (thus doing little to raise per capita living standards). But it was a sharp improvement on the average 1 per cent annual growth in the first half of the century under the British.

of a team from the Massachusetts Institute of Technology, which advised New Delhi on the country's early five-year development plans. At the same time India was also advised by Gosplan, the Soviet Union's economic planning agency.

The idea, combining India's critique of the imperial economic system with a widespread global distrust of free trade following the disasters that had afflicted Europe and elsewhere during the 'hungry thirties', was to give the state a primary role in an economy aiming for self-reliance, or *swadeshi* – the second most important rallying cry of India's freedom movement after *swaraj*, or self-rule. Of great importance in kickstarting this model would be a series of large projects that would stimulate further economic activity – much as the widely admired Tennessee Valley Authority had in the United States. Nehru liked to call such projects 'temples of concrete'.

Nehru's plans for a closed economy dominated by the state came with the blessing of Britain's post-war Labour government, which had agreed to Indian independence and nationalised far more of its own industrial base than Nehru did in India. Many of the Labour government's Fabian advisers were accorded a warm welcome in New Delhi. Indeed, it was not until fifteen to twenty years after independence that international praise of India's economic model was outweighed by rising concerns about its effectiveness. Until then, the country's trajectory was uncontroversial and relatively unexceptional.

Yet, in retrospect and in comparison to other developing economies in Asia, Nehru's economic policies served India poorly. In 1950 South Korea, which was yet to emerge from its war with communist North Korea, had the same living standards as India (roughly fifty US dollars annually per head in 2005 prices). Fifty years later South Korea's per capita income was above ten thousand US dollars, more than ten times that of India. Similar contrasts can be found between India and most of the countries of East and South-east Asia. Even China, which devoted much of the first thirty years of its revolution to countrywide terror, now has double India's per capita income, having started at about the same level from its revolution in 1949.

Why did Nehru's approach fail? In the answers can also be found the explanations for why India's economy today is developing in such a curiously lopsided way. At independence, India was an overwhelmingly rural, agricultural and impoverished country. Almost nine out of ten Indians lived in villages and depended on the meagre yields of farming, mostly on a subsistence level, to live from day to day. In 1951, when India conducted its first census after independence, the country had a literacy rate of only 16 per cent – which means little more than one in seven of its 320 million people could even sign their name. Average life expectancy was just thirty-two years, an extraordinary but credible figure which gives a fair picture of the abysmal quality of life for most of India's villagers. Common descriptions at the time talked of emaciated peasants with visible ribcages, 'coolies' bent double from a (short) lifetime of manual labour, and children with potbellies from protein deficiency.

India was desperately in need of rural land reform and measures that would drastically boost crop yields so it could feed its people and build a launch pad for future growth. Instead, it got public steel plants and aluminium smelters, which, for the most part, were heavily loss-making and ate up India's precious foreign-exchange resources. The Indian farmer needed local irrigation projects to help insulate him against the vagaries of India's wildly erratic annual monsoon. Instead, Nehru unveiled grand dams, most of which are now crumbling and some of which were never completed. The average Indian also needed to learn how to read and write and have access to antibiotics and anti-malaria drugs, without which it was virtually impossible to escape poverty. Instead, Nehru's Congress governments poured resources into universities for the urban middle classes and into new public hospitals in the cities.

Hindsight makes it easy to dismiss as hopelessly optimistic Nehru's belief that devoting most of India's scarce financial resources to grand projects would propel the country to industrial status within a generation. Yet even at the time there were sceptical voices who questioned whether higher education should receive the same budgetary allocation as elementary education in a country where 84 per cent of people were illiterate.[2] There were also a few critics who wondered whether the amount New Delhi spent on agriculture should be as low as a third of the total spending in India's first five-year plan, which was launched in 1952. It plummeted to less than a fifth of spending in the second plan in 1957, when more than four-fifths of people depended on farming for their survival.[3] But these voices were drowned in a sea of utopian rectitude. The disparity between the Indian policy elite's dreams for tomorrow and what most Indians needed today was stark.

To be fair, Nehru had tried land reform and to some extent succeeded in eradicating the most feudal end of the spectrum. The notorious Zamindari system, set up by the British in most of northern India, under which large landholders, the Zamindars, were responsible for collecting taxes for the British from a penurious peasantry, had virtually been abolished by the end of the 1950s. But in most parts of India Nehru's land reforms were either watered down or sabotaged altogether by the local Congress Party elites, who, to the Prime Minister's growing frustration, were drawn disproportionately from the ranks of upper-caste landowners and notables. Nehru also tried and failed to establish cooperatives among the smaller farmers, whose plots were too small for mechanisation and fertilisers to be affordable. These reforms, which were influenced by China's policies of the same era, were also shot down by Congress bigwigs at the local level – where it mattered. An impeccable democrat, Nehru at times expressed envy of China's ability to push through whatever it wished, whether the people wanted it or not. But he never gave any hint of a tendency to authoritarianism. 'Let there be no doubt,' he told India's parliament in 1959, 'I shall go from field to field and peasant to peasant begging them to agree to it [cooperative farming], knowing that if they do not agree, I cannot put it into operation.'[4] But even if he had succeeded, it is doubtful cooperative farming would have made much of a difference in a country where caste divisions are most bitterly experienced at the grassroots.

The failure of Nehru's overall model became apparent at two specific moments, a generation apart. The first was in 1967, when Indira Gandhi, who had taken over as Prime Minister the previous year, was forced to devalue the Indian rupee under pressure from the United States and the International Monetary Fund (IMF). India's relative neglect of agriculture had been compounded by the incomplete success of Nehru's land reforms – many Indians remained landless. In exchange for larger international aid to enable India to import food following a succession of poor harvests, Mrs Gandhi was compelled to swallow some unwelcome economic medicine. In devaluing the currency, the aim was to prevent future payments crises by stimulating greater exports and so earning more foreign exchange.* But it marked a symbolic defeat for *swadeshi*, the centrepiece of Nehru's masterplan for India.

Worse, the devaluation followed several years of humiliation in which India's malnourished poor had been kept alive by fleets of US ships carrying surplus grain as food aid. The joke was that India was living from 'ship to mouth'. But Indira Gandhi – who, unlike her father, did harbour dictatorial tendencies, which were revealed in 1975 when she suspended democracy for nineteen months amid mounting protests over her failure to 'remove poverty' (as she had promised in the previous election) – remained committed to *swadeshi*. She also had a less subtle grasp of what her father had meant by socialism: 'The public sector was

---

*In addition to mounting food imports, India was importing more capital goods to sustain its heavy industry, in spite of the fact that the policy was known as 'import substitution'.

conceived as the base of Indian industry so that the country might have more machines, more steel,' she said two years after the 1967 devaluation. 'It also ensured India's freedom. To the extent India depended on imports its independence was compromised.'[5]

The second and even more dramatic moment came in 1991, when India's economy went into a tailspin after its foreign-exchange reserves dropped almost to zero in the aftermath of the first Gulf War, which had triggered a steep rise in oil prices that technically bankrupted the country.* Iraq's decision to put a torch to the oil fields in Kuwait was the straw that broke the camel's back for India's economy, which was already living beyond its means. Unlike in 1967, when the lives of tens of millions of Indians depended on foreign aid, by 1991 India was more than self-sufficient in food, having roughly doubled its agricultural yields in the 'green revolution' of the 1970s and 1980s. Scientists from India and abroad had developed much better yielding varieties of rice and particularly of wheat, the two principal staples of the Indian diet, which had boosted harvests dramatically. But the successes of the green revolution were little comfort in 1991, which sounded the final death knell for India's *swadeshi* hopes. In exchange for emergency balance of payments assistance from the IMF, India again devalued its currency and was required to move much of its gold as collateral to London. Nehru's socialist dream of creating an economy that would be immune to the influence of the former colonial powers had culminated in bankruptcy, and worse, a bankruptcy in which it was London that played the symbolic role of pawnbroker in saving India from collapse.

Like almost everyone in his circle, Alok Kejriwal went to an English-language school in the 1980s in Mumbai. Nehru had done

---

*India's reserves fell to just $1 billion, covering less than one month's worth of imports. Economists say financial reserves should cover at least six months of balance of payments needs, preferably a year.

his best to move India away from Britain's economic influence (at least until the Fabians came along). But with the English language, which he once described as the 'glue of India', and which he ensured remained the principal medium of government and courts after independence, Nehru's love affair was lifelong. At school in the 1980s, Alok might have been introduced to *The Discovery of India*, Nehru's *Autobiography* and *Glimpses of History* – books in English that Nehru wrote mostly during his long years of incarceration by the British. Some of Nehru's prose is exquisite.

But India's great statesman would have been puzzled by Alok and the tens of thousands like him who are thriving in today's India. At thirty-six, Alok is a dollar millionaire, in large measure because of India's facility with the mother tongue of its former imperial rulers. The fact that India's middle classes speak fluent English has given India a huge competitive advantage over China in the service sector, where the ability to converse in the world's business language makes a large difference.

Nehru also bequeathed another legacy with consequences as unintended as his championing of English: his governments created five elite universities of engineering, the Indian Institutes of Technology (IITs), many of whose graduates now play leading roles in Silicon Valley, California. These were the country's high-flying engineers who were supposed to lead India to *swadeshi* by building heavy industries. There are several thousand Indian millionaires in Silicon Valley, many of them 'IITans'.

Coming from a traditional business family that makes socks, Alok did not attend an IIT, but he found sock-making and dealing with unionised shop-floor workers too predictable, so, to the horror and deep scepticism of his father, he struck out alone. Bathed in primary colours and adorned by retro posters of early Bollywood films, the cheerful walls of Alok's company offices radiate the signature decor of India's new economy. Situated in midtown Mumbai in a district that was formerly dominated by textile mills, most of which went bankrupt in the 1980s, Alok's surroundings reminded me of Clerkenwell in London, or Haight-Ashbury in San Francisco. The decor is what some people call post-modern. I spent a lot of time talking to Alok and some of his sixty employees at C2W.com – contest-to-win.com, an outfit that markets brands through the Internet, mobile phones, interactive TV shows and other new technology.

The company's principal clients are global multinationals who are desperate for converts among India's rising class of spenders. India's consumers, said Alok, are tired of crude television commercials and other traditional marketing ploys. They want their marketing to be savvy and lateral. His diagnosis, which must be right because Alok is very rich, reminded me of Coca-Cola's ill-fated return to India in the early 1990s (having been kicked out in the 1970s): 'We're back!' proclaimed the Americans. Indians shrugged and carried on drinking Thums Up, Coke's local imitator, which never went away in the first place.

Alok, whose start-up capital came from Citibank and Rupert Murdoch's News Corporation, provided an example of his methods. Garnier, the French cosmetics company, wanted to introduce Indians to hair conditioner, a habit that was confined to a tiny travelling elite. So Alok created a game for Garnier's Indian website in which contestants are awarded a year's free supply of L'Oréal if they win. It involves an interactive contest in which you attempt to climb up the long hair of Rapunzel, the fairy-tale princess, who is locked in a tower. If her hair is either too dry or too oily you fail.

Another game which C2W developed for Jockey, the underwear maker, involves removing the knickers and shorts of lots of models. A cackle of electronic laughter greets those who succeed. In a third game devised for Yamaha motorbikes you attempt to pick up your girlfriend by negotiating sharp turns on narrow roads. 'Some curves demand attention,' says the caption, once you have collected your animated girlfriend. All of this is slightly risqué in a country much of which still outwardly pays homage to Gandhi's values. But it is also a wild commercial success that is stretching the horizons of marketing in India. Stanford University has even done a business study on C2W's mobile-phone marketing strategy.

I asked Alok about whether he was deliberately needling the Gandhian values of his elders. 'I don't really care about Gandhi – Gandhi is retrograde,' he said, over an espresso in his open plan office. 'Most of these people protesting against short skirts and foreign influences are hypocrites. Half of them send their children to English private schools and go abroad if they need a medical operation. These people are retrograde.' Alok engages in conversation with an intensity he presumably uses on potential clients, peppered with the terminology of a world that consists of 'ecosystems', 'last miles', 'mindshare' and 'optimum space'. When I asked for the bathroom I was pointed to a door with a placard that says 'gentstogo.com'. And when I asked him whether this work is intellectually challenging enough for him, Alok replied: 'Wow! that is an awesome question!' He never really answered it.

Yet, the world of which Alok is part (admittedly a relatively privileged part) – of the Internet, of information technology, of software maintenance and of call centres, back-office processing units and research and development hubs – is in other respects very serious. The success of India's IT companies in attracting ever more impressive flows of offshore business from the United States and Europe has reverberations way beyond the air-conditioned offices in Bangalore, Hyderabad, Delhi or Mumbai. It has convinced sceptics across India, who were raised in a culture of what economists called 'export pessimism' – a consequence of Nehru's *swadeshi* philosophy – that Indian companies can, after all, compete and make profits in global markets. This demonstration effect is increasingly visible in India's manufacturing sector and among businesses that have no connection to IT or to the service industry.

India's software prowess has also helped revolutionise the country's foreign exchange situation, which in 1991 had almost broken the country's economy. Then India's reserves were less than $1 billion; by 2006 they had climbed to $140 billion. This is as good a barometer as any of India's newfound spirit of confidence. India's software sector clocked up a milestone in 2003 when it earned more dollars that year than the entire cost of India's oil imports – the erratic energy bill that has haunted the country's economy for decades. Rising prices from the deteriorating situation in Iraq following the US-led invasion of Iraq sent India's oil bill shooting upwards in 2004 and 2005, but this time it had minimal impact on the country's balance of payments situation.

Having kept a straight face in the late 1990s while it profited from the west's paranoia about the Y2K computer bug, which provided the lift-off for India's software companies, India's IT and IT-enabled sector had also boomed to such an extent that it was changing the face of India's urban economy. The employment of hundreds of thousands of young engineers, scientists, economics and English graduates on pay scales that often exceeded those of their parents nearing retirement age created a new generation of consumers with little time for India's traditional pace of life. They were also impatient with the time-honoured verities of their parents: Be Polite to your Boss, Work your way up the Hierarchy, Don't Spend more than you Earn, and so on.

Alok said his employees, most of whom were dressed in the style of their counterparts in San Francisco, never talk about money in cash terms. They measure their pay in EMIs, or equal monthly instalments. These are monthly deductions from your bank account that continue for years, enabling you to pay off the car, motorbike, microwave, deep freeze, air-conditioning units and flats that you have not yet earned. You can even have an EMI holiday. Most go to Thailand or the Maldives. 'Holiday now, pay later,' says the commercial. The number of EMIs you have depends on what you earn, and what you want to buy in advance. Alok also provides stock options as an incentive for employees to stick around until the company is listed on the stock market in a world where people are constantly job-hopping – another novelty for India, where a secure job is conventionally something you cling on to for life. But stock options are not much incentive for an employee who slices up his or her (almost half of Alok's employees are female) income into exact bytes of EMI. 'Saving is the last thing on these guys' minds,' Alok said.

The rapid ascent to affluence of Alok's employees and those like them across metropolitan India explains why the country so quickly became a market that western and Asian exporters could no longer ignore, no matter how much bureaucratic torture they had been subjected to during previous forays into the Indian market. One of the first things I read when I arrived in India was an agonised article in one of the leading English-language dailies about the small size of India's mobile-phone market. In 2000 India had a grand total of just three million mobile-phone users, the precise number that neighbouring China was adding to its subscriber base every month. By the end of 2005, India itself was adding four million users each month, and had exceeded a total of 100 million. Retail explosions like this do not happen very often.

Alok and I got along fine. But what struck me most was his single-minded ambition. All he wanted to do was make a lot of money. 'My ambition is to make C2W a billion-dollar company,' said Alok. 'I am greedy, I have no trouble admitting to that.' We had returned to his flat on Pedder Road, one of Mumbai's smartest addresses. The walls of Alok's flat are adorned with contemporary Indian art; modern art is the abiding passion of Chhavi, his wife, who works at C2W in the mornings. 'It is a relaxed set-up,' said Alok. 'Chhavi doesn't have any KRA [key responsibility area].' Their two charming young daughters were playing in the living room, one of them wearing a T-shirt that said 'Miss Behave'.

I suggested Alok's real role in life was to sell globalisation to Indians: G2I, perhaps. 'People live brands and eat brands – if you can understand them and what people see in them, then you are in the right place,' he said. 'In today's world brands are the new religion.' I said that I thought I was an agnostic, but now Alok had left me nowhere to go but atheism. He laughed: 'You know, at thirty-seven, you're just out of reach of our target age bracket [seventeen to thirty-five].' Twenty years ago, Alok's overt pursuit of money, and his honest admission to it, would have marked him out as tasteless or unusual, even in Mumbai, which has been India's financial capital since the Victorian era and is home to the oldest stock market in Asia. But India has changed, in some respects quite radically, since 1991. 'You know I have some friends from Tamil Nadu [India's southernmost state] where the culture still frowns on you if you talk about money,' said Alok. 'But they are the unusual ones nowadays.' I told Alok it was interview2end.time and he laughed, although this time politely, because I was beginning to repeat the joke.

India, as many Indians like to remind you, is a unique country. But what makes it particularly unusual, especially in comparison to China, is the character of its economy. In spite of much breast-beating in the west, China is developing in the same sequence as most western economies have done: it began with agricultural reform, moved to low-cost manufacturing, is now climbing up the value-added chain, and probably, at some stage in the next ten to twenty years, will break into internationally tradeable services on a larger scale. India is growing from the other end.

Its service sector accounted for significantly more than half of its economy in 2006, with agriculture and industry accounting for roughly equal shares of what remained. This resembles how an economy at the middle-income stage of its development, such as Greece or Portugal, should look. But Greece and Portugal do not have to worry about a vast army of 470 million labourers in their hinterlands. India's problem, and its peculiar way of addressing it, presents the country with a daunting challenge. The cure may be economic, but the headache is social.

When India started to liberalise its economy in 1991, there was effectively only one television channel on offer: Doordarshan, the state broadcaster. By 2006 there were more than 150 channels and three or four new ones were being added every month. In 1991 Doordarshan reached just a small minority of homes. Such is the electricity supply in much of rural India that even villages that had a TV set would only intermittently get good reception. India's general election of 2004 marked the first national poll in which the majority of the electorate could watch the spectacle on television. Roughly a third of these, more than 150 million people, had multi-channel cable television piped into their homes.

What today's villagers and small-town dwellers in India see seductively paraded before them as they crowd around their nearest screens are things most of them have little chance of getting in the near future: the cars, foreign holidays, smart medical services and electronic gadgets that dominate TV commercials. Most of these products are not meant for them at all but are targeted at – and often by – people like Alok. Such items are well beyond the reach of the majority in a country where the average per capita income in 2006 was still below $750. Sooner or later, if you are unable to get what you are repeatedly told you should want, something has to give. India's more far-sighted policy-makers frequently remind themselves that if the country is to forestall a social backlash, rising crime and further lawlessness, which blights life in many of its poorer states, they must ensure that economic growth keeps accelerating. On every occasion I have interviewed Manmohan Singh, the quiet, bespectacled Sikh who was India's Finance Minister in 1991, when the country began to loosen its regulatory stranglehold on the economy, and who became Prime Minister in 2004, he emphasised the same argument: 'The best cure for poverty is growth.' Judging by India's own record, it is hard to disagree.

India's economy has on average expanded at 6 per cent a year since 1991, almost double the 'Hindu rate of growth' it experienced in its first four decades after independence. This sharp economic acceleration has coincided with a steady fall in the rate of India's population growth, so the relative growth of individual incomes is even better than the economic growth figures would suggest. Put vividly: the difference between India's abysmal decade that began in 1972 and the more impressive decade that began in 1995 is the difference between countrywide unrest – which led Indira Gandhi to declare the Emergency, in which she suspended democracy amid an epidemic of national strikes, protests and rising violence – and the relatively normal functioning of democracy after Dr Singh ushered in economic reform. In the first decade India's economy grew by 3.5 per cent a year while its population grew by 2.3 per cent. In the second the economy grew by 6 per cent a year while population growth fell to just 2 per cent. It would have taken fifty-seven years for an Indian family to double its income in Gandhi's decade. In Dr Singh's decade it would take just fifteen years.[6] In an age when you can watch exactly how the other half lives on a flickering screen, it is the difference between anarchy and stability.

Yet, on its own, faster growth is not enough: growth, as economists say, is a necessary but not sufficient condition for removing poverty. Equally important is the quality of growth – whether it is capital intensive, as it has been in India, in which case it will not employ many people, or labour intensive, as in China, which will give much larger sections of the television-viewing population a stake in the growth they see dangled in front of them.

Before he became Prime Minister, I used to talk to Manmohan Singh quite regularly. Because of his pre-eminent role in India's policy-making history (since the late 1960s he has held almost every important economic portfolio in New Delhi), it is worth reproducing his diagnosis of India's economic situation. After he became Prime Minister, he measured his words more carefully.

For the first forty or fifty years of India's independence we were plagued by two shortages: a shortage of food and a shortage of foreign exchange. These were the twin problems that dominated everything. Now we have solved both, the first through the green revolution and the second through higher export earnings and a more liberal trade regime. Today we have plenty of food and plenty of foreign exchange. Today our key problems are quite different. But there is an old mindset that refuses to face up to them and is still fighting yesterday's battles. Our biggest single problem is the lack of jobs for ordinary people. We need employment for the semi-skilled on a large scale, and it is not happening to anything like the degree we are witnessing in China. We need to industrialise to provide jobs for people with fewer skills. Why is it not happening on the scale we would hope? Because we are not as single-minded as China in pursuing our goals in a clear manner.

Dr Singh was outlining India's twin economic challenges of today: the need to modernise agriculture and the related objective of providing more manufacturing jobs for India's under-employed peasantry. In his characteristically polite way he referred to 'mindset problems' that were making it more difficult to reach these goals. Perhaps the biggest mental hurdle to both is the Indian elite's continuing love affair with the village. It has become popular for journalists and academics in India to write off Gandhi's philosophy as officially dead. Certainly, as a political ideology, Gandhianism in today's India is an orphan: none of India's many political parties officially endorses the Mahatma's philosophy of the village. But as a social attitude his view of the village lives on notably in much of India's civil service; it can be heard coming from the mouths of many of India's senior diplomats and judges, and it is still mainstream among India's non-governmental organisations, the tens of thousands of charities which in many parts of rural India provide the village schools, basic medicines and the arts and crafts livelihoods which the Indian state often fails to deliver.

Gandhianism can also be taken as shorthand for an even more deeply rooted attitude that is quite common among privileged and upper-caste Indians, who, at many levels – some not openly stated – view the brash new world of metropolitan India as a challenge to their traditional domination of culture and society. This attitude is also a continuing echo of the anti-colonial struggle against the British, in which the village and the home were seen as those parts of Indian culture which were least touched by colonial influence. Even those who argued with much of Gandhi's philosophy, such as Rabindranath Tagore, the great Bengali writer, poet and educationalist, still attributed to the Indian village an almost holy status – an attitude that is not as noticeable among those Indians who live in villages. 'We have started in India, the work of village reconstruction. Its mission is to retard the process of racial suicide,' said Tagore. 'The villages are the cradle of [Indian] life, and if we do not give them what is due to them, then we commit suicide.'[7]

Devdoongri is a tiny hamlet in the drought-prone west of Rajasthan, the largest of India's twenty-nine states. But Rajasthan's population, most of whom are dependent on the unpredictable annual monsoon to feed their crops, is relatively small at just fifty-two million people. Parts of the state, particularly the eastern sectors that are closer to New Delhi, are quite well irrigated, but the districts around Devdoongri, which are home to the western section of the arid but strikingly beautiful Aravalli range of hills, are lucky to get good rains every three years. The government provides very little in the way of reliable irrigation to make up the difference. When I visited in July 2005 the long-suffering villages of this area were praying for good rains. Their prayers were only partially answered.

I had come to stay with Aruna Roy, one of India's most admired and effective social activists, who made Devdoongri her home in the late 1980s. Although from a privileged and Anglophone upper-caste family background, and although she joined the Indian Administrative Service in 1969, Aruna abandoned all this for a life among the people. Ms Roy is a Gandhian to the tips of her fingers: her saris are always made of cotton; she is a vegetarian; she lives ascetically among the villagers; she uses the occasional hunger strike, and more frequently the *dharna*, or sit-down protest, to pressurise the authorities – both tactics Gandhi pioneered against the British. And, although she concedes that escaping your caste identity is much more difficult in the village than in the town, she sees the former as the key to India's future.

Coming from an air-conditioned residence in New Delhi was not the best preparation for a stay with Aruna. Her base is a collection of small mud huts which, until a few months earlier, had home-baked tiles for their roofs. These had been replaced with manufactured tiles because, as she told me only half jokingly, the cobras would occasionally drop on to the ground during the night while stalking rats across the roof. But, on account of the heat, which is always most oppressive before the break of the monsoon, we all slept outside in a row on the ground and on *charpoys* – the traditional wooden beds held together by a maze of woven jute thread, on which farmers like to take their afternoon siesta. (My presence was a bonus for the mosquitoes.) Each meal was a nutritious vegetarian mix of rice, *roti* (Indian bread), *dhal* (lentils), and a variation of potatoes, aubergine and okra, with a glass of buttermilk. Afterwards we rinsed our hands and plates in a parsimonious trickle of water, which, owing to continuous shortages, is strictly conserved. We sat cross-legged on the ground and ate with our hands.

Aruna's 'left-hand man' is Nikhil Dey, an intelligent and articulate man in his early forties who has been with her since the move to Devdoongri, and who comes from an equally privileged background in the city. His father was second-in-command of India's airforce. There were many others, too, in what seemed like a tightly knit but ever extending family. Aruna's followers greet each other with a clenched fist and say, '*Zindabad!*', meaning 'long live!', in place of '*namaste*' or '*salaam alekum*', the more conventional Indian hellos (for Hindus and Muslims respectively). Their group, the MKSS (Mazdoor Kisan Shakti Sangathan – the Organisation for the Empowerment of Workers and Peasants) agitates to secure the basic rights of ordinary villages from an often impervious bureaucracy.

I had been curious to understand what motivated Aruna, since I thought this would help explain her attitude to the village. 'I have had long conversations with my friends about whether it is politicians or civil servants who are more corrupt,' said Aruna, who is in her fifties, but has the zest and intensity of a much younger woman. Occasionally her stern, headmistressy expression gives way to infectious laughter. One of her followers had earlier read out a sycophantic letter from a small-town academic in which the correspondent cringingly begged Aruna for permission to write her biography. 'These *chamchas* [hangers-on],' she said. 'Where do they come from?' Aruna said she thought that civil servants should be blamed more for corruption, since they usually came from more privileged backgrounds than the politicians. 'That's why I left,' she said. 'I couldn't take it any more. I wanted to live among and work with villagers, to join them in their struggles for change.'

Nikhil took me to Sohangarh, a typical Rajasthani village, in the same district as Devdoongri. MKSS had conducted a survey of the income and living standards of the eight hundred village residents, which gives a fairly accurate picture of how a villager lives in most of northern India. Like many such villages, it is centred on a small and dusty public square through which the occasional sacred cow wanders on its afternoon rounds. The village is dotted with modest shrines to Hindu gods. A few of the richer peasants have electricity, but at best for only three to four hours a day. Most villagers make do with hurricane lamps to nego-tiate the dark. There is, of course, very little water, so people can only change their clothes every few days. Like anywhere in India, you see adults washing themselves decorously while fully dressed in their white tunics, for the men, or more colourful saris, for the women. The average landholding is just half an acre, barely enough to feed the family and very rarely significant to produce a surplus for the market. The plots will become progressively smaller as they are divided among the sons of the next generation. There is little prospect, on any commonsense assessment, that such a small area of farmland could bring material security, let alone prosperity, to the growing population of the village in the future. Unless there were significant migration to the city, which would enable the consolidation of farm holdings through voluntary sales, the further subdivision of the plots down the generations would only make the situation worse.

What little income the villagers receive is earned mostly from outside in the form of weekly cash payments from menial and casual jobs in Beawar, a local town, Jaipur, the capital of Rajasthan, or larger cities outside the state. Contrary to the image of an India in which its villages rely wholly on the soil for their survival, its men are escaping the village because it cannot sustain their families. By 2001, more than a third of India's rural house-holds depended on non-farm income for their livelihoods.[8] This suggests a pent-up demand to migrate to the city. According to Aruna's survey, the village of Sohangarh had earned 5.1 million rupees (about $120,000) the previous year, an average of $150 per person. The average daily surplus to spend on extra food supplies was six rupees (about ten cents) per person, and three rupees on what Nikhil smilingly referred to as the un-Gandhian habits of tea and *bidis* – the popular hand-rolled cigarettes of the poor.

Nikhil gathered a group of the local men to tell us about their lives. The village women held back at a polite distance, although curious to eavesdrop on the exchange. Most of the men were wearing the striking red turbans and sporting the handlebar moustaches which are the trademarks of the Rajasthani peasant. At Nikhil's request, one by one they stood up and announced their profession. It was a roll-call of agricultural failure. The first was a well-digger who travels from village to village. Another worked as a security guard for Reliance Industries, one of India's largest companies, in Delhi. The next was a cloth worker who had lost his job in the city. The fourth had been trying for years without success to join the army. The next two were both menial workers at a hotel in the city of Ahmedabad in the neighbouring state of Gujarat. And so on. Barely any of the men remain in the village because farming is not enough to make ends meet. While they are away, the women and children tend to the family cow and the small plot. But very few of the men can find secure jobs in the city. The nature of city employment is not enough, either in terms of a secure contract or a decent income, to persuade them to sell their land and migrate. The men of Sohangarh and those living in hundreds of thousands of villages like it naturally hold on to their plots because they are the best insurance they have.

I asked Nikhil whether he believed the village – Sohangarh or any other – could provide an economic future to all its inhabitants. Like Aruna, Nikhil is one of those self-sacrificing activists that keep emerging from urban India. Gandhians might be non-violent, but some are as tough as leather. 'It is funny,' said Nikhil, 'but even when I was a teenager living in my parents' house in Delhi leading a consumer lifestyle with all the mod cons, I wanted to live in a village and do something like this. I did not find the move to the village in the slightest bit difficult. In fact when I go back to stay with my parents that is a much harder adjustment to make. I don't want air-conditioning or electricity or the other elements of the affluent lifestyle.' But if the villagers decided to move to the city would they be sacrificing their culture? Nikhil took some time to reply. 'That would be too simplistic,' he said.

'But I believe we should not risk losing all of this [pointing to the village]. We can make the village work through better farming and cottage industries. If people leave the villages then they also lose the rootedness that comes with living where you are from, and the strength you draw from your natural surroundings.'

The more I talked to Aruna and Nikhil, the more I felt that although they care deeply for the welfare of the villagers and have done as much as anyone to give them the courage to fight for their rights, their work is also about something larger. They have a vision of society in which the land will sustain the majority of the population, albeit after profound social reform at the grassroots level. Perhaps *swadeshi* would best sum up their point of view: they want India to buck the universal trend in which society urbanises as it develops. 'In some respects we are Gandhian and in other respects we are Marxist,' said Nikhil. 'But we prefer to avoid being labelled.' However, it is hard to imagine any of these villagers voluntarily turning down the opportunity to have electricity or the other comforts of a consumer lifestyle. Nor is it easy to imagine a rural economic model that could sustain 700 million Indian villagers in security and in a condition of social enlightenment, which is what Nikhil and Aruna are fighting for. Indians will continue to move to the city. Many more would move if there were secure jobs to be found.

India's culture also lives in its cities. A hundred years ago, France was predominantly rural; now it is predominantly urban. But French culture lives on. Aruna and Nikhil's view of today's world is that it consists of multinational companies who wish to exploit India's people and resources for hit-and-run profits. In essence, it is a world whose companies are modern versions of the East India Company, the British outfit which used its royal charter to colonise India in the eighteenth century, a 'neoliberal' world that profits from the entrapment and immiseration of the developing world's poor – and in which moving to the city in today's India, whether it is from Sohangarh or any other village, happens not voluntarily but because you have – in Aruna and Nikhil's view – been brutally uprooted by new technology and the profit motive. This new globalised form of capitalism forces people to migrate to the city by replacing their skills and traditions with the work of large machines. Once urbanised, they are slotted in as microscopic cogs in the giant apparatus of globalisation. In short, they believe India can and should resist the forces of modernity, including urbanisation.

Less than 7 per cent of India's dauntingly large labour force is employed in the formal economy, which Indians call the 'organised sector'. That means that only about 35 million people out of a total of 470 million have job security in any meaningful sense; and only about 35 million Indians pay income tax, a low proportion by the standards of other developing countries. The remainder, in more senses than one, are in the 'unorganised economy'. They are milking the family cow, making up the seasonal armies of mobile casual farmworkers, running small shops or street-side stalls, making incense sticks and *bidis*, driving rickshaws, working as maids, gardeners and nightwatchmen, and bashing metal as mechanics in small-town garages.

Of the 35 million or so Indians with formal sector jobs – which are, to some extent, registered, monitored, measured and audited – 21 million are direct employees of the government. These are the civil servants, the teachers, the postal workers, the tea-makers and sweepers, the oil sector workers, the soldiers, the coal miners and the ticket collectors of the Indian government's lumbering network of offices, railway stations, factories and schools.

This leaves around fourteen million working in the private 'organised' sector. Of these, just over a million – or about 0.25 per cent of India's total pool of labour – are employed in information technology, software, back-office processing and call centres. Software is clearly helping to transform India's self-confidence and the health of its balance of payments situation with the rest of the world, but the country's IT sector is not, and is never likely to be, an answer to the hopes of the majority of its job-hungry masses. Nor do foreign companies employ large numbers of Indians – estimates vary between one and two million people, depending on the definition of a 'foreign' company. The remainder are employees of Indian private sector companies.

Understanding the difference between organised and unorganised India is the key to realising why the country's economy is so peculiar: at once confident and booming yet unable to provide secure employment to the majority of its people. Contrary to much conventional wisdom in the west, which often quite wrongly sees Indian employees of foreign multinationals as exploited sweat-shop labour, the fourteen million who work for Indian or foreign private companies are the privileged few – India's aristocracy of labour. In 1983, as India was entering the twilight of its *swadeshi* phase, the average labour productivity of the worker in the private organised sector was six times that of his counterpart in the unorganised sector. By 2000, that had risen to nine times.[9] The disparity in earnings was similar. This is a world of difference. Crossing from one world to the other requires good education and skills, or a huge dose of luck. It does not happen often enough.

If India is to build a better bridge between the old world and the new it must provide jobs for unskilled and semi-skilled employees in its manufacturing sector. In terms of scale, India can be measured only against China. In 2005 India employed just seven million people in the formal manufacturing sector, compared to more than a hundred million in China. Given the large investment and the priority that Nehru accorded to industrialisation, many people find it puzzling that sixty years later India's manufacturing sector employs so few people. That is because Nehru's strategy was essentially capital intensive: he aimed to develop India's technological capacity, rather than employ the maximum number of people. But it does not follow that Indian manufacturing is correspondingly weak or uncompetitive. Measured by quality, if not quantity, many of India's home-grown private sector manufacturers are considerably more impressive than their counterparts in China. Again, in this respect, India finds itself higher on the ladder than one would perhaps expect it to be. It is just that most of its population are still standing at the bottom.

This very Indian paradox is visible everywhere. One of the best places to see it is the impeccably maintained and clean-swept company town of Jamshedpur in the eastern state of Jharkhand. Jamshedpur is almost a museum of India's industrial history from its nationalist beginnings at the turn of the twentieth century (long before the British departed) to the early twenty-first century, where galvanised steel is exported to China and auto-components to America and Japan. The plant was established in 1902 by Sir Jamshed Tata, founder of the Tata Group, India's largest private sector company. At the beautifully kept park in the centre of town, fourth- and fifth-generation menial employees of the company can be seen leaving rice or flowers, or doing *puja* (small prayers), beneath the imposing bearded statue of Jamshedji, as he is still known.* The sight is reminiscent of Rudyard Kipling's description of lower-caste Hindus and Muslims worshipping at 'each other's wayside shrines with beautiful impartiality'. But the prayers are well deserved: for the poor, a job with Tata is a job worth having. With it comes access to high-quality company medical care, *pucca* (good-quality) housing with clean, drinkable tap water, and good schools in which to educate your children. But there are fewer and fewer.

Like many large Indian manufacturing companies, Tata's balance sheet has gone from respectable in 1991, when a new world

---

*'-ji' is an honorific suffix that is given as a mark of respect. If you want to get something done in India, and all else has failed, adding '-ji' to the end of the person's name often has an open-sesame effect.

was opened up by Manmohan Singh's abolition of the industrial licensing system, to world class today. Yet its payroll count has gone in the opposite direction. In 1991 the imposing steel mill in Jamshedpur turned out just one million tonnes of steel a year and employed 85,000 people. In 2005, it made five million tonnes but employed just 44,000 people. Tata Steel's turnover has risen from $800 million to $4 billion in the same period. 'We could probably get the labour force down to twenty thousand and move up to a production of ten million tonnes,' said one of the Tata executives.

Tata Steel's story – in which it transformed itself from a labour-intensive company which supplied low-cost steel to the domestic market in 1991 to a capital-intensive company that supplies world-beating automobile steel to Japan's shiniest car companies today – parallels that of other successful Indian manufacturers. Until 1991, Tata made everything it possibly could in its own backyard, since it was always too much of a struggle to import spare parts or new machinery under India's 'import substitution' regime. Naturally this was a distraction from what the company was supposed to be doing and added greatly to its labour force. Tata also employed large numbers of lobbyists and 'gofers' who hung around ministries petitioning bureaucrats. Companies such as Tata needed the permission of bureaucrats for even the smallest investment decisions on what they could produce, and when and where they should produce it.

Another questionable legacy of the well-meaning society Nehru wanted to build is that India has some of the strictest labour laws in the world, making it virtually impossible to sack an employee, even if the person you want to fire is a chronic absentee. Some parts of Nehru's model, such as the Orwellian Licence Raj, have now been dismantled, but others, such as the absurdly strict labour laws (which became even stricter under Indira Gandhi in 1976), remain. This means that companies are reluctant to hire large numbers of people even when they are expanding because they fear being stuck with boom-era payrolls during the next recession, which would push them into bankruptcy and endanger everyone's job. But it also means companies prefer to outsource as much of their work as possible to small, unaudited outfits in the 'unorganised sector' so they can escape the labour laws, which are effectively unenforceable in India's labyrinthine informal economy. Other legacies also have yet to be abolished, such as the 'Inspector Raj' of constant inspections that plagues much of Indian business. As Gurcharan Das, former head of Procter & Gamble India wrote: 'In my thirty years in active business in India, I did not meet a single bureaucrat who really understood my business, yet he had the power to ruin it.'[10]

There are also unintended consequences to another of Nehru's critical legacies – the decision to pour as much money into English-medium universities for the middle classes as he did into primary schools for the villages. The elite Indian IIT engineering graduates who are not in Silicon Valley or Massachusetts, are working for companies like Tata Steel and Reliance Industries. Because of its impressive university system, India's scientific and technical capacity is ranked third in the world,[11] behind the United States and Japan but ahead of China. In contrast to India, though, China has invested much more heavily in elementary schools for those at the bottom of the social ladder. India produces about a million engineering graduates every year, compared to fewer than 100,000 in either the United States or Europe. However, India's literacy rate is only 65 per cent whereas China's is almost 90 per cent.[12] 'We have some of the best engineering graduates in the world working for us,' the Tata executive had told me, after a tour of the company's state-of-the-art production line. 'And they come much cheaper than engineers in Japan.'

The fortunes of Dinesh Hinduja, who owns Gokaldas Exports, one of India's most successful garment-makers, illustrate India's paradox even more vividly. Businessmen such as Hinduja in India and China are the reason why so many in the west fear the economic resurgence of Asia's two giant neighbours. Situated in Bangalore, the booming capital of the south Indian state of Karnataka, Gokaldas Exports turns out two million garment pieces every month for twenty-six brand labels around the world. Prominent clients include Marks & Spencer, Banana Republic, Gap, Pierre Cardin and Abercrombie. They even affix the barcode and the price tag before the clothes leave India.

Hinduja's highly trained workforce can turn out clothes in nine hundred different styles, switching production techniques as fast as youth fashion changes in the west. They embroider and print exclusive fabrics for the older generation, and batter and tear jeans for the young. Watching the bemusement of the employees as they jump all over denim to give it that couldn't-care-less look made this one of the more entertaining factory visits I have made. 'They find it very hard to understand why they should make such a nice pair of jeans and then kick them around afterwards,' he said. Hinduja picked up a sensible cotton shirt that already had its £85 price clipped on to it and the Marks & Spencer label. 'If this had been made in the UK, it would have cost three or four hundred pounds,' he said. 'The moment your competitor shifts production to India or China, you have no choice but to follow, otherwise you would go out of business.'

By the standards of other developing countries, including China, Hinduja's outfit is defined as 'complex manufacturing'. India's garment exports are not made in the large, labour-intensive warehouses you find in China, which employ millions of people, but in small units like those of Gokaldas Exports, which employ tens of thousands. Hinduja employs 33,000 people. If he could operate in China, where there are millions of literate workers, his workforce would be closer to 200,000, he says. His Indian factories are staffed mostly by women. There is a medical centre and a crèche. 'We try not to hire men, because they are less reliable,' he said. 'We had one case of a man who was a drunkard and we fired him. He appealed and it took us fifteen years and huge amounts of management time before we won the appeal.'

Dinesh Hinduja's competitive edge in complex manufacturing is an almost perfect illustration of India's economic paradox. He can hire any number of highly qualified graduates who will be instantly at home with fashion software, so they can design the clothes on computers. Since they will also be fluent in English, they can then market the designs at the grand garment fairs in Paris, New York, London and Milan. As a result, Hinduja probably makes more money than his counterpart in China. But he is careful not to expand his payroll count too much, since labour in India is a sunk cost. Hiring workers in India is a decision that you can reverse only if you have great patience for *dharnas*, and deep pockets for litigation. 'When I expand, it is always in a capital-intensive and not a labour-intensive direction,' he said.

There is another idiosyncracy to Mr Hinduja's operations, which can also be found across India's textile sector. Small-scale cottage industries receive big financial and regulatory incentives for remaining small, so Hinduja has broken up his production lines and spread them to many smaller units across Bangalore. He must also pay much higher excise and tariff duties than his Chinese counterparts on all of his fabrics, except for cotton, which remains a talisman of India's national identity. Since his competitors in China do not pay such duties and are not encouraged to fragment their production lines, Hinduja has no choice but to produce luxury garments, which means using more complex techniques. In effect, he has been forced to go higher up the economic value-added chain. 'We compete because we have a better pick of highly educated English-speaking graduates than China,' he said. 'We couldn't possibly compete on price with China by making the cheaper garments.'

My second most entertaining visit to an Indian garment factory was to a site near Chennai, the capital of Tamil Nadu, India's southernmost state, which faces the island of Sri Lanka. The company makes underwear for Victoria's Secret, America's popular lingerie chain for women, and other lingerie companies. Again, almost all the employees are women. Their company dress is as conservative and decorous as the Madonna bras and crotchless knickers they make are not. Like the workers at Gokaldas Exports, the employees of Intimate Fashions, a part-German, part-Sri Lankan company, have to switch techniques at a moment's notice; and they have to import most of their material, including lace from France and microfabric from Germany. 'We have Valentine's Day, then the summer collection, then the winter collection – all the time the orders are changing,' said the manager. Unlike in India's northern states, almost all of Tamil Nadu's workforce is literate. It is a much better-governed state. The government of Tamil Nadu has also managed to relax some of the national labour laws locally, since India's federal constitution gives considerable leeway to the provincial capitals. As a result, Intimate Fashions has expanded its workforce more rapidly than it might have if it had been located elsewhere. But to the evident puzzlement of many of its well-proportioned seamstresses, the underwear they make keeps getting smaller.

India's growing manufacturing reach is also visible in its pharmaceutical and biotechnology sector, which again draws its personnel from the country's serried ranks of science, engineering and technical graduates. In the cite of Pune (formerly Poona), in western India, the Serum Institute, which is owned by the Poonawallah Group, supplies almost half the United Nations' annual order of vaccines, which inoculate tens of millions of children every year in the developing world. The institute began as an offshoot of the Poonawallah family's horse-breeding concern and is situated next to the town's racetrack. Horses naturally produce the serum used to inoculate humans against tetanus. Today, every other child in the developing world is inoculated with one or other of the institute's products – shots for rabies, meningitis, polio, measles, rubella and tetanus are manufactured. The workforce for this globally crucial institute numbers just a few hundred, almost all of them college graduates. But India's advantage in medicines and drugs is no longer just about making cheaper generic drugs than the west. Indian drug companies have more applications for patents pending with the US Food and Drug Administration than any other country.[13]

Bharat Forge, India's largest auto-components manufacturer, is located just a few miles from the Serum Institute. The company, which exports engine components and chassis parts to Europe, China and the US, bases its advantage on the software and engineering talents of its workforce. The average shop-floor worker in China is paid less but produces more than his or her Indian counterpart: China's unit labour costs for basic manufacturing are much lower. Like Gokaldas, Bharat Forge has moved to higher-skilled production in order to gain an advantage. It is competitive because it uses information technology and engineering skills to design more sophisticated vehicle components. This is typical of the industry as a whole. India's auto-components exports are expected to surge from about $3 billion now to over $20 billion by 2012.[14] But it is capital intensive. Bharat Forge proves that India can compete on world markets. It does not yet prove that India can lift its masses out of poverty.

India has a highly unusual economy. Its complex steel plants are helping put their Japanese and American counterparts out of business. Its elite private hospitals conduct brain surgery on rich Arab clients and perform hip replacements on elderly British 'medical tourists' who are frustrated by the long waiting-lists in Britain's National Health Service. Employees at India's call centres are empowered by telephone or computer to accept or reject insurance claims of up to $100,000 from American policy-holders half a world away. And its drugs sector is on the cusp of producing new products as a result of indigenous research and development skills. Yet large numbers of India's farmers still subsist at African standards of living. Fewer than one million Indians annually produce more in IT and software export revenues than several hundred million farmers earn from agricultural exports.

It is true that India's higher economic growth rates in the last fifteen to twenty years have helped lift more people out of poverty than was the case in previous decades. According to the government of India, the proportion of Indians living in absolute poverty dropped from 35 per cent to just over 25 per cent between 1991 and 2001. The percentage is likely to have dropped further since then. Some parts of India, particularly its southern states and the west of the country, where the system of administration is widely regarded to be of a higher quality, have generated many more jobs than before, in both the organised and the unorganised service and manufacturing sectors. As is so often the case in India, the picture cannot be reduced to one simple snapshot.

However, contrary to what demographers would expect and what has happened in other developing economies, India's rate of urbanisation has actually *slowed* while its economic growth has accelerated. In 1981, 23.7 per cent of India was urban; by 2001, this had risen only to 27.8 per cent.[15] Of course, the numbers of people moving to the cities are still large by the standards of other countries: seventy million Indian villagers migrated between 1991 and 2001. Nevertheless, 'The surprise is that just when the urbanization process was expected to accelerate, it slowed down,' writes Rakesh Mohan, the deputy governor of India's central bank and one of the country's leading economists. 'This has been caused by both faulty national economic policies that have discouraged urban employment growth, particularly industrial employment, and by rigidities that have inhibited urban infrastructure investment.'[16]

Some of India's business leaders believe the economic gap between rural and urban India cannot persist without eventually provoking a backlash. In 2004 Manmohan Singh asked Nandan Nilekani, the chief executive of Infosys, one of India's most successful IT companies, to join a task force on urbanisation. Unusually among Indian leaders, Singh believed more rapid urbanisation and a stronger manufacturing sector were essential to India's future success. Nilekani, who had put one million dollars of his own money into a project to improve urban governance in Bangalore, where Infosys is based, accepted without hesitation.

'Much of the elite in India still attach great importance to the village, even though none of them actually lives in one,' he said over a cup of tea in his Bangalore office.

> In my view they are dangerously wrong. India must urbanise much more rapidly and much better than we have done so far. This is what is happening in China. And this is what has happened in every developed country on the planet. India cannot buck this trend. And even if it could, why should we want to? There are fundamental problems with the Indian village. The village is unable to give its people jobs and it never will, because reform of agriculture will mean mechanisation of farming and fewer jobs. The village is a trap for the lower castes. It is a kind of prison. We cannot modernise the Indian economy – or Indian society – unless we urbanise more rapidly and urbanise better than we have done so far.

Many people who visit India are struck by the squalor of the urban slums that assault their senses almost immediately after they leave the airport. They find it hard to understand why so many Indians would voluntarily want to live in such conditions when they could be milking the family cow back in the village. But most of the migrants have voted with their feet (some have been involuntarily displaced by natural disasters or dams). In their view even the most squalid slum is better than living in a village. In spite of the inadequacies of India's urban planning and the absence of secure employment, the city offers economic and social opportunities to the poor and to the lower castes that would be inconceivable in most of rural India. More than 100 million rural Indians do not own any land, and many of them are likely to move to the cities in the years ahead, whether slum conditions have improved or not.

'The answer is not to send people back to village, which anyway you can't do in a democracy,' Nandan Nilekani explained.

It is to improve the quality of urban governance and to provide the poor with real jobs. The urban elites feather their nests with the best of comforts. Then they want to pull up the ladder and deprive everyone else of the same opportunities. Unless we start to provide the masses with jobs and increase the rate of economic growth, then everybody's security will be threatened. We have to embrace the future.

India's economy offers a schizophrenic glimpse of a high-tech, twenty-first-century future amid a distressingly medieval past. But even more perplexing is that it is among India's elites – those who have been the largest beneficiaries of the liberalisation of the economy since 1991 – that you find the most robust defenders of an old mindset that could be described as modernity for the privileged, feudalism for the peasantry. It would be unfair to Aruna and Nikhil, whose vision for India's villagers is centred on grassroots 'participatory democracy', to class them as defenders of feudalism. They are at the progressive end of a wide spectrum that includes every type of village romantic, from upper-caste civil servants who block attempts at better urban planning to colleagues of Nandan Nilekani in the IT industry who sometimes seem to believe that if only the digital revolution could be extended to the villages then people would not want to move (this is a widespread sentiment).* However, most of the evidence

---

*Given the lack of water, electricity and paved roads in many of India's villages, the idea that India's principal social and economic gulf is the digital divide seems strange. It gives the impression that some of India's urban leaders are insufficiently acquainted with the economic realities of rural India.

suggests that the peasantry – including those in north India – does not necessarily acquiesce in this view. Many poor farmers get informal jobs in the city that enable them to send money to their families back in the village. The families remain behind because the jobs are not secure. This is one reason why India's official rate of urbanisation has slowed.

I was accompanied by my mother-in-law, Aparna, an academic who was head of the history department at Delhi University before she retired. We were visiting a village in Uttar Pradesh, India's most populous state with 170 million people, crammed densely into the plains around the Ganges, India's holiest river. The suggestion for the visit had come from Virender Singh, Aparna's driver, who, like many of Uttar Pradesh's peasantry, helps to sustain his family by working as a menial in New Delhi. Virender had been asking me for years to come and see what his village was like.

The village is about a three-hour drive from Delhi along pot-holed roads that are chock-a-block with scooters, bicycles, donkey carts and antique tractors that have been reincarnated, bizarrely, as what must be the slowest taxi service in the world. You often see twenty or thirty people crammed on to the back of the tractor and stuck to each other like glue, chugging along patiently at fifteen miles an hour. As it is across most of the Gangetic plain, which dominates northern India, the landscape is flat and monotonous. The villages seem infinite. It is hard to recall a view in which humans do not dominate both foreground and back-ground. Every few miles you see the Dickensian silhouette of an ailing sugar factory, supplied from the unending sugar-cane fields of western Uttar Pradesh. During the harvest, traffic can stop for miles around as the farmers queue for up to three days in their tractors and on their donkey-drawn carts to get their cane weighed at the mill. That the mill-owners do not open more queues and provide more weighing machines, and that the farm-ers appear to be calmly suffering this trial of patience, is testimony enough to the balance of power in rural Uttar Pradesh. To the out-sider, there is what looks to be an almost limitless tolerance to the Indian farmer, honed presumably by generations of practice. But there are strong new undercurrents beneath the still surface.

Virender's family home is like any other in the villages of Uttar Pradesh. There are six buffaloes kept within the small family com-pound, which is flanked by mud walls and covered by a straw roof. The dung of the buffaloes is put to multiple uses – as build-ing material for cementing the house, as fuel for cooking and as antiseptic flooring in the rooms. Cow dung is even used as an anti-septic in childbirth, which for families like Virender's still takes place at home. Maternal mortality in Uttar Pradesh, which is home to 8 per cent of the world's poorest people,[17] is among the highest in India.

Aparna and I were asked to sit on the family's only *charpoy* while Virender boiled some buffalo milk for us to drink. The roof and walls of the small kitchen, which also doubles as a sleeping area for eight people, were blackened to charcoal with the soot of the family hearth. The tubercular hacking cough is as common a sound in the north Indian village as the lowing of the cattle or the ringing of the temple bell. Virender said he was the only member of his family to work in Delhi out of four brothers. His small monthly salary accounts for 90 per cent of the family's income. The two-acre family plot, on which the brothers mostly grow jawar, a north Indian gram, or pulse, is just enough for the family's subsistence. The same story applied, in varying degrees, to all the neighbours in the village, he said. At least one member of each family remits income from the city.

We decided to visit the largest house and one of the few *pucca* constructions at the other end of the village, near the main road. As with many unannounced intrusions I have made in India, the family was quite happy to welcome strangers into their home without explanation. They were the *Thakurs*, or upper-caste land-holders, of the village. They said they had fifteen acres, some of which they rented out, but this would still barely account for their stupendous home, which flanks a large marble-paved courtyard in the centre of which sits a garish fountain. They said their family land had shrunk to about a third of its size following Nehru's land reforms in the 1950s and 1960s.

In another wing of the house they had constructed a small private temple to Sai Baba, a medieval savant who has a large following across the country. The ceilings of their living room were bordered with bright blue and white alabaster floral motifs, which reminded me of a stately ballroom in Regency England. Unlike most of the rest of the village, which makes do with kerosene lamps, the house was fully electrified and air-conditioned.

But like the rest of the village, this *Thakur* family depended upon the remittances of one family member to keep them afloat. 'My son works for MTNL in New Delhi,' said the mother of the house, as if no other explanation were needed when I had asked how they had built their inimitable home. Mahanagar Telephone Nigam Limited is the main urban state-owned telecom company in India. Its pay scales are dictated by civil service norms, so an executive would receive a salary of between $500 and $1000 a month, cushioned by plenty of non-cash benefits, such as free or subsidised housing, electricity and telephone calls. Although it is a princely sum by the standards of the rest of village, it could not possibly account for the family's opulent style of life.

But then almost nobody who has had dealings with MTNL, or any other public utility in India, would believe that the majority of its officers subsist on their salary alone. The pay cheque is mere pocket money. Their real earnings come from bribery. Although the company plays no part in this, its employees variously ask customers to cough up to get a new telephone line installed, to get an extortionate and unitemised bill reduced, to reinstate a line that had arbitrarily been cut, and so on.

For all but the Anglophone elite, who have exploited new opportunities for themselves since 1991, a job with the government is the most coveted there is. 'Government job,' said Virender, when I asked what career he most wanted. 'Government job,' had said his nephews and nieces, who seemed surprised I needed to ask. 'Government job,' said every villager introduced to me by Nikhil and Aruna in Sowangar a few months earlier. For the overwhelming majority of Indians, having a government job is not merely a question of security, although the fact that you cannot be sacked is a large incentive. Nor is it just a question of gaining a higher social status, though this is also a big attraction to most people. To the majority of Indian villagers, a government job is in the first place an instant leapfrog into a much higher standard of living. One might say it is the difference between a rickety hut built with buffalo dung and a house that is furnished with the finest marble from Rajasthan.

CHAPTER TWO

THE BURRA SAHIBS

The long tentacles of India's state

Just as it is impossible to know when a swimming fish is
drinking water, so it is impossible to find out when a
government servant is stealing money.

Kautilya, *Arthashastra* (*The Science of Wealth*),
c. 300 BC, India's classical political text

From the imperial corridors of New Delhi's loftiest ministry to the
sleepiest rural magistrate's court, India's government offices and
courtrooms share a number of instantly recognisable characteristics. These are the trademarks of a state that is never absent from
your life, except when you actually need it. If you were to assess
India's economic situation by walking through its corridors of
power, it would be impossible to guess the country was undergo-
ing a software revolution. Instead of computers, you have armies
of men shuffling paper. Instead of vacuum cleaners, you have
lower-caste sweepers carefully redistributing the dust beneath
your feet. As a substitute for a specific appointment, you are told:
'Just come.' Yes, but at what time? 'Don't worry. Just come.' In
place of waiting rooms, you have queues of supplicants spilling
over into the corridors and the courtyards outside, each hoping
to snatch a moment with the VIP whose mere word or signature

can put an end to a hundred sleepless nights and a thousand wasted phone calls. Instead of servants – civil or otherwise – you have masters.

Which is why, when I visited the offices of V. J. Kurian, a senior IAS officer who heads the highways department in the southern state of Kerala, I had to ask twice before I was sure I was in the right place. I had come to talk to Kurian about his much-admired feat of building an international airport for Cochin, a colonial-era port near the southernmost tip of India. The moment we walked into his department I was certain we had been misdirected. There were no peons clutching dusty files tied with string. In place of the noisy, antique telex machines there were sleek, wide-screened computers. And there were no petitioners lurking outside the office of the *burra sahib* (big boss), hoping for a chance encounter. My confusion was both resolved and compounded when Kurian came out of his office and said: 'I'm sorry I've kept you waiting. Do please come in and sit down.' The appointment had begun two minutes late. Fortunately though, Kurian was happy for it to run well past schedule. Fortunately also, Mr Kurian, like so many people in India, found it almost impossible to be reticent when talking to a foreign journalist. This is a trait in which I have constantly delighted.

Building an airport, or undertaking any public project in India, is relatively straightforward if you are not squeamish about corruption and do not mind too much about the quality of the end product. In this respect Kurian, who took charge of Cochin airport in 1992, was – and is – an eccentric. As a result of his obdurate refusal to play by the usual rules of the game, Cochin now has a clean and efficient international airport. Unlike most other airports in India, it also makes a profit. But Kurian had to negotiate an assault course of hurdles to achieve this. 'The most difficult moment was when I was called by a very senior politician,' he said, as we munched banana chips and drank the sugary office tea. 'The politician wanted me to choose the second-lowest bidder for the contract to build the airport runway and that I should discard the lowest bidder. When I said I would not break the rules, he said there was one *crore* [ten million rupees, about $200,000] in it for me. I stood my ground. The politician did not know what to say.'

Shortly afterwards, and to nobody's surprise, Kurian was transferred to an obscure job with little appeal or glamour. In India it is almost impossible to sack a civil servant, so if the carrot fails politicians usually transfer the offending official to an isolated district or a marginal department. But within two years, Kurian was recalled because the airport was making heavy losses. By 2005, it was achieving profit margins of 70 per cent, principally by having contracted out the retail services, most profitably the duty-free outlets, to private companies for hefty fees.

Arriving at Cochin airport is as disorienting as pitching up at V. J. Kurian's office. It is clean, modern, sleek and, unlike its counterparts in Delhi and Mumbai, which provide the first view of India to most arriving foreigners, the foyer does not appear to need twenty-four-hour crowd control. Yet, in spite of having a reputation for being professionally managed, Kurian continues to be plagued by 'requests' from ministers and other civil servants. 'On one occasion the Minister for Corporations and Electricity lost his temper with me because I refused to hire two hundred of his people as airport labourers. I told him that I had contracted out almost every single job to the private sector and so I had no control over who was hired or fired.' On another occasion the project was almost torpedoed when Air India, the state-owned carrier, said it would refuse to fly to Cochin unless it was given the contract to manage the ground-handling operations – a traditional source of patronage. On that occasion, Kurian had no choice but to concede, but elsewhere he has prevailed. 'If you stand firm and you don't mind where you get transferred to, then usually there's nothing they can do to you,' he said.

Kurian, though, is a rarity in India – a senior bureaucrat who has consciously minimised his own discretionary powers and those of his colleagues so that he can do his job better. I reminded him of a widely cited equation in India: $M + D = C$, Monopoly plus Discretion equals Corruption. For the youthful forty-five-year-old, who earns 42,000 rupees (about $1000) a month, a fraction of some of the offers he has received from the private sector, mention of this Einsteinesque formula was a cue to open up. As with many impressive people in India, he invoked the divine. 'I can only explain my luck and survival by fate and by divine providence – I have been blessed,' he said. I reminded him that he had also made the earthly decision to take anything they could throw at him. Why did so few other IAS officers do the same? 'It is hard to say,' he replied. 'The honest IAS officers deal with corruption by not doing anything – if you don't do anything then you are not corrupt. The problem with this is that there is so much to do.' He said that in Kerala some people even admired corrupt officials. 'They say if you're not making money, you must be really stupid.' Keralites have a word for honest officials – *pavangal*, which means a highly moral person of good intentions, but it can also be defined as naïve and gullible. Likewise, those who know how to give bribes are described as *buddhi*, which means cunning and implies the 'power of discrimination which distinguishes adults from children'.[1] It is a revealing vocabulary.

Kurian claimed most people underestimated the difficulties in cleaning up India's system of administration.

When I talk to left-wing friends I tell them they have got it so wrong: 'The true exploiter class in India is the bureaucracy. About one or two per cent of the population work for the government and they live off the people. These are your exploiters.' If you look at the new recruits to the IAS they are worse than my generation. They want

money straight away. They want to be wined and dined in
the most exotic holiday resorts and they make no attempt
to disguise their love of money. Nowadays they can see
how much money their friends and peers are making in the
private sector. That is why it is getting worse.

As if to keep his conscience dancing, Kurian was constantly interrupted by telephone calls during our conversation. One caller was
an official from another department who wanted Kurian to use
his influence to secure an upgrade to a business-class seat for his
flight that afternoon. Another was an official from the notorious customs and excise department who wanted free parking for
himself and his colleagues for an evening reception at the airport.
Kurian complied with both requests. 'What can you do?' he asked
me sheepishly. 'These are little, little things. There is no harm.'
I laughed at the relevance of the interruptions but also at his
honesty. If he had to pull 'little, little' strings, at least he was transparent about it.

And yet our conversation prompted thoughts of how difficult
it is in India to tame a creature that in many ways remains
out of control, in spite of the drastic curtailment of many of the
central government's powers since 1991 when Manmohan Singh
began to dismantle the 'License Raj'. It also reminded me of a
comment by Arun Shourie, who was Minister for Administrative
Reform in New Delhi from 1999 to 2002. Talking about his
efforts to reform the bureaucracy, he said: 'It is as if we were
to start hacking a path through the Amazon forest. By the time
we have proceeded a hundred yards, the undergrowth takes over
again.'

Shourie provides an example of the farce that sometimes
results from efforts to reform a system that will go to great
lengths to thwart even the smallest of changes.[2] In April 1999
India's Ministry for Steel submitted a formal query to Mr
Shourie's Ministry for Administrative Reform. The grave matter,

which was to take almost a year to resolve and would consume the valuable time of some of India's most senior officials, concerned whether civil servants should be allowed to use green or red ink, as opposed to the blue or black normally used to annotate documents.

After several weeks of meetings, consultations and memoranda, the IAS officers in Shourie's department concluded that the matter could be resolved only by officials at the Bureau of Printing. Another three weeks of learned deliberation ensued before the bureau returned the file to the Ministry of Administrative Reform, but with the recommendation that it should consult the Ministry of Training and Personnel. It took another three weeks for the file to reach that ministry since the diligent mandarins at Administrative Reform needed time to consider the expertly phrased deliberations of the Bureau of Printing. And so this question of state meandered for weeks and months, in meeting after meeting through ministry after ministry, before the following Solomonic compromise was struck: 'Initial drafting will be done in black or blue ink. Modifications in the draft at the subsequent levels may be made in green or red ink by the offices so as to distinguish the corrections made,' said the new order. Hierarchy also had to be specified: 'Only an officer of the level of joint secretary and above may use green or red ink in rare cases [duly set out, with appropriate caveats].' As Shourie noted, it was 'A good bureaucratic solution: discretion allowed but circumscribed!' If Franz Kafka had inserted this into one of his novels, critics would have accused him of going too far.

As for V. J. Kurian, he has received handsome offers to join prominent companies in India's private sector, but so far he has not been tempted. 'It might sound naïve in this day and age to say I am motivated by public service, but it is true,' Mr Kurian said, as I was finally leaving. For a moment I wondered whether I might ask Mr Kurian to arrange an upgrade for my flight back to Delhi the following day. The moment passed.

India has had more time than most parts of the world to get used to the state. Historians estimate that states began to form in India from at least the sixth century BC, when Buddha was emerging in northern India as the great philosophical sceptic of early history. *Arthashastra* (*The Science of Wealth*) was written between 300 and 200 BC for the Mauryan dynasty, whose most acclaimed scion, the Buddhist emperor Ashoka, is seen as perhaps India's greatest ruler.* In his potted history of the world H. G. Wells said: 'Amidst the tens of thousands of names of monarchs that crowd the columns of history the name of Ashoka shines, and shines almost alone, a star.' Scholars have estimated that Pataliputra, Ashoka's capital, whose ruins are beneath the modern city of Patna in northern India, had a population at least as large as that of imperial Rome. At a time when the Roman Empire had yet to be born and northern Europeans were not even at the stage when Romans would call them barbarians, Ashoka could draw upon the *Arthashastra*, a manual of governance that scholars consider the equal in sophistication and subtlety of Machiavelli's *The Prince*, written more than 1700 years later.

The tome, penned by Kautilya, can still evoke a shiver of recognition in early twenty-first-century India.[3] We are introduced to the idea of *mandala*, in which the kingdom views its diplomatic interests through ever widening circles, always allying itself with the next but one circle to unite against the circle in between. This is probably the earliest formal exposition of the doctrine of 'the enemy of my enemy is my friend'. Kautilya also lists the duties

---

*The deciphering by the British of the famous Ashokan edicts, which were carved on to pillars the length and breadth of India, brought to life a figure that time had virtually forgotten. Strictly Buddhist, Ashoka's edicts exhort his subjects to be kind to animals, to refrain from violence and to provide shelter for travellers. These are perhaps the earliest examples of public service announcements.

of each caste in minute detail. His description of the Vaishya, or merchant, caste as 'thieves that are not called by the name of thief' is one that can still be detected. At another point he elegantly suggests that the king's tax policy should resemble a bee's extraction of nectar from a flower: no enterprise should be taxed more than once; then it can flourish, profit and so be taxed again another day. (This evokes slightly less recognition in contemporary India.) He also recommends detailed rules of order for the bureaucracy: all departments of state should be headed by more than one person, to prevent their capture by selfish interests; officials should be transferred frequently for the same reason; and no decision should be taken by any official before having consulted a network of superiors. More famously, Kautilya lists forty ways that a bureaucrat can cheat a king of his revenues.

Many ages have passed since Kautilya penned his curiously bloodless vision of how a good government should operate. And it would, at the very least, be odd to project sentiments from India's ancient manuals on to its modern character, if only because so much time has elapsed. Yet there is a cultural – rather than a political – continuity to India that can be found in few other places, except China. When A. L. Basham, the British classical historian, wrote his still widely admired book *The Wonder That Was India* in 1954, he tried to persuade his American publishers to make a minor alteration in the title.[4] The book was part of a series that included the Aztecs, the Greeks, the Mayas, the ancient Egyptians and so on. Professor Basham said that in India's case 'was' should be changed to 'is', since its civilisational story was unbroken. Although his publishers would not concede the change, it was a good argument.

In contrast, the story of the state in India after Ashoka's empire had disintegrated is one of almost continual fragmentation, warfare and dissolution until the Mughal dynasty swept into northern India from Central Asia in the early sixteenth century. It was only when Emperor Akbar took the throne in the 1550s and held it until his death in 1605 – a reign almost exactly corresponding to that of Queen Elizabeth I of England – that most of what is present-day India was again united under one dynasty covering roughly the same territory Ashoka had ruled. The contrast with China, which has been governed from the centre for most of the last 2500 years, with only brief interludes of fragmentation or civil war, is stark. So too is the historical contrast between the Indian and Chinese systems of bureaucracy. China had a nationwide system of competitive examinations in which even a lowly peasant could become a mandarin on merit. Until the British colonised India in the eighteenth and nineteenth centuries, positions in the administration there were almost all hereditary and were mostly held by upper-caste Brahmins.

The chief influence that continues to shape India's state today is British – with some lingering traces of the Mughals. Remote from the people and Olympian in its self-image, the British colonial administration aimed to be 'minutely just and inflexibly upright'.[5] It has become fashionable since independence for historians in the west and India to dismiss the Indian civil service of the Victorian era as racially aloof and overtly imperialist. But this overlooks the progressive and in many respects radical impact that a civil service which professed equality before the law and the impartial administration of justice had on the Indian mindset. Although Indian judges were almost never allowed to try British defendants, British rule marked the first time in India's history that Indians were defined as equal to each other in the eyes of the law. The fact that in early twenty-first-century India there is still a debating society of lower-caste Hindus named after Lord Macaulay, the imperialist who authored the still-existing Indian Penal Code, is testimony to this. Nor is it surprising that B. R. Ambedkar, the lower-caste leader who framed India's constitution, hinted at times that he was more fearful of an independent India ruled by upper-caste Hindus that he was of continuing British rule.

For more than two hundred years Britain's cadre of district collectors saw themselves as 'Platonic Guardians',[6] an elite which remained deliberately aloof from the masses but which governed in their interests. This suited imperial purposes well since it was an efficient way of collecting taxes and of maintaining law and order. But it left a tradition of detachment and paternalism that remains evident today. To most modern Indian villagers, the following description of late nineteenth century India by a celebrated Indian writer looking back on his childhood might still fit quite well: 'Overhead there appeared to be, coinciding with the sky, an immutable sphere of justice and order, brooding sleeplessly over what happened below.'[7] Others have detected in today's India a popular attitude that thinks of the state 'like the monsoon, as an aspect of nature'.[8] Few people believe they can fight nature.

I have visited many of the colonial whitewashed bungalows inhabited by district collectors across India and wandered into numerous district 'collectorates' – the local headquarters where the official presides both as the local magistrate and as the local arm of the executive. Although the portrait hanging in the collector's office is of Mohandas Gandhi rather than King George IV, a nineteenth-century British colonial official would feel immediately at home. The collector is surrounded by a beehive of peons and never moves anywhere within the district without a phalanx of sidekicks. At every village he (or increasingly she) will be garlanded like a film star with carnations, jasmine or marigolds. Since the average population of each Indian district is almost two million people – larger than many of the member states of the United Nations – the village will only rarely, if ever, play host to the collector. So the village leaders will do their utmost to impress the *burra sahib* in the fleeting time they have. Even the collector's mode of transport, a colonial-era white Ambassador with an insistent red light flashing on top, is unchanged from the later days of the Raj.

Many of today's IAS officers are of high calibre and are motivated by the desire to uplift the lives of ordinary people. But very few hold on to the idealism with which they started their careers. I have lost count of the number of district collectors who have described their job as fighting a losing battle to fend off an ever rising tide of petitioners, supplicants, complainants, plaintiffs and sycophants. Like King Canute they cannot stem the tide. Like their British predecessors, they usually come from elsewhere and are far removed from their friends and peers. They work all day and sometimes all night, since there is little else to do in *mofussil* (small-town, rural) India. Many of them, especially since the 1970s, when corruption appears to have become widely accepted as normal in India,* have themselves become corrupt. Many even accept it as a legitimate part of the job. Since they are unsackable, there is almost nothing local people can do about a corrupt IAS officer, even if they believe the official is doing anything wrong in the first place.

In the last chapter we met Aruna Roy, Nikhil Dey and the MKSS, which fights against corruption in some of the poorest districts of India. Their campaign to hold the Indian civil service to account is one of the most impressive challenges so far to a cadre which owes much of its ethos to an imperial era that took its curtain call more than three generations ago. I accompanied Aruna and Nikhil to the main public square in Beawar, the district capital in their corner of Rajasthan, where they had spent forty days staging a *dharna* to embarrass the local authorities into providing information on public spending. The exercise, which caught the nation's attention, was far from academic. In a part of

*Indira Gandhi, who was Prime Minister for most of the 1970s, famously said of corruption: 'What can you do about it? It is a global phenomenon.' But India consistently ranks among the worst countries in the annual 'Transparency Index' of corruption conducted by a non-profit group in Germany.

the country where public relief works are sometimes the only difference between starvation and survival, tens of thousands of men and women had been denied the daily minimum wage of 73 rupees ($1.75) after performing months of back-breaking manual labour. Others found that their names had been included on the government's muster rolls when they had not provided any labour. Corrupt officials were pocketing the wages of these 'ghost workers' for labour on relief works, such as filling in pot-holes or building small 'check dams', which were themselves often fictional. Having forced the authorities to publish details of how much it had spent on what, the MKSS then set about verifying the state's own information. They discovered in one administrative sub-unit covering a group of villages that 4.5 million rupees out of a total of 6.5 million of public spending was entirely fictional. The name of the *panchayat*, or local council, is Janawad.

'It was high comedy,' said Nikhil. 'The government officials took us to a check dam that we knew had been registered as four different dams on their spending accounts. Then they took us to the same check dam three more times by three different routes hoping we wouldn't notice it was the same one. We weren't even angry. We were laughing too much.' Their inquiry yielded fictional muster rolls, imaginary health clinics, schools that did not exist and tens of thousands of people who had never been paid for their work. Embarrassed by all the media attention, the Rajasthani government reluctantly agreed to carry out its own inquiry into the allegations. Although this upheld the MKSS's findings, not one civil servant was fired, let alone convicted. Nevertheless, the case of Janawad has become a symbol in Rajasthan of how to combat bureaucratic venality. 'We never despair because we are making real progress,' said Aruna. 'It is becoming more difficult for the bureaucrats to be corrupt in the future. We have raised the cost of corruption.'

During their regular protests and agitations, Shankar Singh, the group's puppet-wielding and folk-singing mascot, keeps thousands of peasants entertained with compositions that are now well known in many villages throughout Rajasthan. 'They [the officials] are as fat as water melons,' Shankar sings in Hindi to the protesters. 'Their faces are as red as tomatoes. All they know how to do is give false assurances. Cut the noses off these high-nosed characters! They fed false names on to the muster rolls and they stole our money for development. Cut the noses off these high-nosed characters!' Shankar's show, conducted under the noses they want to cut off, causes hilarity among the villagers. It is a humorous and irreverent display of Indian democracy in action. In India the more local you get, the worse the corruption seems to be and the more control civil servants have over people's lives. This is reflected in voter turnout, which shows an ascending scale of participation the further down you go, with national elections evincing the least interest. Voter turnout for the *panchayat*, which covers just a handful of villages, is often higher than for national polls. When I visited the home of Virender, my mother-in-law's driver, I was surprised to discover that nobody knew the name of their member of parliament. But almost everyone knew the name of their representative in the state legislative assembly.

Nikhil took me to the offices of a nearby *panchayat*, Vijaypura, where the elected head, Kalu Ram, is a member of the MKSS, a Dalit (untouchable) and is not affiliated with any of the established political parties. His office contained a few plastic chairs and one temperamental fan. We were plied with a continuous flow of milky tea in small metal containers. Ram told me: 'When I started this job I went alone to see the collector to ask for the money that is supposed to be spent on the *panchayat*. He said: "Let's negotiate." I realised it was not worth going alone. If you go in a group to see any officials they cannot deny later what he has agreed to.'

Outside his office, which he will inhabit for four years, there was a bright yellow board that listed all the local public works projects, which included spending on road repairs, maternity clinics, new wells and recreational centres. Each item stated the amount spent and the date on which it would be completed. There were also large muster rolls painted on the walls so that people could check whether their names had been included and whether the wages they received were accurate. All of this was the result of the group's right to information (RTI) campaign, which forced the Rajasthani government to enact a law in the late 1990s. This law quickly gained recognition in other states, and in 2005 New Delhi passed a right to information act to cover all of India. Arun Shourie, the former Minister for Administrative Reform, would probably have been amused to learn that New Delhi excluded from the act some of the annotations written in the margins of official documents – regardless of ink colour. Aruna and Nikhil did not find it so funny. Bureaucratic obfuscation often flourishes in the margins.

'It is very hard to get people out of the habit of paying for what is theirs by right,' said Kalu Ram. For example, people often want a copy of their birth certificate so they can obtain a food ration book – something they should get for free. But they still routinely try to slip in three or four hundred rupees. Similarly, a widow might try to bribe an official for her husband's death certificate so she can qualify for assistance. As we spoke, two panic-stricken men in white turbans rushed in looking desperate for help. They were petty local officials who feared the police would file charges against them because they had misplaced public property. The property in question was a long piece of paper containing the names of those on the next muster roll. It had been eaten, they claimed, by the next-door neighbour's goat. I found it hard to contain my amusement at what seemed to be the Indian equivalent of 'The dog ate my homework'. But everyone else appeared to believe the story. 'The neighbour's goat could well have eaten their muster rolls,' said Nikhil. 'At this time of year before the monsoon there is no grass, so goats eat anything, including paper.' This was clearly not the moment to crack a joke about scapegoats.

Having reassured the two men that the goat would indeed take the blame, Ram was then approached by an old lady who was spitting with so much anger that her veil kept falling from her face. It took several minutes to calm her down and work out what had so enraged her. She showed us her food ration book and said the manager of the local Fair Price shop, where people who are classified as below the poverty line receive subsidised wheat and rice, had ripped out four coupons in exchange for only one coupon's worth of grain. Ram started taking notes. 'While you are worried about your stupid formalities,' the lady yelled, 'what about my stomach?' We stood up and marched down the road with her to the Fair Price shop. At first Ganga Singh, the food dealer in question, strenuously denied having stolen the coupons. Then, realising we were not going to disappear, his demeanour transformed and he smilingly handed over another three portions of wheat to the old lady. But the wheat was of such poor quality that even the local camels would have thought twice before eating it. Like many such food dealers, Singh had sold the good-quality government-supplied wheat on the black market and replaced it with inedible chaff. After more elaborate discussion, Singh cheerfully admitted this too in the full knowledge that nobody present could do anything to remove his licence. Eventually the lady departed with four rations of good wheat. It was an average day in a typical village in Rajasthan. 'This is what life is like for the poor in India,' said Nikhil. 'The government does not behave well towards them.'

In the Soviet Union there used to be a joke about people who were employed by the state: 'You pretend to work and we pretend to pay you.' In India the joke should be: 'You pretend to work and we will pay you handsomely.' It is true that India's elite IAS officers are underpaid relative to their increasingly well-remunerated counterparts in the private sector. However, unlike most private sector employees, they are entitled to many perks, including free housing, telephone, electricity, first-class travel and so on. More than 90 per cent of India's 21 million public sector employees are in the Class III or Class IV category of civil servants – such as junior officials, teachers, government drivers and peons. They are paid almost three times the salary of their peers doing equivalent jobs in the private sector. Only Ghana and Côte d'Ivoire in Africa have a higher ratio than this.[9] Furthermore, public employees have cast-iron job security. Under the curiously drafted Article 311 of India's constitution, it is virtually impossible to demote a corrupt civil servant, let alone to sack him.[10]

Probably the biggest non-salary benefit for many civil servants is the opportunity to make money on the side. Rajiv Gandhi, who took over as Prime Minister from his mother, Indira, in 1984 after she was assassinated, before he was himself assassinated in 1991, was among the biggest critics of corruption. He estimated that 85 per cent of all development spending in India was pocketed by bureaucrats. Some accused him of exaggeration, others of misleadingly precise guesswork. But his calculations are not challenged by those who are best acquainted with the system – the civil servants themselves. 'Corruption has reached such proportions in India that I sometimes wonder how much longer we can bear it,' Naresh Chandra, a former cabinet secretary, the most senior civil service job in India, told me in an interview. Another former cabinet secretary T. S. R. Subramaniam, told me: 'Many people, especially foreigners, do not appreciate the extent of corruption in India. They think it is an additional nuisance to the system. What they do not realise is that in many respects and in many parts of India it *is* the system.' Perhaps the best description comes from Pratap Bhanu Mehta, one of India's most respected political scientists, who heads a prominent think tank in New Delhi: 'At almost every point where citizens are governed, at every transaction where they are noted, registered, taxed, stamped, licensed, authorised or assessed, the impression of being open for negotiation is given.'[11]

One reason why such corruption does not provoke greater outrage is because most of India's middle class and the country's larger private businesses were liberated from the worst excesses of state interference when the Licence Raj was abolished in 1991. Those in the elite, who control the media and therefore shape public opinion, are least affected by it. Many believe that corruption is therefore on the retreat. What is less appreciated is the extent to which India's Licence Raj of quotas, permits and hair-splitting regulations continues to exist outside India's organised economy. Beyond the manicured lawns of middle-class India, the tentacles of the Licence Raj continue to reach into the lives of vast numbers of impoverished Indians.

For example, in New Delhi there are an estimated 500,000 bicycle rickshaw drivers, yet there is a ceiling of just 99,000 permits to operate a rickshaw. These are some of the poorest slum-dwellers in India. But rather than raise the permit ceiling or abolish the quota altogether, the state ensures that more than 400,000 people continue to operate illegally. In order to do so the rickshaw drivers have to pay regular bribes to the police each month.[12] Worse, a Delhi by-law specifies that the owner of the rickshaw must also be its driver. This means that budding entrepreneurs from the slums usually remain there because they are forbidden from buying more than one rickshaw and employing others. Naturally, those who do own more than one rickshaw pay the police handsomely to turn a blind eye.

For the same reason, New Delhi's 600,000 street hawkers are deliberately kept in a state of legal limbo. Many of the city's middle classes complain that the hawkers are occupying public space for free. But they each pay between 800 and 1000 rupees a month in bribes.[13] In spite of losing up to a third of their meagre earnings this way, the hawkers are often raided by the police or by the customs and excise department. Their goods – fruit juices, sunglasses, steaming samosas, imported cigarettes and T-shirts – are 'confiscated'. They almost never get them back. These are some of the benefits-in-kind of working as a policeman or a customs inspector. Life can be very cruel to the poor in India.

The country has managed to avoid famine since independence chiefly because it is a democracy, as Amartya Sen has argued. At times of acute shortage or crop failure, electoral pressure and the free media provide the state with an incentive to ensure the rapid and well-targeted distribution of emergency relief. India's last instance of mass starvation occurred in the early 1940s under the British, when millions died of hunger. The country's record since independence stands in striking contrast to that of China, where up to thirty million perished during Mao Zedong's 'Great Leap Forward' in the late 1950s. But India's democracy has a much less impressive record than authoritarian China at protecting its poor from other afflictions such as illiteracy, tuberculosis and malnutrition. One of the Indian state's most important functions, which was spelled out in the 1950 constitution, is to eliminate hunger and provide all with access to clean drinking water. New Delhi's failure to accomplish this is less glaring now than it was twenty or thirty years ago. Higher rates of economic growth have contributed to a steady reduction in poverty: the proportion of Indians living below the official poverty line fell from more than 40 per cent of the population in the 1980s to just under 26 per cent by 2001. But that still means that in 2006 almost 300 million Indians can never be sure where their next meal will come from. They also live with the probability that more than one of their children will die from easily preventable water-borne disease. Almost a million Indian infants die of diarrhoea every year.

India's failings have nothing to do with a lack of resources. Poorer countries, such as Bangladesh and Botswana, have better human development indicators than India.[14] New Delhi has enough funds not just to develop and maintain an arsenal of nuclear warheads but to embark on a race with China to send an unmanned space mission to the moon – something that both countries hope to achieve by 2010.

Yet India's state seems unable to provide even the most basic of amenities to many of its poor, such as public toilets for the urban slums, chalk for primary school teachers in the countryside or clean syringes for its doctors in the country's *mofussil* health clinics. In light of the growing threat of an HIV–Aids pandemic in India, the poor quality of most of the country's rural clinics is particularly worrisome. India spends less on primary healthcare as a proportion of gross domestic product than almost any other developing country.[15]

Chief among the Indian state's failings is its system of food subsidies for those living below the poverty line. As Amartya Sen pointed out, food distribution is highly effective in India when there is a threat of famine. Yet 47 per cent of India's children who are under five years old are 'chronically malnourished' by United Nations standards.[16] A malnourished child is likely to be stunted both mentally and physically for the remainder of his or her life – the majority of malnourished children in India are girls. When she becomes an adult, a woman will pass on many of her mineral deficiencies to her unborn children.

How can a state that achieves feats of genuine technological prowess fail in such a basic objective? Observing the workings of India's food subsidy system in greater detail brings us close to an answer. The problem is not lack of food: India's grain production has more than quadrupled since independence, while its population has tripled. The Indian government also holds vast food surpluses: at one stage in 2003 India was storing more than sixty million tonnes of grain in its public warehouses, enough to provide a tonne of rice or wheat to every single family living below the poverty line. (This amounted to more than a fifth of world grain stocks at the time.) Nor does the answer lie in spending limits. India spends almost as much on defence than on all its anti-poverty programmes put together. The answer, unfortunately, is to be found in the mentality of India's civil servants and in the general public's inability to translate its frustration with the bureaucracy into genuine reform of the system through the ballot box. It is a complex problem, but India's ability to find a solution will have serious implications far beyond its national borders.

One of the most disturbing experiences I have ever had was visiting the slum of Sunder Nagri, which ironically means 'beautiful town', in New Delhi. Situated just a few miles from the genuinely beautiful and imposing buildings of political Delhi, which were designed by Edwin Lutyens in the 1920s, Sunder Nagri is home to tens of thousands of people living in conditions that ought to have disappeared long ago. I was accompanied by members of a group called Parivartan, which translates as 'renewal', who are as much of a nuisance to officials in India's capital as Aruna Roy's people are to the bureaucrats of Rajasthan. They took me to see a group of local women in a small hall off one of the slum's narrow but cheerfully decorated side streets. A large sign in Hindi in the centre of the hall said: 'Silence is death.'

Each of the women had experienced unimaginable horrors. One had visited the police station to register a case of rape. She was taken to one of the cells and raped again by those to whom she had turned for help. Another had lost a child who was playing outside on the street when he fell into a channel and drowned in the sewage. The local member of Delhi's legislative assembly had promised to enquire into the matter but she never heard from him again. Another, a widow, had been trying and failing for years to obtain a certificate proving her husband had died in order to benefit from a small state pension. She could not afford the bribe that would secure the certificate. These were isolated horrors.

I do not want to give the impression that the lives of India's poor consist of nothing but tortuous endurance. Like many other visitors, I am often struck by the sense of community, colour and laughter that one sees in India's slums; and I am always humbled by the generosity of their inhabitants both to outsiders and to each other. However, many of the women to whom I spoke, and many of the poor Indians whom I have met in villages and slums across the country, have been deprived of their right to sub-sidised food. India's government can be both negligent and callous, but the state's army of statisticians regularly churns out reports that supply incriminating evidence of its own guilt, as does a wealth of independent studies.[17] They vary in their details, but all point to a glaring and massive 'diversion' of public food from those to whom it is supposed to be targeted. Rates of theft vary widely from state to state, with the better ones, such as Kerala and Tamil Nadu, getting more than 80 per cent of sub-sidised food to their poor. However, in the northern state of Bihar, India's second poorest with a population of 75 million, more than 80 per cent of the food is stolen. The all-India aver-age varies between a quarter and a half of all food depending on the survey. It conveys a pattern of routine larceny at all levels of the state.

One of the women described how she had tried to secure a BPL (below poverty line) card so she could acquire the subsidised grain, kerosene and sugar to which she and her family were enti-tled. Government surveys show that up to 40 per cent of those who possess BPL cards are not themselves poor; they have obtained the cards through bribery. So up to half of India's sub-sidised food is stolen, and almost half of those who gain access to what is left do so fraudulently. 'They would not even give me the correct application form unless I bribed them,' said the woman, who was a migrant to Delhi from Bihar. 'Then when I bribed them, they gave me a form in English, which I do not under-stand. So I had to pay somebody sitting outside the office to write out my application.' Having finally received the card at great expense, she then visited the local Fair Price shop. It was almost never open, and when it was, all they had was mildewed old wheat grain. The woman showed me a sample that was crawling with insects.

On this occasion I forgot to ask what jobs the women would like to see their children get when they were older, but I have little doubt that most of them would have wanted them to work for the government. It is hard to argue with so common an aspiration even though the aspirants are implicitly condoning the corruption of which they are so often victims. Pratap Bhanu Mehta describes the ambivalence of Indians towards the state as a 'civil war within our souls . . . In a society that does not often acknowledge the worth and value of individuals, where the visible means of proving one's worth through substantial achievement are open only to a few, corruption is a way of saying you are somebody.'[18] A government job confers status, money and opportunity. For those who live in slums such as Sunder Nagri it is the most obvious way of moving up to a better class. To the poor, the state is both an enemy and a friend. It tantalises them with a ladder that promises to lift them out of poverty, but it habitually kicks them in the teeth when they turn to it for help. It inspires both fear and promise. To India's poor the state is like an abusive father whom you can never abandon. It is through you that his sins are likely to live on.

I was having a quiet lunch with Sanjoy Dasgupta, a senior IAS officer, in Bangalore when something unusual happened: he burst into tears and remained in this state for several minutes. We were dining at the Bangalore Club, a traditional members-only institution founded during the Raj. The club has prominently hung a framed copy of a large unpaid bill in the name of Winston Churchill, who was stationed here as a military officer in the 1890s. Perhaps because of its starchy traditions, nobody appeared to notice Dasgupta's discomfort. He had been telling me about Captain Thomas Mun, a British district collector, who in the late nineteenth century had apparently transformed the lives of hundreds of parched villages in a nearby district. Riding on horseback almost continually for several years, Mun had covered vast tracts of the south Indian countryside in search of the best places to sink wells. Even today, over a century later, the local villagers still celebrate his legacy by leaving small offerings at the wells that he sunk. In the late 1990s Dasgupta took the same job that Mun had as district collector of Kolar, in what is now the southern state of Karnataka. So moved was he by the affection in which the long-dead official was still held that he set about finding Mun's gravestone. Having located it and cleaned it up, he invited his predecessor's descendants and a representative from his former military regiment in Britain to a small commemoration in Bangalore. 'The love and dedication that one man showed to poor voiceless villagers should be an inspiration to us all,' Dasgupta told me. 'He died serving them.' Then he started to cry.

Decades from now, the inhabitants of Kolar, a ruggedly beautiful but impoverished district that suffers from very sporadic rainfall, might well see Sanjoy Dasgupta in a similar light. Motivated by a sense of public service, he made use of the latest technology to improve the water situation for villagers in the area. Whereas the Victorian district collector used his own amateur (but effective) knowledge of geology to locate the right spots to dig, Dasgupta commissioned satellite imagery from the Indian Space Research Organisation (ISRO), which is based in Bangalore. ISRO's images revealed more than four thousand ancient 'tanks', or small reservoirs, that had fallen into disuse and become silted up. These had been the lifeblood of a once-efficient system of irrigation for the farmers. Dasgupta set about restoring them.

I visited one of the villages that was benefiting from his scheme. They told me nowadays only wealthy farmers could count on regular supplies of irrigation water for their crops, since only they could afford to install the electricity connections and buy the equipment to sink bore holes that are needed to pump water from the ground. As a result, the area's water table had dropped from 40 feet below the surface in the 1960s to more than 600 feet underground. The natural wells on which the poorer farmers rely are useless at such depths. The ancient habit of harvesting rainwater as it falls and feeding it through hundreds of channels into tanks has also disappeared. The tanks and their feeder channels were maintained by a family in the village, whose specific task was hereditary. But after independence the government said it would take charge of all irrigation to bring development to the people. The people I met did not seem very impressed. It is a story that is repeated across India. In the name of the poor the state provides free electricity to farmers so they can pump water from the ground, but it is usually only the rich farmers who benefit. Their modern pumps suck out the groundwater, draining the water table that had once been available to all. Since they pay nothing for the electricity, their pumps are constantly in use. 'If you give something for free then people will always overuse it,' explained Dasgupta.* As is so often the case, the gap between the Indian state's rhetoric and its actions is vast. In the name of the poor the poor are deprived of water.

Yet, as Sanjoy Dasgupta discovered with ISRO, some arms of the Indian state are both efficient and impressive. The space agency, which was set up in the 1960s by Vikram Sarabhai, an inspirational figure from an old industrialist family in the western state of Gujarat, is in charge of a satellite programme that is considered as good as any in the developing world, if not better. Other countries, such as Malaysia and Thailand, rent India's satellites for meteorological purposes, as do UN scientists studying global warming.

Some, including the United States, have long alleged that the science behind ISRO's satellite-launch vehicles is supplied directly to India's military establishment for its nuclear missile programme, which requires similar technology. ISRO denies the charges and insists it is wholly separate. 'It is like asking: "Have

---

*I was very saddened to learn that Sanjoy Dasgupta died suddenly of a heart attack in late 2005.

you stopped beating your wife?"' said S. K. Das, the senior civil servant at ISRO. 'We cannot prove a negative.' What ISRO does prove is that the Indian state can be efficient and accountable when it wants to be. Another example is the Election Commission, which organises and monitors fully computerised national polls involving more than 600 million voters, and presides over free and fair elections that western observers say bear 'comparison with any third world and most first world countries'.[19] Each successive Indian general election is by definition the largest democratic exercise in history. Nobody has ever alleged the overall result was hijacked. Likewise, the policing and sanitation for India's grand *Kumbh Mela*, a Hindu religious gathering which takes place every twelve years at the confluence of the Ganges and Jamuna rivers, is unparalleled. Somehow the state manages to ensure the safety and health of more than ten million people who camp on the river banks. It is a very impressive logistical feat.

Evidently India's problems with governance have more to do with the state's priorities than with its capabilities. S. K. Das believes ISRO owes its efficiency to the fact that it was granted independence of action. 'ISRO is accountable only to the Prime Minister, so we don't have all these ministries interfering with our day-to-day operations. Because we are treated well and given autonomy, people very rarely leave,' he said. Likewise, the Election Commission has statutory powers granting it independence, and civil servants who work there cannot be transferred if they displease the politicians. This does not apply to bureaucrats working in normal government departments. Immunity from transfer gives the election commissioners the confidence to take tough decisions and to ignore the pressure of those who want to stuff the ballot boxes. In ISRO's case, there is an additional reason: 'Launching satellites is such a difficult and precise technology and it is so hard to get it right that if there was even one per cent corruption the satellite would come crashing down to earth,' said Das. 'We cannot afford to be corrupt. It is a national priority.' As indeed are free and fair elections.

Contrast these success stories with the notorious inefficiency of the highways department in Uttar Pradesh. This state has some of the worst roads in India: they are so pot-holed that most of the villages cannot even get their farm surplus to market. *Kutcha* (sub-standard) roads are one of the main reasons why only 2 per cent of India's farm output has any value added to it beyond being harvested or milked. More than a third of the country's vegetables and fruit rot before arriving at market. The government cannot blame lack of manpower: the highways department employs one worker for every two kilometres of road, among the highest ratios in the world.[20] But many of them do not bother to turn up for work because they cannot be sacked; and any attempt to offer voluntary redundancy to public sector workers prompts an outcry about abuse of workers' rights. (There is little such outrage about what happens every day to the produce of Uttar Pradesh's far poorer and far more numerous farmers.) But even if the road maintenance gangs did regularly report for duty, the government in Lucknow, the historic state capital, would still be unable to equip them with enough tools and material for the job, such as steamrollers and tarmac, because it spends most of its road budget on salaries. The employees of Uttar Pradesh's highways department are paid more than three times the market's going rate.

The same pattern is visible in numerous public sector departments across much of India. Perhaps uncoincidentally, it is particularly visible in the poorest states of the north. In their development programmes India's poorest states have a ratio of seventy rupees of direct spending to every hundred rupees that go on salaries.[21] This is before accounting for what is euphemistically described as the cost of 'leakage', otherwise known as corruption. To put it starkly, the amount spent on the salaries of a few million employees is far greater than what is spent on all the anti-poverty measures for hundreds of millions of people.

There is an even bigger example of fraudulent accounting on India's books: public subsidies. We have already seen what happens to food subsidies. The same applies to fertiliser subsidies, which is the second-largest subsidy item in New Delhi's annual budget. If all of India's 'pro-poor' subsidies are added together and evaluated, two-thirds of subsidy spending is 'non-merit', in the felicitous words of the Indian government.[22] In other words they go to the 'non-poor', and often to the very rich. Most of the rest of India's annual budget is spent on interest payments to service the government's debt, on salaries and pensions for its employees, and on the military. As a result, India's central government and its states have a combined budget deficit of almost 10 per cent of gross domestic product. Since the state borrows so heavily to fund expenditure, which it mostly lavishes on itself, there is a continual shortage of capital for everyone else. This increases the cost of borrowing, which sharply lowers the overall level of investment in the Indian economy, costing millions of potential jobs. Furthermore, after spending so much money on itself, the state has very little left over to spend on better infrastructure, which would create many new jobs directly and even more indirectly. Better roads, electricity supply, railways and ports would stimulate higher investment by private businesses, which would expand overall employment. The difference between these vicious and virtuous circles is the difference between lifting hundreds of millions out of poverty within a generation, and leaving the majority as they are, to watch their vegetables rot and hope their children have better luck.

At a certain stage, anyone describing the gap between what the Indian state says it is doing and what it actually does starts running out of appropriate vocabulary. Hypocrisy is too mild a word to describe those who defend this system in the name of the poor. More diplomatically, Amartya Sen has compared the outcomes of the Indian state's policies to 'friendly fire',[23] when soldiers accidentally shoot their own men. He illustrates this 'lethal confusion' with his appraisal of India's support system for farmers, which is designed to reduce poverty. Under this policy, the government buys wheat and rice from farmers at a higher price than the market would pay in order to increase their incomes. This 'minimum support price' system sounds reasonable in theory. But in practice it is a *maximum* support price system.* A small proportion of wealthy farmers in the well-irrigated states of Punjab and Haryana collect almost all the subsidy, because they produce much higher surpluses of grain than those in other states and because they operate a ruthlessly effective lobbying system in New Delhi. The government's intervention sharply raises the purchasing price of food, which inflates its selling price. Higher food prices hit everybody, but they hit the poorest hardest, since they spend almost all of their incomes on food. In theory the Fair Price shops should shield the poorest from higher prices by supplying them with cheaper food. But, as we have seen, they do no such thing in practice. India's food policy might be aimed at an enemy called poverty, but it ends up shooting the poor.

By the same token, India's judicial system is supposedly blind, but it often has eyes for the rich and powerful.

It was one of those beautiful Indian dawns in which you savour every drop of mist before the heat of the day forces you back indoors. I was at the Madras Club in Chennai, having breakfast with Sriram Panchu, a senior advocate at the High Court, who was offering his views on the Indian legal system. We were outside on the veranda between neoclassical stone pillars and

---

*It reminds me of a joke. An adviser tries to convince a bureaucrat of the merits of a policy and ends by exclaiming: 'And it works in practice.' The bureaucrat replies: 'That's all very well, but does it work in theory?'

beneath the lazy whirring of a giant ceiling fan. On the river across from the club, you could spot the occasional fully crewed boat flitting through the mist and the flash of early morning sunlight on their oars.

I had been introduced to Mr Panchu the previous weekend up in the Nilgiris (Blue Mountains) in the small town of Coonoor, a former colonial summer retreat, surrounded by tea gardens. We were with the family of a mutual friend, Ramachandra Guha, one of India's best-known historians, and his talented wife Sujata, who owns her own design company. We had met for lunch at the club in Ooty, another colonial hill station which, like Coonoor, has become a favourite weekend haunt of the middle classes of Chennai and Bangalore. All of us had been amused by the portraits of red-jacketed colonial fox-hunters and their hounds that covered every available square inch of the club's yellowing walls. The game of snooker was invented in the Ooty Club by what I presume were extremely bored British military officers. 'Does all of this make you feel nostalgic for home?' Panchu had asked kindly. 'No,' I said truthfully, through a mouthful of heavily boiled peas and carrots.

Over breakfast at the Madras Club, Panchu and I agreed that India has preserved aspects of traditional British culture in far greater detail than Britain itself. One such aspect was the mania among India's Anglophone elite for belonging to exclusive clubs. I had observed in my time in India that most Indian judges live a very genteel life. For a judge the normal day in court begins at 10 a.m. and winds up at 4.15 p.m., with at least one hour for lunch. The judge's holiday leave is extensive, and in addition most Indian courtrooms adjourn for all of the nation's religious days. India has more religious holidays than any other country in the world: in addition to the mainstream Hindu and Muslim festivals, there are days commemorating key moments of the national freedom struggle, and festivals for Sikhs, Christians, Buddhists, Jains and Parsees. Many of these holidays

are voluntary. But Indian judges seem to be compulsively ecumenical.

The Indian judicial system's leisurely approach to life is exacerbated by the fact that so many judicial posts remain unoccupied.
While India has one of the lowest ratios of judges to population in
the world, the senior judiciary appears to be in little hurry to fill
the large number of vacancies below them. In some parts of India
a quarter of all judgeships are empty.

It is important to underline that just as there are many self-
sacrificing officers in the IAS, there are also many Indian judges with
a strong reputation for integrity. And there are some, particularly
in the senior appeals courts, who give rulings that are both timely
and courageous, which regularly check the powers of an executive
that has lost its sense of balance. India should be thankful for
having a legal system that often attracts people of quality. China,
for one, has much to envy India for its independent judiciary.

But like the IAS, which since the early 1990s has had ever
greater difficulty in attracting qualified people because there is so
much money to be made in the private sector, the best-quality
(and best-paid) Indian lawyers are increasingly reluctant to accept
judgeships. A judge in India gets an Ambassador car with a chauffeur, an official residence with gardeners and cooks, a full waiver
from utility charges, and a large amount of kudos. But a judge's
formal salary looks smaller and smaller as the years go by. At
around 30,000 rupees (about $700) a month, a high court judge in
the autumn of his career is paid the same as a twenty-five-year-old
engineer in the software industry or a young graduate in the media
or advertising. 'The lifestyle is great, but if you want to send your
children to a good university abroad or even in India, the judge's
salary is next to useless,' said Panchu. 'The pension is a percentage
of the salary, so once you have retired and given up your official
residence and your chauffeur, you have to think of other sources
of income. Many judges look to remunerative legal work after
retirement.'

Unsurprisingly, then, a minority of judges succumb to corruption. While some punitive action is possible in the case of the lower judiciary, judges of the superior courts can be removed only through impeachment by Parliament. A two-thirds majority of votes is needed for this, precisely what is required to amend the constitution. This has never happened. In spite of serious concerns voiced by senior judges about corruption in the judiciary, India has yet to put in place an effective mechanism to investigate and prosecute corrupt judges.

An even bigger problem in the Indian judicial system is the gigantic backlog of suits, which in 2006 amounted to twenty-seven million cases. At the current rate at which India's courts go through proceedings, it would take more than three hundred years to clear the judical backlog.[24] 'The motto of our judiciary really ought to be "Justice delayed is justice denied",' said Panchu. This is hardly a new problem for India. There were similar complaints about the slow wheels of justice during the era of the British, many of whose laws, like their clubs, are unchanged. But complaints about slow justice stretch back even further than that. One of India's ancient texts warns its readers of a legendary King Nrga, who was reborn as a lizard because he kept two litigants waiting for too long over a cow dispute.[25] There would be many a lizard presiding over India's courtrooms today.

The cost to Indian society of its sclerotic legal system is steep. Although the higher courts, and particularly the Supreme Court, allow important cases to jump the queue, it takes as long as fifteen years for some murder trials to be heard. By this stage many of the witnesses are dead and most of the rest cannot remember much that would be admissible in court. A very low proportion of criminals is therefore convicted. There is also an economic cost: almost $75 billion is tied up in legal disputes.[26] This is roughly 10 per cent of India's gross domestic product in 2006. This money could be invested in jobs and growth.

Predictably, legal disputes between different arms of government, or between one ministry and another, account for a significant proportion of the twenty-seven million cases that are in the pipeline; India's state has a knack of clogging itself up. One of the largest backlog of cases is civil suits within families, such as disputes over inheritance, family property, divorce and custody. At least here there is greater prospect for reform. Panchu has recently set up India's first court-annexed mediation centre, which is inspired by a similar system in parts of the United States, and which he hopes will take hundreds of thousands of civil cases out of the Indian legal system.

Another innovation in India's legal system is for courts to accept petitions from any member of the public to hear cases of public interest – so-called PILs, public interest litigations. The Supreme Court has said it will even accept petitions on a postcard from somebody in prison. Such cases tend to jump the queue, and they provide important redressal to a bureaucracy and a political system that is often deaf to questions of public importance. The PIL has grown in importance since the 1980s, partly because India has moved from one-party majorities to a seemingly permanent condition of coalition government. This has fragmented the legislature and enhanced the political power of the courts to intrude on the terrain of the executive. The Supreme Court has ruled on PILs ranging from the right to clean drinking water to the state's alleged complicity in communal riots and the removal or demolition of illegal structures in cities. In spite of the many inadequacies of India's legal system, the PIL offers a real alternative when citizens feel that other arms of the state have become deaf to their rights. However, its growing popularity has clogged up the judicial system even further. India needs many more civil mediation centres if it wants to provide anything approaching timely justice. 'We are persuading people that they will save hugely both on cost and time if they go to a mediator and avoid the courts,' said Panchu. 'Civil cases account for up to a fifth of the judicial backlog. So if we can succeed in persuading people of the merits of mediation, it would be a big help.' I could only wish him luck. By this stage the sun had risen and a searing heat was starting to intrude.* We retreated to our vehicles.

A couple of weeks later, at a very different kind of meeting, I was given a jolting reminder of Sriram Panchu's views on the price India often pays for its slow-moving legal system. I was in Dadar, a nondescript district in mid-town Mumbai, drinking coffee with a senior policeman in a seedy hotel. The police officer, who was head of the crime unit for a zone covering about a quarter of this vast metropolis of sixteen million people, had recently been suspended pending an investigation into his role in the extra-judicial killing of a terrorist suspect. The policeman, whose name, for obvious reasons, I promised to withhold, had the standard Indian policeman's moustache. His thinning hair was oiled and brushed carefully over a bald patch. He wanted to talk. 'They have given me six months' paid leave, so I have plenty of time on my hands,' he said. Like a small number of senior policemen in Mumbai, he is an encounter specialist, an officer who kills criminals in 'fake encounters'. Indian newspapers often describe the criminal as having tried to 'flee the scene', which leads to 'an intense shoot-out'. They usually result in dead criminals and unscathed policemen. Often the bullet holes are found in the back of the corpse.

My interviewee was happy to explain how encounter specialists operated. He was equally candid about his own role in killing suspects whom he believed the courts would either absolve or never get round to trying. However, he flatly denied any involvement in the killing of the alleged terrorist, a man who had been detained for questioning after a bloody terrorist incident in 2003: two car bombs were detonated near Mumbai's seafront and killed fifty-seven bystanders. The Indian government

---

*So intense is the summer heat in most of India that at one dinner party our hostess said, in full seriousness: 'Please sit down to eat or the soup will get hot.'

said the bombing was facilitated by Pakistan's Inter-Services Intelligence Agency, Islamabad's equivalent of the CIA, but the case remains open.

'It is ironic that the one time I didn't actually kill the person in question, I get suspended,' said the policeman. 'Why would I want to kill a key witness who could have led us to the organising network behind the bombs?' I did not have an answer, but I felt it would be wise to agree with whatever he said. I asked how many encounter killings he had carried out. 'About fifty,' he said, 'which, compared to X [the head of the anti-crime unit in another zone of Mumbai], is not very many. He has been involved in about eighty.' My goodness, I replied, that is many more than you. 'I always have to be one hundred per cent certain before I agree to anything.' Did he also have to get approval from a superior beforehand? He gave me a patient look. 'It is very rare that you get a freelance encounter killing,' he said. 'I have never been involved in a killing that hasn't either been approved or requested by the senior commissioner of police. We do not break the chain of command.'

I found this insight both reassuring and unsettling. Although the encounter system has been widely chronicled in the Indian media and elsewhere, and although I have spoken to other policemen about it, I had not fully understood how organised and hierarchical it was. He then explained that the killing of the alleged terrorist had been carried out by a policeman in Mumbai's anti-terrorist unit who had been bribed to kill the witness. My interviewee claimed he was being framed, which he said was another part of the deal struck by the bribed officer. 'He [the anti-terrorist officer] paid a lot of money to get transferred to the job in the anti-terrorist unit, which is highly coveted and very prestigious,' he said. 'Naturally he has to find ways of repaying his debts.' I believed his story, although he had no evidence to back it up. Nevertheless, Dnyanesh Jathar, a veteran Mumbai-based journalist who had arranged the interview, told me the case against our policeman would probably fizzle out.

And what were the ground rules for agreeing to an encounter killing? The suspended policeman gave me an example of the type of case that might result in an order to kill the suspect. It involved a very grisly murder that had taken place in 1992; he had been the chief investigating officer. He said he assembled a clear-cut case against the alleged culprit, but the trial was postponed for a couple of years and the defendant was granted bail. As the new trial date approached, some of the key witnesses 'turned hostile' – either changed or withdrew their testimony. Another key witness was killed in a car accident. 'It is a waste of time and it is damaging to our morale,' he said. 'All the defendant needs to do is find a corrupt judge to buy him time and he will do the rest. If you see the nature of some of these murders, if you see how these *goondas* [thugs] terrorise people in the slums, then you would want to do the same. Even if the judge is honest, the case usually takes too long to come to trial. We end up with useless witnesses who can't remember anything of value.'

The day-to-day lives of Mumbai's senior police officers are bound up with the city's notorious mafia gangs. The city's best-known mafia don has an Interpol arrest warrant against him and is alleged by New Delhi to be living in Karachi, Pakistan. His rivals, like most celebrity dons, are often spotted in Dubai, in the United Arab Emirates, but are unlikely ever to be brought to justice in India. Most of the bigger dons who have fled Mumbai control proxy dons from exile, but their power is declining. They made their money in the 1970s and 1980s smuggling goods that were easily available in other countries but which were closely regulated under India's strict regime of import controls. 'The mafia dons were making most of their money from smuggling gold and electronic goods,' said the policeman. 'Since the 1990s restrictions have been lifted so there is much less money to be made in smuggling. They still have protection rackets and prostitution rings, but they are not as lucrative.'

In the last few years the Indian government has relaxed the rules governing the finance of the film industry, which means that Bollywood producers can tap sources of mainstream finance much more easily nowadays and do not so often have to rely on backing from the underworld. As the anti-prohibitionists argued in America in the 1930s, the simplest way to get rid of crime is to get rid of the controls on the things people want. 'Ten years ago we would have two or three gang killings every day,' said the policeman. 'Now it is a few each month. It has definitely improved.' He said the work of Mumbai's police was now increasingly focused on tackling the two new frontiers of organised crime: Islamist terrorist groups and battles for control of the city's most expensive real estate. Although India has dismantled many of its trade restrictions, the country maintains a very detailed system of property market controls in its largest cities, particularly in Mumbai, which has some of the highest land values in the world. In the past people talked of the 'Bollywood mafia'. Now they talk of Mumbai's 'land mafia'.

The only time the policeman's bonhomie gave way to anger was when I asked him about the entry of mafia dons and *goondas* into mainstream politics. By standing for election, criminals hope to gain respectability and to protect themselves from possible encounter killings by the police. But these strongmen also fill a gap that is left by the state. Many of Mumbai's slum-dwellers, who account for a majority of the city's population, receive next to nothing from the state, so they turn to the dons. We talked about Arun Gawli, one alleged mafia don, who is now a member of the state assembly of Maharashtra and with whom I had spent the previous evening. Gawli, whose constituency is in mid-town Mumbai, had denied ever having been involved in a murder. I passed this on to the policeman. He erupted in laughter, then began to enumerate the multiple cases 'pending' against Gawli, most of them alleging murder. I asked why the police had not arranged an encounter with Gawli, since they clearly believed him to be guilty. 'So far we have not had a good opportunity,' he said.

I thought a great deal about this unusual conversation over the following days, and I shared its contents with some better-informed people. In spite of having a Westminster-style system, in which employees of the state are required to be politically neutral, India is no stranger to partisan civil servants, biased judges and pliable policemen. When a policeman crosses the line and becomes a vigilante, he often acquires a taste for it. It would take a strong character never to misuse the power of life and death over others. Later we will look at an incident that took place in Gujarat in 2002 in which up to two thousand innocent Muslims were massacred by Hindu militants while the local police stood by and watched, allegedly, on the instructions of their political masters. It has happened before, even in Mumbai. I wondered how many years of incremental compromises and accumulated cynicism it would take before you could watch children and their mothers being burned alive without intervening.

Away from such horrors, in the everyday policing of rural and urban India, it is relatively common for the police chief to take orders from a local political faction or an ascendant rural caste leader. In the ranks below the elite Indian Police Service, which is a parallel stream to the IAS, India has hundreds of thousands of police constables who have minimal training, low average levels of education, and a weak sense of belonging to an institution. Unlike the Indian military, which instils a much greater *esprit de corps* in its recruits, the loyalties of India's police often appear to be open to negotiation. 'Procedures [for bribery] are organised in networks that are built around key individuals,' according to one account of life in rural Uttar Pradesh.[27]

Whatever your social standing, and from whichever corner of India you come, your experience of the Indian state is too often governed by your dealings with 'key individuals' rather than with key institutions. In India men are still often stronger than laws. It would be hard to deny that most of the poor in today's India can only rarely expect to be treated with respect by the state, let alone in the same way as their social or economic superiors. India has been described as a 'rich–poor nation' with a 'weak–strong state'.[28] The writ of the state is visible almost everywhere you look. But it is a state whose powers are easily hijacked by groups or individuals for their own private gains. Sometimes they claim to be acting on behalf of the poor, but the poor do not always take this literally. Often they sign away their allegiance to independent strongmen who operate private fiefdoms like parallel mini-states. Such as Arun Gawli.

'There is no pillow as soft as a clear conscience,' said the slogan on the poster, with a picture of Mecca behind it. The poster was hanging on a wall in the waiting room of the five-storey head-quarters of Arun Gawli in the heart of Mumbai's textile district. Many of Gawli's supporters, who are drawn mostly from the work-ing classes, see him as a hero. In the *chawls*, the working-class tenements around his constituency, which is now dominated by the empty hulks of bankrupt garment factories, he is seen as a benefactor. People call him 'Daddy'. At the back of his headquar-ters there is a sprawling *chawl*, a warren of hundreds of apartments that each measures ten feet by twelve. Families of up to ten people sleep side by side in a space that is probably smaller than the average American linen cupboard.

The young men of the *chawl* exercise in a sweaty gym that Gawli donated to the community. In front of his headquarters, which doubles as his residence, he maintains a medical dispensary which gives free antibiotics and other drugs to anyone who walks in off the street. In front of the dispensary is a Shiva temple, whose bells ring for prayers every hour or two. Gawli also main-tains a small *gau shala*, or cow shelter. The smell that wafts up to his residence from below is a mix of cow dung, temple incense, the scent of cut flowers, traffic fumes and a mouth-watering hint of baking bread.

I was shown up to the top storey, where Gawli sleeps and prays. On the terrace outside there was an artificial garden whose flower beds were arranged around a depiction of Mount Kailash, the Himalayan home of Shiva, which dispensed a small waterfall into a pond below. Inside the terrace rooms the walls were covered with representations of Krishna, Shiva, Lakshmi and other gods. There were also pictures of large mosques. If someone had not tapped me on the shoulder and pointed out that Gawli had arrived, I would have mistaken him for a tea-boy or a sweeper. A small man in his fifties, he was wearing a white tunic and seemed completely unprepossessing.

'That is all in the past,' said Gawli when I asked him about his alleged mafia role. So how did he make all this money? 'My father used to own a large cattle pen. Then cattle were banned from Bombay and he made a lot of money from selling the land. We built this on a portion of the land,' he said. Even his flunkeys, who were seated with us on the terrace, looked a little surprised to hear such an eccentric declaration of income. Gawli then claimed he had twice falsely been imprisoned for life and twice been acquitted on appeal. He spent a very long time explaining which mafia don had been in and which mafia don had been out, and who had killed whom and when and why. I quickly lost track of all the details, there were too many names. But the gist of the story was plain enough.

Strongmen like Gawli came into their own in the 1980s and 1990s when Bombay's textile industry started to crumble. The mill owners, who had been backed into a corner by a fatal combination of excessive regulation and militant trade unions, used people like him to break strikes and recruit *badli* – or casual labour – replacements. In the west they would have been called 'scabs'. Behind India's privileged working classes – those who have formal sector jobs – lies a vast reserve army of unemployed labourers who are willing to step in with few preconditions. India's social divisions make it easy for large employers to split the unions. But this is a double-edged sword. The unions themselves keep splitting of their own accord, which can cause confusion and add to indiscipline in the mill. There are few workplaces in India where there is genuine labour solidarity. Bhimrao Ambedkar used to complain that the left-wing-dominated trade unions who controlled the shop floors of the textile mills in the 1930s refused to work alongside Dalits. This was because the work involved the use of saliva on the threads, which other castes considered too polluting.

The political space vacated by an easily fragmented working class was mostly filled by the Shiv Sena, the army of Shivaji, a right-wing Hindu chauvinist party whose rallying cry is 'Mumbai for the Mumbaikars'.* The rest was filled by men like Gawli: underworld figures who spoke the slang of the working classes, but whose goals were money and power. After the textile industry collapsed, the mill owners wanted to sell their land, which is situated in prime zones of central Mumbai and is valued very highly. Mumbai's powerful class of property developers needed people like Gawli with the muscle and credibility to help them get around the city's network of regulations governing the redevelopment of land. Gawli would step in to 'persuade' slum-dwellers to leave so that land could be redeveloped for more lucrative uses. Yet in the *chawls*, Gawli is still a working-class hero. 'They are my people. I give them free power and water and medicine because the state gives them nothing,' he said. 'I am the friend of the Hindus, the Muslims, and all the working classes.' But did he go into politics to protect himself from any more criminal cases? 'The poor are ignorant but they suffer terribly,' he said. 'They need someone to speak for them in politics. All these bureaucrats are just in it to line their own pockets.'

On the street below us, the temple bells started to ring. It was

---

*Shivaji was a seventeenth-century Maratha general who fought and frequently defeated the encroaching Mughal empire. The name also coincides with the popular god Shiva.

sunset. Gawli politely asked if I could excuse him while he attended evening *arti* (prayers). He disappeared and within a few minutes the terrace had been engulfed in the scented smoke of sandalwood, which is traditionally burned for Hindu ceremonies. From the terrace I watched the sunset bleed slowly across Mumbai's crowded horizon. In between there were the sprawling slums and sleek high rises that give this city its unsettling but pulsating quality. The temple bells were joined by the sudden eruption of Muslim calls to prayer from the minarets of a dozen mosques around us. The noises merged into a strange cacophony that was surprisingly haunting against the crimson sky. It is a blend you find only in India.

'I owe my life and my success to the blessings of Shiva,' said Gawli on his return. It struck me that I had rarely met a politician or a strongman in India who had not claimed divinity was on his side. Gawli also delivers God to the doorsteps of his constituents, making sure always to make generous donations to the local mosques for Eid, the feast that comes at the end of Ramadan, and money for the Ganapati procession, in which the elephant-headed Ganesh is paraded through the streets. 'The people want it,' he said. 'Religion is important to them.' Then two large, besuited men arrived with large briefcases. Gawli introduced them as his lawyers. They help him to keep the state at arm's length. 'In my line of work you need lots of lawyers,' he said. 'Everything is paperwork.'

The lingering scent of sandalwood was suddenly replaced by industrial quantities of insect repellent, which small vehicles below were pumping into the streets. Mumbai had just suffered one of its worst floods in decades after receiving a record 947mm of rainfall in a single day. The authorities, who had wasted valuable years failing to upgrade the city's sanitation system, feared an epidemic and were taking no chances. As ever, the state was waking up too late to a problem that had long since been highlighted by the media and activists. We were quickly enshrouded in a cloud of fumes and were forced to retreat indoors. After it had cleared, Gawli took me to his lift and clasped his hands together in the conventional Indian goodbye. 'It has been a pleasure and an honour. May you take the blessings of Shiva,' he said, as the doors were closing.

CHAPTER THREE

BATTLES OF THE RIGHTEOUS

The rise of India's lower castes

> The liberation of spirit that has come to India [since 1947]
> could not come as release alone. In India, with its layer below
> layer of distress and cruelty, it had to come as disturbance. It had
> to come as rage and revolt. India was now a country of a million
> little mutinies.
>
> V .S. Naipaul[1]

There is a Sanskrit word, *dharma*, which appears frequently in
India's ancient Hindu texts. It is usually translated as 'duty' or
'religion'. Someone who is *dharmic* is 'righteous'. But the word
has many layers of meaning.[2] The ancient texts talk of a *dharma* of
life, in which the individual should always be truthful, be respect-
ful of their elders, obey the law, and live generously and selflessly.
There is also a *dharma* of governing, in which the king should
uphold harmony and stability. And there is a *dharma* of the uni-
verse, which underlines the unity and spirituality of all things.

But it is the *dharma* of castes that perhaps gives us the best
insight into how India's traditional society saw itself. Each caste
possessed a different *dharma*, which specified separate duties and
abilities depending on the caste to which you belonged. At the
summit was the *dharma* of the priestly Brahmin caste, which gives

them control over all spiritual and religious aspects of society. They also possessed the 'sacred power' of the word, and were the only caste permitted to read and write. Next there was the warrior Kshatriya caste, whose *dharma* was to command the military and to rule the secular world as kings. If a new dynasty came from the wrong caste background then the Brahmin priests would invent the necessary Kshatriya family tree for it: 'Whoever rules is a Kshatriya,' say the texts.[3] The merchant Vaishya caste follows in the traditional ranking. As we have seen, the Vaishyas were viewed by some of their betters as a caste of 'thieves who are not called by the name of thief'.[4] But they had an important *dharma* to take care of the material needs of society. One of their original roles was to look after the principal currency of ancient India: cattle. The cow gradually evolved into a holy animal. Fourth, there is the Sudra caste, the farmers, servants and sometimes the foot-soldiers at the bottom of society. They kept their distance from other castes and were not even permitted to hear the recitation of the sacred Vedic texts. The ancient laws of Manu, which set down caste duties in detail, teach that each caste must rigidly stick to its own *dharma*: 'It is better to do one's own duty badly than another man's well.'

Beyond these rankings, and beyond the pale of society, were the outcastes or untouchables, who were not even given a caste name. The texts mention them only in the context of pollution: no other caste should have contact with them. It was forbidden to eat food prepared by an untouchable. Their role was to perform tasks that no other human would consider, such as removing human waste, usually referred to as 'night soil', tanning leather (from the hide of a cow that had died of natural causes), or sweeping the streets. So polluted were the outcastes that in some parts of India they were required to forewarn others of their approach by clapping together two blocks of wood. Fa Hsien, a Chinese Buddhist traveller to India in the fifth century AD, recorded his observations of the 'pollution on approach' of untouchables. He also noted that only the untouchables and the other lower orders were permitted to eat meat.[5]

India's ancient texts prescribe different punishments for the same crime, depending on your caste. For example, a Sudra who insulted a Brahmin faced death, but a Brahmin who killed a Sudra was awarded the same light penalty – usually just a fine – as he would receive for killing a cat or a dog. One text states that a Sudra who 'arrogantly teaches Brahmins their duty shall have boiling oil poured into his mouth and ears'.[6]

Such are the conventional accounts of the origins of traditional Indian society. However, more recent scholarship has shown that the ancient texts should not always be taken literally. There is historical evidence to show that in practice, as opposed to what is described in the pages of the manuals, ancient India was less rigid than many supposed, and that castes could and did change their ranking through either luck or alliance. For example, the great Mauryan dynasty, which was headed by Emperor Ashoka, is believed to have been Sudra originally. Nevertheless, caste as a system was rarely transcended, even if groups or individuals could improve their ranking. Thus, the Mauryas were reclassified as Kshatriya (in spite of the fact that they were Buddhist and therefore rejected caste). The gradual spread of Islam and its militant sense of equality after the eighth and ninth centuries AD inspired a wave of anti-caste movements within Hinduism during what is called India's 'medieval' period. These breakaway cults were known as *bhakti*, or devotional, movements, and they stressed worship of a particular deity and equality of all before God. They generated great ferment and attracted adherents from all castes. But over time they gradually morphed into new castes themselves and were quietly absorbed into the traditional hierarchy. Hinduism has a way of pacifying and accommodating its challengers. It is simultaneously rigid and flexible.

*

In many respects the town of Aurangabad, in an arid corner of Maharashtra, India's second-largest state, is unexceptional. Aurangabad's dilapidated old town, which dates from the days when it was ruled by the princely state of Hyderabad, several hundred miles to the south, is surrounded by the nondescript sprawl that can be found in so much of contemporary India. Its narrow waterways are choked with rubbish. Flies proliferate in the searing dry heat of summer. A puff of wind can scald your skin. Traffic, mostly scooters and motorbikes, collects lazily at railway crossings, and now and then is halted altogether by a noisy wedding procession. On the main commercial avenues you pass the provincial bank branches, roadside tea stalls and chain sweetshops that are to be found all over small-town India. Then there are the sacred cows, feeding on piles of rubbish and whatever else has been discarded on the streets. The town somehow manages to be both colourful and drab.

Aurangabad also happens to be a centre of the Mahar community, an untouchable caste, one of whose members was Bhimrao Ambedkar. The caste's duties included being porters, messengers, watchmen and guides for their social betters. Although other Dalit groups were required to perform more humiliating tasks, the Mahars were never permitted to enter temples, or to draw water from the same well as the rest of the village.* Ambedkar helped them to reject the roles to which they were born. Other lower-caste leaders, along with Mahatma Gandhi, were agitating for Dalits to be given access to temples and wells, but Ambedkar was dismissive of the chances of bringing about any real change in the mentality of upper-caste Hindus. He declared that he did not

---

*Dalit is a generic term. In practice India has hundreds of untouchable sub-castes, including the Mahars, who traditionally lived separately from each other and did not intermarry. The same applies to the four *varnas* – the traditional name for caste. Each *varna* – the Brahmins, Kshatriyas, Vaishyas and Sudras – has hundreds of *jatis*, or subcastes, who traditionally married only within their own communities. In today's India many *jatis* are now merging to form larger sub-castes.

want to enter their temples at all. 'I was born a Hindu,' he said, 'but I will not die a Hindu.' It took Ambedkar many years of studying before he chose Buddhism, which he believed was the most egalitarian of the world's religions. Other virtues included the fact that Buddhism was Indian in origin, so he could not be accused of lack of patriotism, as might lower-caste converts to Islam or Christianity. And, most importantly for Ambedkar, who rejected all forms of superstition and ritual, Buddhism was also the religion that came closest to atheism. He based his sense of the religion on Buddha's original teachings – rather than subsequent interpretations – in which the philosopher had rejected the existence both of the soul and of the afterlife. Ambedkar officially converted to Buddhism in the town of Nagpur in 1956, along with half a million fellow Mahars, at what must have been one of the largest ceremonies of mass conversion in history. He died shortly afterwards.

Ambedkar's statue and likeness is visible all over Aurangabad and in countless other small towns across India. I visited Milind College, on the road that leads out of the town towards the world-renowned Ellora Caves, which boast some of the most enchanting and dramatic Hindu and Buddhist temple art in India. Ambedkar named the college after the legendary Greek King Milinda, who challenged any priest or scholar to beat him in philosophical debate. For years, nobody succeeded, then a Buddhist monk called Nagsen arrived on the scene. In their debate the monk tied Milinda up in knots. The King conceded defeat, gave up his throne and followed Nagsen for the remainder of his life. 'For Ambedkar, King Milinda was a symbol of intellectual honesty, which was a virtue he felt was lacking in Hinduism,' said Indrajit Alte, the principal of Milind College.

Ambedkar was obsessed with education. A colonial survey in the early twentieth century found that only 0.13 per cent of India's untouchables could read or write.[7] There are no more recent statistics because caste-specific questions were banned from the census after independence, but it is estimated that at least a third of Dalits in today's India are now literate. It would be safe to say that a majority of Ambedkar's Mahar community can read and write. As a result, Mahars have captured a far larger share of white-collar jobs and government sinecures than any other Dalit group. There is a sizeable Mahar middle class, much of it living in Aurangabad, and a Mahar working class in the town's factories and assembly lines. Most Mahars have left their villages, never to return.

As a child, Indrajit Alte sat outside the temple in his village hoping in vain to be permitted entry. Then his family converted to Buddhism and moved to the city. 'In Aurangabad, or Bombay, or any town, you are treated with respect. You can walk down the street and nobody knows your caste,' said Alte, about half of whose 3600 students are Dalits. 'But when I return to my family village, people of other castes who cannot even read and write will not allow me into their homes, or even to share a cup of tea. This is how they treat the head of a college from the city. You cannot escape your caste in the village even if you have changed your religion.'

Professor Alte took me to a room overlooking Milind College where Ambedkar used to sleep and study after he had resigned as Minister for Law in Nehru's government in 1951. He tendered his resignation partly in protest at the delay in passing the Hindu Civil Code Bill, which he viewed as essential to promoting gender equality (such as giving daughters inheritance rights). It was broken up into four bills, which were finally enacted in the mid-1950s. The room, which stands alone on the college roof and is shaped like a *stupa*, the steeple of a Buddhist temple, contained some of Ambedkar's belongings, including a long bamboo stave with eight notches, which represented Buddha's eightfold path of righteousness. There were faded black-and-white photographs of Ambedkar wearing his trademark horn-rimmed spectacles and western suits talking to various other statesmen.

Garlands of flowers were hung over each of his monsoon-stained pictures. The professor told me the story of an educated Mahar village boy who had apparently humiliated a group of orthodox village Brahmins in the area. He said the local Brahmins hold an annual ritual to determine whether the coming monsoon will be a good one, which they divine by filling a *linga* – a phallic representation of Shiva – with water. The boy used his scientific education to debunk the ritual. 'This is what Ambedkar meant by fighting against caste,' said Alte. 'It was also a battle against superstition.'

But the gulf between the lives of the Mahars who still live in villages and those in towns like Aurangabad is large. In the villages Buddha has become just one more god to be placed alongside the popular Hindu deities in the Mahar household, such as Shiva, Krishna, Ram and Vishnu. Some households even keep a small figurine of Ambedkar among their pantheon. When the women are menstruating, they remove Ambedkar's likeness so as not to pollute him. It is hard to imagine the Dalit leader would have been flattered by this. By the same token, village Mahars greet Hindu villagers with the phrase '*Jai Bheem*' (Long Live Ambedkar), to indicate they should no longer be seen as untouchables. But when Mahars greet each other they say '*Ram Ram*', the traditional Hindu greeting.[8] Many of the Brahmin households claim Buddha is an incarnation of the Hindu god Vishnu. Some of the Mahars seem to agree. Converting to Buddhism appears to have changed very little in the lives of village Mahars.

The city is a world apart. I visited the neighbourhood of Amit Sudarkar, a young activist, in a Mahar area of Aurangabad. Although this was a poor area, I was immediately struck by the cleanliness of the streets compared to other parts of town: everything was neatly swept and washed. Above each house fluttered the multicoloured flag of international Buddhism and the blue flag depicting the Ashokan wheel, named after the great Buddhist emperor. Inside the homes there were pictures of film stars and cricketers. But I did not see any gods, only small framed pictures of Ambedkar and Buddha. Like many urban Dalit neighbourhoods in other parts of India, the Mahars lived next to a Muslim locality. 'We get along much better with the Muslims than the caste Hindus because we look out for each other,' said Sudarkar. 'Before we converted to Buddhism we used to eat beef with the Muslims.' As was the case with many Mahars I met, I was struck by Sudarkar's self-confidence. They are a literate, educated people. Almost everyone I met was either the first or second generation of educated Mahars and they radiated self-confidence. It is hard to overstate just how radical a change this represents for people whose parents, grandparents and ancestors stretching back hundreds – perhaps thousands – of years were born to a lifetime of bowing and scraping.

A crowd gathered, as so often happens when outsiders are in the vicinity. They dragged me to their local temple. All it contained was blue walls and paintings of Buddha and Ambedkar. I was amused by the fact that Ambedkar's portrait always depicts him with rosy, thick lips, much like those of Buddha. But there were no bells, no incense and no candles. 'We do not pray to Buddha, because we believe he was a human being – not a god,' said Sudarkar. 'We pray for peace, or else we just meditate. Sometimes we just come here to read.' Then he wanted to introduce me to the local dentist, another Mahar, whose surgery was near by. The clinic was air-conditioned and spotlessly clean. 'People from other castes come to me regularly for treatment,' said the dentist. The others in the clinic, wishing to make sure I understood the full import of the fact that upper castes were now routinely permitting an untouchable to stick a finger in their mouths, muttered: 'Imagine that?', 'Very good dentist', 'Mahar dentist'. Most of them spoke some English in addition to Hindi and Marathi, the principal language of Maharashtra. Sudarkar said: 'There is still discrimination against us – we do not live in mixed communities and we go to our own schools – but we are free and we know our rights.'

Once under way, it was hard to resist the pressure to visit other sites that illustrated some accomplishment or other of these proud Mahars. The tour was gathering a momentum of its own. The next stop was at a museum devoted to Ambedkar's life, although half the books in the library were about Malcolm X's Black Panthers in America. After Ambedkar died, his Republican Party of India disintegrated into squabbling factions. A group of Dalits, inspired by Malcolm X, set up the Dalit Panther movement, which still exists, although it has never got very far. 'We feel a lot of kinship with what blacks suffered in America before the civil rights movement and what blacks suffered in South Africa under apartheid,' said the museum curator. But in some respects what untouchables have suffered – and still do – is even worse. During apartheid, and in the deep recesses of the American south, white families would often employ black cooks and black wet nurses. 'Upper-caste Hindus would rather have died than let an untouchable cook their food or suckle their babies,' said the curator. 'It would have been polluting.'

After the museum, I visited Ambedkar University, which until the early 1990s was called Aurangabad University. Even then, the change of name prompted riots by angry caste Hindus, although they failed to overturn the decision. Then I was taken to a small Buddhist seminary that was situated under one of the rocky hills that encircle the town. The monks, who were mostly in their twenties and thirties, appeared sterner than the Mahars I had met in town that day. They all wore maroon robes. They talked to us about why Buddhism had virtually disappeared from India, the land of its birth, while it had thrived in so many other parts of Asia. They said the great Indian Buddhist centres of Taxila and Nalanda (in modern-day Pakistan and Bihar respectively) had been plundered by Brahmins, who feared that Buddha's egalitarian message would undermine their stranglehold on society.* 'They destroyed Buddhism because it had no caste,' said one militant young novice. 'Where are the Brahmins without caste?' I asked why so few of India's other Dalit groups, such as the Chamars, the traditional leather-workers, or the Valmikis, the scavenger caste which removes the excrement of other castes, had converted to Buddhism. The monks said that many of the other Dalit groups felt rivalry with the Mahars, though they still erect statues of Ambedkar. 'The upper castes are experts at brainwashing and intimidating the lower castes into remaining within Hinduism,' said the young novice. 'Many lower-caste people do not understand that it is impossible to change Hinduism. Hinduism has no pope or Vatican. The Brahmins are too slippery.'

It was an interesting diagnosis. And it was hard not to feel sympathy with their anger. My conversations with the monks and the other Mahars had also helped to clarify something that many foreigners, including myself, find hard to understand: the fact that Dalits and other lower castes are often as bitterly divided against each other as they are against the Hindu upper castes. It was something Ambedkar tried to overcome. But now, fifty years after his death, even his limited success in helping to unite some Dalit groups with each other and with other lower castes is open to question. India, as V. S. Naipaul has said, has become a land of a million mutinies: some are mutinies of lower orders against the upper orders, but there are also mutinies of upper orders (and some lower orders) against Muslims, and mutinies of lower orders against each other and upper orders against each other. But India is also a land of unexpected alliances: between enemies of enemies, between Muslims and lower castes, and between people who disdained each other yesterday and may do so again tomorrow. In one large Indian state there is even an alliance between Dalits and

*In fact, the great monastery of Nalanda was probably plundered by a Muslim dynasty, but there is plenty of evidence to show that Hindu dynasties in an earlier phase of India's history took steps to suppress Buddhism too.

Brahmins (against almost everyone in between). Indian politics, like the shifting caste alliances below it, bubbles in a strange cauldron of its own, defying easy comparisons with anywhere else.

I was in Patna, the capital of Bihar in India's north, to observe an important state assembly election that would choose the next government of India's third-largest state. I had just come from the buzzing city of Hyderabad in the southern state of Andhra Pradesh, which is a magnet for much of India's software investment. The contrast between the two cities could not be greater. In Hyderabad there are as many five-star hotels as you would find in any western city. Most of them offer a cutting-edge 'wifi' service so you can log on to the Internet by laptop from anywhere in the building. At Patna's best hotel the crackle on the internal phone system was so noisy you could not communicate with the receptionist. 'Hello, hello, is this a long-distance call?' No, I am calling from room 212. 'Hello, hello? Do you have a reservation?' Naturally, Internet access was unthinkable. Likewise, although often clogged with traffic, Hyderabad's roads are paved and smooth. Meanwhile, in Patna, a city of three million people, there is not a single functioning traffic light. Such is the reigning inertia, the city has not even changed the colonial names of its streets. I got a kick out of driving up and down Boring Road. It was named after a British official.

Patna is actually a very interesting place. Many people used to refer to it as the capital of 'Laluland', named after India's most celebrated and witty lower-caste leader, Lalu Yadav. He and his wife, Rabri Devi, had been ruling the state since 1990 courtesy of a powerful electoral formula known as 'MY' – or Muslim–Yadav – an alliance between the state's Muslims and the Yadav caste. The Yadavs are one of India's largest 'other backward classes', a government term that covers most of the Sudra castes. They are the traditional cow-herder caste of north India and are relatively low down on the traditional pecking order, but not as low as untouchable Mahars or Chamars. In a state that is probably more bitterly divided by caste than any other in India, the 'MY' combination had delivered an impregnable 30 per cent of the vote to his in four successive elections. But in this election Lalu's alliance appeared to be fraying. Other caste alliances were beginning to pick off some of the wealthier Yadav and Muslim voters, who were growing tired of Lalu's caste-identity politics, which had come at the expense of economic growth and law and order.

The week I was visiting Patna, the news was dominated by the kidnapping of a young pupil from the town's elite English-language private school. It was the fifth kidnapping in as many months. Bihar's kidnapping industry is closely connected to the state's other main industry: politics. It is no coincidence that the number of kidnappings increases sharply when elections are on the horizon. Running an election in one of Bihar's 243 provincial constituencies costs between 10 million and 50 million rupees ($200,000 to $1 million), an absurdly large sum for a state with an average annual income of less than 15,000 rupees ($300) a person.[9] Apart from its output of succulent mangoes and lychees, which are exported to other parts of India, Bihar has virtually no industry. Its principal sources of income are the grants it receives from New Delhi, and remittances from the millions of Bihari villagers who go to Delhi, Mumbai or Punjab to do casual jobs in the informal sector. Most of Bihar's middle classes have fled.

'If I had known then what I know now, I would never have returned to Bihar,' said Dr Ajay Kumar, who runs his own medical practice in Patna, and who had just stepped down as head of the Bihar Medical Council. He had been working as a doctor in Britain's National Health Service when he decided to return to Patna in 1984. Dressed in a blue boating jacket with gold buttons, he looked out of place in a town where it is wise not to stand out. As a Bhumiyar, the caste of traditional Bihari landowners, and a qualified doctor, he is both upper caste and middle class (the two do not always coincide: there are many poor Brahmins living in the villages). In the eyes of the lower castes he is a 'feudal', and in the eyes of the kidnappers he is a primary target. 'I sleep with a gun under my pillow,' he admitted, as we chatted over tea at his clinic, while he kept a wary eye on the closed-circuit TV that monitors the entrance to his surgery. 'All the time I am getting threats of abduction or extortion. It is desperate here. Most of my colleagues have left. They won't come back.'

Dr Kumar alleged that the kidnappers and the police were often one and the same thing. He also said the police behave as though they are the personal staff of their political masters. Earlier in my visit I had talked to D. P. Ojha, who had been head of the police for the entire state of seventy-five million people when he was shunted into early retirement. One of Ojha's transgressions had been to arrest Mohammed Shahabuddin, a member of parliament for Lalu's party, who faces multiple charges of murder, kidnapping and extortion. In an interview on national television Shahabuddin had casually threatened Ojha's life. Almost 100 of India's 545 members of parliament in New Delhi have 'criminal backgrounds', which means they have been indicted for one or more crimes, but not convicted.[10] Once elected, it is virtually impossible to convict them, which is often a primary incentive for entering politics in the first place. In turn, the wealth and muscle of the mafia dons give an incentive to political leaders, such as Lalu, to adopt them as electoral candidates. Of the hundred or so alleged parliamentary criminals, Bihar and Uttar Pradesh account for by far the largest share. Anyone who gets in their way, such as D. P. Ojha, risks the consequences. Like Kumar, Ojha said he was too old to think of leaving his home state, so he runs a one-man show to combat political corruption. 'We have excellent laws, even in Bihar. Our problem is the people who are supposed to be upholding these laws,' the retired police commissioner told me. 'When the gamekeepers are poachers in disguise, why should anyone else take the law seriously?'

It was a good question, which I thought was worth putting to Lalu Prasad Yadav. Lalu, as everyone calls him, is also a member of parliament in New Delhi. He was indicted in the late 1990s for alleged corruption in a fodder subsidy scandal. Having been briefly imprisoned, he stepped down as Bihar's Chief Minister in favour of his wife, Rabri Devi, who had presided over the state ever since. But the indictment did not prevent Lalu from becoming India's Minister for Railways in 2004, a senior cabinet position in the government headed by Manmohan Singh. Lalu's party was the second-largest partner in Singh's multiparty coalition government, after the Congress Party. The cabinet was a curious mix of urbane technocrats, such as Singh, and earthy rural leaders, such as Lalu. Some despaired of its incoherence, but others were more philosophical. At a party shortly after the election, one of Singh's colleagues told me: 'I think we should all be studying the history of how corrupt American politics was in the early twentieth century. It proves that you can still rise to become a great power.' The analogy was reasonable enough: India's economy has continued to grow at 7 per cent a year since 2004.

However, Bihar's economy has gone from bad to worse. It is India's most rural state with more than 90 per cent of the people living in villages. For most Biharis the countryside is far from a rural idyll. Fewer than one in ten Bihari households have electricity; only one Bihari in twenty can afford a scooter; and life expectancy is the lowest in India, with the average Bihari living fifteen years less than his counterpart in the state of Kerala, where most people have access to medicine, schooling and electricity.[11] There are no real jobs. Bihar's economy is so anaemic that it collects only 0.7 per cent of India's national sales tax revenues, despite accounting for more than 7 per cent of India's population. Fewer than one in forty Biharis possesses a television.[12] For entertainment, many rely on Lalu, whose public speeches draw crowds of several hundred thousand people. He can be very witty. During the most recent election campaign, a reporter informed him that

Hema Malini, a glamorous Bollywood actress, had said she was a fan of his. 'If she is my fan, then I'm her air-conditioner,' Lalu shot back.

This was only my second meeting with Lalu, and I was a little nervous. After my first interview a couple of years earlier, I had written an article that Lalu had publicly criticised. He had been sitting in his garden with a large collection of cronies and it was night-time. He was talking in a continuous banter which generated much laughter, and I had written: 'There was the unmistakable whiff of marijuana in the air.'[13] I believed I was right as the smell is hard to confuse, and the person accompanying me had agreed. But Lalu had not taken kindly to it.* He told the local media and anyone else who cared to listen that western journalists were always out to defame him: 'They are in league with the Brahmins,' he claimed.

On this occasion, getting into Lalu's compound proved difficult, although not because of my previous article. His residence was surrounded by hundreds of people shouting slogans. It was a winter evening and the air was thick with fog. Our car had to crawl myopically for fear of hitting someone. It was hard to make out what they were shouting about. I found Lalu amid a thicket of microphones and cameras, giving a press conference in his garden. Once he had dismissed them, I joined him and his wife around a fire on the veranda. Lalu sprawled on a rattan chair with a blanket around his shoulders and occasionally warmed his hands on the fire. Rabri Devi served lemon tea and Bihari sweets. I asked Lalu what he thought he had achieved for Bihar in the last fifteen years. 'Our two biggest achievements are social justice and communal harmony,' he said. 'We have given courage to the downtrodden. Dalits can now hold their heads up high. They are no longer oppressed by the Brahmins and by the landowners. And

---

*Marjiuana is legal in most parts of India and in many states, including Bihar, it is sold at licensed government outlets. However, it is meant to be used only during holy festivals.

Muslims are safe. We have defeated the Hindu nationalists.' Much of this was true. But Bihar had no rule of law. Lalu said: 'Whenever anyone writes about Bihar they talk about law and order problems or they talk about caste violence. That is because we have an upper-caste media in India. Even foreigners are fooled by these things.' Then he said that two years earlier a journalist from the *Financial Times* of London had written that marijuana had been smoked in his presence. 'That was me,' I told him. 'No, no, it definitely wasn't you,' he said, looking a little flustered. 'He didn't look at all like you, he was, he was . . . ' But it *was* me, I insisted. 'Oh, it doesn't matter,' he said, looking genuinely uncomfortable. 'I am sure it was a cultural misunderstanding. It can happen very easily.' I confess I was charmed by Lalu's embarrassment. He is celebrated up and down India for his perfect one-line insults. During the 2004 national election campaign, he suggested the poll should be resolved by a running race between the leaders of the two main parties, Sonia Gandhi, the fifty-nine-year-old Italian-born widow of Rajiv (with whom Lalu is allied), and Atal Behari Vajpayee, the septuagenarian Hindu nationalist Prime Minister. Vajpayee had recently had operations on both of his knees so could barely walk, let alone run. But even Mr Vajpayee's friends laughed at Lalu's joke.

I asked Lalu about the noisy crowd outside his residence. 'They are my people and they are shouting pro-Lalu slogans,' he said. It turned out the mob was packed with aspiring candidates for the Lalu party ticket in the forthcoming poll. 'When I drive through the crowd,' he said, to the merriment of those inside the compound, 'I draw the window curtains so I don't have to look at their faces.' The interview then descended from banter into circus. Lalu insisted on showing me around his compound, which he had converted into a menagerie for his favourite animals, mostly cows, of which there were two hundred. There were also two white Arabian horses. During his spell in prison in the late 1990s, Lalu said he had a vision in which the Lord Krishna, the god most beloved of Yadavs, told him to become a vegetarian and to be kind to cows. Lalu had complied ever since. 'It sounds like you are trying to become a Brahmin,' I said. He ignored my joke. Lalu was born to acute poverty in a Bihari village and spent his childhood in rags and without shoes, tending the village herd. His nine children have all been educated at English-language schools. One of his daughters lives in Singapore and is married to a senior software executive. We were now inside the cow shelter and Lalu was introducing me to his favourites, each of which had a name. Dozens of full-time attendants were assigned to look after the cows. 'This is my favourite,' said Lalu, patting its head lovingly. Then he put both his hands in front of the cow's face and said: 'This hand is for Lalu and this hand is for Ram Vilas Paswan [Lalu's fiercest electoral competitor].' The cow did not move when Lalu raised the hand that represented Paswan, but then something peculiar happened. When Lalu raised his other hand – the one that represented himself – the cow slowly but emphatically nodded its head. I looked in vain for an attendant who might be pulling the cow's tail or tugging on a piece of string. But the trick was authentic. It must have taken Lalu hours and hours of practice.

A few months later, Lalu's party was ejected from office in Bihar, although it retained its pivotal role in the national coalition and Lalu remained India's Minister of Railways. Many people hailed the 2005 election result as a vote for 'good governance' after fifteen years of misrule by Lalu and his cronies. But the coalition of lower- and upper-caste parties that defeated him was stitched together in much the same way as Lalu's had been, and used much the same appeal to caste identity as he had. It was led by Nitish Kumar, a former Railways Minister and a member of another lower-caste called the Kurmis. Kumar and his allies fielded even more candidates with criminal backgrounds than Lalu. Even in defeat, Lalu's logic lived on. I have little doubt that he will be back.

*

It has taken India's lower-caste leaders decades of practice to master the complexities of Indian democracy. Now they do it better than anyone else. In Indian politics lower-caste voters have an advantage that is of little help in other spheres of life: sheer weight of numbers. About half of India's population is lower caste, in one form or other. If you add 150 million Muslims and the tens of millions who live outside their home-language area, more than half of India's population is officially classified as 'minority'.[14] Lower-caste parties have another advantage: their non-caste competitors have to pitch their message as wide as possible. The Congress Party aims to appeal to everyone by stressing a secular and inclusive Indian nationalism and centrist economics. The Hindu nationalist Bharatiya Janata Party tries to appeal to almost every voter, except for Muslims and Christians. (Hindus make up 85 per cent of India's population.) The lower-caste parties, on the other hand, can ruthlessly target their message at their narrow slices of the population, so they are more efficient at garnering their respective 'vote banks'. However, this limits their overall electoral tallies to their own caste populations. If all the lower castes were to make common cause with each other and merge into one umbrella lower-caste party, it would probably govern India in perpetuity. What prevents them?

A small clue might lie in Lalu's constant references to Krishna. Lalu's unique personality has often prompted contrasts with rebel leaders throughout history, few of whom consulted astrologers and soothsayers, or had much time for religious imagery. They sought to unite their people against the monarchy, the Church, the landed aristocracy or foreign rule. Their rhetoric was universal and they promised equality. Lalu and the leaders of India's six or seven other nationally significant lower-caste parties aimed at a specific category of people. They ignore others who live in exactly the same kind of poverty. Some foreign and Indian observers describe India's lower-caste parties as left wing because they represent the underprivileged, but this misses the trees for the wood – to reverse the aphorism. Each lower-caste party represents only one section of the underprivileged. Lower-caste politicians do not unite the lower orders by stressing what they have in common but rather keep them fragmented by focusing on what divides them. This is much closer to ethnic politics than it is to class politics.

Lalu's numerous Yadav caste is also quite visible outside Bihar, particularly in the large states of Uttar Pradesh and Madhya Pradesh. His counterpart in Uttar Pradesh is Mulayam Singh Yadav, whose key right-hand man, Amar Singh, we will meet later on. Like Lalu, Mulayam's party relies on the support of an alliance between millions of Yadav and Muslim voters who are united in antipathy to Brahmins and increasingly to Dalits. It has also garnered the votes of many Rajputs, a sub-caste of the traditional warrior Kshatriya caste, to which Amar Singh belongs. It is one of India's new-fangled caste alliances.

Lalu and Mulayam are both members and former presidents of the All-India Yadav Mahasabha (assembly). The Mahasabha has developed an interesting ideology: it claims all Yadavs are descended from Krishna, the god who is depicted in the epics as a cow-herder, the traditional caste function of the Yadavs. According to this view, the genes of Yadavs are as pure as – or even purer than – those of the Brahmins. The Mahasabha has also pronounced both Mulayam and Lalu to be incarnations of Krishna. But it has left unsaid any view it may have on the blood-lines of other lower castes, who presumably remain as polluted as they were before. This is what one of the speakers said at the Mahasabha's annual conference: 'We have assembled here from different parts of the country. We speak different languages . . . our habits and customs are different but we feel oneness and brotherhood because the same blood is running in our veins.'[15]

Like other 'caste-origin myths', the Yadavs say they were denied by trickery or historical injustice their rightful place in the upper layers of the hierarchy, among the righteous rather than the polluting castes. Almost all of India's larger sub-castes have constructed similarly proud mythologies of an elevated ancestry that was robbed from them in the mists of time by scheming Brahmins or thieving Kshatriyas. With the notable exception of the Mahars, whose outlook remains heavily influenced by Ambedkar, most of the other untouchable castes, including the Chamars, also claim descent from either a god or a great saint. Perhaps the most intriguing claim is that of the Bedias, a caste of prostitutes who are shunned by everyone, at least during daylight hours. Bedia women say that caste identity comes from the bloodline of the father, and since most of their clients are Rajput men, they argue that their true caste is Rajput, which is relatively high on the scale. The Bedias even hired a Brahmin priest to support their claim. He duly pronounced, somewhat elliptically, that it is the seed that is sown on the field that matters, rather than the soil of the field.[16] Rajput men tend to disagree. The opinion of their wives is not recorded.

In much of rural India caste discrimination is as rampant as ever and hundreds die every year from caste violence, some at the hands of the police. According to the Indian government, violence by the police against Dalits whom they have falsely arrested is still routine in village India: 'During interrogation, injuries sustained by the arrested person are so great that he usually dies.'[17] Equally, Dalits are still often denied entry into temples. But it is perhaps more noteworthy that so many Dalits want to enter temples in the first place. Seventy years ago Ambedkar wrote: 'Hindu society is a myth. The name Hindu is itself foreign. It was given by the Mohammedans to the natives for the purpose of distinguishing themselves. Each caste not only dines among itself and marries among itself but each caste also prescribes its own distinctive dress.'[18] This may have been accurate at the time, but in today's India it would be hard to distinguish someone's caste by what they wear or where they eat.

Beneath the radar, there have been fairly dramatic changes in the lifestyles of the lower castes over the last few decades.

Ordinary Yadavs may believe they are descended from Lord Krishna. But Yadavs and other lower castes have increasingly adopted the private habits and beliefs of the upper castes. Indian scholars call this 'Sanskritisation', in reference to the classical language that was the preserve of the Brahmins.[19] It stands for a trend in which the lower orders are now copying the culture of the upper orders by following the same gods, attending the same temples and celebrating the same festivals. In urban India it is often only by the name that you can distinguish the caste of a person. Other attributes, such as dress or dietary habits, have become increasingly general to all castes. In their lifestyles the wealthier lower castes – farmers who may have profited from the green revolution or those who have found secure jobs in the city – are reinventing themselves. If you enter an urban home in today's India it would be hard to tell the caste of its occupants. The gods depicted in most small household shrines are the same. They follow the same traditional upper-caste rituals.

However, in the political world India's lower castes are moving in the opposite direction to 'Sanskritisation'. Instead of seeking to emulate their Brahmin role models, they use politics to play out their revenge against the upper orders and to extract compensation for their low social status. Usually they get want they want. India's affirmative action programme is the largest in the world. It is far larger and more extensive than that of America. In India half of all government jobs are reserved for three separate categories of underdog: Adivasis, Indians of tribal origin who make up almost 10 per cent of the population; Dalits, officially accounting for 12.5 per cent of the population; and 'other backward classes', including castes such as the Yadavs, who account for 27 per cent of the population. Together, 50 per cent of India's public sector jobs are allocated to these groups. In addition each state has its own system of reservations and in some, including Rajasthan and Tamil Nadu, the quota for provincial government jobs is as high as two-thirds. Few are allocated by competitive examination. In practice many of the jobs are dispensed by the relevant caste leaders and their networks of hangers-on, or they are put up for sale to the highest bidders.* It is the most extensive system of patronage in the democratic world.

Expanding this system is the *only* serious item on the agenda of the lower-caste parties. None of them publishes manifestos at election times setting out policies on the economy, foreign policy or defence. All they offer their supporters is the ability to extract greater powers of patronage from the larger parties in exchange for making up the parliamentary numbers in multiparty coalitions. That is why Lalu, whose party helped bring Manmohan Singh's government to power in New Delhi, was given the Ministry of Railways, which oversees a workforce of almost 1.5 million people (second only to China's People's Liberation Army as the largest employer in the world). Since they dispense few jobs, neither the Foreign Ministry nor the Ministry of Finance would have held the same appeal. Likewise, when Mulayam Singh Yadav's party helped prop up an earlier coalition government in New Delhi in the 1990s, he became Minister of Defence. Most of India's large defence industry is publicly owned. Neither Lalu nor Mulayam has submitted anything resembling a coherent plan on how to manage India's economy. But both are hostile to privatisation of state enterprises since any reduction in the public sector would shrink their means of patronage. Both also support extending the system of public job quotas to the private sector. This, though, remains an unlikely prospect, in spite of evidence that many of India's older private sector companies do practise caste and religious discrimination in their hiring policies. Mere mention of reserving jobs on grounds of caste rather than qualifications sends shudders of horror through India's company boardrooms.

*

---

*The *Financial Times*' driver in Delhi once applied for a job as a government driver. He was told it would cost 100,000 rupees to get the position. Each job has a fixed price.

What can be said about Lalu and Mulayam is true many times over for Mayawati, the leader of India's largest untouchable political party, the Bahujan Samaj (Majority of the People) Party. Like many Dalits, Mayawati has only one name, but in recognition of her status as their 'tallest leader', many of her fellow caste members refer to her as Behenji Mayawati, which means 'honoured sister'. Mayawati has been Chief Minister of Uttar Pradesh three times. When she first took power in 1996, she was the first untouchable in India's history to take charge of the state. She quickly gained a reputation as someone who delighted in causing great discomfort to her upper-caste civil servants. Within the first year of her administration she ordered fourteen hundred transfers of IAS officers, which was – and remains – a record. Some of the senior IAS officers had to move station every few weeks at great cost to their children's schooling. There appeared to be no logic to Mayawati's mini-revolution. Some accused her of trying to humiliate the Brahmins. Others alleged that she was trying to raise money from IAS officers who were prepared to pay bribes either to stay put or to move back to where they had been stationed before. 'Mayawati likes to keep the Brahmins dancing,' one of her advisers told me. 'Our people in the villages enjoy watching the spectacle very much.' Other observers, including the World Bank, whose development projects in Uttar Pradesh were badly disrupted by this game of musical chairs, were less amused.

Mayawati has never granted me an interview, since she has little interest in speaking to the English-language media, foreign or Indian. But on one occasion I came close. There was a large Dalit rally in the north Indian town of Gaya, near the famous Bodhgaya temple, which was built on the spot where Buddha was reputed to have achieved enlightenment under a *peepul* tree. Mayawati's public meeting took place in a large *maidan*, or park, in the centre of the town and was attended by thousands of cheering supporters. After she had finished speaking she left the podium and moved towards a waiting Ambassador car, which would whisk her to a helicopter a couple of hundred yards away. Waving my press pass, I managed to enter the enclosure and approach Mayawati. But before I could get further, my path was barred by four men, whose standard-issue sunglasses and handguns identified them as political musclemen. I managed to shout my request to Mayawati, who glanced suspiciously at me for a couple of seconds before getting into the car. Then her cavalcade of vehicles proceeded for all of thirty seconds to the waiting helicopter, with her security men running alongside, brandishing their guns. Mayawati gave a brief, imperious wave from the hovering chopper to the crowds below. Then it nosed off into the distance to another rally at another *maidan* teeming with star-struck supporters.

Few, if any, leaders in today's India can bank on as much loyalty from their voters as Mayawati. Electoral analysts say her BSP (not to be confused with the Hindu nationalist BJP) has the most disciplined vote bank of any party in India. Whatever the circumstances, and whatever her record in office, the BSP can rely on the votes of one-fifth of the Uttar Pradesh electorate, which roughly corresponds to the proportion of Dalits among the state's 170 million people. Even after Mayawati was accused in 2003 of awarding contracts to her favourite construction companies to build a large shopping complex around the resplendent Taj Mahal, her voting tally did not fall. Mayawati was forced to abandon her plans to bring Las Vegas to India's greatest monument.

Mayawati's overriding agenda is to bring more Dalits into government jobs. Her mentor, Kanshi Ram, founded the BSP in the 1980s after he had been refused a day's leave from his government job on the occasion of Ambedkar's birthday, a public holiday. The incident ignited years of pent-up frustration, with Ram claiming that Dalit civil servants were routinely denied promotion and respect by their peers. The new party's agenda was meant to give Dalits self-respect and to create more government jobs for them: 'Political power is the master-key with which you can open any lock,' he said.[20] Following in his footsteps, Mayawati uses power with a fury that makes Lalu and Mulayam seem like consensus politicians. Her campaign speeches often consist of a long list from which she reads out the caste origins of each of her candidates. She makes no attempt to present policies or opinions on more general subjects. In one closely studied campaign she devoted 91 per cent of her speeches to the issue of 'social justice', which is code for 'government jobs for Dalits'.[21] In contrast to most of her competitors, she did not once refer to issues such as 'good governance', 'nationalism', 'prices' and 'corruption'.

Dalits routinely list these issues as major concerns in their lives, but when it comes to casting their votes, their choice seems to be dictated solely by the caste of the candidate. Essential services, such as roads, electricity and jobs, are in short supply in the rural economy of Uttar Pradesh, so the voter, especially the lower-caste voter, needs access to the people who have control over them. Sharing a caste background with the politician helps. Evidence you have voted for the politician helps even more. Kanchan Chandra, a scholar at MIT who conducted these surveys, argues persuasively: 'Elections in a patronage-based democracy [like India] are in essence covert auctions in which basic services, which should in principle be available to every citizen, are sold instead to the highest bidder.'

Elections in Uttar Pradesh are also about muscle power. Both Congress and the BJP have been virtually eclipsed in the state, which is by far the most important of India's 29, since, with 84 of the country's 543 constituencies, it is home to almost a sixth of India's parliamentary seats. Eight of India's thirteen prime ministers have come from Uttar Pradesh. But nowadays neither of the national parties can match the ruthlessness of the state's two principal lower-caste parties.

*

One of the most extraordinary pieces of Indian electioneering I have observed is the sight of Mulayam's Samajwadi (socialist) campaigners driving through Allahabad in a cavalcade of about forty vehicles, consisting mostly of Mercedes and Toyota Safaris. Thickets of guns poked out of each vehicle. Doubtless voters were meant to be intimidated. But they would also have been impressed. The electioneering was for a by-election in Allahabad itself, a city of four million people that was an important metropolis for the Mughals and the British, and remains one today.

The by-election had been triggered by the assassination of Raju Pal, the BSP member of the legislative assembly, who had been gunned down in the city's main commercial street opposite a car showroom at midday. Pal was hit by more than twenty bullets. Mayawati's party alleged that the murder had been carried out on behalf of Ashraf Ahmed, the brother of Atiq Ahmed, who is the area's member of parliament in New Delhi for Mulayam's party. Ashraf was immediately imprisoned. But that did not stop him from standing in the election from his jail cell. His opposing candidate was Puja Pal, the pretty, twenty-five-year-old widow of Raju Pal. The contest – the young widow battling against her husband's alleged murderer – had all the makings of a Shakespearean tragedy.

The first to grant me an interview was Puja Pal. Having driven out on dirt tracks at night to a village on the outskirts of town, we were greeted by Pal dressed in white, the colour of mourning. She had married Raju only a few weeks earlier. Fifty or sixty of her supporters crowded round us in the courtyard of the house to observe the interview. Every time I asked Pal a question, someone else would answer it for her. So I requested that she answer directly. The Samajwadi had claimed the BSP was running an Islamaphobic campaign, since Pal's opposing candidate was a Muslim. They also alleged that she was blaming the criminalisation of politics in the city on the Muslims.

I asked Ms Pal whether she was running an anti-Muslim campaign. 'Look around at all these people,' said Pal, having finally been permitted to answer for herself. 'He is a Muslim, he is a Muslim, and he is a Muslim. Ask them.' The three men nodded happily. Pal then said she had not been allowed to see her husband's body, since it had been burned by the police the same day he was killed, ostensibly to forestall a potentially riotous funeral procession. She claimed that Mulayam, the Chief Minister, had ordered the police to dispose of the corpse in this way. She also mentioned lavish sums of money that had allegedly changed hands to bring about the murder of her husband. None of this could be verified, but I could not help admiring the young woman's courage. As we departed, her supporters hung garlands around us, as if we were the politicians. It would have caused offence to refuse. She narrowly lost the election, which took place in June 2005.

Getting to see Atiq Ahmed was much trickier. Everybody wants to see him. Access to him is closely regulated. After persistent telephone calls, I was eventually allowed inside his heavily guarded compound, which was opposite the local mosque in the densely populated Muslim quarter of Allahabad. There was a fleet of tinted-glass cars parked in front of the entrance to his mansion. Once inside, the first thing I saw was the household armoury, with row upon row of guns stacked against a wall. As I waited for the appointment, Atiq's octogenarian father sat and chatted to me. His beard was dyed red with henna. He had just completed his third and final Haj (pilgrimage) to Mecca. Neither Atiq nor Ashraf had yet been on the Haj. 'They are still children,' said the father about his middle-aged sons. We were interrupted by a young man who said our interview was being postponed because Ahmed had to rush to join Mulayam, who had landed by helicopter in the centre of town to address an election rally. I got to see him at his party headquarters in town later in the day. He was seated in a tiny room on a plastic chair and was shouting at someone on his mobile phone. I was a little anxious about questioning

Slum residents fetch water in today's Mumbai *(Getty Images)*

Call-centre workers, Bangalore *(Getty Images)*

Nandan Nilekani, chief executive of Infosys, one of India's most successful
IT companies *(Getty Images)*

Social activist Aruna Roy and some of the Rajasthani villagers with whom she campaigns *(Sohail Akbar)*

A typical traffic scene in rural India *(Sohail Akbar)*

A passenger jet comes in to land over the slums of Mumbai *(Getty Images)*

Slum shacks in amongst Mumbai's tower blocks *(Getty Images)*

Lalu Prasad Yadav, one of India's most celebrated and witty lower-caste leaders
(Sohail Akbar)

At prayer before Bhimrao Ambedkar, who gave hope to those marginalised
in Indian society *(Sohail Akbar)*

A queue of villagers waiting to sign up for paid election work *(Sohail Akbar)*

Sri Sri Ravi Shankar,
one of India's most
successful gurus
(Empics)

Members of the Hindu nationalist Bajrang Dal train with bamboo staves *(Sohail Akbar)*

A Muslim man surrounded by Hindu rioters begs for his life during the Gujarat riots, March 2002 *(Reuters/Corbis)*

A Hindu activist armed with an iron bar, Gujarat, February 2002 *(Getty Images)*

him, but he waved a friendly hand towards some chairs and ordered tea and sweets. His face was dominated by heavy jowls, a thick moustache and bulging eyes. His teeth were stained red with *paan*, an addictive mix of betel nut, lime and tobacco that you chew for hours. He was quick to laugh. I asked why he had alleged that the Dalit party was running a Hindu nationalist campaign. 'Dalits are very simple people,' he replied. 'They are nice people also. But you know some of them think that if they fall sick they can cure themselves just by tying a yellow string around a tree. In politics, they follow one leader in the morning and another in the afternoon. They are very easily misled. Mayawati is wooing the Brahmins because the Brahmins don't like the Muslims or the Yadavs. So this is what has happened.'

I said most people thought the election was really a contest between two rival mafia gangs for control of the city. Politics was incidental. Ahmed looked surprised, then revealed a broad, betel-stained smile. He seemed to appreciate the question. 'Oh, that is all false propaganda spread by the Hindu nationalists,' he said. 'Pay them no attention. Such nonsense is talked.' 'But what about all your guns?' I asked. 'They are not my private guns,' he replied. 'They belong to the intelligence agencies who have been assigned to protect me.' I did not believe him, but there was no point in pursuing it. I said people claimed he had done nothing to contribute to the development of his state. 'It is very difficult to bring development to India,' he said, looking suddenly thoughtful. 'It is such a complicated and diverse country. If you drive in your car fifty miles south of Allahabad, you will find the customs change. Our customs are very diverse. We [the Samajwadi Party] are adding new castes to our political equation. We are not just Yadavs and Muslims but also Rajputs. The more castes we add, the more we will be judged by voters on our performance and not on our identity.'

This prediction may or may not prove true in the coming years. Certainly, the tendency of lower-caste parties to woo one or other of the upper-caste groups is growing. It was an alliance such as this that proved to be Lalu's undoing in Bihar. In Uttar Pradesh Mayawati is selecting Brahmin candidates in areas where upper castes are concentrated. But the logic behind her electoral arithmetic is unrelated to development. In their daily lives many Dalit farm labourers feel more oppressed by wealthy Yadav farmers than they do by distant Brahmin civil servants. Few Brahmins farm for a living – the caste's ancient *dharma* forbids them to touch a plough. Most Yadavs are farmers. So Dalits and Brahmins both resent and fear Yadavs (Brahmins because they are losing their traditional domination of society). Any development agenda that might result from such an unholy alliance would be purely incidental.

But there was little time to probe Ahmed further and he seemed uninterested in the issue of economic development. He stood up and led me through his party headquarters to the waiting car outside. A hundred or more men who had been lounging outside the small office immediately sprang to their feet. Many of them were armed. It felt like we were strolling through an army camp. Instead of a parliamentarian, it was as if a general were waving me off. I felt no surprise a few weeks later when I heard that his brother had prevailed in the Allahabad campaign.

As a journalist, I have been inside the homes of many wealthy people. But nothing has compared to the interior of 27 Lodhi Estate in central New Delhi. It is the official residence of Amar Singh, a member of parliament for Mulayam Singh Yadav's Samajwadi Party. The airy bungalow, one of 204 similar residences in the capital allocated to the nation's most senior politicians and officials, is officially protected under New Delhi's heritage laws. It was designed, like much of the city, by Edwin Lutyens. Amar Singh, who had agreed to allow me and a mutual acquaintance to look over the property, had generated controversy in the newspapers for carrying out extensive alterations to the bungalow. During our guided tour, he was keen to stress that the changes he had made were in fact 'improvements'.

Although himself a Rajput, a relatively high caste, Singh is one of the two or three most powerful leaders among India's lower-caste parties. A portly man nearing fifty and sporting the obligatory moustache, he was accompanied by Jayaprada, a former Bollywood actress, who had been recruited into politics in the 2004 election. In spite of being an MP herself Jayaprada at all times referred to Singh as 'sir'. He told us: 'I was not very enthusiastic to show you my residence after what the media has been writing about me. They come here, eat my food and write what they like.'

The same month that I visited the bungalow, Mulayam Singh Yadav, in his capacity as Chief Minister of Uttar Pradesh, had appointed as his chief secretary a person who had been voted by her colleagues (at an annual convention of civil servants) as the second most corrupt civil servant in the state. Her appointment caused a furore. Allegations against the Samajwadi Party include selling electoral tickets to the highest bidder, accepting bribes from civil servants wishing to be moved to more comfortable post-ings, handing out industrial licences in exchange for favours and fixing supposedly blind lotteries to allocate prime urban land to friends. Amar Singh is the founder and head of the Uttar Pradesh Development Council, a group of politicians and businessmen that the media has labelled 'crony capitalist'. Other prominent members include Anil Ambani, who controls Reliance Infocomm and Reliance Energy, two of India's largest companies, and Subroto Roy, who owns the Sahara Group, a diversified private company with an airline, TV channels and sprawling private res-idential estates. 'If this is crony capitalism then we should all be crony capitalists,' Singh told me, pointing out that the UP Development Council had brought in much new investment for his state. What about the corruption allegations against his party, though? 'There might be a little corruption here and there,' Singh conceded. 'You cannot check everything.'

Our tour of the bungalow began with the garden. Singh took us along the outer perimeter, whose walls had been recast with white marble bas-reliefs of gambolling cherubs and nubile winged angels, a curious hybrid of classical Greek art and modern pornography. Next we entered a prefab annex Singh had erected which contained a modern gym with the usual Nordic Trackers and cycle machines. In the adjoining room there was a large marble jacuzzi with gold-plated taps. Singh then took us across to the main building, against the exterior of which he had constructed a sweeping *Gone with the Wind* staircase that took us up to the terrace, which had been converted into a roof garden with grass turf and rose beds. 'Are you liking this?' he asked. Next we went inside. The main room was dominated by a vast portrait of Singh and his family. Next to it were gold, jewellery-studded depictions of Krishna. No corner of the room remained unadorned by some trophy item or other: a silver *Ravissant* receptacle here, a priceless antique vase there. In each of the main rooms Singh had given pride of place to one of the most expensive items of home entertainment in the world: the sixty-inch plasma-screen Bang & Olufsen TV. Each retails for as much as $60,000 in India.

But the grandest cut was reserved until last. Singh, whose excitement had been mounting as the tour progressed, took us into the main dining room. At the side of the room he had demolished a portion of the wall to create a small alcove that jutted into the garden and which was protected by a glass screen. Behind the screen was a small, illuminated marble basin, out of which gurgled a soothing stream of water. Singh took out what looked to be a giant TV remote control and pointed it at the high ceiling above the dining table. I half expected another TV screen to pop out. He pressed the button and something started to happen to the heavy stone Lutyens ceiling. Slowly but noiselessly, it began to divide. It was impossible to guess what was about to be revealed. We seemed to be characters in a Bond film, with Singh about to feed us to birds of prey. After the ceiling had fully parted we were greeted with a dazzling view of the roof through the prism of a small glass pyramid that was clearly modelled on what sits above the Louvre in Paris. The shimmering glass refracted the verdant foliage of the terrace beyond. Everyone gasped, half of us in shock, the other half in admiration. 'Now,' said Singh, turning towards us, beaming from ear to ear, 'do you think these are improvements or just alterations?'

Most of this chapter has focused on the deep caste divisions of north India and the corruption that often goes with it. A majority of Indians live in the north, which gives the region a correspondingly larger impact on the character of national politics. Many who despair of the area's sometimes pathological caste relations glance longingly towards the south, especially to the state of Tamil Nadu, which seems to have put the worst excesses of caste conflict behind it. Caste still exists in Tamil Nadu, and as in the north its two principal political parties seem to sit up all night thinking of ways to break their opponent's caste alliances. As in Uttar Pradesh neither the Congress nor the BJP has much of a presence in Tamil Nadu, accounting for less than a fifth of the state's representation between them. However, guns only rarely play a part in Tamil Nadu politics, and there are far fewer politicians with 'criminal backgrounds' in its legislative assembly. The state provides basic services with a much higher degree of efficiency to most people. Things appear to function, at least to a minimum standard of acceptability. 'We estimate that roughly thirty per cent of public resources are diverted in Tamil Nadu, compared to about seventy per cent in the north,' the chief secretary of Tamil Nadu told me. As a result, the state has paved highways, large inflows of both foreign and domestic private investment, and an economy that generates jobs on a significant scale. It is no coincidence that Tamil Nadu is the most urbanised state in India, with almost half of its people living in towns. (Bihar is the least urbanised, with fewer than 10 per cent living in towns.)

Tamil Nadu, which was among the first regions in India to be ruled directly by the British in the eighteenth century, has a much longer experience than the north of lower-caste political agitation. As long ago as the 1880s, when the British were starting to classify Indians by caste for their census, the city of Madras was already a hive of lower-caste radicalism. The government of Madras, as the whole of Tamil Nadu was then known, conceded public sector job quotas to lower castes in the 1920s, thirty years before India allocated similar quotas to Dalits, and almost seventy years before New Delhi extended national reservations to 'other backward classes'. Tamil Nadu holds the record in India for the highest proportion of reservations, amounting to 69 per cent of its government jobs. This has good and bad consequences. The bad is that it is very hard to reform the state's bloated bureaucracy or instil a system of meritocracy. Most quotas are supposed to be temporary, but as the saying goes: 'There is nothing as permanent as a temporary government measure.' The good side is that the state's upper castes have had many decades to grow accustomed to 'social justice' as a normal part of politics, even if they do not particularly like it.

Another positive aspect is that almost 90 per cent of Tamil Nadu's sixty million people are literate, compared to just half of Biharis. This owes something to the fact that lower-caste agitation began in Tamil Nadu long before India became a democracy, which meant lower-caste leaders had to focus on other arenas to empower their followers. As a result, there was a much greater emphasis on educating the masses as the most obvious way of raising their social status. Other reasons could be that Tamil Nadu, like neighbouring Kerala, had far more experience than the north of Christian missionary activity in the eighteenth and nineteenth centuries, which meant there were many more opportunities for the lower castes to attend schools. Furthermore, Bihar and Uttar Pradesh are deep in India's landlocked interior, while Tamil Nadu is a coastal state, so it was always more open to foreign influences. It also has a relatively low proportion of Brahmins, amounting to just 3 per cent of its population, compared to between 15 and 20 per cent in the northern states. This unusual caste demography meant it was easier for everyone else to unite against the upper orders and release their stranglehold on society. Finally, Tamil Nadu has a completely different language and script to the rest of India, so it is linguistically shielded from many of the less savoury trends that are visible in the 'Hindi-belt'.

Tamil Nadu gave the rest of the world an impressive display of its efficiency after the devastating tsunami of December 2004. India is no stranger to large natural disasters: thousands died in the coastal state of Orissa in 1999 when it was hit by a large cyclone; earthquakes claimed thousands of lives in the western Indian state of Gujarat in 2001 and in Kashmir in 2005. But none of these states responded with anything like the alacrity of Tamil Nadu in 2004, whose disaster was as devastating as anything India has seen in recent decades. Between fifteen and twenty thousand people were killed by the giant wave that hit the state's coastline.

I visited the district of Cuddalore, about a hundred miles south of Chennai. The district had suffered several hundred deaths and tens of thousands had been made homeless. However, within a year of the disaster, the state government had rehabilitated almost all of Cuddalore's displaced people in *pucca* accommodation. By contrast, in 2006 there were still people living in camps in Orissa who had lost their homes seven years earlier in the cyclone. Most of those I met in Cuddalore were lower caste, but they were fully aware of their rights. 'In Orissa the women were too afraid to come out of their huts and talk to me,' said Joseph Williams, a Tamil doctor who had assisted in both disasters. 'In Tamil Nadu it is difficult to get the women to stop talking.'

In one village that had been particularly badly hit I was taken to the temporary shelters in which many of the three thousand villagers were now housed. The shelters were rudimentary, but they were still more impressive than the makeshift dwellings in which millions of people live permanently in the slums of Bombay, Delhi and Calcutta. The refugees also had the use of toilets that were cleaned daily. Dozens of people had gathered to answer my questions and the women frequently interrupted the men. This is rare in the north. Literacy can do wonders for people's self-confidence. Some of the women had been cross-checking the assistance and financial compensation they had received against what had been announced in the newspapers. 'Where is the three thousand *crores* [about $750 million] that the World Bank pledged?' one woman asked me. Another said: 'We have only been compensated for eighty-four boats but we lost ninety-six.' I asked who had lost a relative. Everyone raised their hand. Then I asked how many had received the 200,000 rupees' compensation for their dead. Everyone again raised their hand. All had already been allocated free housing in the new township that was under construction a few hundred metres inland.

Inevitably, the village was divided along caste lines. My guides, who were working for Action Aid, a non-governmental relief organisation, told me there was a 'greater fishermen's' caste, and a 'lesser fishermen's' caste and they had lived in different parts of the village. But the new village was providing mixed housing. Unusually, the caste least affected by the disaster were the Dalits, who were too low down in the pecking order to live near the sea. The worst affected were the 'greater fishermen', who lived on the edge of the sea in the prime spots. Amid the swaying palms was an endless stretch of rubble from the devastated housing set against the azure backdrop of a now-becalmed sea. I asked the women how quickly they had received aid. In the Gujarat earthquake of 2001 much of the assistance had been held up, sometimes fatally, by the eagerness of national VIPs to be photographed visiting the disaster zone. Their private planes clogged up the small airstrips that were also being used by relief agencies to bring in supplies. In addition, the relief effort was compromised by an unseemly competition between different aid agencies to get to the scene. The government of Gujarat had clearly lost all control of the situation. Conversely, in Tamil Nadu the state government allocated different aid agencies to different villages and retained an iron coordinating grip on the whole relief effort. There were consequently no epidemics. 'We got assistance quite quickly,' the women acknowledged.

It is not just Tamil Nadu's disaster-response system that is relatively efficient. The state also has one of the best records of delivering everyday services to the poor. One of the most important is the 'midday meals' programme, in which children are given an incentive to attend school by the availability of free cooked food. In this state it works most of the time. In many other parts of India, though, the midday meals rarely arrive, partly because education is valued less highly than in the south but also because upper-caste families will not permit their children to eat food which they suspect has been prepared by lower-caste cooks. In Tamil Nadu this no longer appears to be a problem. Marrying within your caste is still the norm, but the majority of people, except for some among the state's small enclave of Brahmins, who have a reputation for being even more finicky about caste rules than others, have overcome the more offensive aspects of caste pollution rules. Much the same contrast applies to health centres. Jean Drèze, one of India's leading economists, in a survey of Tamil Nadu's rural clinics, said: 'They were clean, lively and well staffed. Patients streamed in and out, evidently at ease with the system. It was a joy to see this, in contrast with the bare, deserted, gloomy, hostile premises that pass for health centres in north India.'[22]

I do not aim to glorify Tamil Nadu. It suffers from chronic problems, such as poor water supply in its cities and abysmal irrigation for its farmers. It also has a militant civil service that refuses to be reformed. It took the state's police more than twenty years to apprehend Veerappan, Tamil Nadu's most celebrated criminal. Veerappan, whom some saw as a Robin Hood-type figure, had plundered the state's beautiful tropical parks of wild elephants and sandalwood and his gang was alleged to have killed hundreds of innocent people over the years. He was reputed to have many police officers and local politicians on his payroll, which would explain why he eluded the law with such ease for so long. Eventually, though, in 2004 he was cornered and shot. Jayalalithaa, Tamil Nadu's Chief Minister, and a politician who is as intimidating as Mayawati, handed out rewards to 752 policemen. Each of the policemen was given 300,000 rupees (about $7000), a plot of land and a promotion. More than ten thousand police in the neighbouring state of Karnataka, who also claimed to have played a role in Veerappan's demise, demanded similar consideration, in spite of having 'just missed' Veerappan on numerous occasions. In turning down their request, B. N. Alburquerque, Karnataka's chief of police, was the only senior figure in either state to show a sense of humour about this absurd demand. 'If the operation had been botched, no one would have claimed responsibility,' said Alburquerque. 'Success has many fathers, while failure is an orphan.'[23]

But Tamil Nadu's problems pale in comparison with those of most of northern India. Although the state has yet to confront the issues of a large administrative service that lacks accountability, it possesses something very valuable that is not evident in most of the north: a civic society. It is much more difficult to hijack public space in Tamil Nadu because there is a large urbanised middle class which accepts the need for rules that everyone should follow, even if they are not followed all of the time. At a trivial level it is evident in Chennai's enforcement of everyday regulations such as no-smoking zones, which in cities like Delhi are blithely ignored. More importantly, as we have seen, it is also evident in the routine provision of basic public services to people from all backgrounds. Tamil Nadu's civic culture may be hard to measure, but it is an invaluable asset which gives the state a decisive economic edge over most of the north.

Many Indian modernisers hope that Tamil Nadu points the way that the north is heading – towards a more moderate and civilised clash between the castes in the field of politics and elsewhere. Tamil Nadu proves that caste sentiments can be diluted, especially in urban settings. But caste has far from disappeared even in urban India. In a detailed nationwide poll conducted in January 2006, 74 per cent of respondents said they did not approve of inter-caste marriages.[24] Among the educated – and overwhelmingly urban – respondents, 56 per cent of graduates agreed with this statement. Likewise, 72 per cent of all respondents agreed that parents should have the final say in their children's choice of marriage partners. Among urban respondents, 59 per cent agreed with this. Certainly, in an urban setting it is easier to escape the traditional caste functions and taboos that are still likely to govern your life in the villages. It is easier to be anonymous in the city. But that does not necessarily mean you transcend your caste. You are still likely to vote for your caste party, marry within your caste and live in residential areas where your caste congregates. It is true that you are much less likely to be born into a particular job or caste function, as would still be the case for most villagers. But in other respects – not least in the world of politics – caste in India shows few signs of withering away.

CHAPTER FOUR

THE IMAGINARY HORSE

The continuing threat of Hindu nationalism

Oh Rama be wise. There exists no other world but this. That is certain.

Advice given to Lord Ram by Javali, a sceptical priest,
in the Hindu epic the *Ramayana*[1]

I had never heard of 'biofuturology' before. But for two hours this strange science held me spellbound. I was in the central Indian city of Nagpur, at the spacious residence of a prosperous industrialist whose company makes packaging materials. It was his friend and mentor, Dr Ramachandra Tupkary, who was doing most of the talking. A retired engineer, Dr Tupkary was one of the leading intellectual thinkers of India's large 'family' of Hindu nationalist groups. The parent of the family is the Rashtriya Swayamsevak Sangh (RSS) – the Organisation of National Volunteers – which has between two and six million members, depending on whom you ask (it does not publish membership rolls). Even the lower number would make the RSS the second-largest political movement in the world, after the Chinese Communist Party. One of its offspring is the Hindu nationalist Bharatiya Janata Party (BJP), which led India's coalition government between 1998 and 2004.

A soft-spoken man, Tupkary had been both the editor of the RSS intellectual journal and the leader of its annual 'officers' training camp', a semi-militarised gathering of senior volunteers held in Nagpur every summer. I thought his views might give me a better insight into the Hindu nationalist way of thinking. It was one of the hottest days of the year in India's hottest city and it took a while for me to regain my bearings after coming in from what felt like a Turkish sauna on the streets outside. Tupkary started by defining biofuturology for me: it is a science that gives you an intellectual master-key to understanding the development of the human race. He said the human brain is divided into two halves: the right side is equipped to deal with diversity and the left side with uniformity. The typical Indian has a 'right-side brain' and the typical European a 'left-side brain', although he conceded there were plenty of exceptions to this rule. Cultures which have a strong right-side brain are good at dealing with complex thoughts and tend towards a democratic and decentralised society. Their minds are original but disorganised. People who have a strong left-side brain are more disciplined but tend to develop autocratic and centralised societies. They are better at organisation but lack imagination. Hindus are right-side, Muslims are left-side. Polytheistic Indians are right-side, monotheistic Europeans are left-side; the software of human development comes from India. The hardware comes from the west. 'Are you following?' asked Tupkary. I was indeed.

After independence, India had gone badly astray because it was run by people with overdeveloped left-side brains who had been educated in western ways. They had believed in simplistic notions such as a secular constitution and the industrial society. They had taken India further away from itself. But now India was slowly moving back to its natural mental state, in which diversity, complexity and – another new term – 'demassification' were again the ascendant forces.[2] Demassification stood for India's tradition of small cottage industries, which harnessed the creativity of right-side Indian people, as opposed to the regimentation of large factories, which corralled its victims into a mind-numbing left-side way of life. The global pendulum was now swinging back India's way. 'Many people in the west and even in India fail to realise this,' said Tupkary.

> India was a developed society long, long, long before it was colonised by Muslims and by Europeans. We had a developed economy thousands of years ago. We had demassified oil production, we had sophisticated medicine and science. We had a very high standard of living. Civilisation was born in India at least ten thousand years ago and from India it spread to the rest of the world. Hindustan is a microcosm of the universe. It contains every contradiction and tendency. Now history has turned full circle. Once again India is in a position to help the world.

I must have seemed out of sorts because Dr Tupkary was looking at me indulgently. My head was beginning to throb on its left and its right sides. 'It is quite complicated to understand all in one go,' he said to me gently. 'Would you like another *nimbu panni* [lime juice with water]?'

India's cultural pedigree is indeed ancient. One of the world's earliest civilisations existed in the Indus Valley in what is now Pakistan between approximately 3100 and 1700 BC. It coincided with the other early city-state cultures of Mesopotamia, in what is today's Iraq, and the Yangtse Valley in China. Unlike the other two, though, scholars have been unable to decipher the fragments of script engraved on the various Indus Valley pots and seals that have been uncovered at the main archaeological sites of the Harappan civilisation.* However, although the Harappan script

---

*The first site was discovered in Harappa, near modern-day Lahore. The largest site at Mohenjodaro (meaning 'Mound of the Dead'), was excavated in the 1920s.

remains elusive, scholars have revealed some tantalising characteristics about the civilisation: the Harappans maintained probably the most advanced system of sanitation and drainage known to the ancient world; they had a strikingly uniform culture across dozens of cities separated by hundreds of miles and many centuries; they were obsessive town planners, replicating their standard grid network of streets in each city; they maintained a kind of loose federal republic with no apparent system of monarchy or dynasty; they buried their dead; and they were unfamiliar with the horse. These last two characteristics are particularly important.[3]

At some stage in the early part of the second millennium BC, the Harappans disappeared. Initially historians thought their cities had been ravaged by horse-riding Aryan invaders who swept down into the subcontinent from Central Asia some time between 2000 and 1500 BC. Some still argue that this is what happened – and there is evidence, in the form of sites containing masses of smashed human bones, that might indicate the Harappans met a violent end. But others now believe that the Harappan civilisation was fizzling out when the Aryans began to migrate peacefully into India early in the second millennium. Both accounts draw upon archaeological evidence (coins, pots, bones, brickwork and terracotta seals) and clues contained in later literature. Their dispute centres on how the Aryan-speaking peoples arrived in India, not in the fact of that arrival, nor in its timing. There is substantial overlap between the two accounts. But the question of whether the Harappans were already in decline or whether they were pushed into oblivion by the incoming Aryans remains unresolved. Perhaps it will never be answered conclusively. But academics are at least agreed on the rules of evidence for debating it.

In 1998 the whole discipline was turned on its head when the BJP came to power. With little evidence but with very clear motivation, the intellectuals of the Hindu nationalist movement argued that the Aryans had in fact come from India and had migrated to the rest of the world. The Harappans themselves must therefore have been Aryan. Furthermore, they argued that the Harappan era and the following Vedic era had been dated far too recently and ought to be pushed back a few thousand years. The objective was straightforward: to establish that India was the sole cradle of civilisation, long pre-dating the Greeks, Chinese, Babylonians and others. India had exported civilisation to the rest of the world through migration. If true, this theory would shoot to pieces not only all accepted scholarship on ancient India but much of the foundations of classical archaeology for the rest of the world. It was bold, but it lacked one vital element: the support of any accredited and respected scholars.

Murli Manohar Joshi, the BJP's Minister for Education between 1998 and 2004, spent a lot of his budget on projects that he hoped would give the theory more respectability. Joshi, who had been a professor of physics at Allahabad University before he went into politics and had been a lifelong supporter of the RSS, packed the boards of New Delhi's various historical and social-science bodies with people who agreed with him. Established scholars who refused to trim their sails to the new winds did not have their contracts renewed. Some, such as Romila Thapar, probably India's best-known classical historian, were subjected to very personal hate campaigns by the RSS. Expatriate Indians belonging to American chapters of the RSS tried to prevent Thapar from speaking in public during her year in the United States as a visiting scholar. 'Almost all other research projects were sidelined,' said Ms Thapar. 'Everything was crowded out by the drive to prove something that had no empirical support.'[4]

Although the Hindu nationalist account of India's history has so far failed to achieve any academic breakthroughs, the view-point has seeped into mainstream public opinion. India's school textbooks were rewritten to present the Aryan–Harappan theory as fact and were then distributed in thousands of schools across the country. The textbooks said new evidence had proved that the Harappans did after all possess horses, which meant the Indus Valley civilisation must have been Aryan. In support of the contention, the textbooks mentioned the recent discovery by two academics of the unmistakable depiction of a horse on one of the Harappan terracotta wax seals.[5] It did not seem to matter that in 2000 the discovery had been exposed as a simple case of fraud. Michael Witzel, Professor of Sanskrit at Harvard University, showed how the two men had manipulated computer-generated images of the seal to conjure up a horse. The textbooks were neither withdrawn nor amended.

The BJP's textbooks also put a new slant on more recent periods of Indian history. For example, they showed Islam as having come to India at the point of the sword during India's medieval period without reference to its peaceful spread through trading links in south India much earlier. Before the arrival of Muslims, Hindu society had been contented and peaceful. There was no mention of what happened to Buddhism in India. Indian Christians, meanwhile, spent their time torturing people in the Inquisition. The word 'caste' did not appear once in the history textbook. In the section on modern Indian history, the assassination of Gandhi in 1948 by Nathuram Godse, a right-wing Hindu nationalist, was simply omitted. Taken together, the changes amounted to an overhaul of what was conveyed to children about their society and its history. The message was that India was Hindu and Hindu was India. There was no room for other identities. The experience of the lower castes was simply airbrushed out of the picture. Imaginary horses could fill only some of the blank spaces.

The BJP government also painted much of India's higher education in saffron (Hinduism's holy colour and naturally the background tone on the BJP's electoral logo). Joshi introduced courses in Vedic mathematics and Vedic science at Indian universities. Composed between 1500 and 1000 BC, the Vedas were passed down orally from generation to generation until at some stage in the first millennium BC they were set down in writing. They are religious incantations, some of which are hauntingly poetic while others are intricately sophisticated and subtle in their theology. India produced some of the world's greatest astronomers between AD 100 and 900, and is credited with introducing the binary system, which is the basis of modern mathematics. But the discovery of the zero came many centuries after the Vedic era, which produced little of scientific value. 'Despite the richness of the Vedas in many other respects, there is no sophisticated mathematics in them, nor anything that can be called rigorous science,' writes Amartya Sen.[6] Even if the Vedas had made great breakthroughs in knowledge, the rules of scientific evidence are universal, so it makes no more sense to talk of science as 'Vedic' than it would to label Newtonian physics 'Christian'.

The Hindu nationalist government invested a lot of capital in seeking both to shift the Vedas back into a much earlier stage of pre-history and to locate the earliest prototype of human learning within these incantations. So far, the project has found no supporting evidence in scholarship. Many decades ago, A.L. Basham said the Vedas offered romantic nationalists the perfect opportunity to indulge their fantasies because so little could really be known about the Vedic era. 'Around these phantoms later tradition draped glittering mantles of legend,' he wrote. 'But when the mantles are removed only vague shadows remain.'[7]

The political scientist Benedict Anderson describes nation states as imagined communities: '*Imagined*,' he writes, 'because members of even the smallest nation will never know most of their fellow members, meet them, or even hear of them, yet in the mind of each lives the image of their communion.'[8] Most people think of their nation as a natural entity awakened by history, oppression or revolution.

But this overlooks the way in which a nation seeks to establish its identity by defining itself against other nation states. One of the principal tools of nation-building is the selective rummaging through history for events that can provide rallying stories or myths. Every country, including the oldest nation states, such as Britain and France, tailors its national holidays, educational systems and public monuments to these ends (largely at the expense of each other, in the case of Britain and France). But India is unusual in that it retains two competing and very opposed ideas of the nation: the first, largely conceived by the Congress Party during the freedom struggle, stresses a plural, secular and composite India (in contrast to Islamic Pakistan); the second, represented by the Hindu nationalist movement, pushes for a more exclusive and Hindu definition of India (in an unintentional echo of Pakistan). It is only in the last twenty years that the second has provided a serious challenge to the first.

The 1990s were a turbulent and disorienting decade in Indian politics and government. The sharp and rapid decline of the once-dominant Congress Party created space for a new kind of politics which was far more fluid and less predictable than what it replaced. Between 1947 and 1989 India had just six prime ministers. Between 1989 and 2004 it had seven. Some of the vacuum created by a declining Congress was filled by the emergence of a small platoon of lower-caste and regional parties. As we saw in the last chapter, they have little idea of India beyond their own particular status within it. They do not challenge the Congress-dominated freedom movement's definition of Indian nationhood, even though they present a strong electoral challenge to the Congress Party itself. The rest of the vacuum was filled by Hindu nationalism, which is a much more coherent force. The main aim of the *Sangh Parivar* (the 'family of the RSS', of which the BJP is the political arm) is to reconstruct India's national identity along Hindu lines. Rewriting India's history is a key element in that project.

The RSS was founded in Nagpur in 1925 by K. B. Hedgewar, a medical practitioner. Whereas Congress was dominated by lawyers and journalists, the RSS was dominated by those with a scientific background. Both groups were almost exclusively Brahmin in their formative years. Even today the RSS and the BJP are dominated by the upper castes. Hedgewar was the RSS's first *sarsangchalak*, or leader. Three out of his four successors were also from scientific backgrounds: M. S. Golwalkar, perhaps the most influential Hindu nationalist of the twentieth century, was a zoologist; Balasaheb Deoras, the odd one out, was a lawyer; Rajendra Singh was a physicist; and K. S. Sudarshan, the current head of the RSS, who took over in 1999, is an engineer. Unsurprisingly, given this history, the Hindu nationalist idea of India abounds with scientific imagery. Much like the German and French romantic nationalists of the late nineteenth century who influenced them, RSS supporters see the nation as a living organism that is deeply rooted in the national soil. They reject the fictional 'social contract' between individuals that underlies most western ideas of the nation state because it implies the individual has a choice in the matter.

The way the RSS is organised was inspired by European fascism. Its principal organisational unit is the *shakha*, a group of individuals who gather each morning to perform exercises and recite nationalist stories in tens of thousands of neighbourhoods across India. Every day several hundred thousand, possibly upwards of a million, Indian men gather at their local *shakhas* for a dawn routine of martial training and indoctrination. The uniform they put on is a mix between the khaki outfit that was worn by the British colonial police and sartorial details taken from Mussolini's Fascist Black Shirts, who were icons to Hindu nationalists when the RSS was founded in 1925. The *shakhas* are equivalent to the semi-militarised cells that formed the building blocks of both Mussolini's Fascists and the Nazi Hitler Youth in Germany.

Golwalkar, whose books *We, or Our Nationhood Defined* and *Bunch of Thoughts* are the bibles of today's RSS volunteers, wrote:

'The ultimate vision of our work . . . is a perfectly organised state of society wherein each individual has been moulded into a model of ideal Hindu manhood and made into a living limb of the corporate personality of society.' He likened the *shakha* to a cell in the human body: 'Each cell feels its identity with the entire body and is ever ready to sacrifice itself for the sake of the health and the growth of the body.' The main aim would be to create a Hinduism that was masculine so that it could prevail against the muscular cultures of Islam and the west. It sprang from the diagnosis that India and Hinduism had become too 'effeminate' over the centuries. The frailty of the Hindu body had enabled outside powers to dominate the country with ease. The aim, therefore, was to copy the unity and organisation of the monotheistic or 'Semitic' cultures, the better to repel them. Christophe Jaffrelot, probably the best scholar of Hindu nationalism, describes the RSS strategy as 'emulate then stigmatise'.[9] In other words, copy the strengths of your enemies while also demonising them. This explains why Gandhi, who in so many respects was an inspiring exemplar of Hinduism, was so hated by Hindu militants. He stood for non-violence, which they saw as effeminate, and he preached love of other religions, which made him a traitor.* Nathuram Godse, the man who shot Gandhi, came from an RSS family.

The main aim of the RSS is to create a Hindu society in its own image. Each cell in the body of Indian society would have to conform to the whole. In its imagined community an Indian would be defined as someone who saw India not just as his fatherland but as his holy land. This would obviously exclude Indians who looked to Mecca or to Rome for their spiritual sustenance. 'The foreign races in Hindustan must either adopt the Hindu culture and language, must learn to respect and hold in reverence Hindu

---

*Although Gandhi shared some of the facets of the Hindu nationalists. Both took their cue from the British who liked to classify castes and religions. 'The Hindu is by nature a coward,' wrote Gandhi in 1924, 'whereas the Muslim is a bully.'

religion, must entertain no ideals but those of glorification of the Hindu race and culture . . . or may stay in the country, wholly subordinated to the Hindu nation, claiming nothing, deserving no privileges, far less any preferential treatment – not even citizen's rights,' wrote Golwalkar.[10]

According to this view, Muslims and Christians were not just 'foreign' but belonged to different 'races'. It is worth stressing here what might be obvious to most readers: India has an extraordinary hotchpotch of different races, languages and cultures. Even the Aryans are nowadays described by scholars as a language group, rather than a race. But even if the Aryans were a race, they too came from elsewhere. Very few of India's Christians and Muslims are descended from Christian and Muslim immigrants to India: the overwhelming majority are descendants of lower-caste Hindus who converted in the (mostly forlorn) hope of escaping their low status. Christianity has been present in India since the first century AD, when large-scale conversions took place in the southern state of Kerala. Islam has been present since the eighth century, when it spread through south Indian ports which had trading ties with Arabia. Christianity's Indian pedigree therefore significantly predates its arrival in most of Europe. Islam's history in India begins several hundred years before Protestantism was born. However, the RSS still allows a crack in the door for India's religious minorities. Lal Krishna Advani, the Deputy Prime Minister during the BJP government and an RSS *swayamsevak* (part-time volunteer), said he approved of 'Hindu Muslims' and 'Hindu Christians', meaning those who accept, as do most Hindus, that there are many paths to God. The RSS also runs a programme called *Ghar Vapasi* – or 'welcome back to Hinduism' – for Muslims and Christians who wish to convert to Hinduism.*

*

*According to India's census, Christians formed 2.8 per cent of the population in 1951 but only 2.3 per cent in 2001. Yet the Hindu nationalists maintain that India is rife with Christian proselytisation.

Interacting with members of the RSS is never quite what I expect it to be. Often they are very charming. I once caused some puzzlement while dining at the home of a very hospitable RSS sympathiser in Ahmedabad, capital of Gujarat. His other guest was Manmohan Vaidya, the head *pracharak* (full-time volunteer) for the state. The dinner had been arranged to educate me about the movement. Vaidya described what it was like to be an RSS *pracharak*: he should take a vow of celibacy, which ensures he will remain married only to the movement. He sleeps in dormitories in the network of rest-houses and centres the RSS maintains up and down the country. He cannot drink alcohol, smoke cigarettes or eat meat. His whole existence is bound up with the cause. To me, this life sounded tough and self-denying. 'Apart from vegetarianism,' I said, 'you seem to have quite a lot in common with Islamic fundamentalists.' Vaidya looked startled, but then he laughed: 'We are very dedicated. I suppose you could say we have some things in common, but they are very superficial. We are Hindus.' 'Just Hindus,' I asked, 'or Hindu fundamentalists?' 'We are not fundamentalists, we are nationalists,' he stressed. 'There is a big difference.'

Some months later I visited the headquarters of the RSS to observe its annual 'Officers' training camp. The main RSS building, which is located in the heart of the industrial central-Indian city of Nagpur, overlooks a large, dusty parade ground, which is where the RSS volunteers conduct their daily drills. It is a kind of giant *shakha* for the RSS national leadership lasting for thirty days. I was accompanied by Ram Madhav, the talkative and engaging national spokesman for the organisation. We observed two thousand men of all ages marching up and down the parade ground, each wielding a *lathi* – a long bamboo stave also used by the police. They were dressed in the standard kit of the RSS volunteer: a plain white shirt, khaki shorts held up by a sturdy black belt, yellow socks and black shoes. They also wear the trademark RSS black cap, an inversion of the traditional white Congress cap. The RSS salute, which is frequently rendered, is unmistakably fascistic: standing to attention, you move your right arm across your chest with the palm of your hand facing down. At dawn each day the trainees gather in front of the fluttering saffron flag of the RSS to salute it and then sing 'Vande Mataram' – 'Hail Motherland' – the Hindu nationalist anthem. For the rest of the day, until 10 p.m., they undergo martial training and 'character building', punctuated by discussion groups and traditional games such as Kabbadi, which involves two teams breathlessly trying to tag each other while shouting, 'Kabbadi, kab-badi.'[11] Individual sports and games are discouraged, even those that originated in India, such as chess. Although a team game, cricket is also banned, as it is of foreign origin.

Having observed the drill, we were taken to the RSS official headquarters in the heart of Nagpur's old town. This is where the senior leadership lives, with the head and deputy head sharing a small suite. Their bedrooms, which both adjoin a compact living room, are bare and monastic. Some people argue that the RSS is not technically fascist since fascist ideology is built around the personality cult of a single leader, whereas the RSS stresses collective leadership with the sarsangchalak playing nothing more than the role of 'guide and adviser'. The distinction strikes me as a moot point. But certainly the RSS could be described as ascetic. I was fascinated by the sarsangchalak's simple bedchamber. It seemed like the living quarters of a Carthusian abbot, or perhaps of a very abstemious pope. 'This is the bed the sarsangchalak will probably die in,' said my guide, a pracharak. Then we were taken to the family home of Hedgewar, the first sarsangchalak. It was a beautifully restored Chitpavan (Hedgewar's sub-caste) Brahmin home, typical of how the well-to-do Hindu classes used to live. Hedgewar's family had moved in the nineteenth century to Nagpur from Hyderabad, which was ruled by a Muslim nizam who was intolerant of dissent.* This

---

*About a third of British India was ruled by separate princely states. Most of the five hundred or so principalities were too small to matter, but several, such as Hyderabad and Kashmir, were significant enough to give the impression of being independent states in their own right. They were not.

family history must have had something to do with Hedgewar's Islamaphobia. 'Isn't it a beautiful house?' said our guide.

I have always wondered why Hindu nationalists are so keen to win the approval of people who would be very unlikely to sympathise with their outlook. It is hard to reconcile the RSS's aggressive view of the world with the gentle courtesy of many of its members. They convey disdain for foreign ideas and culture yet yearn for the recognition and goodwill of foreigners. It is a complex psychology – far more complex, perhaps, than their ideology. I was accompanied on the visit to Nagpur by Sohail Akbar, a Delhi-based, Muslim photographer. He was a little nervous about how the RSS would respond if they discovered his religious background. But nobody did, or else if they had, they never let on.

It was particularly important to conceal Sohail's full name during our next visit. The most militant offshoot of the RSS is the Vishwa Hindu Parishad (VHP) – the World Council of Hinduism. The RSS is in charge of the overall reform of society, the BJP is its political arm, and the VHP is the arm that deals with reform of the Hindu religion. The VHP's youth wing, the Bajrang Dal, supplies the shock troops whenever there is a communal riot. Named after Hanuman, the monkey god who burned the island of Lanka with his tail in the classic Hindu epic the *Ramayana*, the Bajrang Dal consists of young men between the ages of fifteen and thirty. Between 300,000 and 400,000 are said to have been trained so far.

We visited a Bajrang Dal training session in Nagpur. Unlike the RSS drills, the young men – some of whom had barely reached puberty – were training with swords and airguns, in addition to the *lathi*. 'This', said the trainer, wielding a *lathi* in slow motion, 'is how you kill a man with a blow to the back of his head. It is very simple.' I asked some of the young men, most of whom wore fierce military moustaches, why they had signed up for this kind of training. One, a tribal teenager from an area of India where Christian missionaries are active, said: 'The Christians are trying to proselytise our people. We need to defend ourselves.' Another said: 'In our town the Muslims kill cows and make a huge noise when we are trying to pray. We kill or get killed.' All were very eager to display their skills. The head trainer was equally friendly. 'This is commando training for the defence of Hinduism,' he said. 'We have nothing to hide.' The training session was taking place in full view of the passing traffic on the grounds of a college sports field in the centre of Nagpur. 'If they had known it was a Muslim taking their photographs, God knows what they would have done,' said a relieved Sohail after we had left. His apprehension was perfectly reasonable. The Bajrang Dal played the leading role in two of India's three worst riots of the last quarter of a century, in 1992 and in 2002.*

The riots of 1992 were a direct result of the Hindu nationalist project to rewrite India's history. The three thousand people who were butchered – mostly Muslims – were proof, if any were needed, of how lethal history can be when the identity of a multi-ethnic nation state is under question. The violence was triggered when a large mob of Hindu militants demolished a mosque in the Hindu holy town of Ayodhya, in Uttar Pradesh, on 6 December 1992. Spearheaded by L. K. Advani, who became leader of the BJP in 2004 after it was defeated at the polls, the Hindu nationalists had in 1987 launched a national campaign to demolish the mosque. They claimed the Babri Masjid, or the Mosque of Babur, named after the first emperor of the Mughal dynasty, stood on the site of a temple that Babur had razed in 1528. The also claimed that the site was the birthplace of the Lord Ram, after whom the *Ramayana* epic was named. There is no evidence of the existence of Ram, whom most educated Hindus take to be a mythical figure (Rabindranath Tagore thought the *Ramayana* was 'a marvellous parable'[12]). Meanwhile, the holy

---

*The other major riot was directed by Congress Party supporters against the minority Sikh community following the assassination of Indira Gandhi by her Sikh bodyguards in October 1984.

texts date Ram's birth to several hundred thousand years ago. Nor is there any clear proof that a temple had once stood on the site. These twin theories of Ram's birthplace and the missing temple only gathered momentum after India had gained independence. A sceptic might see in the Ayodhya campaign a good example of what Benedict Anderson meant by the power of imagination. In 1984, before the Ram temple campaign had been launched, the BJP had just 2 seats in India's 545-strong parliament; two years after the campaign was launched, the BJP's strength had risen to 84 seats. Its peak came in 1999, when it won 183 seats, before falling to 138 seats in the 2004 election.

The 2002 riots in Gujarat were directly related to the massacre that had followed the demolition of the Babri Masjid a decade earlier. They were triggered by the incineration of fifty-eight Hindu train passengers in the town of Godhra on 27 February. Godhra, which has a large Muslim population, is an important stop on the train journey from Gujarat to Uttar Pradesh. In the previous weeks the train had been full of VHP militants travelling to Ayodhya as part of a new campaign to pressurise the government into building a Ram temple on the ruins of the demolished mosque.* The Muslim community, many of whom work as hawkers and 'coolies' at the Godhra railway station, claim the trainloads of Hindu militants had been taunting them for weeks. Government inquiries into the incident have failed to reach a firm conclusion about how the fire was started in the compartment where the passengers lost their lives. But all eyewitnesses agreed that a large and angry mob of local Muslims were present when the burning occurred.

The BJP state government of Gujarat, headed by Narendra Modi, an RSS *pracharak* who had become Chief Minister a few

---

*The campaign has yet to achieve its aim. For once, India's judiciary could be forgiven for taking so long to hear what is an insoluble case to determine which religion should have legal entitlement to the site.

weeks earlier, declared a day of mourning on 28 February so that the funerals of the passengers could be held in the streets of Ahmedabad, Gujarat's largest city. This was a clear invitation to violence. The Muslim quarters of Ahmedabad and other cities in Gujarat turned into death traps as thousands of Hindu militants converged on them. As the rioting unfolded, Modi quoted Newton's third law: 'Every action has an equal and opposite reaction.' His words served as a green light for the killers. But the reaction was substantially more than equal. In the tidal wave of blood that was unleashed hundreds of separate incidents were chronicled by eyewitnesses and some of the killings were recorded by television cameras. The most disturbing feature of the riots was the treatment meted out to Muslim women and children. Mobs gathered round and raped the women, then they poured kerosene down their throats and the throats of their children and threw lighted matches at them. Hundreds stood by and cheered these gruesome incinerations, which symbolised revenge for the burning of the train passengers in Godhra. The male family members were forced to watch their wives and children burn to death before they too were killed. These pogroms appear to have been planned: the rioters possessed electoral registers and were able to single out the homes of Muslims living in mixed communities, leaving the homes around them untouched. They were also able to pinpoint Muslim-owned businesses which had taken the precaution of having a Hindu business partner and adopting Hindu names on the shop front. Hundreds of Muslim shops were destroyed. There was a pattern and efficiency to the killings that implied some degree of foreknowledge.*

The second-most disturbing aspect of the riots was the role of the Gujarat police, who stood by and watched the slaughter take

*History has a way of producing strange coincidences. February 27 – the date of the Godhra burnings – was also the date of the notorious fire in the German Reichstag in 1933 that gave Hitler the opportunity to seize power.

place. In some instances they allegedly even assisted the rioters by giving them directions to the addresses of local Muslims. In others they allegedly turned fleeing Muslims back into the arms of the mob. Numerous inquiries into the riots that have been conducted by Indian and international human rights groups have produced evidence that the Gujarat police were under instructions not to interfere.[13] 'The mob caught my husband and hit him twice on his head with the sword,' Jannat Sheikh, a Muslim housewife, testified to an independent legal inquiry.

> They then threw petrol in his eyes and burned him. My sister-in-law was stripped and raped. She had a three-month-old baby in her lap. They threw petrol on her and the child was thrown in the fire. My mother-in-law was unable to climb the stairs so she was on the ground floor with her four-year-old grandson. She told them to take away all the money and jewellery but to spare the children. They took the money and jewellery then they burned the children. Unmarried girls from my street were stripped, raped and burned. The police were on the spot but they were helping the mob.[14]

This was one of hundreds of corroborated eyewitness accounts taken by human rights groups. In almost every case the police had refused to record witness statements.

One BJP minister, Haren Pandya, a rival of Narendra Modi, had agreed to testify to a commission of inquiry in 2003 about the instructions that had been given to the police. But he was assassinated by an alleged Muslim terrorist shortly beforehand. No trial has taken place for his murder. At the time of writing, in 2006, only a handful of people have been convicted for murders during the Gujarat riots, while more than two hundred Muslims remain incarcerated without trial under India's anti-terrorist laws for the killing of the train passengers in Godhra. Not one Hindu has been detained under these laws. The defeat of the national BJP-led government in 2004 did little to change the situation. Under India's federal constitution, law and order is principally a state concern. Narendra Modi's state government was re-elected with a sweeping two-thirds of the seats in December 2002, nine months after the riots had taken place. Modi's campaign theme was the 'Pride of Gujarat'. On the campaign trail he equated Gujarat's Muslims to a 'fifth column', an enemy within, whose loyalties were to Pakistan.

Another unsettling feature of the Gujarat riots was the response of the national government in New Delhi. Atal Behari Vajpayee, the Prime Minister at the time, did not visit the scene of the violence for a full month after it happened. According to people in his office, Vajpayee, who was generally seen as the moderate face of the BJP, attempted to sack Modi after the riots but was overruled by his colleagues. Having failed to do the right thing, the Prime Minister chose to swim with the tide: 'Let us not forget how the whole thing started. Who lit the fire? How did it spread? he asked at a party conference in the beautiful coastal state of Goa a few weeks later. 'Wherever in the world Muslims live, they tend not to live peacefully with others. They want to spread their faith by resorting to terror and threats.'[15] Others openly celebrated the restoration of 'Hindu pride' the riots had apparently brought about. The RSS hinted that any future incidents would result in equally bloody outcomes. M. G. Vaidya, the RSS spokesman at the time, issued the simple statement: 'Let the Muslims understand that their real safety lies in the goodwill of the majority.' Such statements were usually accompanied by the rider that Hindus, unlike Muslims, were a tolerant people. Most Indians I know, whether Hindu or Muslim, and in many cases friends of mine who reject any religious label, are strikingly tolerant. It is part of their national heritage. It would require a considerable leap of imagination to place the RSS within the same heritage.

One final, equally upsetting, aspect of the Gujarat riots was its aftermath. More than 200,000 people were made homeless and ended up in refugee camps. The government provided little or nothing in the way of compensation for the loss of relatives, homes or businesses, while the state provided only a trickle of relief to the camps. Most of the makeshift schools and shelters for the refugees were provided by the Islamiya Relief Committee, a charity run by an orthodox and relatively hardline branch of Sunni Islam.* Many of the Muslims targeted in the massacre had been either Bohra or Ismaili, esoteric sects from the minority Shia Muslim strand of Islam. Neither sect would remotely identify with Sunni-dominated Pakistan, where the Shia minority are often treated as second-class citizens. Yet they had been deserted by the Gujarat police, the state's system of justice and its welfare officers. Many young and angry Muslim men, both Shia and Sunni, therefore found a new lodestar that had helped them when they needed it most. 'It is bitterly ironic that young Muslim men who had no radical instincts before the riots came out of the riots very radicalised,' said Hanif Lakdawala, a Muslim based in Ahmedabad, who runs a charity for women who live in the slums. 'If the state had done something for the Muslims – if it had shown any concern at all for their welfare or for the principles of justice – then they would have had something else to turn to.' Imagined communities tend to beget other imagined communities. Then they draw strength from each other.

What can be said about imagined national histories can apply just as much to religious traditions. Just as Christians in medieval Europe imagined Jesus as a blond and embraced the concept of Deicide (murder of God) when it suited commercial interests to persecute Jews, and just as liberal Muslims today scour the *Hadiths* for evidence of equal opportunity rights for women, so Hindu

---

*It is important to mention that thousands of young Indians, most of them Hindu, also went to Gujarat to volunteer to help the victims in the aftermath of the riots. The many journalists who took great risks to record what happened in the riots were mostly Hindu.

revisionists reinvent the past for contemporary purposes. One such tool is the sacred cow. Mere mention of this theme is enough to provoke great anger among Hindu nationalists, so I will be careful. I was once on a television panel in India sitting next to the BJP Minister for Information and Broadcasting. There were upcoming elections in various states, as there almost invariably are in India, and inevitably the BJP had raised the issue of banning cow slaughter. I pointed out that most Indians I had spoken to worried much more about prices, jobs and water supply. Issues such as cow slaughter and banning forcible religious conversions were red herrings dreamed up by electoral strategists to divert people's attention from the real problems. The minister was incandescent. Wagging his finger at me, he said: 'Do not disrespect the cow. It is a sacred animal. Are you disrespecting the cow?' Of course not, I said, fumbling for an adequate response. The minister had succeeded in diverting the issue.

D. N. Jha, a historian at Delhi University, got it much worse. In 2001 Dr Jha, a diminutive man in his early seventies, wrote *The Myth of the Holy Cow*, which submitted evidence that beef was eaten by large sections of Hindu society – including Brahmins – in the ancient past. Many on India's left have sought to portray India's Hindu–Muslim problems as an invention of the British, who maintained their rule by dividing Indians into artificial categories. Some have even claimed caste was invented during the colonial era.* Clearly, then, there is questionable scholarship on both the left and the right. I have no means to judge the authenticity of Dr Jha's arguments but India has free speech and Jha was denied it. His book was immediately banned by the BJP government and has not resurfaced in India (I picked

---

*It is one thing to manipulate existing religious and caste divisions, which the British undoubtedly did, but quite another to conjure them out of thin air. One unintentional effect of such scholarship is to rob Indians then – and now – of any role in making their own history. It also elevates the British into geniuses, a description with which few who study the imperial era in India would readily agree.

up my copy in London). For a while Jha was also confined to his campus residence at Delhi University because youths from the Bajrang Dal and right-wing student activists were threatening to kill him. 'Nobody stood up for me, not even the publishers,' Jha has said. 'When you use the word "cow" people lose all reason.'

Cow protection movements emerged in the late nineteenth century in northern India, where there were large concentrations of Muslims. The Arya Samaj, a militant Hindu reformist sect, which, because of its asceticism and militancy, could be compared in some ways to Calvinism, chose the supposedly endangered holy cow as an emotional tool to create a feeling of Hinduness among the masses. The sect's aim was to bring lower-caste Hindus into the fold, in an almost precise foreshadowing of the strategies of Hindu nationalism today.

I decided to visit the Cow Product Research Centre near Nagpur. Run by the VHP, the centre seeks to build on the five traditional village products of the cow: milk, *ghee* (clarified butter), butter, urine (for religious purposes) and dung (for fuel). I was accompanied by Sunil Mansinghka, a senior VHP activist. The centre, which draws on the research skills of dozens of young men with Ph.D.s in medicine and biology, also runs a hostel and a school for the local tribal population that is named after Swami Vivekananda, a widely respected Hindu philosopher and social reformer. 'Please remove your *chappals* [sandals],' said Mansinghka as we approached a vast cow shed. 'What, barefoot?' I asked, with an eye on the puddles of cow urine and cow dung that covered the ground. 'Yes, barefoot,' he replied. 'Cow dung is an antiseptic. If you have athlete's foot, you will be cured.'

Outside the cow shelter there was a notice which said: 'Do not tease the cow, give it love. Spitting is prohibited inside. Give any donations or offerings to the worker not to the cow.' I stepped gingerly into the shelter, trying not to slip. Mansinghka said: 'These cows are the pure cow breeds of Hindustan. We have spent a long time separating the foreign cow breeds from the indigenous breeds, which are much superior in every way.' He wheeled me face to face with a very fierce-looking bull, whose vast dangling testicles were the size of cricket balls. I recoiled. 'Do not worry,' said Mansinghka, wheeling me back to face the bull, 'it is a pure Indian breed. It cannot hurt you. Not like the bulls in the west.' I was pushed eyeball to eyeball with the bull for a snap second. Then I was somehow manoeuvred through the two-inch layer of cow product to the middle of the herd. I was handed a silver tray with candles on it and also turmeric, rice, flowers and red paste. I had to circle the tray a few times above the head of one of the cows before smearing the paste on the cow's forehead and my own. 'Now you are praying to the cow. She is my mother. She is your mother,' said Mansinghka. Mother seemed unfazed by all the attention.

Then I was taken to the laboratories. The first room hit me about twenty metres before we arrived. It contained hundreds of bottles of cow's urine, stacked up, one upon the other. There were Bunsen burners and some of the urine was bubbling away in beakers. 'This is an antioxidant that will cure cancer,' said one of the lab researchers, waving a capsule under my nose. Then there were urine-derivative products which cured bronchitis and obesity, one which gave energy, and another that purified blood. Next we were shown cow-dung products. Cow dung, too, conceals an impressive range of world-beating cures. My favourite product was cow-dung soap. There was also a cow-dung shampoo for dandruff. Mansinghka said the centre had submitted a number of cow-derivative applications to the US Patents Office and other countries. 'God lives in the cow dung,' he said. 'All of these recipes are contained in the holy texts.'

Mr Mansinghka, a Rajasthani in his late thirties, told me that there was no medicine outside of the Vedas that was worth using. It occurred to me that he was utterly sincere. Taken together, his beliefs amounted to textbook fundamentalism – a modern condition in which you take the beliefs that people in the past had on some level accepted as symbolic and hold them to be literally true, and even scientifically demonstrable: God made the world in six days; Eve was formed from Adam's rib; Ram was born on this precise spot; and so on. But the Cow Research Centre did have some impressive uses for cow's product. Mansinghka showed me several trees, each of which had been fertilised with specially enriched cow biomass. Every leaf emitted a concentrated odour of the fruit of the tree – be it mangoes, lemons or oranges. This seemed very pleasant. And for all the science I know perhaps cow's urine really can cure cancer.

At the end of the tour Mansinghka, who had been looking throughout for some sign that I had been converted to the merits of the holy cow's products, said: 'When you write, please be kind to the cow. She is our mother.' I was happy to promise not to disrespect cows. When we had returned to Nagpur and were dropping Mansinghka off at the VHP offices, on the street just outside the entrance there was a cow with its head stuck in a large pile of rubbish, chewing through plastic. It was an everyday scene, even in Nagpur, the capital of the cow protection movement. Nobody seemed to mind.

On 15 October 2002 five Dalit men were lynched by a large mob of upper-caste Hindus in the town of Jhajjar, near New Delhi. The men had been found carrying the carcass of a dead cow which they had purchased in a nearby village. Although, as members of the Chamar sub-caste, this was part of their hereditary profession, someone had alleged they had killed the cow before going to work on its skin. So they were strung up and left twisting in front of a large crowd. After the murders, the traumatised local Dalit community insisted the cow had already been dead. The overwhelming majority of Indians were horrified at the medieval cruelty of this rare incident. But Giriraj Kishore, the VHP's national leader, merely said: 'According to our *shastras* [holy texts], the life of a cow is very important.'[16] By implication, it was more important than the lives of five lower-caste Hindus.

*

The hot-and-cold relationship between Hindu nationalism and India's lower castes is key to understanding the fortunes of the BJP. It explains why the party is unlikely to gain an overall majority in India's national parliament until it finds an effective way of winning sustained support from lower-caste voters. Membership of the RSS and the BJP has always been overwhelmingly upper caste. In the 1990s some attempts were made to co-opt prominent lower-caste – and even Muslim – political figures into the BJP in order to broaden its electoral base. This met with limited success. As we saw in the last chapter, the narrower a party's social base in India, the more effective it is at targeting its vote bank. The BJP lost credibility when it suddenly started to promise all things to all people.

The BJP was propelled to national prominence by an upper-caste backlash against the growing trend in the 1980s (and ever since) to reserve government jobs for different categories of lower-caste people. In Ahmedabad, the capital of 'saffron politics', upper-caste men rioted in 1981 and 1985 against the Congress state government's extension of public sector job quotas to other backward classes. The controversial policy led to the unravelling of the Congress Party's traditional domination of Gujarati politics, in which, since independence, it had consistently relied on the support of the state's upper castes to win re-election. Their votes were diverted to the BJP and have never returned. What happened in Gujarat was then played out on the national stage in 1990 when V. P. Singh, the Prime Minister of a short-lived minority coalition government, embraced the report of the Mandal Commission, which recommended the reservation of 27 per cent of all national government jobs for other backward classes. Singh's decision sparked riots in the streets of New Delhi and several upper-caste students immolated themselves in full view of the TV cameras.

More significantly, it led to a collapse of V.P. Singh's unwieldy coalition. His government had consisted of all those parties that hated Congress, which effectively meant everyone else, including the BJP and the parties of both Lalu Yadav and Mulayam Yadav. Hatred of Congress was the only sentiment that united them. After Mr Singh had embraced the Mandal recommendations the BJP withdrew its support, prompting the coalition's disintegration. L. K. Advani, the BJP leader, then launched a national *rath yatra*, or chariot procession, to Ayodhya. This culminated in the demolition of the Babri Masjid two years later. The ostensible target was Islam. But the fuel that kept Advani's chariot on the road was upper-caste anger against lower-caste politics. His strategy for overcoming the problem was to unite both sides of the divide under the banner of Hinduism behind the goal of building a Ram Mandir (Temple of Ram) in Ayodhya. To some extent, this worked: from 1990 onwards the twin poles of Indian politics were Mandal versus Mandir: lower-caste politics against Hindu nationalism. The Congress Party occupies an uneasy middle ground between the two.

I was passing through Mumbai in 1998, shortly after the BJP had come to national office. Although the BJP was only one of twenty-four parties in the coalition, it dominated the government. Its grip was tightened after it won fresh elections in 1999. The BJP-led coalition lost power at the polls in 2004, but for the first – and, to date, the last – time in India's modern history a non-Congress government had governed for a full term. Atal Behari Vajpayee, the septuagenarian leader, was also the first Indian Prime Minister not to be either a current or a former member of the Congress Party.

Many people I met in Mumbai in 1998 were nervous about what the BJP would do now it had finally gained power (save for a thirteen-day interlude in 1996, when Vajpayee had barely had a chance to get his feet under the desk). The BJP lived up to expectations. Within a few weeks of coming to office it tested five nuclear weapons under the Thar Desert of Rajasthan. Many Indians who had opposed nuclear weapons and cherished the moral foreign-policy position that Nehru had fashioned after independence suddenly found themselves waving the Indian tricolour. I was at a party, talking to a novelist who described himself as a liberal. 'I do not support the BJP, but this is a very special moment in Indian history,' he said. 'For the first time in more than a thousand years we have a Hindu government, and it had the courage to take on America with the nuclear tests.'

Vajpayee had soothed the worst fears of his coalition partners by agreeing to put on ice three of the BJP's most cherished goals: the creation of a common civil code, which would have meant the abolition of the separate personal laws that Nehru had conceded to Muslims; building the Ram Temple in Ayodhya; and abolishing an article in the Indian constitution that gives a greater degree of autonomy to the state of Jammu & Kashmir – the divided Himalayan state, all of which is claimed by Pakistan.*

But in 1998 some of India's middle class and many foreign investors were still apprehensive. Like every other political party in India, the BJP has a strong emotional attachment to the independence movement's rallying cry of *swadeshi*, economic self-reliance. Manmohan Singh had done away with the main elements of Nehru's economic framework from 1991. But the BJP and others still rallied to the old cause, and *swadeshi* remains a strong element of RSS philosophy, which frequently describes foreign products as 'polluting'.

In 1995 the BJP city government in New Delhi had closed the capital's only branch of Kentucky Fried Chicken after health inspectors had found a fly in the kitchen. Those familiar with standards of hygiene in the typical Delhi restaurant were a little sceptical about the BJP's pretext. The closure was anyway unnecessary since Indian consumers almost unanimously consider plain fried chicken to be the opposite of *finger lickin' good*. But the closure

---

*Jammu & Kashmir is comprised of two principal parts: Jammu, which is predominantly Hindu, and the valley of Kashmir, which is mostly Muslim. A third part, Ladakh, is mostly Buddhist. From now on, I will refer to it simply as Kashmir.

sent a clear political message. Likewise, in 1998 the BJP promised in its election manifesto that it would accept foreign investment, but only in areas where new technology was needed: 'Microchips not potato chips,' said the slogan. So there was understandable concern that the BJP would reverse Manmohan Singh's reforms. However, Vajpayee's government soon enthusiastically embraced economic liberalisation, although it had better luck attracting investment in potato chips than in microchips.

The greatest hope of the BJP's electoral supporters – probably only a minority of whom could be described as genuine Hindu nationalists – was that it would uphold its promise of being 'the party with a difference'. This very effective electoral slogan sent the clear message that the BJP would not succumb to the corruption that was enveloping so many areas of Indian public life. It served as an effective way of differentiating the BJP from both Congress, which had created the system of corruption, and the lower-caste parties, which had perfected it. People might not approve of the BJP's communal hatreds, but they could at least look forward to a period of clean government.

This hope proved optimistic. The BJP satisfied some of the bloodlust of its hardcore supporters, as we saw in Gujarat, and the RSS, which had been voicing mounting disaffection with the government's liberal economic agenda, was partly mollified by the BJP's decision to 'saffronise' much of India's educational curricula. However, in the day-to-day workings of government the BJP proved just as corrupt and opportunistic as any other political party. The only real difference to be found in 'the party with a difference' was its open disdain for minorities. And even here it sent mixed signals. In 2004 Vajpayee could not resist appealing to the Muslim vote when elections loomed. He became the butt of many sardonic jokes during the campaign when he donned green ceremonial headgear to stage photo opportunities with Muslim dignitaries. Evidently the strategy failed as the BJP was thrown out of office. It was an unexpected ending for a government that appeared to have gone from strength to strength.

Before I moved to India, a colleague at the *Financial Times* who is very familiar with the country told me: 'Remember, in India things are never as good or as bad as they seem.' One of the most striking aspects of the 2004 elections was that both of India's national parties suffered a decline in their vote share. In the next chapter, we will look at the fortunes of the Congress Party and the Nehru–Gandhi dynasty. But amid all the euphoria in the Congress Party, people overlooked the real winner of the 2004 election. The BJP's vote share fell from 24 per cent of India's voters in 1999 to 22 per cent in 2004. The Congress vote fell from 28 per cent to 26 per cent.

The true victors in 2004 were the plethora of small lower-caste and regional parties, whose collective share of national representation continues to rise and now exceeds half of all national votes. None of these parties has an economic pro-gramme and few are interested in foreign policy or peace initiatives with Pakistan (or in war, for that matter). At rare moments of national crisis the BJP has the ability to overcome caste differences and unite a large number of Hindus around their religious identity. But only at rare moments. When normality prevails, Hindus return to their narrower caste or linguistic iden-tities. In the battle between Mandal and Mandir the former increasingly appears to have the upper hand. 'Fragmentation rules!' might be a good summary of India's political direction.

During the 2004 election campaign I visited Gujarat to observe the fortunes of the BJP in its heartland. The party had decided to downplay Hindu nationalism and talk about the success of its economic reforms: India had achieved a growth rate of 8.4 per cent the previous year and was on target to emulate that figure in 2004. In spite of the pogroms in 2002, Gujarat was one of the principal beneficiaries of India's liberal economic reform. Gujarat's standard of living is among the highest in India. It is also India's most globalised state. A large proportion of software entrepreneurs in Silicon Valley and the thriving Asian middle class in Britain are from Gujarat. Yet enthusiasm for the BJP's 2004 election slogan, 'India Shining', was hard to find.

While in the state I managed to locate Lal Krishna Advani, the Deputy Prime Minister and the man who had devised the Ram Mandir strategy that had propelled the BJP to national prominence in the 1980s and 1990s. Mr Advani was sheltering from the midday heat in the spacious residence of a local businessman in Ahmedabad. A few weeks earlier I had visited the home of a VHP leader who had expressed bitterness about the moderate tone of the BJP's election campaign. He had said the Ram Temple was still a pipedream and he felt particular resentment towards Advani and Vajpayee. 'They rode to power on the chariot of Ram, but when they got to the throne they abandoned Ram,' he had said. It was a complaint that had been echoed increasingly by hardline activists as the BJP's term in office had worn on: where was the Ram Temple?

In 2002 Hindu nationalist hardliners thought the government had finally found its soul when it rallied to the support of Narendra Modi, Gujarat's Chief Minister, and allowed him to call a snap state election in which open hatred for Muslims was the dominating theme. During the campaign Ashok Singhal, a VHP leader, said: 'What happened in Gujarat will be repeated all over the country.'[17] The BJP won the state election comfortably. But it was held against the tense backdrop of a military stand-off between India and Pakistan. This was especially significant for Gujarat, which is on the border with Pakistan. After 2002, tensions between the two countries receded and economic growth and regional stability became the national government's main priorities. The BJP sent its attack dogs back to their kennels, tossing them the occasional bone.

I was fortunate to stumble across Advani in the 2004 campaign. Unlike Vajpayee, who had given me several interviews, the Deputy Prime Minister had avoided my requests. Now seated in the corner of a large room, he looked as though he were attending a wake. Arun Jaitley, the BJP's Minister for Law, was also present. Both Advani and Jaitley represent Gujarat in parliament. Advani was born in Karachi, which was then part of a united India ruled by the British. His life had been built around hatred of Pakistan and distrust of India's Muslim minorities. His symbolic chariot procession across India had left a trail of dead Muslims in every town through which it passed. Yet during the 2004 campaign even Advani, like Vajpayee, had donned Muslim headgear for the TV cameras.

I said to him the RSS had been complaining that he had abandoned saffron politics. 'Ever since I was a child, the RSS has influenced me and my philosophy,' said Advani. 'I will never abandon the *sangh* [organisation]. But our biggest achievement in the last six years has been to strengthen the system of federalism in India. We have proved that multiparty coalition government does work, it can provide stable government for India. That is our biggest achievement'

He refused to be drawn on the question of whether he had abandoned Hindu nationalism. I quoted some of the rude things people in the RSS and the VHP were saying about him. Everyone was expecting the BJP to win the 2004 election. They were also expecting Vajpayee, whose eightieth birthday was looming, to stand down in favour of Advani as Prime Minister. But the heir apparent, who at seventy-seven was only a little younger than Vajpayee, looked exhausted. Either he had an inkling that all the opinion polls were inaccurate and that the BJP was going to lose, or the man could not muster any enthusiasm for the moderate election campaign he was running. 'Not the RSS, I don't believe they said that about me,' he protested weakly. 'Maybe some people in the VHP would say that, but not the RSS. It is a very disciplined organisation.' During the 2004 election the RSS was disciplined only in its apathy. Very few of its hundreds of thousands of members in Gujarat volunteered to do election work for the BJP, a decisive source of strength for the party in earlier elections. The RSS wanted shock and awe. But the BJP confined its campaign messages to economic growth rates and the soaring stock market index.

A few months after the BJP was defeated, one of the most powerful priests in orthodox Hinduism was arrested on suspicion of murder. Dubbed by the media (a little dramatically) as the 'Hindu Pope', the Shankaracharya of Kanchi was shown on TV screens up and down the country being bundled like a common criminal into a police van and taken to prison. Advani, who by this stage had become the leader of the opposition BJP, scented a perfect opportunity to revive the war cry of 'Hinduism in Danger'. It would also help appease the RSS, who were still muttering bitterly about Advani's supposed betrayal of the Hindu nationalist cause. The Shankaracharya – an official title that means 'wise teacher' – had allegedly arranged the murder of a temple official who was blackmailing him about an affair he was having with a young woman. He was also alleged to have laundered money from the accounts of his temple in Kanchi, a holy town in Tamil Nadu.

There were also suspicions that Jayalalithaa, the Chief Minister of Tamil Nadu, who had ordered the arrest, was inflating the allegations against the Shankaracharya for political reasons. Jayalalithaa's Tamil nationalist party had been allied to the BJP in the national elections and her party's representation in New Delhi had been wiped out. It was left with no seats out of the state's forty parliamentary constituencies. As a ruthless political operator, many believed Jayalalithaa had deliberately engineered the high-profile humiliation of the Shankaracharya to signal her rejection of Hindu nationalism and the end of her alliance with the BJP. A few weeks earlier she had repealed a state anti-conversion law (targeting Christian and Muslim proselytisers) that had been enacted only a year before.

To add to the suspicion, Jayalalithaa ordered the arrest of the Shankaracharya on the eve of Divali, the Festival of Lights, probably the most holy day in the Hindu calendar. She could have chosen any other day. It was like waving a red flag at a (western) bull.

Advani seized the opportunity to put the Hindu juggernaut back on the road. He and his colleagues went on a three-day hunger strike and staged a *dharna* outside parliament in New Delhi to protest against the humiliating treatment of the Shankaracharya. The BJP leader said that the patience of Hindus was close to snapping. He compared the Shankaracharya's arrest to Indira Gandhi's suspension of democracy in 1975: 'The arrest is as significant in the history of the nation as the imposition of Emergency,' he said. 'Even during British rule, Hindu leaders were not treated this way.'[18] The stage was set for a dramatic confrontation between the votaries of saffron politics and India's new secular government. But to the surprise even of his detractors, Advani's protest was a flop: hardly anyone showed up. After a few hours even the TV camera crews went home.

The reluctance of most Hindus to express outrage over the arrest of the Shankaracharya was striking. Perhaps people felt there was some truth to the allegations (the case had yet to come to trial in 2006). Irrespective of this, the lack of outrage illustrated something more fundamental: there is no such thing as a Hindu pope because there is no such thing as a Hindu Church. In the Shankaracharya's temple in Kanchi all the priests are Brahmin and so are most of the temple staff and worshippers. The Shankaracharya is therefore merely a *Brahmin* pope. In contrast, as a rallying theme, building a temple to Ram appealed to a broad cross-section of Hindus, since all castes are familiar with the Ramayana. In his rush to rouse the Hindu nationalist faithful Advani had forgotten his most basic electoral arithmetic. In January 2006 he stepped down as leader of the BJP in favour of Rajnath Singh, an upper-caste leader from Uttar Pradesh.

Although Singh is drawn from the traditional ranks of the BJP, he appointed a number of lower-caste leaders to senior positions in the party. It seemed he had learned from some of his predecessor's mistakes.

I was still several miles from the ashram. But I could already make out its imposing meditation hall illuminated in shimmering blue and white light. I had come to visit Sri Sri Ravi Shankar (not to be confused with the classical sitar player), perhaps the most prominent of a new breed of highly successful Hindu evangelists, at his Art of Living Foundation in southern India. It was evening and hundreds of devotees had already congregated for prayers. Up close, the meditation hall, built just a few years ago, was even more striking. Rising to five storeys, it had been constructed entirely from marble and was shaped like a lotus. There were 1008 marble petals covering the exterior of the building, symbolising the diversity of human consciousness. The funding for this extravagant construction had come from corporate donations – much of it from the software companies in nearby Bangalore – and revenues the foundation earns from its hugely popular courses in breathing techniques and meditation. 'Come inside,' said the polite young lady assigned to show me around. 'You are just in time to watch the *guruji* take his evening questions.'

The interior, fashioned like a Roman amphitheatre, was even more striking. We sat on polished white marble steps leading down to a stage in the centre. I felt like I had stepped inside a large wedding cake. Above us the walls and ceilings were covered with pink lotuses. On the pillars that supported the dome around the central stage were the symbols of the world's main religions: the Islamic Crescent, the Star of David and the Cross of Jesus. In the centre, much larger than the other representations, was a depiction of Lakshmi, the Hindu goddess of wealth. Alone on the stage on what looked to be a large throne sat a man in flowing white robes with an equally flowing beard and silky locks of hair falling luxuriantly around his shoulders. It looked as if Jesus were shooting a shampoo advertisement. This was Sri Sri Ravi Shankar.

There was some chanting and clashing of cymbals. Then the prayers ended and a hush descended over the hall. It was time for the *guruji* to take questions. I was expecting people to ask about higher consciousness or metaphysics. But the questions consisted mostly of mundane queries about how to deal with recalcitrant teenagers, whether staying late in the office was a good idea, and how to choose a marriage partner. The *guruji* spoke in a quiet, sonorous voice. But his answers were more like those of an agony aunt than a prophet. Someone asked how she could truly know she was a good person. 'You don't need to be sweetie sweetie, goodie goodie all the time,' said the *guruji*. The audience broke into delighted laughter. Puzzled, I looked around to see hundreds of shining eyes and ecstatic expressions. The next question, which had come by email and was read out by one of the *guruji*'s followers, ended with: 'I love you so much, *Guruji*.' Someone asked whether it was always wrong to pay bribes. 'You shouldn't be too idealistic all the time,' said the *guruji*. 'Sometimes you have to make little, little compromises.' Again, the audience erupted in laughter. I was beginning to wonder about the Art of Living's breathing techniques.

After the Q&A session had ended, I was told it was time for my 'audience' with Sri Sri Ravi Shankar. It took a while for the interview to begin because throngs of people had surrounded the *guruji*, seeking his blessing. Half of them were westerners. 'Can I have your blessing, *Guruji*?' shouted a blonde woman as he was approaching the interview room. He turned slowly and placed his hands on the woman. Her young face was a study in beatific joy. Finally, he entered the room. After we had settled down, I asked him what he thought about the arrest of the Shankaracharya of Kanchi. 'It was a shock to me,' he said. 'It was also a shock to hear about all the financial inefficiency in the *mutt* [temple]. But I am not surprised at the lack of public reaction. The

Hindus are a very docile people. We are a non-violent people. But maybe it has also to do with the fact that the institution never really reaches out to people. Other sections of society don't feel any attachment to his temple.'

In contrast to the Shakaracharya's temple in Kanchi, which is dirty, the Art of Living Foundation was spotlessly clean. Its meeting rooms looked like executive boardrooms. There were liquid-crystal displays. People from all walks of life and religions are welcome at the Art of Living Foundation. All major credit cards are accepted. Sri Sri Ravi Shankar has a reputation for being a mystic and a liberal. But what is less widely known is the *guruji's* close attachment to the RSS, or that he has shared a platform with VHP leaders at public meetings. I asked him whether the Ram Temple should be built in Ayodhya. 'Suppose,' he said, 'that it was the birthplace of Jesus or Mohammed. What would you have done? Would you have tolerated another structure on that site? Let us build a temple to Ram and let the Muslims make this gesture as an act of goodwill and then the temple will also belong to Allah and to all Muslims.' 'To Allah?' I asked. 'Yes, as you must have seen, we accept all paths to God. Sometimes we wish other religions would do the same.'

The *guruji's* words reminded me of Advani's desire to see more 'Hindu Muslims' and more 'Hindu Christians'. They also reminded me of an interview I had conducted with Narendra Modi in Gujarat. Modi had said: 'We have nothing against people who are not Hindu. What we cannot accept is when people say "We are whiter than white. Our religion is better than yours".' As we saw, Modi demonstrated his opinion of such people in more robust ways. I wondered whether the *guruji* really believed all this. He seemed courteous and gentle – although I suspected he might also be suffering from a mild case of narcissism. 'Why do people want to convert people to other religions?' he asked. 'It is a great pity. We should protect the cultural diversity of the planet and not try to change it.' I pointed out that the Art of Living Foundation was thriving in places such as California, London and the Netherlands. 'Yes, but we are not a religion. We do not try to convert anyone. There are many paths to God.'

A few weeks later I received a telephone call from Ram Madhav, the national spokesman of the RSS. 'I am calling about Sri Sri Ravi Shankar,' said Madhav. 'I was talking to him the other day and he said he was disappointed with your article in the *Financial Times*. You only quoted his views on politics and the Shankaracharya. He said he was hoping you would quote his views on tolerance and on spiritualism.' It was true my article had lacked the space to quote the *guruji*'s opinions on these matters. But I was surprised that he had chosen the RSS – of all organisations – to convey his complaint. I promised that I would take the next opportunity to quote Sri Sri Ravi Shankar at greater length. Now I have fulfilled that promise.

I confess I did not feel blessed by my meeting with the *guruji*. Yet he does possess knowledge of great importance, as do other Indian celebrity cult leaders, such as Deepak Chopra, Ramdev and many more. In order to flourish again, the BJP and the RSS will need to take lessons from India's modern breed of businessmen-gurus, whose marketing and public relations skills can reach people from many different backgrounds. The Shankaracharya may or may not be guilty of criminal acts, but he can certainly be charged with declining relevance. Figures like Sri Sri Ravi Shankar, meanwhile, are becoming increasingly relevant. The BJP's challenge is to learn from people like the *guruji*.

'It is very clear that the established Brahmanical order is incapable of rising to the challenge,' wrote Swapan Dasgupta, India's best-known newspaper commentator on Hindu nationalism. 'The conclusion is obvious. There is a thriving tradition of what can loosely be called evangelical Hinduism. They are the Pat Robertsons and Billy Grahams of modern Hinduism. The failure of organized Hindu nationalism lies in not being able to link up with the congregations of individual evangelists.'[19]

The era of Brahmin-dominated politics in India is dead. The upper-caste RSS's cult of material sacrifice and self-denial is losing relevance in a country where consumer values are spreading rapidly among all castes in the cities. People no longer automatically associate Hinduism with poverty or celibacy. Whether Brahmin or Sudra, rural or urban, consumers are voting for a new kind of Hinduism with their wallets. Converting these wallets into electoral dividends will be the goal of the BJP in the coming years. Equally, the trend of Sanskritisation, in which lower castes adopt the lifestyles and markers of the upper castes, is a phenomenon that plays to the advantage of the Hindu right wing. The BJP could well govern India again. It is much too soon to write its obituary.

CHAPTER FIVE

LONG LIVE THE SYCOPHANTS!

The Congress Party's continuing love affair with the Nehru–Gandhi dynasty

Power has never attracted me, nor has position been my goal. I was always certain that if I ever found myself in the position that I am in today, I would follow my own inner voice. Today that voice tells me that I must humbly decline this post [Prime Minister]. I appeal to you to accept the force of my conviction and to recognise I will not reverse this decision.

Sonia Gandhi turning down the premiership on
18 May 2004, following her party's election victory

Few individuals in today's India – perhaps none – excite as much adulation and hatred as Sonia Gandhi. Born in a small north Italian town in 1945, there is little about her shy and reticent character that could justify either sentiment. Sonia met and fell instantly in love with Rajiv Gandhi, the son of Indira and grandson of Jawaharlal Nehru, at Cambridge in the 1960s. Rajiv was studying engineering and Sonia was learning English. They married in 1968 and moved to New Delhi to live in the house of Indira, who was Prime Minister at the time. Both Sonia and Rajiv, who became a full-time pilot for Indian Airlines, kept a strict distance from politics in this period. Then, in the first of many tragedies to befall the family, Sanjay Gandhi, Rajiv's younger brother and the heir apparent to Indira, died in a plane crash in 1980. Dynastic duty called. Sonia wrote that she 'fought like a tigress' to dissuade her husband from joining politics, so afraid was she of the consequences. But without success.[1]

Four years later Indira Gandhi was assassinated by her bodyguards and it was Sonia who cradled the dying Prime Minister in her arms as she was rushed to hospital. To Sonia's alarm and despair, Rajiv was sworn in as Prime Minister shortly after his mother had been pronounced dead. Her forebodings proved justified. Seven years later Rajiv himself was assassinated by a Tamil nationalist suicide bomber while on the election campaign trail in southern India. Sonia was not with him. 'I watched him, peeping from behind the curtain, until he disappeared from view, this time for ever,' she wrote of the last time she had seen her husband.[2] For seven years Sonia ignored the pleading of Congress Party loyalists to enter politics. At least once she turned down the offer of the premiership. Then, in 1998, she finally caved in under the relentless tide of flattery, cajolery and pleading to become president of the by-now opposition Congress. Six year of relatively undistinguished leadership ensued before, to the surprise of most Indians, the crown was suddenly hers for the taking again. Against all odds and almost every opinion poll, the Congress-led alliance had ejected the BJP-led government from office. Sonia, and to some extent her children Rahul and Priyanka (whose political debuts were made in the campaign), took the credit. In the eyes of many people, Sonia's position could no longer be written off solely as an inheritance: she had earned the job of Prime Minister. It was an extraordinary outcome for a woman who had spent much of her life in disdain of politics. But she had gradually warmed to the role. India, meanwhile, was blowing hot and cold – and not much in between.

During the build-up to the 2004 election mere mention of

Sonia Gandhi's name could enliven the dullest dinner party, splitting the guests into those who admired the Congress Party leader and those who felt contempt. I have always been baffled by the strength of feeling on either side. Sonia sometimes evokes both sentiments in the same person. I can think of two senior Congress parliamentarians who despaired in private before the election about having an 'uneducated Italian housewife' as their leader. The same men stood up in front of the nation and the world on 18 May 2004 and tearfully pleaded with her to become Prime Minister following her renunciation of the job. Suddenly she was their 'friend, philosopher, guide' and the saviour of the nation. This was not mere sycophancy. Rather it conveyed an acknowledgement of the Congress Party's sole remaining organising principle: the Nehru–Gandhi dynasty. Both (highly educated) men subsequently became cabinet ministers.

The venom reserved for Sonia Gandhi by her opponents is as potent as the adulation of her supporters. During the election campaign Narendra Modi, the BJP Chief Minister of Gujarat, labelled her 'a half-bred Jersey cow' and 'that Italian bitch'. He said that Rahul and Priyanka Gandhi were not fit to drive his car or clean his shoes. Other less rabid BJP figures despaired that a country of a billion people could choose a foreign-born person as its leader. In the days following the defeat of the BJP-led coalition, Sushma Swaraj, a former cabinet minister, threatened to shave her head and become a *sanyasin* (someone who renounces the material world) unless Sonia turned down the premiership. The BJP had planned a nationwide campaign led by a senior Hindu religious figure to protest against the insult of suffering a 'foreign woman' as Prime Minister. In the event, they were outmanoeuvred by Sonia, who got her (very Hindu) act of renunciation in first. She appointed Manmohan Singh as Prime Minister in her stead, a decision which showed good judgement of character. Singh had never uttered an embarrassing word of fulsome praise for Mrs Gandhi in public, but he had always been polite about her in private.

In the photographs of Sonia Gandhi taken before her husband was killed in 1991, she comes across as a smiling, radiant and attractive woman, frequently dressed in the finest Gucci or Prada outfits. She is often gazing adoringly at Rajiv, and seems deeply in love with her husband. After 1991, she always looks glum and funereal. Her occasional smile is lifeless and diplomatic. But her dress sense has altered: she is only ever caught on camera wearing a sari. On 20 May 2004 Sonia Gandhi and Manmohan Singh emerged from the presidential palace in Delhi to announce the latter's appointment as Prime Minister. 'The nation will be safe in Dr Singh's hands,' said Mrs Gandhi. Then it was Singh's turn to speak, but my gaze, like everyone else's, remained riveted to Sonia. Her smile was oceanic. No matter what questions the reporters fired at her, it simply would not go away.

The author Salman Rushdie once described the Nehru–Gandhi family as a 'dynasty to beat *Dynasty* in a Delhi to rival *Dallas*'.[3] That was in the 1980s. At an earlier stage the Nehru family could perhaps have been likened to that which features in Evelyn Waugh's *Brideshead Revisited*. The traditional Nehru family home in Allahabad is the closest thing in India to the heritage properties that punctuate much of the British countryside. The architecture of Anand Bhavan (House of Joy), the larger family building, is Islamicate, but the interior is a hybrid of the traditional Brahmin household and the most aristocratic of British residences. The property was bought in 1902 by Motilal Nehru, who was making a fortune as a lawyer in the courts. Although he was a leading member of the Congress Party, which had been established in 1885, his style and manner were those of a *pucca* English gentleman. Tradition held no appeal for him. He was expelled from his caste for refusing to undergo a ceremony of purification on his return from England.[4] Crossing the 'black waters' was considered polluting. But he shrugged off the excommunication. He was far too busy enjoying the lavish proceeds of his career. Motilal was the first person in Allahabad to purchase a motor car, his consumption of champagne was legendary, and it was even rumoured, albeit falsely, that he sent his linen to Paris to be laundered. However, all of his suits were tailored in Savile Row.[5] Anand Bhavan had more than a hundred servants and the Nehrus enjoyed a royal lifestyle. Many years later, in 1928, by which time the family had switched their dress to *khadi* – homespun cotton – Motilal wrote to Mahatma Gandhi saying he wanted the 'crown' (the presidency of the Congress Party) to pass to his son Jawaharlal. Motilal, who had held the post himself, was already talking in the language of dynasty.

Touring through Anand Bhavan, which is now a national museum, is a disorienting experience. Outside, on the bustling streets of Allahabad, a city of four million people, there are the usual bodice-ripping posters advertising Bollywood films. Inside, you peruse a world that has almost completely vanished. There are Edwardian waistcoats, pith helmets and travelling kits of irons, toasters and early electric shavers to which father and son were accustomed. Their reading habits were those of the English gentry: books by Lewis Carroll and William Thackeray pack the shelves. On his birthday every year the young Jawaharlal would be weighed against a pile of wheat that would be given away to the poor.[6] He is pictured dressed in the snooty outfits of Lord Fauntleroy. This was a family that, as Macaulay had famously wished for Indians almost a century earlier, was 'brown in colour, but English in taste, morals and intellect'.

As you move through the upholstered rooms, a change starts to occur. In place of the matching silk ties and handkerchiefs, you see simple, homespun outfits. During the 1920s and 1930s Anand Bhavan became an informal meeting-place for Congress Party leaders. Mahatma Gandhi would hold strategic meetings there and sit outside on the veranda between sessions spinning cotton at his wheel. There is a framed letter from the Anglo-Irish playwright George Bernard Shaw, addressed, somewhat presumptuously, 'from one Mahatma to another', in which 'Gandhi' is misspelled as 'Ghandi'. The Indians touring through the mansion, which was donated to the nation by Indira Gandhi in the 1970s, seem spellbound. There is a whiff of dynasty and sainthood as well as a world that no longer exists. This is an advantage for royalty. It should have a touch of the foreign and it should excite the imagination.

Motilal Nehru died a couple of years after his son had first become president of Congress in 1928. Jawaharlal was in prison for agitating against British rule when it happened. He was also in prison when his mother, Swarup Rani, and his wife, Kamala, died. On each occasion he was given leave either to visit them on their deathbeds or to attend their funerals before returning to his cell. From prison, he wrote endlessly to Indira, his only child, who was being raised by governesses, stern aunts and at boarding schools. These letters of historical instruction were later collated into *Glimpses of World History*. There has been much debate about whether Nehru deliberately groomed his daughter to succeed him as Prime Minister. The evidence is mixed. As a widower, Nehru requested the young Indira to be his hostess and household manager when he held the premiership in the 1950s. Naturally, his daughter learned of everything that was happening and everyone who was doing it. This awkward and shy young woman gradually became an operator in her own right. In 1959 she became president (for one year) of the Congress Party. Her son Sanjay rose to prominence in the 1970s by leading the Congress youth wing.

When Nehru died in 1964, Indira was invited into the cabinet by Lal Bahadur Shastri, the new Prime Minister, who was both a loyal Gandhian and a Nehruvian, but whose authority was limited. He died in 1966 while attending an international conference in Tashkent. The Congress Party was deeply split between clashing personalities, and Indira was a natural compromise candidate for most of the factions. Ram Manohar Lohia, the socialist leader, notoriously called her a 'dumb doll' who could be manipulated with ease. At first his verdict proved correct. But when it became clear that her position as Prime Minister would amount to little more than providing a rubber stamp for decisions taken by others, Indira began to emerge from her chrysalis. She turned into the most formidable and ruthless political figure India has yet seen. She was supposed to behave like a constitutional monarch. But she wanted absolute power. The contrast with her father's style of governing, which had been scrupulously democratic, was sharp. Indira herself once described her father as a 'saint who strayed into politics'; she, on the other hand, was better known as 'Durga', the wife of Shiva, symbolising feminine power. She gained the epithet after India had defeated Pakistan in the war that resulted in the succession of East Pakistan from West Pakistan in 1971. Indira became prone to hubris. She did not demur when one of her colleagues famously said: 'India is Indira.'

After she had declared a state of emergency in June 1975 and abandoned democracy for nineteen months,* her son Sanjay began to emerge as an even more ruthless operator than his mother. But he lacked her political cunning. In contrast to Rajiv, his professional and softly spoken elder brother, Sanjay was essentially a thug. Although he held no formal position in government, his power was close to total. Even Indira was afraid of him. He spoke rudely to her in front of others and his circle gradually became the power centre towards which anyone with ambition would gravitate. On one occasion he was reported to have slapped his mother around the face six times in a dinner party.[7] One close family friend dismissed this story as impossible, since 'not even God could slap Indira around the face six times'[8] But the fact that it circulated at all reveals much about the relationship

---

*Indira shut down India's independent media, imprisoned up to 100,000 political opponents and bypassed almost all the procedures of constitutional government during the Emergency. It was India's only real taste of autocracy in the modern era.

between mother and son. Indira permitted Sanjay to devise and take charge of the most repressive social programmes India has witnessed since independence. He oversaw the mass clearance of slums in New Delhi and elsewhere in which millions were brutally evicted from their homes. He also devised a draconian scheme in which hundreds of thousands of men were sterilised, many of them forcibly. It was a relief to most when he killed himself in a plane crash (he was an amateur pilot) in 1980.

Rajiv Gandhi brought with him a completely new set of hangers-on and advisers when he became Prime Minister in 1984. Many were childhood friends from Doon School, India's equivalent of Eton College. His manner was seen as modern and breezy. He was famed for his gentle courtesy, and he displayed respect for the rules of democracy. In other words, he was far more his grandfather's grandson than his mother's son. His children, Rahul and Priyanka, were too young when Rajiv was killed in 1991 for a dynastic succession to be plausible, and it was too soon for Rajiv even to have indicated whether he harboured political ambitions. So the mantle fell upon Sonia, who, as we have seen, retreated into mourning for several years after her husband's death before eventually agreeing to become regent. Now the handsome Rahul – who, like his father, was educated at Cambridge University* and who became a member of parliament in 2004 – is emerging as the next heir to the dynasty.

What has the Nehru-Gandhi family given India? Is it possible now to separate Congress from the dynasty? In spite of Mahatma Gandhi's grip on the freedom movement, it was Nehru, through his control of Congress, who exercised the most influence on the formative character of India after independence in 1947. Others,

---

*Unlike Rajiv, Rahul completed his M.Phil., which was in development studies. Nehru was a formidable reader and possessed an acute intellect, but his grandson Rajiv was not a great reader of books. Neither is Rahul. Indira also showed impatience with study: she did not complete her degree at Oxford University. Sonia did not attend university.

such as B. R. Ambedkar (who chaired the committee which framed the 1950 constitution) and Sardar Vallabhbhai Patel (who, as Home Minister, skilfully incorporated the five hundred or so princely states into India and ensured the continuity of the colonial civil service), also played important roles. But Gandhi was assassinated in 1948; Patel, whose sympathies with orthodox Hinduism clashed with Nehru's strictly secular vision for the country, died in 1950; and Ambedkar resigned from Nehru's cabinet in 1951. At which point Nehru still had thirteen years left at the top.

Nehru left three clear stamps on India that endure to this day (a fourth, foreign policy non-alignment during the Cold War, is no longer strictly relevant). These were democracy, secularism and socialism. Each is often still prefixed with the adjective 'Nehruvian' in recognition of Nehru's role in pushing for their acceptance as part of modern India's creed. The first, in spite of Indira Gandhi's experiment with dictatorship, is alive and well. The second has taken some body blows in the last fifteen years but remains intact. The third is dead as an official ideology but continues to live on in various ways, not least in the Congress Party's enduring love affair with an unreformed state.

It is often taken for granted that a country as diverse and plural as India is naturally democratic. But it was not a foregone conclusion that it would embrace democracy in the form that it has. Mahatma Gandhi wanted to restore India to a semi-mythical past in which it would be governed by a confederation of village councils. But he was murdered before the country's constitutional convention got under way. Some argued the electoral franchise should be restricted to literate adults, who made up just 16 per cent of the population at independence. Others wanted it confined to men. A number of extreme Hindu nationalists questioned whether religious minorities should have the vote. India's Communist Party initially wanted a dictatorship of the (virtually non-existent) proletariat. But it called off its ineffectual struggle against Nehru's 'bourgeois democracy' in 1951.

Nehru himself was never in any doubt that India should have a Westminster-style parliamentary system in which every adult would have the vote. His view, which was strongly supported by Ambedkar, prevailed. In retrospect the decision appeared to be a natural outgrowth of the position of the freedom movement, which claimed the same rights for Indians that were available to the British. But at the time Nehru's position was more precarious. Through charisma and force of intellect he persuaded India to take a unique leap of faith into full democracy when most of the developing world was embracing the opposite.

Ironically, though, Nehru had much less success instilling a culture of democracy inside the Congress Party. The factional character of Congress had – and continues to have – consequences for the way broader democracy evolved in the country. India began its journey into independence with only one genuine national party, which claimed to represent all of the country's castes, religions, languages and races. In practice, however, Congress was overwhelmingly dominated by the rural and urban elites who were drawn principally from the upper castes. Although it was open to all, and although senior office-holders were elected by ballots of the members, the system was routinely hijacked on the ground by local notables. This culture persists in Congress today. In the 1980s Rajiv Gandhi was presented with a report on the party's health which estimated that 60 per cent of its membership was bogus.[9] Bigwigs were inventing membership lists to tighten their grip on their local party machines.

Nehru controlled the national party from New Delhi, but in the provinces, where his policies of land redistribution and agricultural reform were meant to be carried out, Congress was in the grip of the traditional landowning elites. A large share of public subsidies was captured by these elites since, in most of India, Congress and the state amounted to one and the same thing.

'Those who could not afford to pay found themselves at the bottom of the list in the allocation of access to "public goods".'[10] An internal Congress report compiled in 1963 in the aftermath of a series of by-election defeats could equally have been written in 2006. It said: 'The pivot around which Congress activity revolves is the personality through whom preferment can be obtained and not the aims and purposes of the party.'[11] In rhetoric Congress was democratic and radical. In practice it was plutocratic and conservative.

The electoral symbol of the Congress Party is the hand.* 'The hand of Congress is always with the poor,' says the slogan. But as the party's tenure in office wore on, the poor began to realise that the hand of Congress was as often to be found in the till, taking what supposedly belonged to them. Gradually, the party's delicately maintained coalition of communities and castes began to break up and form their own constituent parties. However, the disintegration of cross-caste and cross-religious support for Congress was not linear. Whenever there was a national crisis, such as the war with Pakistan in 1971 or the assassination of Indira Gandhi,† the Congress vote shot back up to the levels it had regularly achieved under Nehru, at somewhere between 42 and 48 per cent. The last time Congress received a national vote nearing this scale was in 1991, following the assassination of Rajiv Gandhi when it was supported by 36 per cent of the electorate. Since then, its vote share has remained between 25 and 29 per cent.

Congress regularly squandered its thundering majorities, displaying an inability to live up to the radical and pious rhetoric in

---

*Each party has a visual symbol which enables illiterate voters to know where to place their mark. The BJP has the lotus, Samajwadi has the bicycle, and so on.
†Indira was shot dead by her two Sikh bodyguards. A few weeks earlier she had ordered the Indian army to storm the Golden Temple in Amritsar. The temple, which is the most sacred place for Sikhs, had been under the control of separatist Sikh militants. After Indira was killed, thousands of Sikhs were murdered in riots. Rajiv said: 'When a great tree falls, the ground shakes.'

which it had imprisoned itself. In 1971 opponents of Indira Gandhi shouted, 'Remove Indira.' She countered by saying, 'Remove Poverty.' Neither was removed, although Indira did remove democracy in 1975 after the High Court in Allahabad declared her 1971 election victory illegal on a minor technicality. Rather than resign, she suspended the forthcoming elections. Later, having been advised by admirers that she would sweep the polls, she restored democracy in 1977. For the first time in its history, Congress was defeated. In addition to large sections of the lower castes, Muslims voted against the party in their droves because so many of them had fallen victim to Sanjay Gandhi's slum-clearance and sterilisation programmes.

In 1984 the youthful Rajiv Gandhi began his term amid the kind of optimism that often greets the advent of a new generation. But his inexperience and the corruption of many around him led to an acceleration of the break-up of Congress's support by the next election in 1989 (the second time the party was defeated). Congress was back in power two years later, led by Narasimha Rao, an old-time parliamentarian. It lasted the full five years and took radical steps to turn around India's economy, but it ran out of reformist steam halfway through. When it was thrown out in 1996 economic reform was barely mentioned on the campaign trail.*

As recently as 1999, the Congress Party was still blind to the logic of striking up alliances with other parties in order to regain power. At its annual meeting it proclaimed it would govern alone or not at all. The resolution said: '[The conference] affirms that the party considers the present difficulties in forming one-party governments a transient phase in the evolution of our polity.'[12] It was because of such hubris – and the superior tone in which it was rendered – that Congress had fallen to a low point in its fortunes. It was also a serious misreading of the direction in which Indian

---

*According to a survey by the Centre of the Study for Developing Societies, only 12 per cent of voters in 1996 had even heard of the phrase 'economic reform'.

politics was heading. In 2003 the party belatedly woke up to the reality of an India that was likely to remain politically fragmented for the foreseeable future. At its annual conclave in the Himalayan hill station of Simla, Sonia Gandhi agreed to set up an alternative coalition-in-waiting. Her decision, which reversed fifty years of Congress isolationist tradition, helped bring the party back into office in 2004 with barely a quarter of the national vote.

Nehru's role in the creation of a secular state for independent India, like his influence in its development as a democracy, should not be underestimated. Congress began life as a party that included all shades of opinion, from Marxist to Hindu nationalist. Many on the Hindu right were bitterly opposed to what they saw as Nehru's contempt for the traditions of orthodox Hinduism. But the assassination of Mahatma Gandhi by a Hindu nationalist provided unexpected assistance to Nehru. It forced Vallabhbhai Patel, Nehru's right-wing Home Minister, to crack down on the RSS, which had held spontaneous street parties up and down the country to celebrate the death of India's greatest freedom fighter. Hundreds of RSS leaders and activists were imprisoned.

'The light has gone out of our lives,' said Nehru of Gandhi's death. The Prime Minister skilfully traded on Gandhi's memory to push most of his secular agenda through the constitutional convention. It was not a definition that would be recognised in France or Turkey, which interpret secularism to mean the state should dissociate religion from all aspects of public life. India's version is less militant. The state happily promotes all religions, rather than disdaining them all equally. Nehru permitted each religious community to retain its own civil laws, or 'personal codes', which govern marriages, divorces, births, deaths and inheritances. It was probably not his ideal since it sat uneasily with the principle of equality before the law, which is also enshrined in the constitution. But in the wake of the horrors of partition it seemed a necessary concession to the millions of Muslims who had ignored Pakistan and remained in India. Although the reforms were mostly liberal, retaining separate family legal codes appeased the Hindu orthodox who preferred a Hindu code for Hindus to a uniform secular civil code that would have undermined their hold on tradition.

Yet, by accepting the consensus that Indians should be at least partly defined by the religion of their birth, Nehru inadvertently helped sow the seeds of the communal battles that continue to bedevil India today. The 1950 constitution enshrines the rights of the individual and the rights of groups, whether religious or linguistic. According to one constitutional article, the state cannot alter laws that govern any religious group without the assent of three-quarters of that group's membership. This makes it very difficult for Indian governments to interfere with traditional practices, however objectionable. For example, there is little the state can do to tackle polygamy, which the Muslim personal law permits. In practice only about 2 per cent of Muslim men have more than one wife, but the fact that they are permitted to have as many as four is a stick with which Hindu nationalists can beat the Congress Party and the Muslim minority. So too is the Indian state's continued subsidy for Muslims who go on the Haj to Mecca, even though in practice it amounts to a tiny amount of money. The Indian state also provides subsidies to Hindu temples and trusts.

The decision to classify Indians by their religion in respect of many of their rights also left a questionable political mark on Congress, which the party has yet to transcend: the temptation always to appeal to identity vote banks. Rather than speak to voters in a language that unites them, Congress got into the habit of customising its message for each community. It is not hard to see why this created a backlash, particularly among upper-caste Hindus who resented the alleged mollycoddling of conservative Islam. Congress sometimes appeared to choose Muslim candidates by the length of their beards. It became equally prone to the manipulation of caste to suit local electoral arithmetic.

Furthermore, the adoption of separate legal codes inadvertently put strict limits on the evolution of liberalism in India. When a religious group objects to a book, a film or a piece of art because it allegedly offends their beliefs, New Delhi is quick to ban it. Salman Rushdie's novel *Satanic Verses* was banned in the late 1980s by Rajiv Gandhi because it supposedly insulted the Prophet Mohammed. A few years later the same author's *The Moor's Last Sigh* was banned because it lampooned Bal Thackeray, a Hindu nationalist leader in Mumbai. Barely a month goes by without some book or film being banned or censored. In the India of today the rights of everyone to freedom of expression are junior to the rights of priests and mullahs to protest on behalf of communities that have neither elected nor appointed them. India is certainly a plural country. But pluralism is not the same thing as liberalism.

The contradictions of India are also the contradictions of Congress. In 1985 Rajiv Gandhi was advised to step in and appease the orthodox Muslim community after the Indian Supreme Court ruled in favour of an impoverished Muslim woman called Shah Bano in a divorce case. From the point of view of the orthodox Muslims, the court had interfered with their civil code by ordering Bano's husband to pay his wife a small monthly alimony. The conservative mullahs were outraged, which worried the Congress Party's electoral strategists. In an extraordinary manoeuvre Rajiv enacted legislation that deprived Bano of her monthly payments in order to reassure the mullahs that they remained in control of Muslim personal law. His move was an unexpected gift for the ascendant BJP, which could point to a Congress Party that would go to any lengths for votes. The inevitable Hindu backlash proved equally worrying to Rajiv's electoral advisers, so he was persuaded to appease the Hindu right wing. In a decision that was to reshape the contours of Indian politics he unlocked the gates to the Babri Masjid in Ayodhya.

(Because of the controversy, activists had until then been denied access to the site.) This ill-advised move set in motion the chain of events that culminated in the destruction of the mosque in 1992.

This episode illustrates the peculiar mix of 'naivety and cynicism'[13] that has long characterised the Congress Party. It no longer appeared to believe in anything. First Rajiv alienated liberal Muslims (and virtually and everyone else) by depriving an impoverished Muslim woman of the little alimony she had been granted. Then he alienated all Muslims by opening the Ayodhya mosque to Hindu fanatics. And finally he appalled Indians of many descriptions by signalling that neither he nor his party appeared to possess any impulse other than a hunger for votes. Much like the pursuit of happiness, which is best conducted obliquely, naked pursuit of power for its own sake can be self-defeating. It is little wonder, then, that Rajiv's historic parliamentary majority of 1984 was reduced to a rump opposition the next time voters were given an opportunity to air their views. Rajiv's battered reputation was restored only after his tragic assassination.

It is hard to imagine his grandfather making such chronic tactical errors. Yet, with hindsight, Nehru's generation could be accused of committing a strategic blunder that continues to undercut supporters of Indian liberalism even today. By diluting the principle of equality before the law, Indian liberalism was encumbered with a handicap it has yet to escape. (Although, to be fair to Nehru, he was a democrat who had to give in to the conservative majority on these questions.) As a relative political novice and a foreigner, it is not surprising that Sonia Gandhi is influenced by the Congress Party's electoral tacticians just as much as her husband was during the 1980s. In 2004 Congress won just nine of the eighty parliamentary seats in Uttar Pradesh. Previously the party had regularly won more than half of the state's seats. Among its candidates were orthodox Muslims belonging to the hardline Islamic school of Deoband.

During the Gujarat state elections of 2002 Sonia felt unable to take a strong stand against the aggressive Hindu nationalism of Narendra Modi's BJP following the anti-Muslim pogroms that had taken place earlier in the year. This was surprising because she evidently felt passionately about the issue. The speech she gave to India's parliament following the killings was widely considered to be her best and to mark her growing confidence as opposition leader. Towards the end of it, she fixed her gaze at the government benches of BJP ministers and accused them of turning Gujarat into 'the land of Godse not Gandhi'. Mahatma Gandhi was from Gujarat; Godse killed him.

Nevertheless, true to its character, Congress bent to the prevailing winds, which were howling with saffron rage. Sonia was advised to appoint Shankersingh Vaghela, a former member of the RSS, to lead the party's electoral campaign. In a state where almost 10 per cent of the population is Muslim, only 5 of the party's 203 candidates were Muslim. Sonia spent much of the campaign visiting Hindu temples. She was advised not to visit the widow of Ehsan Jaffri, a retired Congress politician who, as a prominent Muslim, had been butchered – along with the neighbours he was sheltering – in the riots.

I have little doubt that Sonia Gandhi is sincere in her support of secularism. But she often appears to be a prisoner of the Congress Party's network of advisers, courtiers and carpet-baggers, whose efforts have helped to destroy her party's credibility in large tracts of India over the last generation. As we have seen, the BJP won the 2002 Gujarati election by a landslide. In declining to take a principled stand the Congress Party machine had learned nothing from Rajiv Gandhi's mistakes. His widow bore some of the responsibility. As one commentator remarked, 'If you have an A-team, why would you vote for the B-team?'

Nehru's third legacy was socialism. In Chapter One, we looked at the failures of India's 'import substitution' model and the reasons why *swadeshi* was ultimately abandoned in 1991. It is worth adding two points. Indian-style socialism, in which the supposedly altruistic workings of an elite bureaucracy act as a substitute for social reform on the ground, lives on in the habitual tendencies of the Congress Party today. The Indian state was partly Nehru's creation, but his motivations were ideological and, as we have seen, they were in tune with broader international fashion at the time. Sixty years later the persistence of an unreformed state can no longer be attributed to ideology. We have to look deeper for reasons why India's state is still permitted to operate in its traditional form. Some of these reasons are to be found in the habits and character of the Congress Party.

The inefficiencies of Nehru's state contributed a great deal to India's relatively poor economic performance in the decades after independence. But even more of the blame for these failings should be directed at Indira Gandhi, whose policies led the country to the precipice of bankruptcy. It was she who tarnished the neutrality of the civil service when she called for a 'committed' bureaucracy that would be openly socialist. This led to a sharp increase in corruption since it dissolved the conventions of neutrality and impartiality that had until then acted as restraints on the behaviour of public servants. It also made it easier for politicians to transfer civil servants on a whim or a fancy.

It was also Indira who nationalised India's banking and insurance sectors in 1969. Many people think of finance as an esoteric subject that is of little consequence to their everyday lives. But the way a country regulates and allocates its capital is critical to its economy. Finance is to the economy what blood circulation is to the body. In the name of the poor, Indira handed control of finance to an unreformed civil service. But most of the poor continued to go to usurious private money-lenders. Very few of India's farmers possess a formal title to their land, so they lack the collateral even to qualify for a loan. In a survey in 2002 a majority of the country's farmers said they trusted the money-lenders more than they trusted the public bodies that provide electricity and water.[14] They could have said the same of public sector banks. For those lucky enough to qualify for a loan, it takes on average thirty-three weeks to be cleared; and the bribe to effect that clearance costs on average 10 to 20 per cent of the loan. The ultimate cost of servicing a loan is often higher than it would have been if the cash had been borrowed from a money-lender.[15]

Similarly, by imposing a thicket of restrictions on how much banks could lend to whom and when, Indira Gandhi drastically raised the cost of capital for everyone. If you ration something, you increase its price. As a result, India's interest rates have traditionally been far higher than those in other emerging markets. This partly explains why India's rate of investment (and economic growth) has traditionally been lower. Sonia Gandhi's Congress opposes substantial changes to a banking system that was largely created by her mother-in-law. Shortly after it came to office in 2004, Manmohan Singh's government ruled out any drastic reform of the banks, including privatisation. On some estimates, reform of India's financial sector could add two percentage points a year to India's economic growth.[16]

By the same token, Congress also opposes any radical change in the nature of the Indian state. When he became Prime Minister, Singh said reform of the bureaucracy would be the government's first priority. In his first televised address said: 'No objective in the development agenda can be met if we do not reform the instruments in our hand with which we have to work – namely the government and public institutions.'[17] What was the use of pouring more water into a leaking bucket? But it soon became clear Singh did not have the power to make the changes he wanted. With the exception of the right-to-information law, India's bureaucracy continues to work as it always has. In some respects its role has even expanded under Singh's government. We have seen many examples of how policies designed to help the poor often bypass them altogether. India probably has more experience than any other democracy of poverty-reduction programmes that have largely failed to achieve their purpose. Yet Congress in the early twenty-first century remains as addicted to programmes that are entrusted entirely to the bureaucracy as it was in the 1950s. It is hard to believe it is unaware of the fact that over the last few decades India's bureaucracy has been siphoning off enormous sums of money. It is true that India's persistent rural poverty cannot be addressed without effective state intervention. But doing this through an unreformed and unaccountable state can sometimes be worse than doing nothing at all.

Albert Einstein once said insanity was 'doing the same thing over and over again and expecting different results'. The most spectacular example of the Congress Party's continued faith in an unreformed state is the Rural Employment Guarantee Act, which India's parliament passed in 2005. Much of the bill was drafted by Aruna Roy and Jean Dréze, an impressive Belgian-born economist, now an Indian citizen. Their influence on Sonia Gandhi – who continues, in turn, to shape the policy of Singh's government from behind the scenes – ensured the law was pushed through. This flagship piece of legislation of the Congress-led coalition is designed to cover the entire country by 2009. It is probably India's most ambitious attempt so far to alleviate poverty through direct state intervention. The good intentions of its framers cannot be faulted: their aim is to make life better for India's rural poor. Yet there is little, other than its magnitude and its cost, to distinguish it from previous efforts that have failed.

The law is significant because it distinguishes India's approach to poverty very clearly from that of neighbouring China, which has preferred to create jobs indirectly by stimulating high (public and private) investment in the economy. Singh's government has not followed this path. The new law gives one hundred days of manual labour in the countryside to anyone who wants it. Since payment is at the minimum wage, which varies from as little as fifty rupees a day in some states to eighty rupees in others (between one and two dollars), it is assumed only the really desperate will take the jobs. In the jargon, the programme is 'self-selecting'. Payment can be in a mixture of cash and food. The work is almost entirely physical consisting of the type of manual labour India's poor have been requisitioned to do for thousands of years: filling in pot-holes, digging landfills, mending river embankments, and clearing irrigation channels.

Judging by the results of previous schemes, notably the food-for-work programme, which successfully prevented famine in post-colonial India, the quality of the work is not the priority. All of it could be done more efficiently and to a higher standard with modern machines: unskilled and hungry labourers cannot build good roads with their bare hands; pot-holes are filled in only to be recreated by the monsoon the following year; river embankments crumble at the first flush of rainfall; irrigation channels silt up within weeks. If, as expected, the programme spreads across the whole country, it will eventually cost India up to 2 per cent of its gross domestic product and between 10 and 20 per cent of its annual budget.[18] Yet it promises no investment in upgrading the skills of the people it is designed to help. Nor does it invest in genuine rural infrastructure, such as all-weather roads, proper electricity supply or new agricultural technologies. Such investments would stimulate greater economic activity that would be much more likely to create lasting employment for the rural poor.

And this is without having mentioned the 'leakage' and corruption that are likely to afflict the programme as it unfolds in the coming years. When the law was proposed in 2004, it was dismissed by many Indian and international economists as an expensive way of doing nothing to address the perennial condition of India's poor – their consignment to manual labour at miserably low levels of productivity. Yet India's parliament passed the bill unanimously. Many sceptics believe this rare display of consensus was prompted by the opportunity for all parties to siphon off a new source of public funds. One Indian commentator even suggested the law should be renamed the Corruption Guarantee Act.[19]

Nor has the Congress-led government made any attempt to improve the performance of state-owned companies, whose losses give large swaths of the public sector a net negative value – an extraordinary measure of their inefficiency. There are respectable arguments for retaining some enterprises, including much of India's oil sector, in state ownership. But there are no good arguments for packing the boards of enterprises with politicians lacking any business experience, as Congress has done since 2004 (and as its Hindu nationalist predecessor did). A seat on the board of a public enterprise can bring powers of patronage to allocate jobs and win friends and influence. It also brings perks and status.

I once had a long conversation with the head of police for New Delhi about the number of cars that evaded normal traffic restrictions simply by putting a red or a blue light on the roof. (New Delhi suffers from a permanent epidemic of VIPs.) He told me that a majority of the car-owners were not authorised to use flashing lights. But his police, who are invariably junior in social status to the occupants of the car, felt unable to prevent this abuse of privilege. The same system of discrimination can be observed at the dozens of road security checkpoints surrounding the capital. Rickshaws, motorbikes and freight trucks are always getting stopped by the police, while expensive cars are invariably waved through. Few ordinary police constables would feel confident enough to challenge their social superiors.

In his excellent book *The Burden of Democracy*, Pratap Bhanu Mehta quotes Alexis de Tocqueville's observations on the existence of professional values in early America. To a nineteenth-century European, the relationship in the United States between master and servant was something new. 'Within the terms of the contract one is servant and the other is master;

beyond that they are two citizens and two men,' wrote de Tocqueville. But in a traditional society, such as India's, the ties between master and servant apply in all contexts. In India 'your *sahib* [master] remains a *sahib* whether in office or not', says Mehta.[20] What is unusual about India is the durability of feudal social ties in the context of a full democracy. This tension is most visible in the Congress Party.

Congress's love affair with the state is no longer strictly about socialism, to which few Congressmen nowadays pay much lip service. It goes deeper than ideology. It is partly about status. But it is also about preferential access to a wide range of public goods, including free first-class plane and rail tickets, the opportunity to jump queues, the ability to pull strings and the provision of free services for which the poor have to pay. Corruption, as we have seen, afflicts important public services such as food distribution. But it is also deeply integrated into the transactions of daily life.

I once bought a ticket to watch a big international cricket match between India and England at New Delhi's Ferozshah Kotla Stadium. I was with two Indian friends. We had each paid 5000 rupees ($120) for our ticket. But we were denied entry to the ground, along with thousands of other ticket-holders. The Delhi and District Cricket Board, whose president, Arun Jaitley, was India's Law Minister at the time, had printed thousands of complimentary tickets for VIPs for a ground with a capacity of just 26,000. Mounted police charged an angry crowd which had been shut out of the stadium to clear the way for the VIPs in their white Ambassador cars. I wrote a letter to Jaitley complaining about our treatment, demanding a refund and asking for an explanation. Thousands of Indians had bought the expensive tickets; some had travelled by train overnight to see the game. Mr Jaitley's private secretary telephoned the following morning to convey his 'profound apologies' and offer me a complimentary ticket for the next big game. But the next game was against Zimbabwe – not the same thing at all. I turned him down.

Two years later India was scheduled to play Pakistan in an exciting and diplomatically symbolic encounter in New Delhi. Both Pervez Musharraf, Pakistan's President, and Manmohan Singh were to attend the match. Having failed to get tickets by the normal commercial route, I had given up hope of attending the game. Then I received a phone call from Arun Jaitley. 'I have not withdrawn my offer of a complimentary ticket for you,' he said. Shamelessly, this time I accepted his offer. (I also grabbed one for my wife.) By this stage, I was more inured to Delhi's ways. But thousands of others were once again stranded outside with valid tickets. I learned later that Jaitley had been flooded with requests from judges, cabinet ministers and senior civil servants for free tickets. Even Sonia Gandhi's family, including her two children, had requested and received complimentary tickets. Of all the requests, only one, from Gursharan Kaur, Manmohan Singh's wife, had enclosed a cheque for the face value. This, unfortunately, is how New Delhi operates: if you are rich and important, you rarely pay. If you are poor, you usually pay through the nose. And there is no guarantee that you will even get what you paid for.

As for the rural employment guarantee scheme, it is difficult to believe the Congress Party's claim that it is a good-faith attempt to eliminate poverty in India once and for all. It is hard to see how a scheme that requires the poor to provide twelve or more hours of back-breaking physical labour each day for just a couple of dollars will transform their conditions. If you wander around India's provincial capitals, you see perfectly cropped gardens surrounding the large public buildings and official residences. Often you will also see gangs of twenty or thirty labourers, squatting in rows on their haunches, moving gradually forward in a line, plucking the lawns with their bare hands. Inside the buildings there will be dozens of sweepers, keeping their bodies at all times below yours, rearranging the dust in a posture of time-honoured submission. Occasionally, you pause and ask yourself: Is this about employment? Or is it about reminding the sweeper and those for whom she sweeps who possesses status in society and who does not?

It took several months of perseverance to get an appointment with Sonia Gandhi. For understandable reasons, she has always been reluctant to speak on the record to the media. Every word is scrutinised by her enemies for signs that she is not as Indian as she claims to be. Once she told an interviewer, 'Everything I have loved and lost has been in India.' It would be hard to doubt her sincerity. But still the questions about her national loyalties persist. Naturally, she is even more reluctant to speak to foreign journalists, in case her decision would be misconstrued as bias in favour of non-Indians. I once met a group of Italian journalists who had flown to India specially to interview their former compatriot and I did not have the heart to tell them that they would be at the bottom of the list. However, they did eventually secure a two-minute introduction to Mrs Gandhi. They spoke to her in Italian; she replied in English.

During her years of mourning between the death of Rajiv in 1991 and her acceptance of the Congress Party leadership in 1998, even her smallest gesture would be interpreted and reinterpreted for signs of her intentions. A recent biographer, Yusuf Ahmed, said her 'every utterance would make politicians and journalists draw meanings and construct parallels even where none was intended'.[21] After she assumed the leadership, it became important to be aware of who was supposedly close to Sonia and who was not. 'Madam wishes it' was the stock phrase of the favoured courtiers. A number of senior Congress leaders found this level of adulation unacceptable. 'Coteries do not serve the party,' said Jitendra Prasad, who challenged Sonia for the leadership in 1999. 'They encircle the leadership, insulate it from the workers and block channels of communication. They misrepresent all discussions and differences as proof of disloyalty [to the family].'[22] Prasad's bid for the leadership failed. Some of his supporters were beaten up by Sonia loyalists.

It is hard to believe Sonia herself would sponsor or approve of such blind sycophancy. But the system is far bigger and older than she. Even her biographer, who has worked for the Congress Party but tries (with some success) to maintain an objective tone through most of his book, succumbs to an overblown assessment of Sonia's talents. Opponents of Sonia often criticise her for speaking in a wooden manner and complain that her Hindi is heavily accented. Her defenders overcompensate by likening her to a great modern orator. Sonia's biographer wrote: 'Her cadences were balanced with an element of the bellicose, the pauses perfect, equipoise was flashed in abundance, and her words fell like seeds on a fertile and awaiting soil.'[23] Even Nehru, a truly great orator, would have been embarrassed by this.

He would also have flinched at the great outpourings of public adulation Congress officials constantly offer up to Sonia. I once saw a Congress Party billboard in Chennai, featuring a large sepia-touched picture of her. 'Our pride is Mother India,' said the caption. 'Our guide is Mother Sonia.' Shortly after Congress returned to power in 2004, the party held a large rally in Delhi's Talkatora Stadium to celebrate what would have been Rajiv Gandhi's sixtieth birthday. Delhi was flooded with billboards wishing him a happy birthday and for days newspapers were dominated by brassy advertisements congratulating Rajiv and praising Sonia. 'The Uttar Pradesh Congress Party wishes Rajiv Many Happy Returns!' said one double-page spread. 'The Ministry of Rural Development [under a Congress minister] wishes felicitations to Rajiv on his 60th birthday,' said another. The praise for the couple's children is equally saccharine. At the convention in Delhi to celebrate Rajiv's birthday, one seasoned and widely respected cabinet minister took the microphone and started chanting: 'Let Rahul and Priyanka take leadership positions!' Their visibly embarrassed mother requested that the minister stop speaking. The Prime Minister, Manmohan Singh, sat patiently and unnoticed in the audience.

My meeting with Sonia took place three months before the 2004 election, when most people were expecting another defeat for Congress. I was with a senior colleague, whose visit to Delhi helped secure the appointment. We waited for a short while in a small ante-room at her official residence at 10 Janpath Road, a traditional Lutyens bungalow in central New Delhi. Then the door opened and she popped her head around. 'Please come in,' she said. I was surprised to see that Sonia was entirely alone. She took us into her study and we sat down on the sofa. 'Can I pour you some tea?' she asked. In spite of myself, I could not help feeling awkward. It felt like Queen Elizabeth was offering to massage my feet. Sonia appeared even more awkward at the situation. I looked around the room. It had been Rajiv's study before he died. Nothing, whether it was the decor, the gifts from foreign visitors, or the books in the cabinets, seemed to have been altered. A garland of flowers hung around a large picture of Rajiv on the wall. Afterwards, my colleague said the room reminded him of Miss Havisham's in *Great Expectations*, whose clocks were stopped at the exact time her fiancé died.

Strictly speaking, the one-hour interview was off the record, and we wrote nothing in the newspaper. But I feel enough time has elapsed to overlook this formality. Anyway, Sonia said nothing that would cause her retrospective embarrassment. With hindsight, her views seem prescient. At the time they appeared naïve. I asked whether her election campaign focus on rural poverty would be enough to counter the BJP's 'India Shining' campaign, which was dominating the airwaves and the headlines. She spoke haltingly and shyly, kept asking us for the right word, and thanked us when we offered one. But her meaning was clear. 'If you travel around India, you see darkness and poverty in so many places,' she said. 'India is shining in the cities, but it is not shining in the villages, which is where most Indians live. I want the Congress Party to speak for them. Certainly I cannot predict that we will win, but I think the opinion polls are wrong. I travel around India all the time, and the message I have connects with the people I meet. What they say to me also confirms my views.' She talked about the need to give the poor a greater stake in India's economic boom, and she denied her party was opposed to further economic reform. The slogan Congress later adopted was 'Reform with a Human Face'.

The conversation changed direction sharply when I asked Sonia how it felt to be the object of so much vituperation from the governing BJP. She had borne many deeply personal insults. Did she sometimes feel like packing it all in? She took her time to answer. 'You know politics does not come easily to me,' she said. 'I do not enjoy it. I do not even think I am very good at it. Politics killed my mother-in-law and it killed my husband. But when I saw what they were doing to India's secular culture, I felt I could no longer stand by and watch it happen without doing something. Secularism is the most important legacy of my family. I had to stand up and defend it. I could not watch them tear it apart.' Her eyes were brimming with tears. She was not sobbing, but there was intense sadness in her face. 'What they say about me reflects upon them. I have got used to it. It doesn't matter at all.' We both murmured our genuine sympathy. 'Do you know what happened in Gujarat?' she asked. We said we did. 'This was not India.'

Three months later I saw Sonia again, although this time from the thick of a crowd of fifty thousand people at a large rally in a park on the outer periphery of Chennai. There were just two days to go before the fourth and final phase of India's general election,* and it was only five days before the tally from all the phases would

---

*India's elections are staggered to enable the paramilitary forces to concentrate on different areas of potential instability, rather than spreading themselves too thinly for a single poll. In contrast, the result is known within an hour or two of the polls closing since India's voting system is fully electronic and is collated by computer. It makes a pleasant contrast to Florida in 2000.

be counted and declared. There were three unusual elements to the rally. The first was that the Congress flag was just one among six different party flags. This was the first election in which Congress had struck an alliance with other parties. Sonia was just one of several leaders on the platform, although clearly she was the most well known. Since we were in a Tamil-speaking part of the country, she spoke in English, not Hindi. She paused every two minutes to allow a very theatrical translator to convert her words into Tamil. He took twice as long as Sonia and ended each section with a flourish. The second unusual aspect to the rally was Sonia's expression, which was relaxed and happy. She even laughed a few times, mostly when her Tamil interpreter was giving his animated translations. I wondered whether she had sensed the tide was turning against the BJP. Perhaps she was just getting better at doing public rallies.

The third unusual aspect of the rally was the most poignant. One of the other parties represented on the podium was the DMK, a Tamil nationalist party, which had previously expressed sympathies with the brutal Tamil Tiger separatist movement in the nearby island nation of Sri Lanka. It was a Tamil nationalist suicide bomber – a young woman called Dhanu – who detonated the bomb that killed Rajiv Gandhi and several others in 1991. Rajiv had got India embroiled in the Sri Lankan conflict in 1987 when he agreed to send a peacekeeping force to the island. But it quickly turned into a partisan military presence and was involved in numerous clashes with the Tamil Tigers. Following Rajiv's assassination, Congress refused to have any dealings with the DMK. But Sonia eventually agreed that electoral pragmatism should prevail. The Congress-led alliance won all forty of Tamil Nadu's parliamentary seats in the 2004 election, most of them going to the DMK.

Earlier on the day of the rally, I had visited Sriperumbudur, the spot about thirty miles from Chennai where Rajiv Gandhi had been killed. The site had been turned into a memorial with a plaque describing the assassination. Dhanu had been wearing a sari and there were flowers tied to her hair. She bent down to touch the feet of Rajiv in a gesture of honour and submission. Then she detonated the explosives that were strapped to her body beneath the sari. 'So too on another occasion, another assassin bent to touch the feet of the Mahatma,' said the plaque. During the rally that evening, Sonia mentioned the killing of her husband. In a phrase she had used before, she said: 'I stand here on the soil that is mingled with the blood of my husband. And I can assert that there would be no greater honour for me than to share his fate for the sake of our country.' Not for the first time, I reflected that for Sonia Gandhi the political is very personal.

There is much clear blue water dividing the Congress Party from the BJP. One of the most overlooked distinguishing features is the former's flexibility. The BJP sometimes dilutes its message for tactical reasons. But everybody knows what it really believes in. It is often a struggle, on the other hand, to work out what Congress believes in nowadays. This is both a weakness and a strength. It is a weakness because there is no clearly defined cause behind which to marshal party workers, aside from adulation of the Nehru–Gandhi dynasty. But it can be an advantage because it gives the party room to experiment with different strategies in the states that it governs. In some of these, such as Andhra Pradesh, in the south, Congress rules in the traditional style, promising much to the poor while lining the pockets of the well connected. But in others Congress is led by reformist chief ministers who have tried to change the way the game is played.

One of the party's most impressive local leaders is Sheila Dikshit, who is Chief Minister of New Delhi, the equivalent of mayor of the city. New Delhi is one of the world's largest metropolises, with a population of fifteen million. It adds another million people every three years. It is India's largest or second-largest city, depending on where you draw the boundaries. The other contender is Mumbai, which is governed by one of the most inept

Congress administrations in the country. Partly as a result of the contrasting qualities of the two, New Delhi has overtaken Mumbai as a magnet for new investment in the last few years. It is also the wealthiest part of India, with an average personal income that is double the national average. In the 1990s few Indians would have hesitated if asked where they would prefer to live. Their answer would have been Mumbai. Now the answers would probably be more evenly split. Some credit for that should go to Sheila Dikshit.

Like Sonia Gandhi, Sheila Dikshit is a widow. Her husband, an IAS officer, died young. Like her leader, Dikshit is also part of a dynasty. Her father-in-law was a Congressman, and her son, Sandeep, is a member of the national parliament for a Delhi constituency. This has become increasingly normal in the Congress Party; dynasty is not confined to the Nehru–Gandhis. Often, when a senior Congressman retires or dies, one of his offspring inherits the constituency. Congress has also helped to normalise dynastic behaviour in much broader areas of Indian society. Inder Malhotra, a former editor of the *Times of India* and a biographer of South Asia's dynastic families, says that only two senior positions in Indian public life – the governor of the central bank and the army chief of staff – are untouched by dynasties. Many people who attack the Nehru–Gandhi dynasty are living in glass houses, says Malhotra, who describes the 'yawning gap between the words and deeds of the chattering classes that are most active in deploring the cult of dynasties . . . Most such people go to great lengths to promote their own progeny in all walks of life.'[24]

Mrs Dikshit is unusual for a Congress politician. She talks candidly about the corruption afflicting her administration, and complains loudly about the limitations of politics. I asked her why in so many parts of Delhi rubbish is left to fester on the streets in the summer heat. 'It is a question I struggle with every day,' she admitted. 'We have thousands of sanitation workers in New Delhi who often don't turn up to work and there's nothing I can do about it. I have tried to introduce mechanisation but they resist it because they think it threatens their jobs. You have to introduce change slowly in India. You have to take circuitous routes.'

She has similar problems reforming Delhi's water services. In spite of having a relatively good water supply that could provide over two hundred litres a day to each and every person, most of Delhi receives little or no water. The poor often have to pay private water truckers – the so-called 'water mafia' – to get their supply. The water bills that New Delhi's residents pay do not cover even 10 per cent of the cost of delivery. Naturally, there are no funds to extend access to the slums. Since most of the supply goes to the middle class, the poor are effectively subsidising water for the rich. New Delhi's water board has fifteen times as many employees per kilometre of water pipe than the average for a city in an industrialised country. These employees form a powerful vested interest against change.

When Dikshit asked the World Bank to advise on a plan to contract out water distribution to a private company she was accused of fleecing the poor. The World Bank was also accused of interfering with what it said was a flawed bidding process in order to ensure that PriceWaterhouseCoopers, the US consultancy, won the advisory contract over a number of local consultancies. Clearly the World Bank had breached its own guidelines, which was both inept and politically naïve. But it seemed overblown to accuse Dikshit of 'caving in to the forces of neo-liberalism'.[25] When she increased water bills independently of the World Bank controversy there were similar accusations. In a pattern that is familiar to India, the protests were carried out in the name of the poor, in spite of the fact that the poor are the victims in the status quo.

Sheila Dikshit's troubles show how difficult it is to reform the state in India. Yet it is still possible, even in New Delhi. In March 2004 she opened the first eighteen-kilometre stretch of the New Delhi Metro, a mostly underground rail network that, by the time it is completed in 2015, will have 225 stations covering almost every corner of India's sprawling capital. Infrastructural leaps such as this can transform a city. The project, which could boast almost fifty stations by 2006, has so far consistently been ahead of schedule, and the rail service is clean, efficient and punctual. It stands as a shining antidote to the often tardy, corrupt and shoddy infrastructure projects elsewhere in India. The Delhi Metro is a public–private partnership, partly funded by Japanese and German soft loans and managed at arm's length from day-to-day government interference. Dikshit has made every effort to ensure the public corporation retains operational independence.

'Nobody calls me asking for favours,' E. Sreedharan, managing director of Delhi Metro, told me. 'I do not have to kowtow to anybody. That is why we are consistently ahead of schedule. This is a model of how you should manage the public sector in India. It is not written in the stars that it should fail.' Although the Metro could only have been constructed with the benefit of soft loans and subsidies – as has been the case with almost every mass-transit system built in the developed world – it is expected to enhance the city's economic boom over the coming years.

Dikshit was also involved in a successful drive to clean up New Delhi's choking air quality by converting all public transport, including motorised rickshaws, to compressed natural gas (CNG) – a big environmental improvement on the previous diesel engines. New Delhi's air particle pollution count has consequently fallen by 30 per cent since 1999, when the change was introduced. As with the Metro, Dikshit was just one player in a coalition of interests pushing for the change, including the Centre for Science and Environment, an advocacy body, and India's Supreme Court, which delivered the ultimate ruling mandating CNG. But when political leaders in India choose not to get involved in the solution, they inevitably become part of the problem. Dikshit is also unusual in having been re-elected for a second five-year term in December 2003 in a country where governments rarely continue beyond one term.

New Delhi's problems are legion: the city is clogged with dirty slums, very few of which get proper public services. But unlike Mumbai, which has yet to agree on a modern mass-transit system, Delhi has at least taken some steps, however small, to address its problems. As Sanjay Gandhi showed during the Emergency in the 1970s, simply throwing slum-dwellers out of the city not only violates human rights but ultimately fails. People find a way of coming back in even larger numbers. It is estimated that by 2026, New Delhi will be one of a handful of global mega cities with a population of thirty million or more.[26] 'This is a vast, impossible city,' said Dikshit. 'In my job you have to run and run in the hope you might stand still.' She conceded that the more infrastructure is improved, and the more jobs Delhi can generate (in addition to the many it has created in recent years), the more people will want to move there. Already India's internal migration flows have shifted from Bombay in favour of the capital. It is a catch-22. 'We have no choice but to make our cities more livable and more attractive, even if that proves self-defeating,' she said.

Congress state governments in other parts of India are not as fortunate as New Delhi, whose electorate is overwhelmingly urban. In 2004 the mostly rural voters of Andhra Pradesh ejected their state government. The Congress government of Karnataka was forced into an uneasy coalition with a local party. (In January 2006 it was ejected when that partner joined forces with the opposition BJP to form a new administration.) Congress just clung on to power in Maharashtra, of which Mumbai is capital. In all three of these cases politicians interpreted the results as a sign of electoral impatience with the growing gap between rural and urban living standards. The new state governments put most urban infrastructure projects on the backburner. In the case of Bangalore, India's software capital as well as the capital of Karnataka, the state government's indifference to the city's grow-ing congestion problems is beginning to result in the diversion of new IT investments to other cities, such as New Delhi, Pune, Chennai and Chandigarh.

In Hyderabad the perceived rural backlash is even greater. Y. S. Reddy, the Congress Chief Minister of Andhra Pradesh, came to power in May 2004, having promised free electricity to all farmers. He unseated the Telugu Desam Party, a local-language party led by Chandrababu Naidu, who had been widely fêted in the local and international media as 'Mr IT' for his successful efforts in attracting software investment to the city. Google's Indian headquarters is in Hyderabad. Others, including Microsoft and Sun Microsystems, have large research centres there. Naidu had even befriended Bill Clinton, who had visited Hyderabad on his trip to India in 2000, and he was a regular at the annual conference of global economic leaders in Davos, Switzerland. However, much of Naidu's reputation was overdone. He did very little in office to improve opportunities for the state's farmers, or to reduce notorious levels of corruption in his own party. He was also a hate figure among those opposed to reform – again, with some exaggeration, since there was little he could do about the four straight years of drought Andhra Pradesh suffered before the election. Thousands of farmers in the state had committed suicide because they were unable to service their debts when their crops failed.

Naidu's defeat was interpreted as a sign that Hyderabad's booming successes had come at the expense of the poor in the thousands of villages spread out across this large state. But the electoral picture was more complicated than that. Although Congress ran a campaign on behalf of the rural poor, the secret to its success was an alliance with a local party that wants to secede some territory from Andhra Pradesh to create a separate state. The Congress vote share fell. But because of the electoral pact it swept to power with a substantial majority. It also struck a thinly concealed deal with a local group of Maoist insurgents, the Naxalites, who control large tracts of the state. Named after the town of Naxalbari in West Bengal, where they first launched their insurgency in the 1960s, the Naxalites had come within a whisker of assassinating Naidu in a bomb attack in 2003. During the 2004 campaign they targeted and killed several candidates in Naidu's party, but they left Congress alone. Shortly after the election, they received their reward when Reddy, the new Chief Minister, declared a ceasefire with the rebels and promised peace talks. Within a year the process had collapsed, as almost all observers had predicted it would. But the Naxalites, now known as the Communist Party of India (Maoist–Leninist), used the interlude profitably to regroup and rearm. 'The Naxalites are playing a long game with pauses and strategic retreats,' said Jayaprakash Narayan, who runs Lok Satta, a widely respected think tank in Hyderabad. 'The Congress Party was playing a very short-term game to win the election.'

Once he was in power, the consequences of Reddy's promise of free electricity to farmers became apparent. Under Naidu, farmers had paid only a tiny proportion of the true cost of the power they used – about 8 per cent. But only the richest farmers, who possessed electricity connections, benefited from the subsidy. They used the electricity to pump water from the ground which pushed the water table further and further away from the reach of farmers who could afford neither electricity-driven nor diesel-fuelled water pumps. Waiving the remaining small electricity bill has only exacerbated the tough conditions for the poor farmers. Reddy is himself a rich farmer with no fewer than thirty electricity connections on his farm. Providing free power to his fellow farmers adds up to more than the state's spending on primary healthcare and education combined. Reddy's election campaign was therefore a textbook example of the Congress Party's skill at using pro-poor rhetoric while at the same time achieving benefits for themselves.

A few months after the election I visited Reddy in his Hyderabad office. A large man with an equally large moustache, Reddy was every inch the local satrap. The rooms and corridors outside his office resembled a bustling railway station with dozens of local supplicants awaiting the chance to ask a favour of the Chief Minister. I asked him what he was doing to provide irrigation to the poor farmers. 'Every detail is being taken care of,' he replied. 'And what are the details?' I asked. 'Everything is possible,' he said. 'Can you provide me with some?' 'In time, we will fix everything,' he said. And so it went on. At one stage during this singularly uninformative interview, Reddy started scrambling around for a piece of paper. His secretary handed him something. 'Yes,' he said, reading it. 'Sir Arthur Cotton built lots of irrigation for the farmers in this area. He was British. You are British.' 'But what are you doing?' 'We are doing everything possible to ensure irrigation gets to the farmers.'

Later, I had a slightly more illuminating interview with Chandrababu Naidu. He alleged that Reddy's election campaign had been funded by building contractors who had been promised large irrigation projects in return. He produced charts and documents to back up these allegations. At the time of writing, very few of Reddy's irrigation investments have come on stream. But as a seasoned political operator, Naidu could well have been manipulating the facts. And Reddy still has time to deliver.

During my interview with Reddy, I had asked whether Sonia Gandhi had been involved in his plans. 'Madam is very happy,' he said. 'She approves of everything.' It is a stock phrase of the Congress Party. Without 'Madam Sonia's' approval no Congress politician can get very far. But beyond that, the absence of a binding party ideology provides a cover for all sorts of experiments – good and bad – to take place in the many parts of India that Congress continues to rule. At the national level Congress occupies an awkward position somewhere between the poles of Mandir and Mandal, occasionally adopting elements of one or other programme, yet unable to dictate the direction of Indian politics.

As for the future of the Nehru–Gandhi dynasty, it is not yet clear how much appetite Rahul and Priyanka have for the hard realities of Indian politics. Nor is it clear how good they are at fending off the sycophants or inuring themselves to the vituperation from which Sonia has suffered. Shortly after the 2004 election, a tearful Priyanka, who bears a striking resemblance to her grandmother Indira, said: 'We have never owned our family. We always had to share our parents with the nation.' Rahul, who had just been elected to parliament for the first time, merely commented on the BJP's campaign to tarnish his mother. 'These guys are a bunch of jokers,' he said. Since then, he has not played a very prominent role in parliament. Nor has he yet become much involved, as he said he would, in the Congress Party's drive to restore its fortunes in Uttar Pradesh, India's largest state and the home of the Nehru–Gandhi dynasty. Both he and his mother won thundering majorities in their Uttar Pradesh constituencies and drew huge, adoring crowds wherever they spoke. But Congress failed to win almost all of the neighbouring constituencies. The family magic, it appears, is confined to a very narrow base.

Nevertheless, at some stage in the next five to ten years it seems likely that Rahul Gandhi will become leader of the Congress Party and possibly even Prime Minister. His mother, who has signalled ambivalence about her children's future roles in politics – hoping for their success yet fearing for their safety – will most likely retreat further into the background. Then the light will shine on Rahul. (Priyanka declined to run for parliament in 2004 but she campaigned for her mother and brother.) Thereafter, presumably, the light will also start to shine on the next crop of Nehru–Gandhis, as the family moves into a sixth generation.*

The story of the Nehru–Gandhis is a long one, stretching back to the late nineteenth century, and looks set to extend well into

---

*According to feverish Indian media reports, Rahul has a Spanish girlfriend, Veronique, but she has rarely been photographed with him in public. It is presumed she is Catholic, which, if they were to marry, would entail inevitable political risks.

the twenty-first. To many in the villages and fields of India, it provides a political narrative that links their feudal past to a democratic present and hopefully to a more prosperous future. As for the dynasty, it shows no signs of losing appetite for the limelight. Rahul is now at the centre of a continuing drama that offers fairy-tale glory and adulation. He has to fend off sycophants wherever he goes. He must also try to ignore the possibility of that assassin's bullet.

CHAPTER SIX

MANY CRESCENTS

South Asia's divided Muslims

I have not done well to the country or to the people, and of the future there is no hope.

> Aurangzeb, the last great Mughal emperor, and the most controversial, in a deathbed letter to his son in 1707[1]

I had not realised it was possible. But the mullahs of Deoband, the centre of Islamic orthodoxy in South Asia, had managed to circumvent a *fatwa* (Islamic ruling) out of courtesy to me. They did it so that I could drink a cup of coffee. I was visiting Dar-ul-Uloom – the House of Knowledge – a large Islamic school in the town, which is about ninety miles north of Delhi. It was early October 2001 and the *madrasa* was buzzing with anti-American sentiment. The United States was about to start its bombing of the Taliban regime in Afghanistan. The Taliban – deriving from *talib*, Urdu for 'student' – belong to the Deoband school of Islam. Although few senior Taliban officials had visited Deoband, they saw it as their spiritual headquarters. I was sitting on the ground in the study of Maulana (an honorific given to learned Muslim men) Abdul Khalik Madrasi, vice-chancellor of Deoband, with a group of his students. They were telling me that Christians should make an alliance with Muslims against the Jews, who were the real troublemakers. It was Zionists, they said, who had organised the plane attacks on the Twin Towers in New York a few weeks earlier. It was useless arguing.

The burly Maulana, whose beard reached down almost to his rotund belly, then asked if I wanted some refreshment. I said I would like a Nescafé, which is the only kind of coffee usually available in northern India outside of the cities. 'No, no,' he said sternly. 'We have issued a *fatwa* forbidding the faithful from buying any American or British products.' I tried in vain to argue that I was not one of the faithful so the *fatwa* should not apply to me. They laughed. Then I tried and failed to convince them that Nescafé is owned by Nestlé, which is a Swiss company, but they had either never heard of Switzerland or could not see the difference. No, they said, wagging their fingers, as if they had caught me pulling a fast one, Nescafé is *Angrezi*. (In much of India the word *Angrezi* – English – simply means foreign or western.) Then something occurred to the Maulana, who was also a member of the committee that issues Deobandi *fatwas*. 'I have thought of a legitimate loophole,' he announced with a smile. 'The *fatwa* only applies to products bought after 11 September. Does anyone here possess Nescafé that is older?' A student raised his hand. The mildewed sachet of instant coffee that he fetched from his room certainly pre-dated 9/11. It was one of the most satisfying coffees I have had.

Deoband was founded in the aftermath of the failed Mutiny against the British by rebel Indian regiments in 1857. Known in India as the First War of Independence, the uprising was brutally suppressed by the British. The Mutiny had also been vicious in its methods, killing many of the colonial women and children it encountered. In revenge the British laid waste to much of northern India, burning villages and leaving hundreds strung up from trees along the main highways. Lacking a clear strategy and credible leadership, the rebel soldiers had placed the ageing and wholly titular last Mughal emperor, Bahadur Shah Zafar, at its head. Partly as a result, the British blamed Muslims more than others for the Mutiny and targeted symbols of Islam in the reprisals that followed. Parts of Mughal Delhi were destroyed or vandalised; the city's great Jama Masjid – the largest mosque in India – became a camping ground for one of the Sikh regiments that had helped the British defeat the rebels. Prominent Muslim nobles and rebels remained in hiding for years. For them, it was a time of despair. The suppression of the Mutiny was an emphatic and crushing finale to the era of Islamic dynasties in India.

India's Muslim intelligentsia was deeply split over how to respond. One group, led by Sir Sayyid Ahmad Khan, saw reconciliation as the only practical option. But Sir Sayyid's decision to make an accommodation with the British was also motivated by his fear of what would happen to Muslims in an independent India with a majority Hindu population. His expectations of democracy in India were bleak: 'It would be like a game of dice, in which one man had four dice and the other man one.'[2] In 1875 he founded the Aligarh Muslim University, which chose English as its medium of instruction and included modern science prominently on its syllabus. Many of Aligarh's graduates went on to join the imperial civil service. Later they would provide much of the vanguard of elite Muslims who led the movement to establish the nation of Pakistan.

The other group, led by two Islamic scholars, Hazrat Nanautavi and Rashid Ahwad Gangohi, saw the failure of the Mutiny and its bloody aftermath as a sign that Muslims should return to first principles. Maulana Nanautavi's followers believed the downfall of Indian Islam had been brought about by the sybaritic habits of courtly life under the Mughals. Muslims had also been weakened over the previous two or three centuries by adopting too many customs of the Hindu idol-worshipping majority.[3] The simple Arabian message of the Prophet had been forgotten. Nanautavi established Dar-ul-Uloom in Deoband in 1866. It would offer despairing Muslims a 'shore-less ocean for seekers of knowledge',[4] retreating from the world of unbelievers into a world of certainties.

Very few Deobandis approved of the idea of Pakistan, which was first raised in the 1930s. As a separate nation state, Pakistan was seen as a divisive prospect since it would artificially split the *ummah*, or community of believers. Some Deobandis were persuaded to join the Congress-led freedom movement in 1919 by Gandhi, who grasped the opportunity presented by the British occupation of the Arabian peninsula following their victory over the Ottoman Empire in the First World War. There was much Muslim, and particularly Deobandi Muslim, outrage over the presence of the *infidel* British in the holy lands. Gandhi's endorsement of the Indian *Khilafat* movement to restore the Muslim Caliphate, which had been abolished after Turkey emerged from the Ottoman ruins, instilled in Congress a habit of tactical opportunism towards Indian Muslims that still remains. Little else could explain Gandhi's decision to associate the Indian freedom struggle with a purely religious controversy about the fleeting custody of faraway Mecca and Medina. Believing it was wrong to mix religious faith with politics, Mohammed Ali Jinnah, leader of the Muslim League, who would become Pakistan's first head of state nearly thirty years later, resigned from the Congress Party in disgust. Few Deobandis approved of Jinnah, who drank whisky, ate pork and was hardly ever seen in a mosque. It was only in the early 1940s that he swapped his impeccably tailored London suits for an elegant *sherwani* and black cap.

The school at Deoband is a mix of the ramshackle and the splendid, little changed from when it was built. The architecture of the interlocking courtyards and mosque is an unusual combination of classical Islamic and Gothic. I was put up in one of the *madrasa*'s guest rooms and endured an unpleasant night of persecution by cockroaches and mosquitoes. The school has three thousand students, most of them from poor Muslim families, who are boarded and educated almost entirely for free. Some are sent to Deoband at just five years of age, and they stay until their teens or twenties. Their day begins with the first *namaaz* at dawn and is punctuated throughout by the call to prayer. Almost the entire syllabus dates to Europe's medieval period. The only science or mathematics taught is 'Islamic' and stops with the Ptolemaic system of astronomy rather than the Copernican system that replaced it several hundred years ago. Students are principally taught Arabic, Persian and Urdu so they can read the Koran and the commentaries on it in their original language. Much like the regime the Taliban established in most of Afghanistan between 1996 and 2001, Deoband permits little colour, music or celebration, beyond the Islamic festivals.

Yet, unlike the Taliban (or the Deobandis of neighbouring Pakistan, who have their own political party, the Jamiat-e-Ulema Islam, which runs the government of Pakistan's North West Frontier Province with puritanical zeal), India's Deobandis are scrupulously apolitical – at least when it comes to India. 'We are good Indian nationalists and good citizens,' said the Maulana. Who would they support if India went to war with a Muslim country, such as Pakistan? 'We would prefer it not to happen, but we would not betray India,' said the students, after some discussion. So were they Indians first or Muslims first? 'We are both,' said the Maulana. 'There is no contradiction.' I mentioned some outrages committed by the Taliban, including the destruction earlier that year of the ancient Buddhist statues at Bamiyan in central Afghanistan. My comment created a noticeable awkwardness. The Maulana said: 'These people in the Taliban are Pathans [an Afghan ethnic group from which the Taliban were principally drawn]. Pathan culture is much more fierce than Indian culture. You would be wrong to confuse the excesses of Pathan culture with Deoband. We do not have a patent on the word "Deoband".'

I related the criticisms of Deoband that I had heard from many non-practising Muslims living in India's cities. They said that Deoband and the hundreds of Deobandi *madrasas* around India, which are often founded and staffed by graduates of Dar-ul-Uloom, produce students who are poorly equipped to cope with the modern world. Most are unable to get decent employment since the only science, maths and languages they know are remnants of an Arabian golden age that has long since passed into history. In today's Indian job market you needed modern technical skills, such as computing and up-to-date financial literacy. 'Learning Arabic or Persian does not close the mind,' they responded. 'It opens up a large world of untold riches of which you know nothing.' I conceded the point. But which jobs would they go on to do? There was some murmuring. Their answers were unclear. One or two wanted to become Urdu-language broadcasters or interpreters. My guess was that a large proportion would become teachers in *madrasas*.

The bulk of the discussion, which alternated between heated and friendly, was about the looming war in Afghanistan, which was the cause of great excitement among the students. They assumed it would result in a Taliban victory. The Maulana, who had a certain rhetorical flair, spoke more than the students. 'What do Americans believe in?' he asked. 'They believe in nothing. They live for nothing, except themselves. They have no discipline over their lives. In Afghanistan the Taliban has restored law and order. Do you know that not one graduate of Deoband has ever committed a rape?' It seemed like a bold assertion, since Dar-ul-Uloom says it has produced 60,000 graduates in the last 140 years. I asked whether he believed all women should wear the *burqa* – the full veil. 'Yes, we recommend all women should cover themselves, but only for their own safety,' he said. 'Before the *Angrezis* came to India, even Hindu women wore the *burqa*.' Many Hindu women still cover themselves in the villages of northern India. But does this make society stronger? Does it really improve the behaviour of men? 'All you are taught in your schools in the west is worldly education. There are no ethics in your society. There is only self-indulgence. Do you know why the Taliban are unafraid of the American soldiers?' asked the Maulana. He paused before delivering the punchline. 'Because American soldiers are like children. They even eat chocolate.' There was much laughter. As it turned out, the US army delegated much of the eviction of the Taliban to the Northern Alliance.*

After independence in 1947, India's Muslim population lived under a cloud of suspicion. It has never entirely lifted. After partition, which many in India saw as a national 'vivisection', the country was in a state of turmoil. It had been racked not only by the violence of partition, in which between half a million and a million people were slaughtered, but by the 'Great Killings' of Calcutta in August 1946, when Jinnah declared a 'Direct Action Day' to show Congress the futility of opposing his new nation. When asked about the implicit threat of violence behind the Direct Action Day, which left the streets running with blood, Jinnah said: 'I am not prepared to discuss ethics.'[5]

Jinnah had arguably already won Pakistan in 1939 when Lord Linlithgow, the British Viceroy, effectively recognised the Muslim League as the sole spokesman of all Muslims in British India in return for Jinnah's support for India's participation in the Second World War. The Congress Party had refused to back Britain unless it was consulted before war was declared on India's behalf. Linlithgow had announced India's entry into the war without even informing Congress. In retrospect – and even at the time – the Viceroy appeared to have made a monumental blunder. Both Nehru and Gandhi were strongly opposed to Nazism and they were fearful of an expansionist Japan. Both therefore probably would have supported the war if they had been consulted before its declaration. 'How can India fight for democracy if she herself does not have it?' asked Nehru.[6]

---

*A group of former mujahedin fighters drawn principally from the Tajik Afghan ethnic group and backed by several powers in the late 1990s, including the USA, Russia and Iran.

Nevertheless, even after Linlithgow had snubbed Congress and pushed it into opposing India's participation in the war, Gandhi asked Indian soldiers to remain at their posts. Nehru, who had needed only a symbolic request from the British to secure his support for India's involvement in the struggle against fascism, said that he would still fight to defend his country against the invading Japanese. He would even fight to defend India against the widely expected invasion by the Indian National Army (INA), a group of Indian soldiers who had defected to the Japanese under the leadership of Subhash Chandra Bose, a former Congress leader. But the INA got bogged down along with its Japanese overlords in the jungles of Burma and never invaded India. Nehru made sure that no officer who had fought under the INA flag during the war was reinstated in the Indian army after independence.[7]

Some Indians trace the creation of Pakistan as far back as 1909, when Lord Minto, the Viceroy, established 'communal electorates' – reserved constituencies for religious groups – at the same time as he granted limited provincial democracy to propertied Indians. The move, which was presented by the British as a necessary measure to ensure India's largest minority got a fair voice in the debating chambers, helped to embed minority politics in Indian democracy at a very early stage. It ensured there would be a Muslim party that would appeal only to Muslims having little incentive to speak for – or to – anyone else. 'Separate electorates . . . enabled government to work a system of political control which in large part could ignore Congress,' writes Francis Robinson, a leading historian of the era.[8]

Between 1909 and 1947, the British went out of their way to detach Muslims from the Congress Party. Prominent Muslim members of Congress were subjected to particularly close harassment by the authorities. Nehru and Gandhi each spent a total of a decade or so behind bars. Jinnah did not spend a single night in jail. Many British accounts argue that Britain was motivated by the noble aim of protecting Muslims from a majority Hindu culture. But over the years the colonial power did a great deal to stoke the divisions from which they claimed to be protecting its supposed victims. This generous interpretation of Britain's actions is hard to sustain in light of the facts. It is clear Britain was hoping to prolong its rule of India by exacerbating political divisions between Indians.

Even if the British had originally established the 'communal awards' (separate electorates) in good faith, it could not disguise its main purpose as the story unfolded. In 1931 Britain invited Indian groups to London for a round-table conference on India's future. Gandhi submitted a list of the Congress Party delegates he wished to bring with him. The British struck all the Muslim names off the list.[9] In 1936 the British held India's first full-blown provincial elections. Congress won more than half the vote in the most important state, the United Provinces (later renamed Uttar Pradesh). Jinnah's Muslim League won fewer than half of the Muslim reserved seats, and just 4.4 per cent of the vote in India as a whole.[10]

Some historians, particularly from Pakistan, date the inevitability of Pakistan to the aftermath of the provincial elections in 1937, when a triumphant Congress Party refused to enter into coalition with the Muslim League in the United Provinces. Jinnah's party had won less than a quarter of all seats in the province yet his price for entering into a coalition was that Congress must recognise the League as the sole spokesman of all Muslims. This was outrageous, since there were many Muslim members of Congress and many more who had voted for it. Nevertheless, some people argue Congress made a tactical error in spurning the League's coalition overtures because it could have provided an opportunity to defang India's largest communal party. Yet Nehru felt that a coalition with the League might inflame the Hindu communalists whom he saw as a growing threat to an independent (and united) India.

What Jinnah lacked in popular support was more than compensated for by the patronage of the British. In December 1939, after Jinnah had signed on to the war effort, he got his reward. In protest at the British declaration of war on India's behalf, all the Congress provincial governments, including that of the United Provinces, resigned. Jinnah celebrated by declaring 'Deliverance Day'. In March 1940 he proclaimed the 'Pakistan Resolution' in Lahore – the first time he had openly called for a separate country. But the Muslim League still lacked popular support. Right until the brink of Pakistan's creation, Jinnah's party drew most of its backing from Muslim landowners and urban elites. 'What is really the religious or the communal problem is really a dispute among upper-class people for a division of the spoils of office or of representation in the legislature,' said Nehru.[11] Many Indians would agree with M. J. Akbar, Nehru's biographer, who writes: 'Pakistan was a chimera created by an artificially induced hatred.'[12] Naturally, few Pakistanis would concur with this interpretation.

But history turned out the way it did. And so India entered into independence with a large Muslim minority, many of whom went through the agony of watching close family members migrate to Pakistan for ever. Though the decision of those who remained in India ought to have put them beyond suspicion, their loyalties were constantly called into question by Hindu communalists and others. Equally, Indian Muslims who migrated to Pakistan from provinces such as Bihar and Uttar Pradesh are still known in early twenty-first-century Pakistan as *mohajirs*, or immigrants. Their status remains decidedly second class. It is a terrible irony of partition that the Muslims who remained in India and those who left for Pakistan should have as good a claim as anyone to being true Indians and true Pakistanis respectively, given the sacrifices they made; yet the former are subject to more suspicion about their patriotism than any other group in India, and the latter are largely denied access to the power centres of modern Pakistan, not least the army. The contradictions of partition have yet to die out.

Another British legacy continues to bedevil relations in the subcontinent today, and occasionally threatens broader regional stability: the disputed status of Kashmir. Apologists for British imperialism say the accusation of 'divide and rule' is unfair. Their view is that 'Indians divided, Britain ruled'. India, they say, was deeply divided before the British arrived, and the religious divide in particular was not a British invention. There is some truth in this. But few would dispute that Britain withdrew from India in great haste and with much ineptitude. Under the terms of partition, Lord Mountbatten, the last Viceroy, persuaded a reluctant Nehru that the colony's several hundred princely states should decide for themselves which of the two countries they would join. In most cases it was academic, since the maharajah or nizam in question belonged to the same religion as his subjects. But in Junagadh, Hyderabad and Kashmir the ruler's loyalties were contradicted by the religion of the majority of his population. In the case of Hyderabad this was particularly awkward, since it was geographically nowhere near either East Pakistan (which had been East Bengal, and which in 1971 became Bangladesh) or West Pakistan (which consisted of Sindh, the North West Frontier Province, Balochistan and about half of Punjab). At one point in 1948 the Muslim nizam of Hyderabad looked to be on the verge of declaring for Pakistan. But within forty-eight hours Vallabhbhai Patel, India's Home Minister, had flooded the principality with Indian soldiers. Pakistan protested, but Hyderabad's absorption into India could hardly be reversed. Much the same thing happened in Junagadh, where a Muslim prince ignored the sympathies of his Hindu subjects and declared for Pakistan. Again it was absorbed into India.

The valley of Kashmir proved much more problematic for India. Here, a Muslim majority was ruled by a Hindu prince, Maharajah Hari Singh. It also bordered the Pakistani province of Punjab, so its absorption into Pakistan would have been feasible. However, Indians felt this would have left their nation unacceptably exposed, since Kashmir straddles a vital Himalayan high ground of the subcontinent. Furthermore, it would be India's only Muslim-majority province, a point of overriding importance for a Congress government that wished to burnish its secular credentials. Finally, Nehru had a deep emotional attachment to Kashmir, from where his family had originally come and where he had spent many summer holidays.

To the growing frustration both of Jinnah and Nehru, the Maharajah of Kashmir prevaricated hopelessly over which country he should join. They suspected with good reason that he wanted to declare Kashmir's independence from both. He finally signed the instrument of accession of Kashmir to India in October 1947, as thousands of Pakistani guerrilla fighters approached Srinagar, the state capital.[13] Nehru immediately airlifted Indian troops to Srinagar where they managed to defend the city and prevent the mostly Afridi Pakistani tribesman from going further. The two sides eventually agreed to a ceasefire brokered by the United Nations. The ceasefire line, which divided the state in two, was known as the Line of Control (LOC). It remains the border today between Indian-administered and Pakistan-administered Kashmir. Although the line is unchanged, the world around it has altered radically. Today, in spite of the latest peace process between India and Pakistan – which began in 2003, is still ongoing, and which some believe stands a better chance of success than earlier efforts – the LOC is often referred to as the most dangerous nuclear flashpoint in the world.

The first time I visited Kashmir was in November 2001. I had spent most of the previous two months in Pakistan, along with thousands of other foreign journalists, observing the regime's response to the Bush administration's post-9/11 ultimatum. Bush had reportedly told Pakistan's President, General Pervez Musharraf: 'Either you are with us or you are against us.' Unsurprisingly, given the power of the United States, Musharraf quickly decided

Pakistan would support the US in its 'war on terrorism'. He also promised Islamabad's assistance in the ejection of Afghanistan's Taliban regime (which Pakistan had helped bring to power).

It was an extremely tense time in Pakistan. I watched Musharraf's first post-9/11 broadcast to the nation with acute interest. He justified his decision to ally with the United States on three grounds. It would protect Pakistan's nuclear assets (presumably from the United States, if Pakistan had not joined the coalition against terrorism). It would help Pakistan turn around its ailing economy. And it would assist Pakistan's long-running claim to sovereignty over all of Kashmir (again, by ensuring Pakistan maintained good relations with the world's sole superpower). The slogan Musharraf adopted was 'Pakistan First'. These two words signalled something crucial: nationalism was more important than religion. Pakistan should come before Islam.

A few weeks later I was taken with a group of foreign journalists to Pakistan's portion of Kashmir, which the Pakistanis call Azad Kashmir – Free Kashmir – and which the Indians call Pakistan-Occupied Kashmir. We were taken to a small post on the LOC overlooking an Indian position about a kilometre away across some green hills. We observed the Indian soldiers through binoculars and they observed us. Everyone waved at each other cheerily. The Pakistani major who was accompanying us was keen to stress the importance of holding a referendum in Kashmir. 'India should permit a UN-administered plebiscite to allow the people to determine whether they want to be Pakistani or Indian,' he said. 'If they choose to be Indian then we will accept their choice.'

Ironically, considering India's subsequent rejection of any 'third-party' involvement in the dispute, it was New Delhi that requested the UN-mediated ceasefire in 1948, which culminated in a Security Council resolution on Kashmir. That resolution called for Pakistan to vacate all of Kashmir before a plebiscite was held. It is inconceivable Pakistan would vacate Azad Kashmir, so the plebiscite remains a dead letter. In 2004, after the start of the new peace process, Musharraf unexpectedly dropped the demand for a plebiscite. In doing so he abandoned what had been the core of Pakistan's Kashmir policy for more than fifty years.

The week after my visit to Azad Kashmir I dined at the officers' mess of the Rajputana Rifles, an Indian regiment, very close to the spot on the Pakistani side where I had stood a few days earlier. 'Sometimes they shoot at us, sometimes we shoot at them,' said the Indian colonel, who was my host. 'We don't usually hit each other.' The real game was – and, to some extent, still is – the infiltration of Pakistan-backed militants ('freedom fighters' in Islamabad; 'terrorists' in New Delhi) across the LOC to the Indian side. It usually happens at night and the Pakistani army provides covering fire to assist their hazardous nocturnal dash. The Indian colonel claimed he had made many successful 'interceptions' of these infiltrators. The snows would come soon and, with the change in season, infiltration would decline, he said. The small force of Indian soldiers was dug into trenches overlooking the steep valley from their eagle's nest at an altitude of about eleven thousand feet. Already the chill winds of an impending Himalayan winter were whining through the mess. We dined on steaming mulligatawny soup and hot *rotis*. It seemed an arduous existence.

There are approximately 450,000 Indian soldiers and paramilitaries stationed in Kashmir, many of whom spend long winters along the high passes of the LOC. Others, who are often just eighteen or nineteen years old, can be seen at intervals of about two hundred metres along Kashmir's highways and on its streets, sitting in bunkers waiting to be shot at or to shoot first. Their lives are unenviable. But the ubiquity of Indian military uniforms in Kashmir gives the province the unmistakable flavour of being occupied. With a population of just eight million, the ratio of soldiers to civilians in the state is extremely high. The largest number of European soldiers stationed in British India was

100,000 in the aftermath of the Mutiny, when India had a population of more than 200 million. Perhaps it was a measure of how easy it was for the imperialists to divide Indians. Or perhaps it is a measure of how difficult it is for India to win the loyalty of Kashmiris.

There was another angle to my visit in November 2001. A couple of weeks earlier a group of *fidayeen* – trained suicide bombers – had driven through the gates to the compound of the Kashmiri legislative assembly in Srinagar and blown up themselves and their vehicle, killing dozens of people. It was a heavily symbolic attack, and it came just a few weeks after 9/11. At the time the people of Kashmir were in ferment over a campaign by Islamic radicals to change the way they behaved in public. In contrast to Pakistan, where the *burqa* is widely worn, most Kashmiri women are unveiled. The Kashmiri style of Islam draws on rich strands of Sufi mysticism, which bears little resemblance to the orthodox Deobandi, or Talibanised, Islam that is drilled into most of the militants. A number of unveiled Kashmiri women had been agonisingly disfigured in the previous weeks when militants threw acid in their faces. Almost every Kashmiri I met disliked the Islamic radicals and blamed Pakistan for their presence. But they also bitterly resented the Indian security forces, whose presence in their lives often resulted in human rights abuses, including rape, torture and extra-judicial killings. 'We are stuck between a rock and a hard place,' said one Kashmiri lawyer. A plague, they seemed to be saying, on both your houses.

By 2001, the character of the Kashmiri separatist movement had drastically altered since the early days of the insurgency in 1989. The province had been mostly quiescent between 1948 and 1989. But in 1987 New Delhi had blatantly rigged the state assembly election to ensure that a pro-India party would take office. Resentment at Delhi's heavy-handed and corrupt meddling in the state had triggered the insurgency for an independent Kashmir. In the first few years it had little to do with Islam and was not yet fully controlled by Pakistan. But gradually during the 1990s the indigenous Jammu–Kashmir Liberation Front, which sought independence for Kashmir from both India and Pakistan, was supplanted by other groups that had infiltrated the province and wanted Kashmir to become part of Pakistan. Many of the groups were dominated by radical Islamists from the Pakistan side of Kashmir, from Pakistan Punjab and from the North West Frontier Province. There were even some militants from Afghanistan, Saudi Arabia, Chechnya and other parts of the Islamic world. Pakistan was prepared to give free rein to these *jihadi* (holy war) fighters from outside Kashmir if they would in turn assist Islamabad in its mission to undermine India's hold on the province. From Pakistan's point of view, the timing of the Kashmiri insurgency, which took both Islamabad and Delhi by surprise, was highly propitious. It coincided with the withdrawal of Soviet forces from Afghanistan in 1989, leaving in their wake thousands of victorious foreign mujahedin fighters looking for a new cause. The notorious Inter-Services Intelligence (ISI) – Pakistan's equivalent of the CIA – relocated many of the Afghan *jihadis* to Kashmir during the 1990s and more recently.

A few weeks after my first visit to Kashmir in 2001 the world's attention suddenly shifted away from Afghanistan to India and Pakistan. The Taliban had already crumbled after the Northern Alliance had taken Kabul. The Americans were beginning to realise they might not find Osama Bin Laden in the Tora Bora mountain range on the Afghan–Pakistani border, which they were bombing intensively. In a replay of the *fidayeen* attack on the Srinagar assembly two months beforehand, suicide terrorists attacked New Delhi on 13 December 2001. Four men, strapped with explosives, burst through the gates to the outer rim of India's circular parliament and detonated the white Ambassador car they were driving. The attackers, who killed fourteen people, were stopped by security guards just a few metres short of the parliamentary chamber. Parliament was in session. A little further and they would have demolished part of the chamber and likely taken much of the Indian cabinet with it. I got to the scene within half an hour. Already the streets had been cleared. There was an ominous atmosphere. Previously lackadaisical checkpoint guards were waving guns in people's faces. The whole city was echoing with the sounds of screeching sirens and helicopters overhead. The Indians traced the attack to a Kashmiri militant group based in Pakistan called the Lashkar-e-Toiba – the Army of the Pure. Atal Behari Vajpayee, India's Prime Minister, held Pakistan to account and demanded the immediate extradition to India of twenty alleged terrorists harboured by Pakistan. Vajpayee also demanded the immediate cessation of militant infiltration across the LOC and the closure of alleged Pakistan-backed terrorist training camps in Azad Kashmir. Musharraf angrily denied any involvement. It looked as though the two neighbours were preparing for another round of high-octane antagonism. It was to get worse than that.

My parents were visiting India that Christmas. We took them to Ranthambore, a famous tiger reserve in the state of Rajasthan. We did not see any tigers. But we did catch glimpses of one of the largest military mobilisations in modern history. Vajpayee had ordered the relocation of most of India's 1.2-million-strong army to the international border with Pakistan. The states of Rajasthan, Gujarat and Punjab are on this border. We got stuck at Jaipur railway station in Rajasthan. It soon became apparent why our train to Ranthambore had been delayed. For two hours we sat on the platform watching train after train pass northwards through the station carrying tanks, heavy artillery, armoured personnel carriers and thousands of soldiers. Watching India's rusting military hardware chug past us reminded me of what I had read about the preparations for the First World War: mobilisation had followed the dictates of European railway timetables. Now, India's mobilisation, which was later dubbed 'coercive diplomacy', was occurring at the stately pace of the Indian railways. Somehow this made it seem even more troubling. It was an unusual beginning to our Christmas break, and it ruined my short holiday since I felt journalistic guilt at being in the wrong place. But it was far from clear where the right place might be.

As it turned out, nothing happened; or rather, a great deal nearly happened over the next six months before India stood down from what it had called Operation Parakaram (Valour). There were unsubstantiated but widely reported rumours that both sides had fixed nuclear warheads to missiles in anticipation that the conflict, which threatened to break out at any stage, would escalate very rapidly. Twice during the tense stand-off – in January and late May 2002 – India was on the brink of ordering some kind of cross-border military strike. Mercifully, both times it pulled back from the brink. In October 2002 India's railways lumbered back into action, this time to facilitate the massive demobilisation of a very tired and somewhat dispirited Indian army. Perhaps by then Ranthambore's tigers had emerged from their nuclear bunkers.

Somebody once described wars between India and Pakistan as 'communal riots with armour'.[14] It is a catchy phrase. Pakistan is certainly a Muslim country and under its constitution the republic derives its sovereignty from Allah, rather than from the people. But India is a diverse, multi-faith country with a secular constitution. For all its faults, it would be unfair to describe India's army as 'Hindu' since it has Muslim and Christian officers and many Sikh regiments. India's parliament also elected a Muslim head of state in 2002, while General J. J. Singh, who was appointed army chief of staff in 2005, is a Sikh, as is Manmohan Singh, the Prime Minister. India's most powerful woman is a foreign-born Christian.

The phrase 'communal riots with armour' might be misleading for another reason. Communal rioting has the connotation of butchery. But comparatively few Indian and Pakistani soldiers have been killed in wars between the two countries since they came into independent existence. Officially India and Pakistan have been to war three times – in 1947, 1965 and 1971. There was a fourth unofficial war between the two in 1999, when a large, euphemistically labelled 'guerrilla force' – in fact, they were Pakistani soldiers in mufti – occupied the strategic heights of Kargil on India's side of the LOC. They were ejected after Indian infantry stormed the mountain in a bloody four-week encounter. This was similar in character to the full-blown wars, which for the most part have been very short, with only brief moments of intensive engagement. The total casualties of all four India-Pakistan conflicts amount to fewer than fifty thousand killed. There were moments during the First World War in Europe when as many men were killed in the space of seventy-two hours. If you expand the definition of war to include what India calls Pakistan's 'proxy war' in Kashmir – war conducted through nominally independent militants – the number of deaths rises by between forty and eighty thousand. This is a large number. But communal riots in India before, during and since partition have claimed far more lives.

Yet, to many Indians, the very existence of Pakistan is seen as a dagger aimed at the heart of India. This threat is perceived on a number of levels. First, Pakistan claims Kashmir, India's only Muslim-majority province. Pakistan is unlikely to relinquish that claim, precisely because it is majority Muslim. If the so-called 'two-nation' theory (which Jinnah propounded) is wrong then Pakistan should never have been created. If it is right then Kashmir should belong to Pakistan. Given the degree to which Pakistan's military regimes have demanded national sacrifice in both blood and capital in pursuit of the Kashmiri cause, it would be surprising if Islamabad abandoned its stance.

Second, the creation of Pakistan was seen as an amputation of India's natural geographical and cultural boundaries. It is not only the Hindu nationalists who dream of the day when Pakistan will be reincorporated into Akhand Bharat – Greater India. Many Indians, of whatever background, see partition as an unnecessary tragedy that ought, at some unspecified stage in the future, to be peacefully rectified. Naturally, this attitude contributes to Pakistan's own profound insecurities. However, very few Indians would any longer subscribe to Nehru's view that Pakistan was untenable as a nation state and that it would eventually merge back into India. Indian longing for subcontinental unity remains a vague sentiment. It is not a policy.

Third, and most intractably, Pakistan is seen as posing an existential threat to India's secular identity. No matter how stable relations are between the two countries, in the Indian mind the existence of Pakistan will always have the potential to divide the loyalties of India's Muslim minority, which now accounts for almost 14 per cent of the population, or about 150 million people. This, in turn, exacerbates the insecurities of India's Muslims. There is little doubt that Pakistan has on many occasions over the last sixty years sought to stoke this neuralgia. Yet, with the exception of Kashmir, which accounts for less than 10 per cent of India's Muslim population, the expectations of many in Pakistan (and around the world) that India would gradually break up under the weight of its diverse contradictions have been proved wrong. India's Muslims remain firmly ensconced in India, as do most of India's other minorities.* There have been no significant population movements between India and Pakistan since 1947. Admittedly, there have been a few overinflated incidents when Muslim slums in India have flown the Pakistani flag when the two national cricket teams met on the field. But in a different country such displays would barely register. Norman Tebbit's notorious 'cricket test', in which he demanded that British Asians should support England when they were playing India or Pakistan, is now viewed by most Britons as embarrassingly out of touch, rather than patriotic.

---

*India does suffer from a rash of small separatist insurgencies, particularly in its geographically isolated north-eastern states, which border China, Myanmar, Bangladesh, Bhutan and Nepal. But these are geographically confined and most of India's neighbours, particularly China, are thought to have withdrawn the tacit support they once gave to many of the north-eastern separatist groups.

The hardline chauvinists in India and Pakistan have much more in common with each other than they would care to admit: both mistrust diversity; both seek to regulate and control the role of women in society through education and culture. They also share a partiality to the use and abuse of history. According to Pakistan's school textbooks, the history of modern Pakistan goes back to the early Muslim incursions into India, when marauders such as Mehmood of Ghazni, an Afghan strongman, conducted raids on northern India. Pakistan's medium-range nuclear missiles are called the Ghauri, after Mohammed Ghauri, who became the first Muslim to rule Delhi when he defeated a Hindu Rajput prince, Prithvi Raj Chauhan, in 1192. Meanwhile, India's short-range missiles are called Prithvis (*prithvi* also means 'earth' in Sanskrit). In a mirror-image of the textbooks that the BJP introduced when it governed India, Pakistan's schoolbooks stereotype Hindus as 'cunning, scheming and deceptive'.[15] The textbooks that are used in the twenty thousand or so schools operated by the Hindu nationalist RSS in India depict Muslims as cruel and bloodthirsty. The emperor Aurangzeb, who was quoted at the start of this chapter, is depicted as a hero by Pakistan but as a villain by India. His great-grandfather, Akbar, one of India's most enlightened rulers, is downplayed by both Muslim and Hindu communalists. They are two sides of the same coin.

Someone once said that the rivalry between the Soviet Union and the United States during the Cold War was ideological, whereas the enmity between India and Pakistan is biological. Whenever I visit Pakistan, I am struck by the transparent paranoia that the military and diplomatic elites in Islamabad feel towards their neighbour. I am equally struck by the absence of these sentiments among ordinary Pakistanis. The same is broadly true in reverse, although India plays a much larger role in the popular perceptions of Pakistanis than vice versa, partly because of the allure of Bollywood. When ordinary Pakistanis and Indians interact there is usually goodwill and warmth.

In April 2004 I flew to Karachi, Pakistan's commercial capital, to attend the first cricket game in years between the two countries. The match was the first in a series organised by New Delhi and Islamabad after the bilateral peace process was launched in 2003. Thousands of Indians had been given visas to attend the game, making this the most significant 'people-to-people' contact that had been permitted between Indians and Pakistanis since the peace process had begun. I spent most of the day touring the stadium in search of Indian supporters to ask how they were being treated. Most of them seemed stunned. The boisterous Pakistani crowd were chanting 'Akhtar Zindabad, Zindabad, Zindabad!' – 'Long Live Akhtar!' (Shoaib Akhtar is Pakistan's fastest bowler.) However, when an Indian batsman played well, the chant of the Pakistani masses switched seamlessly to 'India Zindabad, Zindabad, Zindabad!' Every Indian I met said he had been treated like a long-lost brother (they were mostly men): shopkeepers had refused to accept their cash; taxi-drivers had declined fares; hotels were waiving bills; and people kept approaching them on the streets to offer sweets and other small gifts. 'It is overwhelming,' said one among a group of Indian men, all dressed in the blue shirts of their national team. 'We didn't know what to expect but we feared there would be hostility.' India won the game and received a prolonged ovation from the vast Pakistani crowd.

In contrast, for Pakistan's military–bureaucratic establishment, India is a migraine that outweighs all its other headaches put together. The perceived threat from India and the need to secure Kashmir have provided the principal justification for military rule in Pakistan for more than half of the country's history. These two issues explain why Pakistan spends a much larger share of its gross national product on defence than India: in 2003 the latter spent 15 per cent of its budget on defence, compared to the former's 54 per cent.[16] Some would describe Pakistan as a home for South Asia's Muslims. Others increasingly see it as a Central Asian Islamic republic, or even as an extension of the Middle East. A more enduring description for Pakistan's national identity might be 'Not India'.

Even during periods of warmer relations between Islamabad and Delhi, the Pakistani establishment routinely uses the perceived threat from India to justify its grip on political power. In October 2005 the region was hit by the most devastating earthquake in living memory, claiming seventy thousand lives and making millions homeless. The worst-affected zone was on the Pakistani side of Kashmir, although the Indian portion was also hit. There was strong domestic criticism by the Pakistani media of President Musharraf's handling of the emergency, with many believing the army had acted too slowly in response to the desperate plight of millions of Kashmiris. This lassitude had given the Islamist charities an opportunity to step in and boost their popularity. One ray of light came when India and Pakistan moved (albeit reluctantly) to open several points along the LOC for the delivery of relief, mostly from the Indian to the Pakistani side. In the midst of all this, dozens of large billboards suddenly appeared in Islamabad which implied there was a new threat from India. The posters demanded that India return Kashmir to Pakistan immediately. One said: 'Kashmiris are not Children of a Lesser God'. It was a reminder of the Pakistan military's instinct of resorting to diversionary propaganda whenever its back is to the wall.

It has become fashionable over the decades to argue that the Kashmir dispute between India and Pakistan is insoluble. From the Indian side, the view is that as long as Pakistan is under military rule it will never agree to a peace deal that falls short of full sovereignty over the province. But if a democratic Pakistani government were to conclude a deal that fell short of the country's maximum demands, the army would use this as a pretext to launch another coup. As with Musharraf's coup in 1999 – which followed the decision by Nawaz Sharif, Pakistan's democratically elected Prime Minister, to retreat from the Kargil heights on India's side of Kashmir – Pakistan's courts unfailingly uphold the legality of army coups. The Supreme Court invariably cites the country's catch-all 'Doctrine of Necessity' (a body of law developed by judges in Pakistan that does not appear in the constitution), which says: 'That which otherwise is not lawful, necessity makes lawful.'[17] In other words, if there is a tank parked outside your courthouse, you tend to go with the flow. So, with good reason, Pakistan is alternately perceived by India as either too aggressive or too weak to conclude a lasting peace settlement.

From the Pakistani side, India is correctly seen as a status quo power that will cling on to Jammu–Kashmir but happily leave Pakistan to its much smaller portion of the divided province. India would almost certainly accept a peace agreement in which the LOC were converted from a ceasefire line into an international border. Pakistan almost certainly would not. There are a few Indian irredentists who would like to regain all of Kashmir. But they are on the margins of the debate. Pakistan's establishment quite reasonably also sees India as a country that often agrees to something and then spends years arguing over what it has actually agreed to. There are not many diplomatic corps around the world that are as accomplished at semantic nit-picking as India's foreign service. Sometimes this approach can be self-defeating. In another context, Narayana Murthy, the founder of Infosys, India's largest software company, said Indian bureaucrats were chronically prone to 'MAFA' – mistaking articulation for accomplishment. It is not just the Pakistanis who have felt frustrated by this. India's habit of approaching diplomacy in the manner of a clever high-school debater has ruffled the feathers of many governments around the world at one time or another. But short of nuclear war, which would annihilate both sides, there is little Pakistan can do to alter the status quo. It has tried conventional war on several occasions and has failed each time.

Ultimately, most observers believe that any credible solution to the Kashmir dispute ought to lie at least partly in the province itself. As the status quo power, India can probably do more than

Pakistan to influence the attitudes of Kashmiris in a positive direction, especially since, in spite of the peace process, Pakistan has retained the option of deploying terrorists across the LOC. There have been signs in the last few years that the population of Kashmir would be ready to accept some kind of settlement that would fall short of independence for the province or full merger with Pakistan. This is not because of any sudden affection for India, which has consistently misread the situation in Kashmir and treated its inhabitants with high-handedness and arrogance. It has been driven more by the growing fatigue Kashmiris feel about the violence and uncertainty that have dominated their lives for so long. The gradual shift in mindset might also be related to India's relative economic success in the last few years compared to the more precarious economic situation in Pakistan.

On my last two trips to Kashmir this shift has been increasingly pronounced. Kashmiris nowadays more often refer to militants as 'foreigners' or 'terrorists'. In the past they had generally called them 'freedom fighters'. Kashmir's bewildering array of separatist leaders, who are grouped under an umbrella movement called the All People's Hurriyat Conference, also talk with less respect for the militant groups than before. Most of these separatist leaders are vulnerable to assassination at any time. Some of them are the sons, brothers or nephews of leaders who have been killed by militant groups for having strayed too far from either the pro-Pakistan or the Islamist line. It is not just Kashmiri separatist leaders or the people of Kashmir who believe the militants are out of control. Some of the militant groups have been involved in assassination attempts on President Musharraf. The closest attempt was in December 2003 when a remotely controlled bomb blew up a bridge that Musharraf's car was about to cross. The attempt took place just a couple of miles from Musharraf's official residence in Rawalpindi, the Pakistani army headquarters. Two Kashmiri separatists were subsequently arrested. There was also a close shave for Shaukat Aziz, Pakistan's military-appointed Prime Minister, whose driver and bodyguard were shot dead when he was on the campaign trail in 2004 in the North West Frontier Province. For Musharraf and the liberal and modernising sections of Pakistan that sometimes support him, these incidents served as a reminder that Frankenstein's monster can devour his creator.

The separatist leader in Kashmir who is most vulnerable to assassination is probably Umar Farooq, who is known as the Mirwaiz, a revered hereditary Sufi title in Srinagar that has been held in Farooq's family for generations. The teenage but highly articulate Farooq became Mirwaiz in 1990 when his father was assassinated. (It is unclear who carried out the killing.) In 2004 Farooq's uncle was killed by militants in Srinagar. When I spoke to the Mirwaiz in 2005 I was startled by how much his attitude had shifted since we had first met in 2001. 'We, as Kashmiris, belong to many different religions,' he said. 'We are Muslims, both Shia and Sunni, we are Hindus, and we are Buddhists. Kashmir has a long and tolerant tradition that bears little relation to the Punjabi Sunni Muslim culture that dominates Pakistan.' This was the statement of a man who had grown tired of weighing every word before he spoke. He said most Kashmiris, including himself, had reached the limits of tolerance for violence, from whatever direction it came. 'In the past when there was a bomb or an assassination, up to ten different militant groups would claim responsibility,' he said. 'Now, nobody claims responsibility. That should tell you something about the changes that are occurring.'

I was equally surprised when I later visited Abdul Ghani Bhatt, another seasoned Kashmiri separatist leader, at his ancestral village near the town of Baramulla, about twenty miles from the LOC. I spotted Bhatt sitting behind a shop window, having a cup of tea in the small high street. It was late winter and he was carrying a vessel filled with hot charcoal under his overcoat to keep warm, as is the custom of Kashmiris. I had met him many times before. He had always come across as one of the most inflexible, albeit charming, spokesmen for Islamabad's point of view. But this time his tone was different. 'The whole thing keeps going round and round and people are getting tired,' he said. 'India says, "I am big." Pakistan says, "But Islam is even bigger." It is the usual civilisational debate. Nobody on the ground in Kashmir wants the peace of the graveyard any more. They want India and Pakistan to pause and be more imaginative.' I mentioned Syeed Geelani, the most hardline Islamic separatist leader in Kashmir, whose Jamaat-e-Islami Party is linked to the most violent militant outfits in the province. Geelani is the most prominent of the remaining separatist leaders who still unequivocally oppose the peace process between India and Pakistan. It would be dangerous to cross him. 'Oh, Geelani is just a malevolent narcissist,' said Bhatt. 'Don't pay him any attention.'

In fact, I had paid Geelani quite a bit of attention a few weeks earlier, when I had visited him at his residence in Srinagar. As was often the case, he had been put under house arrest by the Indians. I went to see him with two colleagues, Simon Long of *The Economist* and Amy Waldman of the *New York Times*. The temperature was close to zero. We were seated in three chairs facing the hardline Islamist. 'Are you sure you're not too cold, my dears?' he kept asking. Disbelieving our replies, he sent a young minion to find a blanket and then instructed the minion to tuck all three of us under it. It was my most intimate collaboration to date with journalistic competitors. Whenever Geelani said something, his minions would echo the last three or four words in unison. He said: 'The Indians kill us mercilessly. They rape our sisters and they rape our daughters.' His chorus echoed, 'rape our daughters', before Geelani resumed his monologue. 'The Indians have no respect for Kashmiri rights. We are human beings, not animals,' he said. 'Not animals,' they echoed. In spite of his grim words, it was hard for us to keep a straight face. Geelani, though, could not disguise his unhappiness over the peace process. He cut a lonely figure.

Later that day we went to the central park in Srinagar, where Manmohan Singh was to give his first address as India's Prime Minister to a rally of Kashmiris. The crowd of several thousand had evidently been corralled into attendance by local pro-India parties. Most of them had been paid a small sum to be there. Security was very tight and there were several helicopters in the sky. But the supposedly organised crowd could not be fully controlled. At various intervals in Singh's speech, a section of it would start chanting slogans and the Prime Minister would have to stop speaking. It was a familiar reception for an Indian politician in a highly dissenting and embittered outpost of the country. But the crowd was not yelling cries of 'freedom' or 'Pakistan' or 'Islam', as they might have done in the past. They were shouting for jobs: 'Remove unemployment,' they chanted repeatedly. Perhaps I drew from this small incident more significance than it merited. But it seemed like another indication that the priorities of Kashmiris were changing.

During my time in India I have constantly been alert for any sign that the loyalties of India's Muslim population might be in question. But outside Kashmir (and even there sentiments are more complex than is often portrayed), I have yet to come across serious evidence of divided loyalties. India's Muslims are a disappointment both to Pakistan, where hawkish types look for signs of oppression of Muslims as something that would reaffirm the logic of their own existence, and to the Hindu communalists, whose ideology tells them that it is impossible to be both a true Indian and a devout Muslim. The reality of life for India's Muslims is often more prosaic.

In 2004 the opposition BJP seized upon new data that had been released by India's Census Bureau. According to New Delhi's demographers, India's Muslim population had grown by 29 per cent between 1991 and 2001, whereas the Hindu population growth rate in the same period had been just 22 per cent.[18] These statistics provided an opportunity for the Hindu right wing to raise the spectre that India was in danger of being swamped by Muslims. This idea fitted with the stereotype that Muslims were a threat to India's balance since they tended to have larger families. Narendra Modi, the BJP Chief Minister of Gujarat, described the refugee camps that provided shelter to Muslims who had been burned out of their homes in the 2002 riots as 'child manufacturing factories'.

But the story behind the census data was more complex. India's population growth rate has declined sharply among all communities, falling from an annual average of 2.2 per cent in the 1980s to less than 2 per cent in the 1990s. It is expected to have fallen to about 1.5 per cent by the time of the next census in 2011. During the 1990s the richer Indian states in the south recorded a more rapid fall in their population growth rates than the poorer states in the north. It therefore seems safe to say that the trends are a function of economics, not of religion. Muslims living in the south had a lower population growth rate than Hindus living in the north. But since a larger proportion of Muslims live in poorer states, their average growth rate was higher.

The question ought to have been why such a large proportion of Muslims live in relative poverty in India. But this is rarely addressed. Its causes are multiple and varied. But the exodus in 1947 of most of India's Muslim intelligentsia to Pakistan was surely a big factor. A large proportion of India's Muslim civil servants, military officers and university lecturers left for the new country, often believing they would have a better chance of preferment there. Poor Muslims barely shifted. In addition, a large proportion of those Muslims who remained in India were involved in traditional artisan occupations, such as weaving and basket-making which have suffered economic decline since the 1950s. So some of the poverty is new.

Nevertheless, poverty among India's Muslims continues to fall, although at a less rapid rate than the average improvements for India as a whole. But averages can mislead as much as they inform. Beneath the statistics and the stereotypes, India's Muslim population is as varied and diverse as the rest of India. It is as rare for a Tamil-speaking Muslim to marry a Gujarati-speaking Muslim as it is for their Hindu counterparts to marry outside their communities. Being a Muslim is just one attribute in the complex menu of identities available to most Indians. Nehru once described India as a palimpsest. It was his way of illustrating the large accumulation of histories and cultures that had left their mark on the country, none of which had been fully erased. Indians themselves, including Muslims, could be described as palimpsests in miniature.

For example, Muslims in many parts of India are almost as prone to caste classification as their Hindu counterparts. In Uttar Pradesh, which is home to the largest number of Muslims in India, almost thirty million, Muslim castes are divided into Ashraf and non-Ashraf.[19] Many of the former, who are upper caste and have noble-sounding names like Shaikh, Pathan, Mughal and Sayyid, claim descent from foreign aristocracy, whether Persian, Arabian, Turkish or Afghan. They are as disdainful of the lower-caste Muslims, most of whom are descendants of lower-caste Hindus who converted to Islam (ironically to escape caste), as Brahmin Hindus are towards Dalits. The only place where Ashraf and non-Ashraf rub shoulders on equal terms is in the mosque. Lower-caste Muslims tend to copy the habits and codes of the Ashraf families in their villages by putting their women in *purdah* – a sign of wealth, because only the rich can afford to remove their women from work in the fields. Meanwhile, the Ashrafs are moving to the cities and in many cases 'westernising' and abandoning *purdah*.[20] The long reach of the Hindu caste system might be another reason why more Indian lower castes have not converted to Islam, or to Christianity*.

Another relatively overlooked complexity is the division between India's Sunni and Shia Muslim communities. In cities such as Lucknow, the capital of Uttar Pradesh, where there are large concentrations of both strands of Islam, the principal communal problems are between Shias and Sunnis rather than between Muslims and Hindus. For years there was violence surrounding the annual Shia Moharram Festival, in which Shias mourn the martyrdom of the Prophet's grandson, Hussain. Being a minority among India's Muslims, Lucknow's Shia community occasionally votes tactically for the Hindu nationalist BJP. This is a prime example of the 'enemy of my enemy' principle in Indian politics. And it suggests limits to which the term 'Indian Islam' makes any sense.

One particularly widespread stereotype about India's Sunni Muslims is that they would rather educate their children in backward *madrasas* than give them a modern education. Many Muslim children are sent to religious schools, particularly in northern India. But this is partly because so many of the state schools around them function only intermittently. According to government statistics, on any given day one-third of teachers are absent from state schools. In Bihar, which has a large Muslim population, less than 3 per cent of state schools have electricity, and less than 20 per cent have toilets for their teachers.[21] Only a few schools have separate toilets for girls. Both Hindu and Muslim parents tend to keep their daughters away. But where there is a meaningful choice Muslim parents appear as keen as any others to take advantage.

I visited the old town of Hyderabad, known as Char Minar after

---

*In most Christian Churches in India, especially the Catholic Church, the caste system is almost wholly reproduced, with Brahmins as bishops and Dalits as their congregations, even though the latter vastly outnumber the former. In some parts of India Dalits are even allotted separate cemeteries.

the four minarets that dominate the skyline of this once Persianised princely capital. The mainly Muslim slums that dominate the still strikingly beautiful old town are abysmally served by the government. Many state schoolteachers are available only for private tuition, so the parents have set up a flourishing network of private schools, staffed by untrained or semi-trained teachers, which charge between 500 and 1500 rupees ($12–36) a month in fees. These schools all teach in English, in contrast to their state-run counterparts, which teach in either Telugu, the language of Andhra Pradesh, or Urdu. The private schools overwhelmingly cater to the children of the Muslim working classes – rickshaw-wallahs, vegetable-sellers, weavers and mechanics. Perhaps the most striking dimension to the schools is that there are as many girls as boys in the classrooms. About two-thirds of the schoolchildren in this area of Hyderabad go to private schools in a zone with a population of more than a million.[22] Very few of the girls are veiled.

They have incongruous names, such as Oxford Public School, Green Valley, California High and Windsor Diploma, that belie their makeshift character and humble settings in the tiny back alleys of Char Minar. However, although poverty is acute, many of the alleyways are spotlessly clean. The Muslim slum-dwellers of Hyderabad appear to have taken more than just schooling into their own hands. At one school, MA Ideal, named after its owner Mohammed Anwar, there was a sign hanging prominently that said: 'If Life Gives you Rocks, it is your Choice whether to Build a Bridge or a Wall'.

I talked to some of the mothers who were waiting for school to finish. Most were veiled, and not one of them was literate. The only schooling they had received had been (oral) training in Arabic schools so they could recite the Koran. They wanted more for their daughters. 'The world has changed since we were children,' said Rizwana Begum, whose husband is a rickshaw-wallah. 'We want our daughters to learn English so that they can get jobs. We want our daughters to have the opportunities we didn't have.' It was a refrain I heard often. Rizwana's husband spends a fifth of his 3500 rupees in monthly earnings on his children's education.

Inside the classroom the girls were reciting a rhyme about Jack and Jill. I asked who wanted a job when they were older. They all raised their hands, so I asked what they wanted to be. Their aspirations varied from doctor to lawyer to astronaut. A couple wanted to be tennis players, which was hardly surprising. Sania Mirza, a teenage Muslim from Hyderabad, had recently entered the top fifty in the WTA rankings and was India's number-one female player. Her poster could be seen everywhere in the city and throughout India. A Deobandi mullah had issued a *fatwa* forbidding her from wearing short skirts on the tennis court. Ms Mirza responded by dressing even more provocatively. As the minor controversy unfolded she took to wearing a T-shirt that said: 'Whatever'. Outside the Jama Masjid Mosque in Delhi, probably the most concentrated area of urban Muslims in India, Muslim street hawkers displayed equal insouciance. Posters of a scantily clad Mirza were on sale outside the hostels for Haj pilgrims. Some of the pictures had been doctored to make her clothes even more revealing. The player herself told the Indian media: 'It shouldn't matter whether my skirts are six inches or six feet in length as long as I am winning.' I asked the girls in Hyderabad what would happen if their husbands did not want them to work. 'Then we wouldn't marry them,' they said before clapping their hands over their mouths and giggling. They did not seem to be lacking in ambition.

Down the road I visited Jamila Amshad, a local Urdu-language poet and a formidable Muslim feminist. She operates a centre for slum women, many of whom are battered wives. 'Muslim women have two enemies who have much more in common with each other than they think,' she said. 'Our main enemy is Hindu communalism. They harbour nothing but ill will towards Muslims. Our other enemies are the Muslim mullahs who think women are just chattels.' Amshad is one among a growing number of articulate Muslim women in India who are seeking to overturn central precepts of the Muslim personal law on the statute books. Chief among their complaints is the custom of 'triple talaq', which permits Muslim husbands to divorce their wives by saying, 'I divorce you,' three times. Amshad reserved particular venom for the All India Muslim Personal Law Board, which, despite having no statutory position, speaks on behalf of the 'Muslim community'. The campaign to modernise India's Muslim personal law has yet to succeed. But it is clear that if Muslim law is to be effectively reformed in India, it must be Muslims who accomplish the change. 'Who elected the AIMPLB?' asked Amshad. 'By what right do they speak on my behalf? They are not defending Muslims. They are defending patriarchy.' On the wall of her office there was a poster that made me laugh: 'Do not give me a bangle, give me a pen.' Well-meaning charities often train illiterate slum women to make cheap trinkets.

My visit to Hyderabad coincided with an unrelated event in Lahore, one of Pakistan's largest cities, which was receiving much airtime in India. A group of Pakistani women had been badly manhandled when they embarked on a marathon run to highlight the restrictions women face in their country. The run was organised by Asma Jehangir, Pakistan's most courageous and well-known human rights lawyer. It was broken up by the police before it even got under way, since it was considered an un-Islamic activity for women. Some of the runners were dragged off by the police and stripped. Jehangir had described the event as an exercise in 'enlightened moderation', in a deliberate echo of a phrase used by President Musharraf to describe the type of Islam he would prefer to see in Pakistan. But the country's military ruler had done nothing to prevent the event from being suppressed. I wondered whether Sania Mirza would be hitting forehand winners if she had been born on the Pakistani side of the border.

The condition of India's Muslims is often presented as hopelessly backward. But democracy is as much ingrained within India's Muslim communities as it is in any other. It became a cliché after the plane attacks on the Twin Towers, which were principally carried out by Saudi nationals, to say India had produced no Muslim terrorists because it is a democracy. This cliché is inaccurate. Muslim mafia dons from Mumbai organised a series of terrorist bombings in the city in 1993 in revenge for the riots that followed the destruction of the Babri Masjid in Ayodhya a few months earlier. The blasts killed three hundred people. And there have been plenty of other bombing incidents, which, if the Indian police are to be believed (although often they should not), were orchestrated by Pakistan's ISI. In 2003 dozens of bystanders were killed in Mumbai by a series of car bombs set off by a group describing itself as the Gujarat Muslim Revenge Force. It was in apparent retaliation for the anti-Muslim pogroms that had taken place in Gujarat the previous year.

However, it is true that only a very small number of Indian Muslims have been recruited to the various global *jihads* that have occurred in recent decades, including the Kashmiri insurgency. In spite of India's proximity to Afghanistan, there were almost no Indian Muslims involved in the *jihad* against the Soviet occupation of that country in the 1980s. In contrast, countries as far away as the Philippines and Morocco, which have a fraction of India's Muslim population, were well represented in the ranks of the Afghan mujahedin. Partly this could have been because the Indian government, in contrast to the governments of most Islamic countries, enjoyed close relations with the Soviet Union and discouraged Indian involvement. But it could also be due to the fact India's Muslims − unlike the citizens of most Islamic countries − possess full freedom of speech, expression, worship and movement. Terrorism is a complex phenomenon: it would be far too simplistic to say it is caused by absence of democracy. But the right to air your grievances peacefully and in public must surely increase the likelihood that you will vent your resentment in a non-violent manner. Pakistan's population of 150 million is roughly equal to India's Muslim population. They share ethnicity, culture and religion. Yet Pakistani nationals are frequently linked to international terrorist networks while Indian Muslims rarely are. Perhaps what really divides India's Muslims from their counterparts in Pakistan is the political system under which they live.

Nevertheless, there are concerns that as India's economy continues to grow many of the country's Muslim communities are becoming more exposed to the type of Islam practised in the Middle East, where the traditions of worship are seen as less tolerant and more orthodox than those in India. This influence is perhaps most visible in the south Indian state of Kerala. Millions of Keralite Muslims have worked and continue to work in the Gulf States, particularly in Saudi Arabia and the United Arab Emirates. I visited 'Mini-Gulf', a leafy district about seventy miles south of the Keralite city of Cochin facing the Arabian Sea. Trichur, which includes the Mini-Gulf enclave, is a few miles to the south of Cranganore, a small town that is reputed to have played host to India's first mosque in the eighth century AD. Arabian dhows exploited the seasonal monsoon winds to ply the short route between the Gulf and southern India, bringing goods and the Word of the Prophet. Nowadays it is Keralite Muslims who cross the waters, bringing hefty remittances from employment in the Gulf.

The first thing that I noticed about Abdullah Kutty, a retired Keralite chef who had worked for almost thirty years in the Gulf, was that he spoke English with an Arabic accent. He gave me a proud tour of his 'dream home', which he had built with his earnings. Like many of his neighbours, who live in large white stucco houses adorned with fake Corinthian columns, Kutty grew up in a small fisherman's shack, built out of bamboo sticks and grass thatch. Now he has an upstairs, a downstairs, spare bedrooms and a large teak door fronting the entrance. The interior of his home is decorated with jackfruit wood. One of his sons owns a hotel and a shop in the Mini-Gulf's booming high street around the corner. Next to the shop is a large new mosque that was built with donations from Kutty and hundreds of other Gulf expatriates. Several times larger than the small place of worship it replaced, the mosque has been designed according to the prevalent Gulf style. Its minaret booms out the calls to prayer to a much larger area than before. 'We wanted to give something back to the community,' said Kutty, who did not otherwise appear to be particularly religious. He said that exposure to the Gulf had changed other things too. Most of the women had become more conservative in their dress. 'Now they are considered vulgar if they do not cover all parts of their body except the face,' he said.

The Gulf is having other, less obvious, impacts on Kerala's Muslims. Kutty has two daughters, one of whom is a software engineer working in the United Arab Emirates. The other was preparing for university entrance exams when I visited. Mrs Kutty, who is illiterate, wished she had had her daughters' opportunities. 'Nowadays the girls have to get a good education, otherwise they would never get a job in the Gulf,' she said. 'All the girls are studying so hard.' Since they are educated and financially independent, a small but growing number of the younger women in Mini-Gulf are now deciding for themselves whom they marry and when. 'In our day none of us had any choice,' said Mrs Kutty. If I had driven through the district and simply observed life on the streets, I might have formed a different impression. In the west we are trained to see *purdah* and the veil as signs of women's oppression. But sometimes they are corollaries of women's emergence from the home.

The newfound wealth of this once-impoverished class of Muslims has had other strange effects, which would have been hard to anticipate. Some Muslim families are paying wedding dowries to the families of their sons-in-law, in the form of cash, jewellery and white goods, such as washing machines. The practice of dowry was once confined to the Hindu upper castes, but it is spreading across India to the lower castes and to other religious communities, including Muslims. This popularisation could hardly be described as progress. But it is a marker of upward mobility. 'People are becoming more greedy,' said Abdullah Kutty.

In the state of Gujarat, which, as we have seen, is perhaps India's least tolerant, Muslims are also changing their dress code. About a year after the 2002 killings I was invited to a conference called Vibrant Gujarat, in which Narendra Modi, the Chief Minister, was showcasing the state's investment opportunities to foreign companies. As was customary with Modi, whom I had interviewed before, he turned aggressive the moment I asked about the treatment of Gujarati Muslims. He gave a blanket denial that there were any communal problems in his state: 'These are lies. You are listening to the propaganda of the pseudo-secularists,' he said.

Feeling somewhat despondent, I was about to catch a taxi to my hotel when a senior police officer introduced himself and invited me to dinner. The officer was in charge of one of the districts of Ahmedabad, Gujarat's commercial capital. My visit coincided with the state's annual festival of Navratri, in which thousands of young women and girls dress up in traditional costumes and compete against each other in picturesque mass dance competitions. The policeman took me to several of these Navratri events. Over the course of the evening he talked about what had happened during the riots. 'In districts where Muslims were killed on a large scale, the police were collaborating with the rioters,' he said. 'In districts where there were very few deaths, such as in mine, the senior police official had decided to uphold the law and protect innocent people. If you want to understand riots in India, that is all you need to know.' I could not be sure of his accuracy. But later I ran his name past a Muslim group in

Ahmedabad and they confirmed his reputation as a professional officer.

Later, the policeman took me to one of Ahmedabad's largest private-membership clubs, where there must have been at least two thousand young women swirling decorously under the floodlights in a large open courtyard within its walls. It was a captivating sight. They were wearing colourful skirts, many of which were decorated with sequins that flashed as they twirled. Thousands more were watching the competition, in which the girls were progressively eliminated by judges until there was just one dancer left. The prizes included Hero Honda motorbikes and a Tata Indica car. 'If I were a betting man, I would bet that there is not one Muslim here,' said the police officer. 'It is the same in the street parties that are taking place across Gujarat tonight. The Muslims have gone. Ten or twenty years ago both Hindus and Muslims would celebrate each other's festivals. Now that has almost completely stopped in Gujarat.' It was a melancholy thought.

The same gradual separation of communities is visible in the clothes Gujarati Muslims now wear. Whereas Muslim women would once wear saris, most now dress in the *salwar chameez*, which cover all of the body. Likewise, Gujarati Muslim men are likelier to grow beards and don a white cap. 'It is a very tragic divorce of two communities which used to be very interlinked and overlapping,' said Hanif Lakdawala, the non-practising Muslim we met in Chapter Four. 'Now the Muslims of Gujarat are standing out and saying: "If you want us to be different, we will be different."' The walls of Lakdawala's small flat in the centre of Ahmedabad are decorated with a picture of the god Ganesh, a painting of Jesus and a scene from the Prophet's life. He is married to a Christian from Kerala. They struck me as a quintessentially Indian couple: hospitable, tolerant and happy for all religions to get at least a passing mention in their lives. Earlier, during my unsatisfactory interview with him, Narendra Modi had said: 'In

Indonesia, which is a Muslim country, they have a picture of Ganesh on one of their currency notes. Why can't India's Muslims be more like that?' At the time I did not have an answer. But it struck me later that Hindus are a minority in Indonesia, just as Muslims are in India. If you were to follow Modi's line of thinking, the correct parallel would be for India to put a Crescent on one of its notes.

Jawaharlal Nehru and Mahatma Gandhi in conversation, 1946 *(Empics)*

Sonia Gandhi and her son
Rahul at the twenty-first
anniversary of the death of
Indira Gandhi *(Empics)*

Indira, 1979. The most formidable and ruthless leader India has yet seen *(Getty Images)*

Manmohan Singh, India's understated Prime Minister *(Olivia Arthur)*

An Indian soldier launches a rocket at armed Muslim militants along the
Line of Control, November 2001 *(Getty Images)*

Pakistan's President General Musharraf, September 2001 *(Reuters/Corbis)*

Indian tanks parade on Republic Day, 26 January 2000 *(Reuters/Corbis)*

Indian policemen form a security cordon around supporters of the
Bharatiya Janata Party (BJP) at a political rally *(Emmanuel Dunand/AFP/Getty Images)*

Delhi's new metro,
September 2005
(Getty Images)

Muslim women talk on their mobile phones outside a McDonald's restaurant
(Sohail Akbar)

Old India: villagers draw water at a well *(Getty Images)*

Bollywood megastar Amitabh Bachchan (far left) dances with Aishwarya Rai, Mumbai's leading lady and his son Abhishek Bachchan *(Empics)*

One of modern India's young couples *(Olivia Arthur)*

Manmohan Singh and his wife, Gursharan Kaur,
with President George W. Bush and Laura Bush *(Corbis)*

CHAPTER SEVEN

A TRIANGULAR DANCE

Why India's relations with the United States and China will shape the world in the twenty-first century

The likely emergence of China and India as new major global players – similar to the rise of Germany in the 19th century and America in the 20th century – will transform the geopolitical landscape, with impacts potentially as dramatic as those of the previous two centuries.

From *Mapping the Global Future*, the 2005 report of the US National Intelligence Council

Continental plates shift at a rate that is imperceptible to non-specialists. Then one day the pressure reaches breaking point. What for decades has gone undetected by almost everyone suddenly becomes apparent to all. Likewise, the ascent and descent of a great power often happens gradually until a single event makes the new situation plain. For Britain, the revealing event might have been the meek surrender to Japanese forces in 1942 of its reputed military garrison in Singapore, or perhaps the ignominious collapse of the planned Anglo-French–Israeli invasion of Egypt in 1956, when America withdrew its support for sterling. America's defining moment might have been in 1898, when it showed its big stick to Spain in Cuba and the Philippines, or in 1917 when

Woodrow Wilson's committal of troops to the Allies in the First World War proved decisive. Some argue the invasion of Iraq in 2003 might in future look like a moment of descent for the US.

For India, the big moment does not seem to have arrived yet, although some nationalists believe the country's ascent to great power status should be charted from May 1998, when New Delhi ordered the underground testing of five nuclear weapons devices. That remains to be proved. India's rise in the early twenty-first century is widely expected, but it is not yet fully assured. The 1998 tests can certainly be read as a signal of New Delhi's ambitions. But there are questions about what precisely India achieved by becoming an openly declared nuclear weapons state. Two weeks later Pakistan followed suit and tested six nuclear warheads (symbolically detonating one more than India). In the perception of much of the international community India's conventional military superiority over Pakistan had at a stroke been converted into a level nuclear playing field. China, meanwhile, which had all but arranged Pakistan's nuclear capability, remains many years – possibly decades – in advance of India's capability.

There is another barometer of the rise of great powers: economic clout, of which military prowess is more a consequence than a cause. Modern textile production and steam power propelled Britain's rise in the eighteenth and nineteenth centuries, while the internal combustion engine, railroads and, later, computers fuelled America's rise. On this measure, India's successes in software and 'complex manufacturing' are pushing the country forward as an economic power, although at a less rapid rate than neighbouring China. If India maintains its current average annual growth rate of about 7 per cent, the size of its economy will double every twelve years and India will overtake Japan some time in the 2020s to become the third-largest economy in the world. India's recent economic expansion is sufficiently credible to have prompted a global reassessment of the country's potential. Before I moved to India, I had been living in Washington, DC. Any mention of India by the US administration or by Washington's community of think tanks was usually followed by mention of Pakistan: it was always 'India-Pakistan'. In the last few years this has changed. As the jargon goes, India is no longer 'hyphenated' to Pakistan (although Pakistan remains hyphenated to India). India is now hyphenated to China: 'China-India'. This recalibration has very little to do with nuclear weapons. By the same token, nobody talks of Pakistan's coming superpower status in the wake of its 1998 nuclear tests.

India and China both possess a third attribute that was lacking in Britain but was present to some extent in the United States – a large population. This can be both a strength and a weakness. The population density of China and India will lead to growing strains on their environments and on their scarce supplies of arable land. Unless they seriously qualify the nature of their economic growth, this could lead to large-scale environmental crises as the century progresses. But if the two Asian giants can sustain their economic growth rates, then sheer weight of numbers will ensure they overtake all other economies, including eventually the United States – although that will take several decades longer. However, the disadvantages of having a large population could check and even reverse this advantage if the two countries permit indefinite environmental degradation. This would also impose an unbearable cost on everyone else. Laos and Bolivia can degrade their resources as much as they wish. But if China and India fail to take environmental sustainability into account over the coming decades, they will export their suffering to the rest of the world. We will look briefly in the final chapter at India's current approach to the environment. But it is worth mentioning in passing that America, China and India – the large nation states to which the twenty-first century is expected to belong – are today probably the three most important obstacles to an international consensus to tackle global warming.

*

In 1947 India viewed itself as a 'moral superpower'. It was ahead of other Third World countries in achieving independence and was the only significant colony to have freed itself through largely peaceful means. The unique qualities of India's freedom struggle and the deep charisma of Mahatma Gandhi inspired people around the world, including Martin Luther King, who applied Gandhi's form of non-violent disobedience to the civil rights movement in the United States. India stood tall because it had won by the power of persuasion rather than through the barrel of a gun. The country's elite believed it could project its power around the world in much the same way. With hindsight, this was overly optimistic. Britain, for all its faults and pomposity, was a relatively flexible colonial power compared to the French, Dutch, Belgians, Germans and Japanese. It was only able to sustain its rule over India because of the acquiescence, or at least the tolerance, of most Indians. When it came to a choice between military suppression or departure, Britain opted to leave – albeit ineptly and too late. One of the great characteristics of Gandhi and Nehru was that the two London-trained lawyers understood that Britain was ultimately vulnerable to argument. Gandhi was an uncannily good tactician of the political situation in which he found himself.[1] But as we have seen with some of his economic ideas, what worked in the context of the freedom struggle did not necessarily translate into good policy for an independent nation state. In foreign policy, if not in economics, Gandhi and Nehru were generally of one mind.

More than in any other sphere of government, including the economy, Nehru dominated India's foreign policy in the first fifteen years after independence. His control was all-encompassing. He held the posts of Prime Minister and Foreign Minister until he died. Nehru was the biggest force behind the creation of the Non-Aligned Movement, which was launched in Bandung, Indonesia, in 1955 and included global statesmen such as Tito of Yugoslavia, Nasser of Egypt and Sihanouk of Cambodia. Chou En

Lai, the Prime Minister of China, and second-in-command to Mao Zedong, was present at the Bandung Conference, which announced that a large chunk of the developing world would be neutral in the Cold War rivalry between the US and the USSR. However, China's support for non-alignment was to prove rhetorical and even, from India's point of view, deceitful. Meanwhile, John Foster Dulles, the hardline US Secretary of State, denounced India's moral non-alignment as 'immoral'.[2] India, in the eyes of western Cold War hawks, was preaching freedom and self-determination to the west while conniving with regimes such as China and Egypt that were snuffing out the freedom of their own people. As time wore on, India moved increasingly closer to the Soviet camp. During the decades of non-alignment, India got most of its armaments from the USSR, and it conducted extensive barter trade with the Soviets, in which the two economies swapped goods rather than trading with cash. Although India was not formally part of the Soviet Bloc, ties were extensive and warm at many levels.

Nevertheless, one of the key pillars of Nehru's foreign policy was condemnation of the nuclear arms race between the US and the USSR. He maintained a constant effort to persuade the superpowers of the merits of nuclear disarmament. But his interventions were increasingly ignored. Perhaps because Nehru came to realise global disarmament was an impractical goal, he authorised the creation of an Indian civil nuclear programme that could at some stage in the future prove useful for developing nuclear weapons. He never formally endorsed the nuclear weapons enthusiasm of his advisers, most notably Homi Bhabha, India's premier nuclear scientist. But it is hard to imagine that someone as intelligent as Nehru could have been unaware of the choices he had created.[3]

Another pillar of Nehru's foreign policy was friendship with China. He believed close relations between the two countries would be the axis around which a post-colonial world order would emerge. '*Hindi-Chini Bhai Bhai*' – Indians and Chinese Are Brothers! – was the oft-chanted slogan in Delhi celebrating what was seen as a new era of friendship. India's language was idealistic. And it was mostly self-delusion. China's leaders were perplexed by India's limited grasp of realpolitik. Although Beijing was communist, it had a more traditional vision of diplomacy than India. Quite early into the new era, two issues began to bedevil relations: China's suppression of autonomy in Tibet; and a dispute over the correct dividing line on the 3500-kilometre border between India and China. In 1959 India gave sanctuary to the young Dalai Lama, who had fled Tibet to escape the People's Liberation Army.* Although India imposed the condition that Tibet's spiritual leader refrain from conducting political activities on Indian soil, the decision to grant sanctuary to the Tibetans needled the Chinese.

More ominously, Beijing started to publish maps that redrew many sections of the lengthy Himalayan border between the two countries. Indians called this 'cartographic aggression'. Nehru, whose idealism had not flagged, found it increasingly hard to read the Chinese. The giant neighbours were rapidly becoming estranged. 'It is difficult to know what is in their mind,' said Nehru. 'They smile when they say the most callous and ruthless things. Mao [Zedong] told me with a smile that he was not afraid of atomic war . . . With the Chinese you never know and have to be prepared for unexpected reactions. This may partly be due to their isolation, but it is mainly in the Chinese character I think.'[4]

In 1962 the People's Liberation Army troops took their Indian counterparts completely by surprise when they flooded across the Himalayan border and drove back India's ill-equipped forces. After a short and one-sided encounter, the Chinese declared a ceasefire along an obscure contour that remains the dividing line

---

*The Dalai Lama is still based in India, in the Himalayan town of Dharamshala.

between the two in India's north-eastern region. The thin slice of territory occupied by their troops lacked any strategic value to the Chinese. Beijing's aim had been to cut New Delhi down to size. It was a humiliation for India. But it was a disaster for Nehru. Political opponents now openly mocked his high-sounding words of non-alignment and peaceful coexistence. Nehru never fully recovered from the shock, visibly ageing and shrinking in stature. Within eighteen months he was dead. Shortly thereafter, China exploded its first hydrogen bomb. It was a tragic postscript to a life of tireless and often inspiring international statesmanship. With ruthless precision, Beijing had ensured that Nehru's fond ideals of Asian brotherhood and nuclear disarmament had amounted to nothing. It was a harsh tutorial in the ways of the world.

A third pillar of Nehru's foreign policy was Third World solidarity, particularly when it came to dealings with the United States, which many Indians saw as a neo-colonial successor to Britain. Encounters between Nehru and his US counterparts, Presidents Truman and Eisenhower, were notable for their frostiness. In addition to his distaste for American capitalism, Nehru carried traits of upper-class British snobbery towards what he saw as America's brash materialism. On one occasion in New York, he disdained a meeting that had been set up with American businessmen, asking his aides why he should waste his time on millionaires. For their part, the Americans found it as hard to deal with Indian diplomats as the Chinese had. At the time, India appeared to believe that the 'power of argument' mattered more than the 'argument of power'.[5] But America was more accustomed to giving than receiving moral lectures. Many in Washington found it irksome that a country that was accepting so much US food aid was pontificating about how Washington should run the world (or how India would run the world). 'Most American negotiators are so taken aback by what they perceive as Indian arrogance that they find it difficult to engage in lengthy and complicated negotiations with New Delhi,' writes Stephen Cohen, a former US State Department official and a leading scholar on India. 'Many American officials hate to deal with the Indians compared, say, with Pakistanis, Chinese, or Europeans.'[6] Nowadays, however, Americans find an India that better understands the uses of 'hard power'. In spite of some lingering prickliness, Washington is much keener to engage with New Delhi at greater length and across a range of security and commercial issues.

However, American diplomacy could also prove to be counterproductive. Indians were given a reminder in 2005 of the degree to which American leaders had once disliked their country when the US National Security Archives released transcripts of conversations between President Nixon and Henry Kissinger, his Secretary of State, dating from 1971. India was by then clearly within the Soviet sphere of influence, while Pakistan was an ally of the United States. China had split from the Soviets and had been coaxed and wooed by Nixon into a rapprochement. Pakistan's military regime played an instrumental role in helping bring about the US–China détente. When it became clear that India would intervene in the Pakistan civil war that was raging in East Pakistan, where the Pakistan army was brutally suppressing the Bangladeshi separatist movement, Nixon ordered the nuclear-armed USS *Enterprise* into the Bay of Bengal to act as a deterrent to Indian action. To Indira Gandhi, India's Prime Minister, who nonetheless did intervene and whose actions helped create Bangladesh, America's implied threat was redolent of Britain's nineteenth-century 'gunboat diplomacy'. The situation very nearly developed into a much wider international war. Kissinger said publicly that the United States would not come to India's assistance if China intervened in the conflict, which was a green light for Beijing to do so.

Nevertheless, Indians were still shocked in 2005 to read what Nixon and Kissinger had said about their country. 'What the Indians need is a mass famine,' said Nixon. 'They're such bastards,' said Kissinger, who then called Indira Gandhi a 'bitch'. Nixon reckoned: 'World opinion is on the Indian side but they are such a treacherous and slippery people.' Kissinger responded: 'I think we've got to tell [the Chinese] that some movement on their part . . . toward the Indian border could be very significant.' Later they agreed to tell the Chinese that 'if you are ever going to move, this is the time.'[7] Fortunately for India, the Chinese did not move, as their intervention would probably have dragged the Soviets and consequently the Americans into the conflict too. There is no guessing where it might have ended. The incident goes some way to explaining India's lingering mistrust of the US and Indira Gandhi's paranoia about America from then on. India has at times been guilty of preachy moralism. But the United States, at times, could be accused of reckless amoralism.

In a more polite phase, Kissinger once said, 'India lives in a dangerous neighbourhood.' This was perhaps an understatement. India watched Pakistan and China move ever closer, proclaiming their friendship with each other to be as 'high as the mountains and as deep as the ocean'. Given the circumstances, it is unsurprising that New Delhi pushed ahead with the development of nuclear weapons. In the decades after 1962 many in India thought China was attempting to 'encircle' their country by building close relations with some of India's unfriendlier neighbours, such as Pakistan, Burma/Myanmar and, to some extent, Nepal, even though the latter is the only officially Hindu country in the world (India's constitution being secular). China supported Pakistan's stance on Kashmir whenever it came to a vote in the UN Security Council. The Soviets would invariably support India. After the 1971 crisis in East Pakistan, which had humiliated Islamabad, split the country in two and led to a collapse of Pakistan's second military regime, China became Pakistan's largest arms supplier, replacing America, whose interest in the region had noticeably waned. In the 1980s the US resumed the flow of preferential arms sales to Pakistan, which offered itself as the frontline state in

Washington's drive to reverse the 1979 Soviet invasion of Afghanistan.

Many in Washington's nuclear non-proliferation community, particularly in the State Department, continue to believe that it was deeply irresponsible of India to develop nuclear weapons. But the United States had at times followed policies in the region that inadvertently increased the likelihood that India would do so. In addition, New Delhi had another, more specifically Indian, reason for going nuclear. This was bound up in the country's acute sensitivity to what it saw as modern forms of colonialism. In 1968 the five nuclear powers – the US, Britain, France, the USSR and China – persuaded most non-nuclear countries to sign the Nuclear Non-Proliferation Treaty. This enshrined the existing five as the world's only official nuclear weapons states, and promised civil nuclear-power assistance to those that pledged to forgo nuclear weapons. Countries as diverse as Iran and North Korea signed the treaty, but India did not. And since India did not, Pakistan did not. Indian diplomats brought to bear all their mastery of detail, love of rhetoric, sensitivity about status and resentments of the west to condemn the treaty as unjust. New Delhi called it 'nuclear apartheid'. Indira Gandhi stepped up India's clandestine programme to develop nuclear devices.

In 1974 she ordered a series of 'peaceful nuclear tests'. India's polite fiction was that nuclear devices could be used for civilian purposes, such as creating tunnels and building dams. Zulfikar Ali Bhutto, Pakistan's Prime Minister, responded to the tests by saying that Pakistan would, if necessary, 'eat grass' in order to match India's capabilities. But all Islamabad needed to do was request help from China, which then supplied Pakistan with much of the technology to develop both nuclear warheads and the missile delivery systems. In addition, Pakistan's notorious A. Q. Khan, who later became known as the father of the country's nuclear programme, had in the 1970s stolen the blueprints from his Dutch employer that outlined the process by which uranium is enriched into weapons-grade material. By 1987, when India and Pakistan almost came to blows following the former's 'Brass Tacks' operation – a large-scale military exercise near the Pakistani border, which India still says Pakistan misinterpreted as a prelude to war (Islamabad claims its interpretation was reasonable) – both were thought to possess rudimentary nuclear devices. It was only a matter of time before they tested them.

Even before the 1998 Indian and Pakistani nuclear tests, there were growing apprehensions about how easy it would be for one to misread the other in the 'fog of war'. The fear was mostly directed at Islamabad, since New Delhi had unveiled a nuclear doctrine which proclaimed India as a 'no first use' nuclear power. This meant that New Delhi would use nuclear weapons only if its opponent had used them first. Pakistan, on the other hand, had proclaimed itself to be 'first strike' power, a stance that mirrored America's in the Cold War, when the US had fewer conventional forces in Europe than the Soviet-led Warsaw Pact. (The Soviets, like India, had maintained a stance of 'no first use'.) As the inferior power in terms of conventional military forces, with a ratio of roughly three to two in India's favour, Pakistan has been tempted to rattle the nuclear sabre every now and then. Many Pakistani strategists believe it is in Islamabad's interests to create doubts among New Delhi's decision-makers about how easily and quickly India might cross Pakistan's 'nuclear red line' should it initiate conventional military conflict. What would happen in practice is anybody's guess. Whenever tensions between the two countries have risen to high levels in the last two decades Pakistan has issued veiled warnings to India about the risks of nuclear escalation.

It was May 2002, arguably the most dangerous moment in the extensive history of dangerous moments between India and Pakistan. India, as we saw in the last chapter, had deployed most of its army along the Pakistani border following the failed suicide attack on its parliament the previous December. After an initial scare in January, when India had been on the verge of ordering some kind of military operation across the Line of Control in Kashmir, tensions had subsided. Under pressure from the Bush administration – which, among other things, feared that a conflict between India and Pakistan would compromise its operations in Afghanistan – President Musharraf had given a national broadcast in which he had pledged to crack down on what he called Pakistan's 'state-within-a-state' of Islamist groups. But the crackdown never amounted to much. Groups such as Lashkar-e-Toiba, which India had specifically blamed for the suicide attack, simply changed their names and shifted their headquarters from Pakistan's province of Punjab to Azad Kashmir, the Pakistan-held section of Kashmir. Once the snows started to melt in late March, terrorist infiltration across the LOC into Indian Kashmir resumed at even higher levels than in previous years. The tension was escalating again.

Then, in mid-May, an Islamist terrorist group carried out a particularly bloody attack on the residential quarters of an Indian army regiment in Kaluchak, a town in Jammu–Kashmir. The suicide terrorists butchered thirty-four people, including wives and children of the soldiers. India's army, which had been twiddling its thumbs on the border for months, pushed hard for New Delhi to retaliate quickly. Atal Behari Vajpayee, India's Prime Minister, flew to Kashmir and delivered a speech to Indian soldiers at an army camp very close to the LOC. He spoke of an impending 'decisive battle' to overcome the forces of terrorism. There was open talk in India of a 'punitive strike' across the LOC on Pakistani army positions and the terrorist training camps they were allegedly protecting. The world's eyes shifted to Musharraf to see how he would respond.

At this point I flew to Islamabad to interview Musharraf. Conflict was expected to break out at any moment. A few days earlier the President had ordered the testing of Pakistan's long-range nuclear-capable ballistic missiles in an unsubtle hint at what might happen if India crossed the LOC or the international border. Pakistani officials, who had honed the language of nuclear threat over many years, had suggested to journalists that Islamabad would consider the nuclear option if India launched a conventional military strike. At the UN, Pakistan's ambassador said: 'If India reserves the right to use conventional weapons, how can Pakistan – a weaker power – be expected to rule out all means of deterrence?'[8] Immediately before my interview, Pakistan's leader gave another national broadcast. He was dressed in full uniform and his voice and expression were deeply sombre. It seemed as though he was priming Pakistan for conflict. But General Musharraf's address included a coded and conditional pledge that Pakistan would suspend infiltration across the LOC if India stood down. He could not explicitly promise to halt terrorist infiltration, since a specific pledge would be tantamount to an admission that the Pakistani army had indeed been sponsoring it all along – a position Islamabad continues to deny. 'As you know, the enemy's forces are deployed on our borders,' General Musharraf told the nation.

> The enemy has brought forward its army, navy and air force. They are being faced by the Pakistani army, navy and the air force and they are serving as a bulwark. The entire nation is with the armed forces and will shed the last drop of its blood but would not allow any harm to come to the motherland. Tension is at its height . . . We do not want war, but if war is thrust upon us, we would respond with full might, and give a befitting reply. I would now like to convey a message to the world community. Pakistan does not want war. Pakistan will not be the one to initiate war. We want peace in the region. Let me also assure the world community that Pakistan is doing nothing across the Line of Control and Pakistan will

never allow the export of terrorism anywhere in the world from within Pakistan.* Now I want to give a message to my Kashmiri brothers and sisters. Kashmir resides in the heart of every Pakistani. Pakistan will always fulfil its duty of providing moral, political and diplomatic support to the cause of Kashmir. Pakistan will always support the Kashmiri struggle for liberation.[9]

Having watched this somewhat unnerving broadcast, I drove with my Pakistani colleague, Farhan Bokhari, to Musharraf's official military residence in the town of Rawalpindi, a few miles from Islamabad. We were shown into a stately living room. A few moments later Musharraf appeared. He had changed his outfit: in place of the military regalia, he was dressed in an open-necked shirt and casual slacks. He was smiling and relaxed enough to crack a few jokes. The broadcast had been aimed at many audiences – Indians, Americans and a cross-section of Pakistanis, including the Kashmiri militant groups and the army – so it had contained a number of contradictory messages. But our one-hour interview was specifically for a western audience. General Musharraf modified his demeanour. I asked him about the threat of nuclear weapons. 'Pakistan is a deterrence country and is very capable of guarding its honour and dignity,' he began.

But I would not like to discuss the nuclear issue. It would be very irresponsible for a statesman to discuss nuclear weapons. There's a lot of tension and war hysteria going on. Nobody wants to go to war. There is no walking over

---

*Musharraf's language was precise. According to Pakistan, Azad Kashmir is not techni-cally part of sovereign Pakistan since Islamabad believes the whole of Kashmir is in dispute under UN law. It is also worth noting the tenses he used: 'Pakistan *is doing* noth-ing across the Line of Control'. If Musharraf had said 'has been doing' or 'will do' the inference would have been different .

here by any side. I am sure the Indians know this. Sanity
demands an avoidance of war but at the same time in
pursuit of peace you can't compromise on honour or
dignity. One has to strike a balance between maintaining
honour and dignity and going for peace.

For a western audience, General Musharraf altered his vocabulary.
Instead of responding with 'full might', Pakistan would maintain
its 'honour and dignity'. However, the meaning remained the
same as that conveyed in Musharraf's TV broadcast: Pakistan
considered nuclear weapons to be a military option; and Pakistan
would resume its support for cross-border terrorism unless India
agreed to talks about the status of Kashmir. The two points were
linked. I asked the President about the apparent pledge he had
made in the broadcast to put a complete stop to the terrorist
incursion, and wondered whether he was using the so-called
nuclear bluff to force India to the negotiating table. He put me
straight about the pledge on terrorism:

I said nothing was happening along the Line of Control
now. Whether India accepts it or not, they cannot be the
accusers and judges both . . . I am a realist. There are very
serious problems between the two countries which are a
cause of tensions which have given rise to three wars here.
Other than wars, there are battles going on every second
day. People are dying on the borders, along the Line of
Control. Why should we not address these problems? This
is no bluff. This is realism. Unfortunately we don't see the
same realism across the border.[10]

At the end of the interview Musharraf gave us each his customary
gift, a mantelpiece clock embossed with the Pakistani national
flag. I am now the owner of three identical Pakistani national
clocks.

I hitched a lift back to New Delhi on a British government plane. Jack Straw, who was then Britain's Foreign Minister, was in the region to try to dissuade both countries from embarking on a conflict. A few days later, Richard Armitage, the US Deputy Secretary of State, travelled on the same route. A former soldier himself, Armitage emerged from his meeting with General Musharraf smiling. Later that day he shuttled to New Delhi, carrying with him a pledge that Pakistan would 'permanently' put an end to terrorist infiltration across the LOC. This beefed-up pledge was enough for Delhi to put an end to the crisis. The following week Donald Rumsfeld, the US Defense Secretary, visited both capitals to put a seal on the new situation. Not for the first time, the Americans, assisted by the British, had managed to pull India's and Pakistan's chestnuts out of the fire. Washington had even persuaded China to have a quiet word in Musharraf's ear. The becalming role that the US administration played in 2002, which demanded skill and persistence, made a pleasant contrast with the high-wire games in which Nixon and Kissinger had indulged thirty years earlier.

India was not a frontline state in the Cold War despite its close ties to Moscow. But the collapse of the Soviet Union opened up new possibilities that New Delhi has done much to exploit. The gradual improvement in relations between the United States and India in the last ten to fifteen years has been matched by a gradual cooling of relations between the United States and China. The logic of diplomacy in today's unipolar world is far more fluid than it was during the Cold War. Over the same period India also started to mend fences with China, although New Delhi and Beijing have yet to agree on where exactly those fences should be delineated. Mindful perhaps of its own (admittedly low-level) separatist problems in the country's north-western province of Xingjiang, Beijing has also watered down criticisms of India's position on Kashmir. Some of China's separatist groups are thought to have links with Islamist groups that are sponsored by Pakistan, even though there is no suggestion that Islamabad has facilitated these links. In 2004 China was given another reason to become more even-handed towards India and Pakistan when it was revealed that A. Q. Khan, the father of Pakistan's nuclear programme, had sold nuclear secrets during the 1980s and 1990s to any country that was prepared to pay. Since much of the technology that Khan sold originally came from China, the revelations were embarrassing to Beijing. Buyers in Khan's 'international nuclear Wal-Mart' included Libya, North Korea, probably Iran and possibly Saudi Arabia. In addition, strategists in Beijing reportedly concluded it would be counter-productive to back a rapid expansion of Pakistan's nuclear arsenal because that would spark a nuclear arms race with India, which would bring India more rapidly up to nuclear parity with China.[11]

There are two even more important reasons why China sought better relations with India and why it is likely to push for further improvements over the coming years. First, India is a much more hard-nosed neighbour now than it was during the years of non-alignment. The May 1998 nuclear tests forced China to sit up and take notice of a different India that had all but abandoned the diplomatic philosophy of Gandhi and Nehru. In the early 1990s New Delhi had asked Beijing to declare China's nuclear weapons were 'no first use' vis-à-vis India. Beijing said there was no point in proclaiming a nuclear stance towards a country that did not possess nuclear weapons.[12]

A few days before the 1998 tests, George Fernandes, India's Defence Minister, stated publicly that China was the biggest threat to India's security. After the tests took place, Atal Behari Vajpayee wrote to President Bill Clinton stating that China, not Pakistan, was the principal motivator in India's decision to go nuclear. Since China had provided Pakistan with most of its nuclear know-how, India's claim had some credibility. In public Vajpayee said:

Millions of Indians have viewed this occasion as the beginning of the rise of a strong and self-confident India. I fully share this assessment and this dream. India has never considered military might as the ultimate measure of national strength. It is a necessary component of overall national strength. I would, therefore, say that the greatest meaning of the tests is that they have given India *shakti* [elemental power], they have given India strength, they have given India self-confidence.[13]

China condemned the tests, but its protests were unemotional. In June 2001 India became one of the first countries to endorse the Bush administration's plans for Theatre Missile Defense – or 'Star Wars II'. China condemned the concept as dangerously destabilising to the established global nuclear order. Washington's plans to build a space-based shield against nuclear weapons have since run into technical and financial difficulties, and the terrorist attacks of 9/11 also made Star Wars II seem irrelevant to the principal security challenges facing the United States. But India's unequivocal stance was not lost on Beijing. China remained critical of India and still insists, somewhat quixotically, that the latter should roll back its nuclear programme and scrap its existing nuclear weapons. But there is now also a wary tone of respect in China's admonitions that had been glaringly absent in previous decades.

The second reason for the thawing of tensions between India and China is economic. China embarked on economic reform in 1978, so it has a thirteen-year head start on India, which began to abolish the Licence Raj only in 1991. Partly because of this, China has roughly double India's per capita income and more than four times India's level of exports. However, in the last few years India's economy has begun to accelerate. In 2000 trade between India and China was less than $2 billion, but by 2006 it was almost $20 billion. Although this is a small proportion of

China's overall trade with the world, India is now China's fastest-growing trading partner, and vice versa. Much of the new trade flows have been driven by China's almost limitless appetite for commodities, including iron ore and steel, which India is supplying in ever larger quantities. But India has also been selling vehicle components to foreign multinationals based in China and providing software design for the next generation of high-tech cars. Today, the monetary value of the software embedded in a vehicle exceeds the value of its hardware. Many of India's software companies have also set up shop in China. India's facility with both the English language and information technology is not matched by China. Many of the foreign multinationals based in China, whose investments account for half of China's exports, use the Shanghai or Hong Kong offices of India's IT companies to supply their software and provide them with systems maintenance. India's competitive pharmaceutical sector has also set up production sites in China.

It was not expected to turn out like this. When China joined the World Trade Organisation in 2000, Indian companies were terrified their domestic market would be flooded by cheap Chinese goods. The Indian media buzzed with stories of Chinese umbrellas, batteries and fireworks that were pricing their local competitors out of business. But India has achieved a modest trade surplus with China for several consecutive years. This has drastically changed Indian perceptions of China from being a commercial threat to a potential partner. So strong is global demand both for Chinese goods and Indian services that the two countries have in many respects ceased to see each other as conventional competitors. 'People in India used to say it was China and not India, then they said it was China against India, but if you look at any number of sectors the real story is China *and* India,' said N. Srinivasan, head of the Confederation of Indian Industry. 'The economies of India and China are complementary.'[14]

Assuming that neither country's economy goes off the rails in the next five to ten years – which is, admittedly, a sizeable assumption – then the growth in volume of trade between India and China will make it one of the most important trading relationships in the world. Eventually, demography suggests it will be the world's largest trading relationship. Both countries have placed trade and economics at the heart of their new diplomacy. Nowadays, negotiations to create 'free trade agreements' dominate much of their diplomats' time. China is ahead of India, but the latter is catching up; both countries have concluded trade agreements with the Association of South East Asian Nations; and India is hoping to emulate China's growing trade relations with South America. At the global level China, India, Brazil and South Africa lead the G20, a bloc of twenty developing countries that has become a weighty player at world trade liberalisation talks. There is also a proposal for a bilateral trade deal between India and China, although this would take years to negotiate.

Does all this mean China and India have entered a genuine era of friendship? Proponents of free trade are fond of the aphorism: 'When countries start trading goods, they stop trading blows.' It might be overstated, but clearly, as economic links strengthen and as increasing numbers of Indians visit China and vice versa, disagreements over the exact position of the international boundary, or the status of the Dalai Lama, become progressively easier to manage. The two countries have held fifteen rounds of negotiations on the border dispute and claim to be within touching distance of a final settlement. At a summit in New Delhi in 2005 India recognised China's sovereignty over Tibet. In exchange, China recognised India's sovereignty over the Himalayan state of Sikkim, a small (and nominally independent) kingdom that New Delhi formally annexed in the 1970s. At the close of the summit between Wen Jiabao, China's Prime Minister, and Manmohan Singh, India's Prime Minister, Singh announced: 'Together India and China can reshape the world.' It was a bold statement. By implication he was also warning that if India and China were again to mismanage their relations, they would both be handicapped in their objective of creating a 'multipolar' world. Talk of 'multipolarity' is a polite way of hoping for a world in which there are stronger limits on America's scope to impose its will on others. This is a goal shared by China and India.

There is, though, another pertinent aphorism (this time Chinese): 'No mountain can accommodate two tigers.' Whether strong trading ties between India and China will remove the threat of conflict between the two, as some western commentators believe is true at all times and of all countries, is questionable. But for the time being the mountain is teeming with easy pickings. At the very least, stronger trading ties between India and China cannot hurt. The two countries have developed very different mindsets to the outlooks that led to war in 1962. India is no longer so idealistic, talking much less of Third World solidarity and much more about its own national interests. Although it has not stated so openly, most observers assume China will require peaceful relations with India if it is to achieve its ambition of becoming a global power.

Tectonic plates are gradually shifting. It is an intriguing phase of international relations that is likely to last for a decade or two before China becomes a genuine political force on the global stage. There are potential obstacles to the parallel rise of India. But the odds are that it will overcome most of them, not least because the United States now explicitly desires the rise of India.

In March 2005 the Bush administration did something none of its predecessors had done: it announced it would play midwife to the birth of a new great power. The country in question was India. Specifically, the US spokesman said America wanted 'to help India become a major world power in the twenty-first century. We understand fully the implications, including military implications, of that statement.'[15] Washington's declaration coincided with the publication of a CIA report that identified India as the key global 'swing state' of the twenty-first century.[16] The CIA also predicted that India would become the world's fourth most powerful country by 2012, as measured by a combination of economic, military and technological strength.[17] The view was that building a strong partnership with India, which US officials had repeatedly described as a 'natural ally',[18] would help prolong American power in the coming decades. This unprecedented statement was unusual not only for its originality but also for its candour. What motivated it?

US government officials offer any number of explanations for their pro-India enthusiasm. The most often cited is that India is by far the largest democracy in the world. When George W. Bush came to office, he offered Robert Blackwill, a senior adviser, any ambassadorial posting he wanted.* Blackwill, who had been a senior arms negotiator during the Cold War, instantly chose India. Bush said to him: 'A billion people and it's a democracy. Ain't that something?'[19] Second, in spite of India's nuclear tests, which had triggered US sanctions on the export of sensitive, or 'dual-use', technology to India, the Bush administration was impressed by India's 'responsible stewardship' of its nuclear arsenal. In contrast to Pakistan, which had been passing on the technology to anyone who had the cash, India was considered to have a good system of export control. Third, almost two million people of Indian origin based in the United States had become a strong new voice in US politics. Indian-Americans are the richest ethnic group in the United States, with an average annual income of more than fifty thousand dollars. India also provides the highest number of foreign students in the US and takes up the largest share of the annual H1B visas for foreign technical workers, principally software engineers. India is also emerging as a potentially

---

*Blackwill was one of the so-called Vulcans, led by Condoleezza Rice, who provided foreign policy advice to Bush's 2000 presidential campaign.

vast new market for American products, albeit not as large as China.

US officials rarely mention China in this context, in spite of the fact that it provides the real motivation for Washington's sponsorship of India's great power ambitions. Because of India's sheer size and the nature of its political system, it is seen as the only country that could counterbalance China's rise as a global power. America has watched China's emergence with growing anxiety even as US companies have made the most of China's economic openness. The expected loosening of the Chinese Communist Party's grip on the country's political system that was expected to come as a result of economic liberalisation has not taken place; nor has China watered down its objective of incorporating what it sees as the renegade province of Taiwan into the motherland. On the contrary, China's national assembly passed a law in 2005 authorising military action against Taiwan should it declare formal independence from China. Taiwan is a military ally of the United States. A series of Pentagon reports have also voiced increasingly strident concerns about China's rapidly accelerating defence expenditure, which some US sources estimate is far higher than Beijing is prepared to admit. There is also concern in the United States, and elsewhere, about China's stated ambitions of developing a 'blue water' (far-reaching) navy that would project China's power into the Indian Ocean and beyond.

Advisers to the Bush administration and former officials are more explicit about linking America's strategy on India to its strategy on China. Ashley Tellis, an Indian-born analyst at the Carnegie Endowment in Washington, was Robert Blackwill's nuclear and military adviser in New Delhi between 2001 and 2003. Among others, he and Blackwill argued successfully that the United States should recognise India's nuclear weapons status. In an influential report in 2005 Tellis wrote: 'There is a real fear that China might some day turn its rising economic and military power against America. In this context the US needs to look at a re-ordering of their relationship with India which today is not only a key ally in the war against terror but a counterbalance in Asia against China's dominance.'[20] Blackwill, who had left the Bush administration a few months earlier, said: 'Why should the US want to check India's missile capability in ways that could lead to China's permanent nuclear dominance over democratic India?'[21]

Their argument won out. In July 2005 Manmohan Singh visited Washington and was offered a nuclear deal that went far beyond New Delhi's expectations. The United States offered to accept India's nuclear weapons status, reinstate the export of nuclear fuel for India's civil nuclear programme and lift all remaining restrictions on the export of sensitive technologies to India. In return India would tighten export controls to prevent the sale of dual use technology to other countries, accept international monitoring of its civil nuclear plants, and erect more credible walls between its civilian and military sectors – particularly in respect to the space programme. (India is believed to have made satellite launch technology available to its ballistic missile scientists.) In other words, India would become the first, and possibly the last, country to be accepted informally into the club of official nuclear states. (Formal international recognition would be beyond reach since that would involve tearing up the non-proliferation treaty.) Singh was accorded the maximum honour bestowed on a global statesman during the visit, receiving a nineteen-gun salute. Bush also gave him an official state banquet at the White House, only the fifth in four years that the President had hosted. And Singh was invited to give an address to the joint Houses of Congress on Capitol Hill.

In March 2006 George Bush paid a return visit to India. To the surprise even of those who had been lobbying the US administration to treat India generously, Bush agreed to pretty much everything the Indians wanted. India would be given access to civil nuclear fuel supplies in exchange for agreeing to put most –

but not all – of its civil nuclear plants under international safe-guards. Many in Washington and among America's partners in the 44-member Nuclear Suppliers' Group, which includes sceptics such as Australia and Japan, wondered why the US had agreed to a deal that would enable India to benefit from all the advantages of belonging to the non-proliferation treaty without paying the full cost. The answer is simple if one ignores Mr Bush's stated reason for agreeing to the deal (to reward India's non-proliferation record and strengthen the international non-proliferation regime) and looks instead at the administration's underlying motive. Using the latter, the deal would give India the fuel and cover to accel-erate its nuclear weapons programme and counterbalance that of China. By this more accurate barometer, the deal made perfect sense. In the annals of American diplomacy, the two US-India summits stand out as highly unusual events. Perhaps in retrospect, they will be seen as an ascending moment for India.

There were many critics of the deal in America, particularly on Capitol Hill, where approval was essential if it was to go ahead. Some said it would act as a green light for other aspiring nuclear states to follow India's example. Furthermore, its timing could not have been more awkward: the US–India summit coincided with a heightened phase of concern about the alleged clandestine nuclear weapons programme of Iran, which Washington wanted stopped at almost any cost, and with the apparently fruitless talks between North Korea and a six-nation group led by the United States and including China over Pyongyang's nuclear ambitions. Others said it would provoke an arms race between India and Pakistan, which would inevitably involve China. Ultimately, they said, the Bush administration had signalled that counterbalancing China was more important to America than repairing the rule-based international system to prevent the spread of weapons of mass destruction.

The process of providing India with the benefits of being a nuclear power without formally recognising it as one (which, among others', would require China's agreement), is likely to be lengthy and uncertain, and will probably entail changes to what Bush unveiled in July 2005 and concluded in March 2006. But even if the deal were diluted by Congressional opponents at home and America's four (official) nuclear partners abroad, it would be unlikely to upset the US strategy of promoting India as a great power. Unrelated to the nuclear deal, US and Indian military forces have been conducting regular joint exercises since the late 1990s, at sea, in the air and on land. In 2004 the two countries staged a large joint military manoeuvre on India's border with China. Beijing said nothing. The two navies have also been conducting joint patrols of the Indian Ocean up to the Malacca Straits near Singapore to combat piracy and protect vital commercial shipping lanes, particularly the oil-tanker route. These and other areas of strategic cooperation between the United States and India, including detailed joint intelligence operations on terrorism, are growing all the time. Barely a week seems to go by without a senior American diplomat, senator, general or admiral visiting New Delhi.

But Washington cannot take everything for granted in its developing relationship with India. Unlike Britain or Japan, India is not a declining power that will happily follow America's lead on most important global issues. New Delhi might have learned to curtail some of its traditional Nehruvian moralising, but sometimes it seems to thumb its nose at America purely for the pleasure of it. Much of India's establishment and the country's influential left-wing parties, which prop up Manmohan Singh's coalition majority within parliament without formally participating in the government, remain deeply suspicious of the United States, in spite of Washington's increasingly warm and unconditional overtures. Even Jaswant Singh, who, as Foreign Minister in Vajpayee's government, was the principal architect of India's improving ties with the US, has voiced bitterly anti-American sentiments. The former army major, who remains a senior figure in the Hindu nationalist BJP, held a series of intensive negotiations with Strobe Talbott, Bill Clinton's Deputy Secretary of State, following India's May 1998 nuclear tests. Talbott's aim was to persuade India to 'cap, roll back and eliminate' its nuclear arsenal. He failed, but the intensive talks with Jaswant Singh, which took place over two years and in many different countries, provided the springboard for the rapid improvement in relations during the Bush years. Talbott wrote: '[The Indian government's] strategy was to play for the day when the US would get over its huffing and puffing and, with a sigh of exhaustion, or a shrug of resignation, accept a nuclear-armed India as a fully responsible and entitled member of the international community.'[22]

Although his strategy worked, Singh does not hold back whenever he feels Washington does not accord India its due respect. When Colin Powell, Secretary of State in the first Bush administration, stepped down in 2004, he recalled Washington's role in helping to prevent war between India and Pakistan in 2002. Jaswant Singh had been Powell's opposite number. To most people who read Powell's account, it seemed uncontroversial. He said he had arranged telephone calls between Bush and Vajpayee and claimed to have set up a dialogue between Musharraf and Vajpayee. In addition, he said he had suggested one or two things Vajpayee might say during this conversation. Finally, he revealed that he thought the dispute could well have escalated into a nuclear exchange.

An incandescent Jaswant Singh called a press conference in New Delhi to rebut Powell's account. Nobody was expecting such wounded pride. 'General Powell's claim that he played a role in Mr Vajpayee's peace initiative – even to the extent of setting up an elocution lesson – is entirely fabricated,' said Singh.

There was never any nuclear dimension at all. It is all very much a part of their [the Americans'] imagination, as was the existence of weapons of mass destruction in Iraq . . . Mr

Powell said: 'We set it up.' So are we to understand the
State Department is now acting as a telephone exchange?
The US bureaucracy is always three steps ahead of India in
obfuscation and finding reasons not to do a thing. The
Americans are world champions at bureaucracy. The State
Department, the Pentagon, the FBI, the CIA don't know
what each other is doing. The Americans do not know
how to assert great power status. They are caught in a web
of their own creation.

This impassioned rebuttal, which strayed into subjects unrelated
to Powell's reminiscences, illustrated a fundamental element of
India's character that the Americans and others are continually
required to relearn. Foreign diplomats sometimes barely get past
their opening remarks if their Indian counterparts feel they are
not being treated with exceptional respect. At times, India's diplomats appear to mind more about etiquette than they do about
substance. India wants constantly to be reminded how important
it is, and to be complimented on the profundity of its civilisation.
Having met many Indian diplomats, I agree with the following
description, written by Stephen Cohen:

> Whether a realist or an idealist, almost every member of
> the Indian strategic community thinks that India's
> inherent greatness as a power is itself a valuable diplomatic
> asset. India's ambassadors are expected to persuade foreign
> officials of the wisdom and moral correctness of the Indian
> position, say, by stating the Indian case and supplementing
> political arguments with information about India's great
> civilization, its cultural and economic accomplishments
> and its democratic orientation.[23]

It would be tempting to conclude that India is rising in spite of its
diplomacy. Any suggestion, for example, that there might be out-

side or 'third party' mediation in the Kashmir dispute is treated as toxic. Similarly, India's elite bristles at the notion that there would be any possibility of nuclear conflict in South Asia. In an interview during the 2002 crisis I asked Jaswant Singh about the nuclear threat. He peered at me in a headmasterly way. 'Just because I am an Asian does not mean I am incapable of being responsible,' he said tartly. I also asked him to respond to speculation that the United States hoped India would play a counterbalancing role to an emerging China. 'India does not play any roles, Mr Luce,' was the extent of his reply. Once, also in 2002, the Indian government issued a statement dismissing a trivial observation from the (lone) United Nations military observer in Kashmir. It was not the content of the observation that offended New Delhi but the fact that it had been offered by an outsider: 'We see no need for *obiter dicta* [remarks] on the Jammu & Kashmir issue from any third parties.'[24] To me, there was something about these seventeen short words that crystallised the weaknesses of Indian diplomacy.

There is a strong perception that India's obsession with status can sometimes outweigh the practical calculation of what is in the country's national interest. A good example is the management of nuclear relations with Pakistan. Put bluntly, New Delhi appears to care more about what it sees as the implicit assumption that South Asians are less responsible with nuclear weapons than others than it does about taking every conceivable measure to minimise the possibility of nuclear misunderstanding with Pakistan. I have yet to come across an example of a western strategist arguing that South Asians are inherently less capable than others of managing their nuclear arsenals responsibly. But international observers have real concerns that New Delhi and Islamabad continue to be reluctant to put in place the kind of essential safety measures that became routine between the US and the USSR after the hair-raising Cuban missile crisis of 1962. 'We used to have a joke that the nuclear establishments of the US and the USSR could swap places for a few weeks and everything would proceed as smoothly as before,' said Robert Blackwill. 'You could not say that about India and Pakistan.'[25]

India's sensitivity to what it sees as the underlying racism of western military strategists has also given rise to some counter-intuitive diplomatic positions. During the height of the 2002 crisis, Indian diplomats regularly briefed journalists that Pakistan would never use nuclear weapons. Pakistan, meanwhile, was busy disseminating the opposite message. The complacency of the Indian diplomats was shared by much of the Indian media. During the most tense moments it was instructive to read western news-paper accounts of the situation, many of which were alarmist to the point of caricature,* and then turn to the Indian media, which was at times more concerned with the Indian cricket team's performance than the threat of conflict with Pakistan. Rabid com-mentaries about the evil Pakistani regime were juxtaposed with reassuring editorials declaring that all would turn out fine in the end. As P. R. Chari, one of India's most thoughtful security ana-lysts, told me at the time: 'India wants the world to believe that Pakistan is an irresponsible power that should never be trusted on anything – except on nuclear weapons.'

There is no suggestion that India would be irresponsible with its own nuclear arsenal. In fact, I sometimes have the impression that India sees its nuclear status as entirely hypothetical. This is reassuring. But it is also vexing, because it means India is relaxed about the nuclear postures of its neighbours, which are of a dif-ferent nature. As a result, India knows very little about the nuclear assets, policies and signalling of Pakistan and vice versa. In matters nuclear, ignorance is never bliss. For example, knowl-

---

*'Westerners Flee as Nuclear War Looms' was my favourite headline that appeared in one of the UK newspapers. In fact, not many westerners fled. And it was a possible cross-LOC military raid that was looming. The threat of nuclear escalation does exist, but the prob-ability remains that it will not happen.

edge of which type of military planes are authorised to carry nuclear weapons could prevent a potentially lethal misreading of signals in a conflict. Since India and Pakistan are immediate neighbours this is extremely important. The major cities of the US and the USSR had a twenty-minute missile warning time because of their distance from each other. For India and Pakistan the gap is two minutes. 'India and Pakistan are ignorant of the basic grammar of each other's nuclear establishments,' said P. R. Chari. 'This raises the possibility that you could completely misinterpret a stray enemy aircraft as a nuclear attack. In a conflict you don't have time to get on the telephone.'

Interestingly, one of Washington's additional motivations in pushing for greater US strategic involvement with India was to help create a more responsible nuclear culture in the region. Ever since both India and Pakistan had refused to sign the Nuclear Non-Proliferation Treaty, this had been a constant dilemma. 'We call it the clean needle dilemma,' said Robert Blackwill. 'If you start handing out clean needles to drug users, then you are encouraging them to continue using drugs. But if you don't, they might die of Aids.'[26] There are signs that the India–Pakistan peace process, which began in 2003, might be leading to a better-managed nuclear environment between the two countries. So far they have agreed on symbolic safeguards: for example, they have set up a telephone hotline between their military commanders; and they have agreed to notify each other of the dates and venues of nuclear tests. But a more substantive exchange of nuclear information remains hostage to the successful outcome of the peace process – a scenario that is not inevitable. This is curious sequencing. It is particularly important to put safer nuclear systems in place while there is a possibility of war. But the goal of establishing nuclear safety appears to be lower on New Delhi's list of priorities than maintaining rigid virtue in its Kashmir position. Progress in talks over Kashmir has often been torpedoed by the slightest variation in words, the tiniest shift of parentheses. In the last decade or two India has become a more practical power, but it continues on crucial issues and at crucial moments to believe that words matter more than weapons.

There are a number of other limitations to the continued development of the relationship between India and the United States. First, as Jaswant Singh stated, India apparently does not wish to play the role of strategic counterbalance to China on behalf of Washington. It wants to remain equidistant from China and the United States, while working for good relations with both. In practice, this would still suit Washington's purposes. All India needs to do is continue to grow economically and become more assertive in its dealings with the world and it would naturally act as a counterbalance to China, whether it intends to do so or not. There is a sneaking suspicion that in practice India wishes to have much closer strategic links to the US than to China, but it would be loath to admit this publicly, for fear of provoking a domestic political backlash and for fear of offending China. In fact, the growth over the last few years of military cooperation between India and the United States, and the possibility that New Delhi will accept Washington's offer of establishing a co-production facility in India to build American F18-A fighter planes, suggests these links are is already in place. If that is the case, India is managing its Chinese relations with tact.

India's relations with other countries, including regimes that Washington has classified as 'rogue', are more difficult for Washington to accept. The most notable example here is India's relationship with Iran, part of President Bush's 'axis of evil' but a relatively close diplomatic partner of India. In the aftermath of the July 2005 nuclear deal between India and Washington, New Delhi immediately diluted its earlier support for Iran's nuclear stonewalling. Some saw this change of stance as an illustration of the timeless maxim that once you join a club you invariably want to close the door to new members. But it is likely that India's new pragmatism was more calculated than that. It was probably an implicit quid pro quo that Washington had requested of New Delhi in exchange for the nuclear deal. Even then, however, India's new position triggered bitter complaints from the country's two communist parties that the government was becoming slavishly pro-American.*

India was also critical of the 2003 American-led invasion of Iraq. Washington had made strenuous efforts to persuade India to join the 'coalition of the willing', and these had come close to succeeding, but the strong likelihood of a domestic political backlash caused Vajpayee to pull back at the last moment. The Prime Minister's senior adviser, Brajesh Mishra, reasonably said: 'India does not have a dog in this fight.' Parliament subsequently passed a unanimous resolution condemning the invasion.

But perhaps the most important limitation to the further strengthening of US–Indian ties is the anaemic growth in trade between the two countries – more specifically, the slow rise in US exports to India. During his time in New Delhi, Robert Blackwill, who has probably done more than any other US diplomat to boost relations with India, often said that America's trade flows to India were 'as flat as a chapatti'. Large American investors, particularly in the power-generation sector, allege they have been mistreated by the Indian government. Their most glaring example is the debacle over the 2400-megawatt Dabhol power plant near Mumbai that was built in the 1990s by Enron, the US energy company that went bankrupt in 2001. The Maharashtra state government refused to buy electricity from the plant, claiming it was overpriced. New Delhi then refused to honour the counter-guarantees it had pledged for the operation during the contract

---

*India's main leftist party, the Communist Party of India (Marxist), is a bundle of paradoxes. It supported China's decision to go nuclear in 1964, but opposed India's decision to do the same in 1998. Now it appears to support Iran's decision to go nuclear. Its position is essentially America-phobic.

negotiations. India has a more robust and independent legal system than China. But Americans frequently feel the need to lecture Indians about the 'sanctity of the contract'.

The US has also complained about the slow progress of Indian liberalisation of its retail, insurance and banking sectors, all of which present juicy targets for American companies. India wants to move at its own pace. But the United States possesses a strong lever to encourage acceleration: it can threaten to impose restrictions on the US economy's openness to India's software sector, which derives more than 80 per cent of its earnings from American customers.[27] 'At some stage,' said a senior US trade official, 'India is going to have to reciprocate the opportunities that America is providing to India.' It is unlikely that the US government would of its own accord significantly restrict the access of Indian IT companies to the American market, not least because American companies benefit so much from the reduced costs and more rapid service Indians provide. But Indian software executives remain nervous about the potential for the US to succumb to a populist backlash against 'offshoring'. During his 2004 presidential campaign John Kerry hinted that he would pursue a more protectionist line on offshoring. He was defeated in the election, but it would be rash of New Delhi to believe that American angst over the outsourcing of jobs to India will not resurface, possibly sooner than it thinks. At which point New Delhi could be faced with the choice of opening up its domestic market to foreign investors in a more decisive way or risking the health of the software goose that has laid so many golden eggs.

In my first interview with Manmohan Singh after he had become Prime Minister in 2004, India's new leader said something very significant. Unlike many of his colleagues, Manmohan talks in an understated way: he is not known for his rhetorical flourishes or for his ability to sway the public. In fact, many of his national addresses have been painfully wooden. But his judgement is widely admired, so when he gives a strong opinion that you have not heard before, it is worth taking note. 'The quest for energy security is second only in our scheme of things to our quest for food security,' he said, almost whispering. 'India is dependent on imported energy, and what goes on in the world today, the growing instability of supplies, gives rise to new challenges. The producers must come to terms with the fact that instability is not something that is conducive to the interest of either the buyers or the sellers . . . Energy security is of critical importance [to India].'[28]

To take a small liberty with Manmohan's pronouncement, energy security is actually a bigger headache for India than food security. In the last twenty-five years India has broken the back of its food-supply difficulties and is likely to become a large food exporter in the years ahead. The country now produces more than enough food to cater to the nutritional needs of its growing population, even though its system of food distribution to the poor leaves much to be desired. On energy, however, India's internal shortfall is large and growing. At the moment it imports 70 per cent of its oil needs, and that is expected to rise to 90 per cent in the next two decades as the domestic economy expands. Likewise, if the dollars being thrown around in overseas acquisitions are any guide, energy security is also one of the most critical issues facing China.

The energy situations facing the two countries are strikingly similar. Both have large reserves of coal, but it is mostly dirty and inefficient. Both have oil, but not in sufficient quantities to give them much comfort. Both – particularly China – have built controversial dams to boost their hydroelectric capacity, but the political cost of building dams is high and rising. Both also have ambitions to expand their civil nuclear capacity, but nuclear plants take years to build and demand a huge amount of capital. Even if India were able to expand its nuclear power capacity to achieve New Delhi's ambitious target of twenty thousand megawatts by 2020 (presumably from now with the assistance of Washington), this would still account for less than 5 per cent of India's overall electricity requirements. On gas, India has an advantage over China, having struck significant undersea gas fields in the Bay of Bengal and elsewhere over the last few years. Again, however, India's internal gas supply is dwarfed by its overall demand, which, like oil, will mostly be met from overseas fields.

In the coming years India and China will both look aggressively for new sources of oil and gas around the world. Competition between the two countries is already intense. China, as would be expected, is several years ahead of India in making overseas energy acquisitions, including stakes in Russian, Latin American and African oil fields, but India is catching up, having taken stakes in Sudan, Russia and Venezuela. In both cases the charge is being led by state-owned energy companies. Contrary to the advice of free-market purists who argue that supplies can more efficiently be tied up in the energy futures market, both countries want to extract the oil or gas directly. China's and India's restless quest for energy security also involves striking deals with a number of rogue regimes around the world. Most importantly, close ties are being forged with Iran. Journalists in Asia have dubbed the India–China race for energy security as the 'New Great Game', a reference to the 'Great Game', a scramble between imperial Britain and tsarist Russia in the nineteenth century to gain sway over the vast tracts of Central Asia that divided the Raj from Russia's southern boundaries. The New Great Game is less romantic, but its outcome will have as big an impact on the shape of world geopolitics as did the Victorian race between London and Moscow.

From the point of view of the Bush administration (and whatever administration replaces it in January 2009), the role of Iran in supplying India's and China's energy requirements is troubling. Iran's vast supplies of gas and oil are sufficient to take care of much of India's energy demands in the next two or three decades. New Delhi has indicated that it will not cave in to American pressure and seek its supplies elsewhere. The same applies to

China. There are a number of US statutes that could trigger sanctions against companies that trade with 'rogue regimes'. It is quite possible that India's hopes of building a gas pipeline to Iran will herald a new era of friction between Washington and New Delhi. But given India's large energy needs, it is doubtful that the US could come up with an alternative that would compensate India for the loss of gas from Iran. Equally, it is hard to imagine that any US sanctions against India would outweigh the economic benefits of securing a plentiful supply of cheap Iranian gas. Many Indian strategists also believe the pipeline would have a strongly beneficial diplomatic effect on the whole South Asian region, since it would have to pass through Pakistan, which also has large and growing energy needs. Although the costs of insuring the pipeline against a possible terrorist attack or Pakistani blackmail during a future conflict would be high, the economic and diplomatic gains would be greater. The pipeline would earn Pakistan up to $1 billion a year in transit fees, giving Islamabad a strong incentive to maintain stability with New Delhi.

Thus, in many respects, India and China find themselves on the same side of the fence, with America on the other, when it comes to energy security. New Delhi and Beijing have even begun to discuss areas of energy cooperation, such as forming an Asian buyers' cartel to match the Middle Eastern sellers' cartel and pressure OPEC to reduce its prices. India and China would compete in some areas of energy exploration but cooperate in others. Academics have coined the ugly phrase 'coopetition' to describe such behaviour. For example, the need to protect the busy shipping lanes linking the Middle East to Asia unites Beijing and New Delhi. It might even put a different gloss on China's 'blue sea' naval ambitions. In some respects India's Petroleum Ministry is a growing, albeit unofficial, rival to India's formal Ministry of External Affairs. Negotiating the construction of vast pipelines from Myanmar, Iran, Bangladesh and Pakistan to India is much sexier than drafting subordinate clauses in statements on Kashmir.

Partly because of its thirst for overseas energy supplies, India is also becoming a giver – as well as a receiver – of foreign aid. Some foreign aid officials see the country's external aid programme as an absurd waste of resources, considering the continuing economic deprivation in large tracts of India. But that might be to mistake the true nature of aid. For most western countries, including the United States, overseas aid is as much a tool of foreign policy as it is an expression of humanitarian concern. Again, India is a long way behind China in providing aid to other countries. But it is catching up. India now has aid programmes in parts of Africa and Afghanistan, and it was a contributor of emergency relief assistance after the tsunami struck South-East and South Asia in December 2004. The first planeload of aid to arrive in Sri Lanka, one of the most devastated countries, was from India, which also extended aid to Thailand, even though India's own death toll was much higher than that of Thailand. In a characteristic episode of Indian prickliness, New Delhi even refused foreign emergency aid for its own tsunami victims, who were mostly concentrated in Tamil Nadu. 'India would like to be part of the solution, not part of the problem,' said an Indian diplomatic spokesman. Many foreign aid officials saw this as another instance of New Delhi putting India's national pride above all else, including in this case the welfare of its most stricken citizens. But in the event, India managed the crisis relatively well. Tamil Nadu has one of the most efficient state governments in the country.

There have been domestic political criticisms of India's decision to pursue a more assertive diplomatic role in recent years. But in spite of the noise from the opposition in parliament (for example, against the BJP's nuclear tests in 1998, or against the Congress-led government's nuclear deal with Washington), there has been continuity in policy from government to government over the last ten to fifteen years. India's diplomatic trajectory looks to be enduring, rather than fickle. For example, it is hard to imagine that a future BJP government would undo whatever nuclear deal finally emerges between New Delhi and Washington. Equally, it is hard to imagine that any future Indian government would abandon the country's strategy of gradual economic integration with the world economy (although at a less dramatic pace than China's). Across all political parties, with the exception of the far left, there is a consensus that India should be aiming for 'great power' status, even if this focus on India's standing in the world sometimes looks unbalanced – even narcissistic – against the backdrop of India's continuing social and economic problems.

In today's increasingly communicative world relations between countries as large as India, China and the United States take place on many different levels and between many different types of people. Indian and American diplomats might be toasting each other with champagne in a hotel ballroom while American trade unions lobby against India's IT sector in the conference room next door. China and India join forces at the World Trade Organisation in Geneva to push the United States and the European Union to reduce farm subsidies while exchanging thinly veiled insults at the International Atomic Energy Agency in Vienna. America regards India as the key bulwark against a rising China while simultaneously keeping Pakistan sweet by selling it fighter jets that could one day be deployed against India.

Naturally, countries such as Japan, Russia, Brazil, South Africa, Germany, France and Britain will continue to be important players in the coming decades. But in many respects the world appears to be heading to a situation where relations between the three big powers will outweigh all other ties as the twenty-first century unfolds. The nodal point in the triangle is, of course, the United States. Short of war, however, the US cannot prevent China from rising as a global power, so it will continue to assist India's rise as a counterbalancing force. India, meanwhile, will want to benefit from America's help without jeopardising its own relations with China. There are many possible moves in this triangular dance. And there will be many opportunities to trip up.

CHAPTER EIGHT

NEW INDIA, OLD INDIA

The many-layered character of Indian modernity

There is not a thought that is being thought in the West or the East that is not active in some Indian mind.

E. P. Thompson

The employee identification tag hanging around James Paul's neck said '4844'. To James's colleagues, the number marks out the twenty-nine-year-old as among the lucky first few thousand people to get a job at Infosys, India's best-known software company. James was hired in 1998, when Infosys was starting to win large contracts to scan western computer systems for the much-feared millennium Y2K bug. People at Infosys worried the boom might end in the hangover after millennium eve. Instead, it accelerated. India's software sector barely skipped a beat when the US dotcom bubble burst in 2001. By 2006 Infosys had expanded more than tenfold from when James had been hired to boast a workforce of more than fifty thousand people. Likewise James – who heads a unit of fifteen hundred employees at the company's headquarters in Bangalore and spends at least half his time visiting clients in places like Houston, Paris and Salt Lake City – has seen his salary grow more than ten times to fifty thousand dollars a year – a princely sum, given India's low cost of living. But James is not among the most fortunate category of Infosys employees. Because of an early equity option scheme for employees, which was diluted shortly before James was hired, anyone at Infosys whose ID tag is '1000' or less has already become a dollar millionaire. For a company that few people had heard of in 1995, the creation of wealth from nowhere and on this scale was extraordinary. Similar stories could be told of other Indian IT companies. Azim Premji, the founder of Wipro, is among the richest men in the world. 'We get more than a million job applications a year,' said Nandan Nilekani, chief executive and co-founder of Infosys, who is almost as rich as Premji. 'It keeps our human resources department busy.'

There is another side to the Indian IT story that is in some ways even more revolutionary than the money: the sector is meritocratic. If a Martian had dropped in on India's top companies in the early 1990s and done a quick census of their white-collar management it would overwhelmingly have found men from urban upper-caste backgrounds. The Martian would see a much more diverse picture today. Upper castes are still preponderant in IT and other new-economy businesses, but much less so than in the more established industries. In its strange way, India is coming to terms with modernity. The practice of meritocracy is not yet widespread, but it is at least being given widespread lip service. And in much of the business world genuine changes are taking place. A large chunk of India's top thirty companies are involved in IT. Until a few years ago, most people had not heard of them. 'We cannot afford to follow the traditional "jobs for the boys" culture,' Nilekani told me. 'We have to survive in a very competitive global industry. Our only criterion is to select the best people.'

The Infosys campus in Bangalore, which is as sculpted and green as any in Silicon Valley, provides daycare, in-house supermarkets, gyms, laundry services and recreational facilities for the families of employees. It has tens of thousands of women on its payroll. Outside each of the buildings there are bicycles for employees to cycle from one part of the forty-acre campus to another. There are clusters of rainbow-coloured umbrellas outside each front door. It feels more like a weekend retreat for wealthy anarchists than a thriving global corporation. 'At the weekend this place is like a holiday camp,' said James Paul. 'Then we have all these "Bring your children to work" days and even "Bring your parents to work". But we also work very hard. Perhaps it is because of this environment that we work so hard.'

To get hired by Infosys, James had to work especially hard. I spent a day sitting with him in his cubicle in the open-plan office that is typical of software companies. Above his desk there is a sign: 'Parking for James only. All others will be towed.' He heads the validation unit, which undertakes stress-tests on the software systems of client companies, mostly global telecoms giants. In order for Infosys to develop and finesse the internal software systems for their clients, they have to get to know their business inside out. Inevitably, Infosys is moving into consultancy, where the fees are many times what you can earn from doing the relatively mechanical tasks of maintaining or repairing basic software code. It is not just western software companies who are suffering from Indian competition: the big consultancies, such as PriceWaterhouseCoopers and Accenture, are also threatened. 'To do software well, you have to understand a lot more than just software,' said James.

Born into a lower-middle-class Christian family in Kerala, James was the first member of his family to get a job outside his home state. His parents are schoolteachers. His grandparents were rice farmers who earned barely enough to make ends meet. James attended a local school and in 1992 he struck lucky. Or rather, he created his own luck. He applied to the elite Indian Institute of Technology in Mumbai (there are five other IITs) and was accepted. He had to sit three four-hour entrance examinations. He came 637th out of the 100,000 people who sat the tests. 'That was the big moment,' he said. 'I had to explain this to my parents, who didn't really understand just how big an opportunity it was.' James's parents were convinced and took out a loan to pay the tuition fees, which were then 5000 rupees a term (about $120). Now James earns more than that every day. He often flies back to Kerala for the weekend to catch up with his family, or stops off there en route back from the United States. 'I show my grandparents pictures of the Eiffel Tower or the Niagara Falls and they seem very happy,' he said. 'But they can't really locate any of these tourist sights. They just get the impression I'm doing well.' Naturally, he sends them some of his earnings. His younger brother works at CNBC, the US business television channel, in Mumbai.

A growing number of James's co-workers are from modest backgrounds. Their good fortune has created a far-reaching change in values. James's wife, Sindhu, is a Hindu from the upper-caste Nair community in Kerala. For both their families, the wedding marked a big departure. 'Initially there was doubt and hesitation because in our family we usually marry other Jacobite Christians [James's denomination],' he said. 'My parents had tried to arrange a marriage to someone within the community, but I didn't really click with the girls they introduced me to. But then they realised Sindhu and I were going to marry anyway, so they accepted it. We had a church wedding in Kerala and then we flew to Bangalore and had a temple wedding there.' James said a large proportion of the people working at Infosys have inter-caste or inter-religious marriages. This remains unusual in India, but in the IT sector it has become fairly routine. 'Every weekend it seems there is some wedding of an Infosys colleague and often it is an inter-communal marriage,' said James. 'Nobody raises an eyebrow. It is quite normal.' Interestingly, inter-caste marriage is not nearly as common among Indian software workers living in the United States. 'Long distance nationalism' is often much more conservative than its parent.[1]

Like James, Mariam Ram is a Christian from Kerala. But

Mariam, who owns her own company in Chennai, comes from a privileged background. Her company – TNQ – typesets, formats, stylises and edits some of the world's most complex scientific journals and other, non-scientific, academic publications. Her biggest client is Reed Elsevier, the Dutch-based publisher. Mariam began from scratch in 1998 with fifteen employees; now she has more than six hundred. In 2005 TNQ produced 300,000 pages; her target is a million pages a year. Apart from some of the university publishers in the United States, which still tend to keep their editing in-house, Mariam and her competitors are hoovering up the academic-journal work that used to be done on site in Europe and elsewhere. TNQ edits at about three dollars a page, compared to the going rate of at least ten dollars in Europe.

Some foreigners still think of Indian outsourcing as repetitive work, but Mariam's company requires its employees to have at least a postgraduate degree in their respective subject field. About a tenth of her employees have Ph.D.s. Publications such as *Cell*, *Tetrahydron*, *Semantics Today*, *Medieval History* and *Polymer* sit on the shelves of the company's main office, which is located in a leafy quarter of Chennai. An elegant and highly articulate woman in her early fifties, Mariam can see few threats on the horizon. Finding Anglophone science graduates in Chennai is no problem. 'China doesn't have the English language, the Philippines doesn't have science, Ireland is too expensive now – almost all the work is coming to India,' she said. 'And this is just the thin end of the wedge. There is no law confining us to academic journals. What about newspapers and magazines? I would love to copy-edit one of the prestige western titles.'

The business model looks robust, and India still seems to be in the relatively early stages of the offshoring revolution in services. There are plenty more tasks and functions, both low skilled and highly skilled, that can be remotely undertaken in places like India for half the price or less of what they cost in the west. But the sociological changes in Mariam's world are potentially even more revolutionary. Wherever possible, Mariam hires women – about half of her workforce is female – and she favours people from lower castes and other minorities. 'Women make much better copy-editors,' she said. 'They are much more conscientious about detail.' I talked to many of her female employees, and with the exception of one, who had only just started her job, each of them earned more than her father. Most were in their mid-twenties, and the majority were the first women in their families to have formal jobs. Unusually in India, some of the married ones had retained their maiden names. Mariam herself is something of a rarity, since she has been married twice. Her second husband, N. Ram, is editor and owner of *The Hindu*, a widely respected newspaper. India being India, N. Ram is also a Marxist. 'Very few of my female friends in my generation work,' said Mariam. 'Most of them sit around doing nothing.'

The women I spoke to at TNQ left me with two very strong impressions. First, they were obsessed with educating their children up to the highest level, whether they were sons or daughters. Second, they did not mind in the least that I was asking intrusive and often very personal questions. Nosiness is practically a virtue in India. 'No, no, it's nice being asked about these things,' said Mehroon Tanjore, a young Muslim woman, when I asked whether she would stop at one child. 'I think I will discuss it with my husband.' Her mother, who lives in the south Indian temple town of Tanjore, has always worn the *burqa* and is not educated. Her father insisted on keeping his wife in *purdah*, yet he did not mind his daughter going about unveiled and working with men. Why was that? 'I don't know,' she said, shaking her head inscrutably, south India-style, as if the anomaly had never occurred to her. 'It's different with me.' Mehroon's marriage had been arranged, but she was ambivalent about whether she would arrange her son's marriage. 'It will be up to him. The most important thing is that he becomes educated,' she said. Another employee, Priya Reddy, whose family was originally from Andhra Pradesh, met her Tamil

Brahmin husband in a government office when they were both applying for a driving licence. 'It was love at first sight,' she said. 'I think I forgot my licence.' Her mother is a housewife. Priya hoped her own daughter would be a professional. For Mariam, who is something of a mother figure to her employees, the order books might be full, but she said it is the 'romance' of the business that drives her: 'This isn't really about money – I don't want to be the richest stiff in the cemetery. It is about being part of a new India that is opening up opportunities for people who never had them before.'

Like Mariam and many of her employees, James Paul's value system is a million miles from what still prevails in most of village India. Barely a week seems to pass without a gruesome caste-related murder hitting the newspaper headlines. One of the most common causes of caste violence in the villages is when a boy and a girl from different castes try to elope and are caught. Often, the resulting killing is carried out by men from both families. Sometimes the young lovers are burned; sometimes they are cut up with knives. Although the phenomenon is much worse in northern India, there have been incidents of this nature in Karnataka. Naturally, such stories disturb James.

Pride of place in his cubicle at Infosys is given to a picture of the Art of Living Foundation and its guru, Sri Sri Ravi Shankar. The ashram is about an hour's drive from the Infosys campus. Alok Kejriwal, the Mumbai-based online entrepreneur whom we met in Chapter One, is also a devotee of the Art of Living. James told me that many of his colleagues at Infosys attended Sri Sri Ravi Shankar's evening classes. 'Mostly it is just meditation and stress-reduction,' said James, 'but it is also the spiritualism. We need to become more Indian, and to improve our self-esteem. For example, I don't see why people drink Coca-Cola when there's beautiful Indian lime juice that they can drink.' I understood his point, but I wondered why he had singled out Coke as the betrayal of Indian-ness rather than, say, working for a company that operates in English and services western clients. James looked pensive, then he said: 'Eventually I would like to work for the poor in the villages. We have set up a group at Infosys called "Good for Nothing", where we help women in the villages learn how to weave baskets. One day I would like to do this full time.'

Going through my notes of our conversation later, it struck me that James was in many respects representative of the new generation of middle-class Indians – highly skilled, wealthy, cosmopolitan and comfortable with people of all religious and caste backgrounds. At the same time, he talked a lot about the need to protect Indian culture and its religious heritage from what he saw as the less attractive aspects of global culture – the break-up of families, disrespect of elders, excessive consumerism, abandonment of religious values and worship of money. Many Indians take as part of their conventional wisdom the view that India's traditional moral values are better than those of the west. This gave a quiet but impassioned underlining to much of what James said. 'I believe very strongly that we must protect India's culture and morality,' he said. 'Because of colonialism we have been made to feel ashamed of our traditions. Now that we are independent we have no excuses any more. Our fate is in our hands.'

Sometimes it seems that in India the modern lifestyle is just another layer on the country's ancient palimpsest, simply adding modernity to what already exists. Most Europeans tend to think of modernity as the triumph of a secular way of life: church attendance gradually dwindles and religion becomes a minority pastime confined to worshippers' private lives. It turns into a branch of the heritage industry, celebrated more for its architecture and history than for its contemporary relevance. That has certainly been true of most of Europe over the last few generations. In opinion polls today a majority of Europeans regularly profess either not to believe in God or to be agnostic. In Europe the past is the past. But in India the past is in many ways also the future.

Europe is no longer the universal standard by which other societies measure their progress. For India, the United States offers a more relevant parallel. Neither India nor the United States suffered Europe's history of state-imposed religion, except, in the American case, in the form of a relatively titular Church of England before 1776. As a result, both societies have a tradition of religious communities and sects coexisting and sometimes competing with one another in civil society without benefiting much from state patronage or suffering from state persecution. The absolutist character of the Catholic Church in Europe gave rise to a correspondingly absolutist counter-attack, initially in the form of Protestantism but latterly in the form of anti-clericalism and atheism. India shares few of these impulses because it has a very different history. Its past continues to be visible in its present. On the few occasions in India's history when the state has attempted to proselytise either the effort has quickly petered out or it has provoked a backlash that has forced the state to retreat.

For example, in the seventeenth century the Mughal emperor Aurangzeb imposed the Islamic *jizya*, a poll tax on the heads of unbelievers, which included the majority of the population. This went against the relatively ecumenical traditions of Aurangzeb's predecessors. Many of India's Muslim rulers paid respect to India's non-Islamic customs. For example, Dara Shikoh, Aurangzeb's brother (whom he had killed since he was a rival to the throne), translated the Upanishads (a series of philosophical tracts on Hinduism) into Persian.[2] Aurangzeb's great-grandfather, Akbar, had tried to fuse Islam, Hinduism and other creeds into a new religion, which he called *Din Ilahi*, but without much success. Hindu nationalists claim thirty thousand temples were destroyed by Islamic iconoclasts, but accredited scholars can find verifiable examples for only a fraction of this number.[3] Even then, the temples that were destroyed were usually associated with the outgoing dynasty.[4] And it was a tradition for new Hindu dynasties to do precisely the same thing. Conversely, Turkish Muslim armies left the provocatively erotic temples of Khajuraho in central India untouched because the Candella dynasty that had built them had already fled.*

Muslim rulers would often use Hindu symbols to legitimise their rule in the eyes of the people. For example, Mohammed-bin-Tuglakh, whose dynasty ruled from Delhi, transported water from the Ganges, the holiest river in Hinduism, south to Daulatabad, when he built a new capital in 1327.[5] Contemporary inscriptions never identified the royal house by religion but by language (such as Turkish, Persian or Afghan). It was also common for Islamic dynasties to repair and provide for the upkeep of prestigious temples. For example, the world-renowned Jaganath Temple at Puri in Orissa was restored during the Mughal era. Because of Aurangzeb's open antipathy to Hinduism and because he tried to stretch his rule too far into southern India, he laid the seeds for the break-up of the Moghul Empire. Sensing this, one of his sons even joined a rebellion against him that was led by Hindu Rajput generals. The vacuum created by a declining and enfeebled Mughal Empire was gradually filled by the British.

The British learned the hard way that imposing its religious bias upon India's population could be dangerously counter-productive. That is one reason why fewer than 3 per cent of Indians were Christian in 1947 after more than two hundred years of British rule (and most come from communities that had converted to Christianity long before British rule began). In contrast almost a third of Vietnam was Christian when the French left the country in 1954, less than a century after they had colonised it. The British tolerated and in some cases sponsored Christian missionary activity in India in the late eighteenth century and the first half of the nineteenth century, although with little success.

---

*Much of the *Kama Sutra*, the classic Hindu manual of sexual positions, is depicted on the exterior of the temples. Other sexual props, including horses, play cameo roles on these unique fourteenth-century stone friezes.

Nevertheless, some Protestant missionary societies believed they could lift India's 'idol-worshipping heathens' out of their ignorance en masse.*

After 1857 the British Raj shifted its policy from lukewarm support for the missionaries to outright disapproval. Many of the rebels in the Mutiny, particularly Brahmin troops from the United Provinces, had allegedly been provoked by rumours that they would have to use a new kind of cartridge that was greased with cow fat. Equivalent rumours about pig fat inflamed Muslim soldiers. The uprising had been preceded by widespread talk in the regiments of official British plans to convert India to Christianity. These were unsubstantiated, but there is little doubt that many of the Protestant missionary groups treated Indians and Indian culture in a way that provoked such resentment. So after the suppression of the Mutiny the British chose to stress the continuity of their rule within Indian history by reviving many of the ceremonial features of the Mughals and eventually shifting the capital back to Delhi (from Calcutta).

Even among many of the Christian and Muslim communities in today's India, their form of worship is more eclectic and unorthodox than that practised by their co-religionists in most other parts of the world. This has positive and negative implications. On the plus side, the tendency to accept there are many paths to God derives from India's long-running tradition of tolerance between religions. On the debit side, caste continues to play an important role in dividing Christian congregations (and Muslim communities) along the lines of their birth. Somerset Maugham once visited what was then the Portuguese colony of Goa (in 1961 Nehru lost patience with the Portuguese and

---

*Some Western Protestant societies still believe India should be converted to Christianity. The methods – which many see as culturally disrespectful – used by various Baptist missionary groups in India's tribal zones and in the north-eastern states remain controversial. With some reason, Verrier Elwin, whom Nehru appointed to take charge of India's north-east, described Baptists as the 'RSS of Christianity'.

annexed the enclave to India). Maugham made friends with a Catholic priest, whose ancestors had been converted by the Portuguese. 'I got the feeling,' wrote Maugham, 'that even though there were 400 years of Catholicism behind him, he was still at heart a Vedantist [a classical Hindu].'[6] In 2004 Priya and I dropped in for tea at the home of a well-known Goan Catholic author. She had just finished a beautiful restoration of her ancestral home, which was in the classic Brahmin style of the region. I naïvely asked her whether there was any Portuguese blood in the family. 'Oh no, that is out of the question,' she said. 'Our family is Brahmin.'

An estimated 70 per cent of Indian Christians come from Dalit or Adivasi (tribal) backgrounds.[7] Generally they are not permitted to forget it. This is partly because conversions to Christianity (and Islam) have tended to take place in groups, usually of whole sub-castes, rather than at the individual level. Instead of escaping their caste, they simply add another prefix: 'Dalit-Christian' or 'Dalit-Muslim'. In urban India such labels matter less, but most of the minorities have not yet entered the urban middle classes. In almost every denomination the Church hierarchy is almost wholly of upper-caste origin. In Tamil Nadu a recent study showed that 63 per cent of all Tamil Catholics, but only 3 per cent of Tamil Catholic priests, were Dalit.[8] Likewise, upper-caste pollution rules dictate that Christian women do not enter the grounds of a church during menstruation or for forty days after giving birth. In many cases, including in Goa, Dalit Catholics have separate churches and separate cemeteries. Somerset Maugham, it seems, had a point.

Many of the progressive trends on caste are to be found within Hinduism, in spite of what is happening in the political arena. As India continues to urbanise and as new technology, such as television and the Internet, begins to influence forms of worship, Hinduism is becoming less segmented. In many ways – and for the first time in its history – Hinduism is turning into a unified mass religion. For example, all castes in northern India now celebrate *Karwa Chauth*, in which wives fast for their husbands for one day a year to symbolise their devotion, and *Rakhi*, in which the sister ties a thread on her brother's wrist to convey her love (both are traditional north Indian upper-caste festivals). Many lower castes are also copying the upper castes by initiating their children into adulthood in ceremonies where they tie a sacred thread on the wrists of their sons before they reach puberty. Brahmins see the initiation as a second birth, which is why upper castes are sometimes referred to as the 'twice born'. Additionally, there are now many priests who are not Brahmin.

As a result, Hinduism – or at least Hinduism as it is practised in the cities – is becoming a much more standardised religion. Foreigners often remark on the unique architecture of the traditional Hindu temple. In contrast to most other religions, it lacks a general area in which the congregation can gather. Traditional Hinduism had no real congregation: it was a religion of different castes. The standard Hindu temple has a small inner room, or *sanctum sanctorum*, in which the god is situated, that is open only to the eligible castes. But the new temples of the growing urban Hindu cults, like the Swaminarain sect, or the late nineteenth-century religious reformist movements of the 'Bengal renaissance', such as the Ramakrishna Mission, have been built with large open areas for people to worship collectively. Furthermore, simply by switching on their televisions, people can now worship as one huge congregation. In the last decade India has seen a mushrooming of the Hindu equivalent of America's 'televangelist' cable TV channels. In contrast to the excluding architecture of the temples, India's 'god channels' are aggressively inclusive, since their main aim is to maximise audience share. Hinduism is also crossing regional boundaries. Festivals such as Divali and Holi, which were traditionally north Indian, are now celebrated throughout most of the country.

Technology undoubtedly assists in the nationalisation of Hindu practice. The popular and increasingly pan-Indian Hinduism of today comes from the *puranas*, the histories of the popular gods such as Shiva, Ram, Krishna and Vishnu that were written many centuries after most of the classical Hindu texts. Festivals celebrating lesser gods, such as Hanuman and Ganesh (the monkey and half-elephant gods), who have grown in popularity over the last century, are spreading across India.* Mainstream Hinduism, which Thomas Mann described as the 'all-encompassing labyrinthine flux of the animal, human and the divine',[9] is growing. In India modernity and religion are marching forward together, sometimes hand in hand. Counter-intuitive it may be (particularly for a European), but there is no contradiction.

One of the reasons why many of India's educated elite feel ambivalent about modernity is because the new wealth and technology of the last fifteen years appear to have exacerbated some of the country's less savoury traditions. In large tracts of northern and western India the so-called 'gender gap' between boys and girls has sharply increased. The average ratio of births of girls to boys for India was 945 to 1000 in 1991. By 2001 it had fallen to 927 to 1000.[10] In some parts of India, particularly in the southern states, the sex ratio remains healthy, at roughly one to one. But in India's north-west and north the ratio has fallen alarmingly: Gujarat has fewer than 900 girls to every 1000 boys; Punjab has fewer than 800. The average in the west is 1050 boys to every 1000 girls.[11] Punjab and Gujarat are among the wealthiest states in India and have witnessed the most rapid increases in disposable incomes since economic reform began in the early 1990s, but they have recorded the steepest falls in the numbers of daughters

---

*The annual festival in which a figure of Ganesh is paraded through the streets before being submerged in the sea is relatively recent, having been launched in 1905 by Tilak, a nationalist leader. It began in Maharashtra, and is most popular in Mumbai, but it is spreading to other parts of India.

born. The poorest states, such as Bihar, have much better sex ratios than the richer ones, and have even seen a slight improvement in the last few years. In many parts of India the sex ratio serves as a kind of grotesque barometer of economic progress. Similarly, the practice of dowry has spread most extensively in the wealthier states, with the family of the groom demanding increasingly extortionate compensation for the apparent burden of accepting a new female member. For many of India's new middle classes, having a daughter is becoming an ever more expensive prospect.

'Are you going to kill your daughter?' asks a television advertisment in Gujarat. This aggressive publicity campaign was launched by Amarjeet Singh, the state's Health Secretary, who told me it was the most distressing job he had ever had. It has been illegal in India since 2001 to provide a 'sex determination' test to pregnant mothers. But since it would be impractical to outlaw pregnancy scans, the law is virtually impossible to uphold. There has been only one conviction so far. Yet India has an estimated forty to fifty million 'missing girls'. A sonograph costs as little as 150 rupees. An abortion costs about 10,000 rupees. 'Some of the fall in the gender ratio is because more and more people can now afford to do sex determination tests and then pay for the abortion,' said Amarjeet Singh. 'So probably we have less infanticide nowadays and more foeticide.' He showed me a chart of the worst-affected districts in Gujarat. In some parts of the state the ratio is below 800 girls to every 1000 boys. Families in these districts are now importing girls from other parts of India to serve as brides to several husbands at once – usually the unfortunate woman is shared between three or four brothers. The imported women have no status and are treated as little better than in-house prostitutes. Doubtless their unborn daughters are never born, thus compounding the problem. Singh hoped that Gujarat's gender crisis will gradually fade as people's mindsets adapt to the modern world. 'The solution is to educate women as highly as possible,' he said. 'This will start to happen as people realise daughters have economic value in the modern economy.'

Naturally, the problem is worse in the villages. For most villagers the economic opportunities and the social flexibility offered by the urban lifestyle and the new economy remain distant prospects. In the village arranged marriages and functional illiteracy are still the norm. India is estimated to have the lowest average age of marriage in the world, with child marriage remaining widespread in many rural districts, particularly in the north. According to one estimate, 15 per cent of girls in India's poorest five states get married at or below the age of ten.[12] Clearly, almost all of this takes place in the villages. Children born in the village are also almost twice as likely to die below the age of five as those born in the city.

As we saw in Chapter Three, the phenomenon of 'Sanskritisation', in which the lower castes copy the values and habits of the upper castes, is growing. Many of India's upper castes have traditionally regarded daughters as a burden and a drain on finances, so the problem is worsening as other castes, which used not to practise dowry, become more upwardly mobile. 'It is a lethal combination of old values and new wealth – old wine in new bottles,' said Amarjeet Singh. The upwardly mobile lower castes have also become more materialist. Nowadays it is normal for the groom's family to demand cars, washing machines and even a US Green Card as part of their dowry. This explains the seemingly odd tendency of newspaper columnists to blame the twin curses of the worsening gender divide and dowry inflation on western consumer values, even though neither problem exists in the west.

In contrast, most of the educated upper-caste elite in India has largely abandoned the practice of dowry. Their daughters go to university, so they have become financially independent. However, this is not true of all upper castes in all parts of India. For example, the survival chances of potential daughters in the

Jain and the Marwari communities, who are the traditional business elites of Gujarat and elsewhere, continue to deteriorate. The Jains, who dominate much of Gujarat's merchant trade, are a strictly vegetarian offshoot of Hinduism. Orthodox Jains can be recognised instantly from the white cotton facemasks they wear to prevent the possibility of swallowing an insect. In 2001 there were 878 Jain daughters to every 1000 Jain sons, according to Amarjeet Singh. By 2003 the ratio had fallen to 848 to 1000. 'Just imagine, these people have a religion that says you cannot even harm a fly or a microbe, and yet they are killing off about fifteen per cent of their daughters,' he said. 'How to explain this?'

The state of Gujarat is a genuine puzzle. In economic terms it is probably the most globalised part of India. Millions of Gujaratis have family in the UK, the United States and other parts of the world. Yet to judge by the gender ratio, which is surely the best measure, the status of women appears to be worsening every year. On a more trivial level, the sexes still appear to be segregated as a matter of routine at dinner parties in Gujarat. I have attended several get-togethers where the men sit down and are served their dinner by the women, who only afterwards eat whatever is left over. I once attended an Indian dinner party in the Philippines. My wife, who is half Gujarati, insisted on joining the men in their separate room. I took this as a cue to join the women. The men took this as a double bonus.

Gujarat, as we saw in Chapter Four, is also the most Hindu-chauvinist state in India. One of the principal accusations levelled at Muslims is that Islam discriminates against women. Yet Gujarat has a worse gender ratio than many Islamic countries, including Pakistan and Bangladesh. It is hard to know what would qualify as a more telling measure of gender discrimination than tolerating mass selective abortion. Renuka Patwa is a midwife in Ahmedabad, in Gujarat, who left her job at the hospital to work for the Self-Employed Women's Association (Sewa), a large trade union for women. Sewa has more than 600,000 members working in the unorganised sector, where they make incense sticks, *bidi* cigarettes and textiles. The union educates its members to value their daughters. Although everyone knows her views, Patwa still receives calls from people asking for referrals to clinics that will perform abortions on female foetuses. 'I got a call from a very wealthy Marwari [the business caste originally from Rajasthan] mother-in-law the other day,' said Patwa. 'After some thought I gave her the number because I knew that the poor daughter-in-law would go through hell if she wasn't allowed to have an abortion. These Marwaris are particularly keen on having sons because they want a son to inherit the business.' The couple in question had received a Mercedes and a honeymoon in Switzerland as part of the dowry for the unfortunate young woman who was about to have an abortion.

'It is difficult for me,' admitted Patwa, a jolly woman in her late fifties, with an operatic laugh. 'I believe in the woman's right to have an abortion, but it is troubling to see the reason most women have abortions. The mother-in-laws are the worst. They were once victims, so now they become culprits.' Patwa, whose living room is decorated with cheerful pictures of Krishna playing with *gopis* (cowgirls), depicting the celebrated erotic phase of the young god's life, has had direct experience of such prejudice. 'In 1972 when I gave birth to my daughter, my mother-in-law came into the hospital room and said, "You have given birth to a stone." It was as if I had committed a crime. But I did not feel guilty. My husband said, "I will never disobey my parents," so I divorced him. I have paid a price because society still does not accept female divorcees, but it was the best thing I have ever done.'

Patwa said the situation was improving for the younger generation of educated women, many of whom were beginning to stand up for themselves, but they are clearly outnumbered by the droves of lower castes that are Sanskritising. 'Society still discriminates terribly against women,' she said. 'Sex discrimination leads directly to sex determination.' She poured scorn on traditional moral values, and likened sexuality to a fixed quantity of water: if one channel is shut off, it will find another. 'If you repress feelings of sexuality in women, then the woman will not give her husband pleasure,' she said. 'So the husband will find his pleasure elsewhere. How moral is that?' Meanwhile, the woman's frustrated sexuality would be sublimated into love of her son, which would reinforce her resentment of the daughter-in-law who would eventually take first place in her son's affections. I was not sure how much of this could be proven, but it was worth hearing.

Indian society as a whole seems to be much more at ease with the topic of sex than before. But this is not necessarily an indicator of women's empowerment. Bollywood films, which have always made the most of their world-famous pelvic dance sequences, have become much more risqué in the last decade. Every day the newspapers are plastered with photographs of sultry women performing 'item numbers' – the most revealing dance sequences in Bollywood films, which generally have nothing to do with the plot. Newspapers and magazines also promote the idea that sexual promiscuity is now a normal way of life among the middle classes. Under any circumstances this would be a questionable measure of women's autonomy. But it is also patently exaggerated. The supposedly serious magazines that have led the trend use polling methodology that is usually highly questionable: most canvass only one or two hundred people, usually in the cities and generally English-speaking. But they still generate cover-story headlines like: 'XXX. Seven out of Ten Delhiites Say Porn is Good for Sex'.[13] My favourite survey appeared in a leading current affairs magazine in 2005. According to the magazine, only 27 per cent of women knew what an orgasm was. In the next box 47 per cent of women said they had had multiple orgasms.[14]

Such polls are the stock-in-trade of publications around the world, but in India they reveal a tendency to mistake the libertine society (however exaggerated) for the liberal society. Everyone in India has met young women who wear skimpy outfits, go to night-clubs and have flings with boys, much like their counterparts in the west. But when asked whether they will choose their husbands, they routinely say they will leave the decision up to their parents. The sociologist Dipankar Gupta calls this 'westoxification'.[15] By this he means a tendency to adopt the brand labels and consumer habits of the west and believe this is what it is to be modern. Perhaps that is all there is to it. Certainly India has far fewer teenage pregnancies than countries such as the UK and the United States. But the vast gap between the lifestyles and values of India's consuming classes and the rest gives India a social tension that, in Gupta's view, has more in common with Iranian society in the 1970s under the Shah (although Gupta is certainly not predicting a revolution in India).

Bollywood and other branches of the Indian film industry, such as Tamil-language cinema, which is almost as prolific as its Hindi-language counterpart, offer more subtle clues about society's attitudes towards women's sexuality. The typical Bollywood film is a blend of brilliantly choreographed titillation, which goes down very well with much of the male audience, and a resolutely conservative ending, which meets with the approval of their mothers and wives. A much-celebrated hit, *Dil Chahta Hai* (*My Heart Wants*), shows a young man falling for an older, divorced woman. Much sultriness ensues before she falls ill and dies. The hero ends up with a girl of his own age. Because the film depicted a divorcee in a sympathetic light (before she died), it was celebrated for having broken a taboo.

Another (not-so-classic) film, *Girlfriend*, inexplicably provoked a nationwide boycott by right-wing Hindu groups. A lesbian, who spends her spare time beating up men in amateur kick-boxing sessions, seduces her drunken and unsuspecting best friend. The latter's wholesome fiancé cottons on to the former's preferences and, in confronting her, is almost killed in a furious, muscular assault before he finally prevails. The final scene shows the conventional Hindu couple paying their respects at the lesbian's

Christian gravestone. Convincing scripts are not Bollywood's strongest point. 'Bollywood is expert at having its cake and eating it,' Dev Benegal, an independent film-maker, told me. 'It shows you some flesh but it always ends by disapproving of such behaviour.'

India expects its actresses to be both sexy and conservative. When a leading actress gets married she is expected to give up her career. She almost always does. Sometimes, as with Hema Malini or Jaya Bachchan, they return to cinema later in their marriage to play matronly roles, as kind but stern mothers-in-law. In a few cases, such as Dimple Kapadia, who married an actor, retired, got divorced and then returned to the screen as a sex symbol, they get a second chance. But these are the exceptions. Mainstream cinema in India owes more to the catwalk than the drama school. The leading stars are first and foremost expected to be beautiful. Next they should dance well and handle the wet sari scenes with appropriate panache. If they can act that is a bonus, but it is not a requirement. They should provoke erotic fantasies without themselves crossing strictly defined lines of acceptable public behaviour.

I once visited Mumbai's Film City, a sprawling 517-acre site next to the Rajiv Gandhi National Park. Situating the film lot next to a jungle was deliberate, as no Bollywood film would be complete without one or two dance sequences in the forest or a lovers' duet on a stone bridge overarching a stream. I was taken to watch a scene being shot. A young girl, dressed in a frazzled night-club outfit, was being harassed by her lover under the shade of a large tree. The shooting over, the young actress headed directly to where I was sitting. 'Would you like to interview me?' she asked, with almost unseemly directness.

Shabana Sultan, it turned out, was a twenty-one-year-old Indian who had been born and brought up in Tripoli, Libya, where her father was an orthopaedic surgeon. She had always dreamed of being a Bollywood actress and this was her first film. 'I am not at all nervous,' she said. 'The camera is my lover.' Her father, who never let his daughter out of his sight ('Even the boys are no longer safe in Bollywood,' he said), proudly handed over Shabana's portfolio. The file contained a series of pictures of her in different costumes – western evening dress, sultry nightclub attire, a sexy wet sari, a more restrained sari, and so on. There was not a written word in the file, not even her name. 'I don't know why they gave me the part,' she said, absent-mindedly. 'There wasn't even an audition.' As I left, her father rushed after me clutching a small piece of paper. 'This is Shabana's mobile telephone number,' he said. 'In case you want to continue the interview.'

Two recent scandals illustrate what is expected of the mainstream film actress in India. One of Mumbai's biggest stars is Kareena Kapoor, whose swaying hips and girlish pout are beloved of audiences up and down the country. Like her co-stars, she would never kiss on screen. With one or two much-publicised exceptions, kissing remains taboo in Bollywood movies. So when a nosy fan caught Kareena kissing her boyfriend and fellow actor Shahid Kapoor (no relation) at a party in Mumbai and took a hazy picture on his mobile phone, there was uproar. Kareena denied it was she who had been digitally recorded: 'I'm not this kind of a girl. I have an illustrious family name to uphold,' she said. More seriously, Kushboo, another actress, this time from the Tamil film industry, provoked even greater public anger in 2005 when she told a magazine interviewer that there was nothing wrong with sex before marriage. Large-scale demonstrations broke out across Tamil Nadu, with the protesters claiming she had insulted Tamil culture and defamed Tamil women. The beleaguered actress, who was briefly taken into custody by the police, had to go into hiding. Until then, Kushboo had been involved in an HIV–Aids campaign to highlight the merits of safe sex.* She too was compelled

---

*We will look in the Conclusion at India's growing HIV–Aids problem.

to issue a statement: 'Even in films, I never undertook roles that lowered the image of women,' she said. 'I have the greatest regard for Tamils, especially Tamil women. If my remarks have hurt anybody's feelings, I tender an apology. I am one among you and will always remain with you.'

Bollywood films are not expected to be realistic. Independent film-makers complain bitterly that the space and finance for films that deal with India's 'social reality', or even rural India, have virtually disappeared. Many films ostensibly based in India are now filmed in plush resorts in Mauritius or even Switzerland, where the scenery resembles Kashmir. Dev Benegal told me: 'When we pitch a film about Indian social reality, the financiers say: "We don't want to do a documentary, we want real acting."' In the 1950s and 1960s, in the aftermath of India's independence, Bollywood sold the dream of development and modernisation: films were often set in rural India and depicted heroes battling against the evils of feudalism. Nowadays Bollywood could more accurately be described as an arm of the consumer goods sector. The contemporary formula – which has left rural India, where two-thirds of the country's people still live, on the cutting-room floor – caters to the tastes of the new consuming classes.

Quite by chance, my tour of Film City coincided with the presence of Amitabh Bachchan, India's most revered film star, whose sixty-second birthday had just been celebrated in dozens of newspaper supplements. I was halfway through an interview with Sanjeevanee Kutty, the civil servant in charge of Film City, when her assistant rushed in. 'Mr Bachchan is ready now,' said the assistant. 'Ready for what?' I enquired. 'Ready for his interview with you.' This qualified as one of Bollywood's more improbable little twists. Having no idea that Bachchan was in the vicinity, I had not requested an interview. Had I done so, it would have taken weeks of faxes and conversations with public relations agencies to secure even the ghost of a chance. Led by Kutty in her official white Ambassador, we piled into a cavalcade of cars and rushed to the set. Like most of Bachchan's shoots, it was a commercial. Wherever you are in India, the chances are that if you close your eyes and throw a dart it will land on a billboard bearing Bachchan's distinguished grey-bearded visage. Whether it is for Pepsi-Cola, Cadbury's chocolate, Parker pens or Maruti cars, no amount of exposure seems to dilute his brand equity. On this occasion, he was starring in an advertisement for Dabur, a health-food chain.

Although we were on the edge of the jungle and the temperature was more than thirty degrees Celsius, Bachchan was wearing a balaclava and looking flushed. Behind him a machine was billowing out fake fog. It was clearly a winter scene. 'Are you wearing that [balaclava] for the shoot?' asked Kutty, evidently awkward in the presence of a living legend. 'Well, obviously, ma'am,' replied the megastar, emphasising the 'ma'am'. My interview was short and to the point. 'Many independent film-makers say that Bollywood ignores the realities of India,' I said. 'Well, yes, of course,' said Bachchan, with the same edge to his tone. 'It's called escapist cinema. Why should somebody pay to see a film with poverty in it when they see poverty in their neighbourhood every day? People don't want to be reminded where they live.' 'Would you like to make more films that remind people where they live?' I asked. 'I really don't see the point. Nobody will pay to go and see a film like On the Waterfront.' He wound up the interview shortly afterwards.

Perhaps the most conspicuous item of consumption in today's India is the wedding, which owes a lot to Bollywood, and vice versa. Vandana Mohan, owner of the Wedding Design Company and New Delhi's most successful wedding planner, told me the smallest metropolitan middle-class weddings start at $20,000, climbing to more than $100,000. In 2003 Subroto Roy, a prominent industrialist based in Lucknow, spent an estimated $10 million on the joint wedding of his two sons. (As a rich entrepreneur, he paid, although this is traditionally the responsibility of the father of the bride.) The event, which many high-level politicians attended, was stage-managed by Bollywood directors, stage managers and choreographers. Alongside the growing cost, the volume of people invited and the number of receptions, ceremonies and related gatherings to accommodate them are also climbing. In the past there would be three or four receptions; now there are a minimum of five and usually eight. The 'intimate gathering' for 'close friends' of the two families often exceeds five hundred people. The main reception has upwards of a thousand guests. 'Sometimes it is hard to take it seriously,' said Mohan. 'But it is seriously good business.'

The wedding boom is also good news for astrologers. Dev Vashishtha, a leading astrologer who charges $120 for a 45-minute session, has seen demand for his consultations grow in recent years. 'Even Muslims are consulting me,' said Vashishtha, who scrutinises birth charts for suitability of partner, timing of the wedding and other aspects. 'It is best to get married when Venus is in the ascendant and Jupiter is strong – Jupiter is such a happening planet.' Even the wedding invitation is a study in changing values – a kind of designer-label one-upmanship between India's rising middle classes. Instead of the simple cardboard box of *mithai* (ceremonial sweets) that had traditionally accompanied the card, the sweets now come in crystal bowls, silver-edged plates or hand-woven baskets. The conventional cardboard invitation has been replaced by expensive fabrics or even handmade paper. It has become fashionable among the poshest families to commission M. F. Husain and Satish Gujral, two of India's best-known artists, to design invitations. The guest list often includes people neither the bride nor the bridegroom has met. The point – which is often misunderstood by foreigners – is for both sets of parents to demonstrate who they can persuade to attend. The more sumptuous the invitation, the more competitive it will be. For the bigger weddings, some invitations (to relatives and friends) are accompanied by Louis Vuitton bags,

Revlon cosmetic kits, Bulgari scarves or Prada accessories. 'The days of giving a good old sari are over,' said Vandana Mohan. 'It is not just about how much you spend; it is how much you are seen to be spending.'

Then there is the catering. In the last few years dozens of specialist wedding caterers have sprung up in Delhi, Mumbai and elsewhere. Hosts no longer offer only Indian cooking. So-called 'multi-cuisine' stalls provide Thai, Moroccan, Japanese and other exotic fare. 'The standard is to have at least seven different cuisines – the more foreign ones the better,' said Mohan. 'The fact that everybody heads for the *tandoor* section is neither here nor there.' Equally important is the originality of the decor, the type and variety of candles, the floral arrangements and so on. Most choose themes for the main party, such as 'lounge', 'Moulin Rouge', a particular Bollywood film or even a country. One much-publicised Punjabi wedding in 2004 had South Africa as the motif. The parents of the bride went so far as to transport eight giraffes from Africa to add that authentic touch. 'It is as if some kind of madness has gripped India's middle classes,' said Mohan. I presumed the giraffes were shipped home after the reception in a state of high confusion.

But what of India's esoteric traditions: the Hinduism of the Rig-Veda, the Bhagavad Gita and the Upanishads? Have they survived the onslaught of modern consumerism? India has an extraordinary history of subtle abstraction, and a chain of free-wheeling philosophical speculation that stretches back for three thousand years. It may not be the religion of the masses, but if the finer and more subtle dimensions of India's traditions have survived for this long, it seems highly unlikely that they would vanish in today's world.

Writing about the India of the first millennium BC, when the followers of Buddha, Mahavira and a thousand diverse sects were active, all putting their ideas forward in a climate of relatively permissive enquiry, A. L. Basham observed: 'The intellectual life of India in the seventh and sixth centuries BC, was as pullulating and as vigorous as the jungle after rains.'[16] Pantheists argued with polytheists, dualists with monists, materialists with spiritualists and atheists with everyone else. The quality of classical Indian grammars, from Pali to Sanskrit, was as sophisticated as any that were ever collated. Those who wish to comment on Hinduism purely as a religion (although some argue it is misleading even to describe it as such) should also grapple with its esoteric traditions. I am certainly unqualified to do so, but it is nevertheless possible to appreciate the complexity of India's philosophical traditions. I was struck by this (not unrepresentative) line from the Upanishads: 'The Gods themselves are later than creation, so who knows truly whence it has arisen?'[17] This could be read both as an admission of ignorance about the origins of creation and as an admission that gods are essentially products of the human imagination.

Some of the texts even contain flashes of nihilism. In the Bhagavad Gita, Krishna, who appears as a charioteer, advises Arjuna, the warrior he is serving, to overcome his doubts about the futility of killing and do his caste duty by going into battle on his chariot. This epic conversation is often cited as an example of the moral code behind caste, since Krishna advises Arjuna that doing one's caste duty is more important than personal considerations. It is also cited as an example of karmic morality: Arjuna can escape the bonds of karma – his past actions – only by acting without regard for the consequences. The emphasis is on intention, not outcome. To a foreigner, what also leaps out from Krishna's words is their bleak consistency. He tells Arjuna: 'Thou feels pity when pity has no place. Wise men feel pity neither for what dies nor what lives . . . I am indifferent to all born things. There is none whom I hate, none whom I love.'

Buddha was recorded as having said much the same thing: 'Those who love nothing in this world are rich in joy and free from pain.'[18] One of the most cited stories from his life concerns a young mother who begs him to restore the life of her young son, who has just died of an illness. She pledges to follow him for the rest of her life if he will do this. Buddha tells the bereaved mother to go to the nearest town and bring back some mustard seed from the first household that she finds which has not suffered a recent loss. The mother leaves her son's corpse with Buddha and goes from house to house in the town. Eventually, as the day wears on, she realises that there is no household which fits the required description. She returns to Buddha as a follower, having accepted the futility of challenging the laws of life and death. Basham contrasts this story with the miracles of Jesus, in which people are raised from the dead and the sick and wounded get up and walk. It is hard to experience the force of many New Testament stories unless you believe they literally happened. Irrespective of whether this small episode from Buddha's life actually took place, it makes little difference to the force of the message.[19] Basham could equally have contrasted its message with the practice of popular Buddhism in which people walk clockwise around the temple, believing each lap earns them extra merit, while chanting the name of an atheist philosopher.

But India's most revered texts contain a message that is profoundly asocial – on a literal reading they sometimes appear to recommend an indifference to the suffering of others. Likewise, there is a tendency to recommend words over action. Traces of this philosophical aloofness can be found in many aspects of contemporary India. I was once eating lunch at a large café in Cuddalore in Tamil Nadu when I realised that all the uniformed waiters rushing from table to table were children – some as young as eight or nine. The café was situated about five hundred metres from the district courthouse and many of its patrons were lawyers. No one batted an eyelid. Child labour was officially abolished in India many years ago, but large loopholes were provided for cottage industries. And so the employment of children continues in one of India's wealthiest states under the noses of lawyers as they are eating their lunches off large banana leaves.

Tamil Nadu was also the site of a controversial battle over child labour in the 1980s and 1990s when matchstick sweat shops in the town of Sivakasi were revealed to be employing large numbers of children. The owners of the factories had secured cottage-industry status, so they benefited from the lax interpretation of labour laws. Their main competitor, Wimco, was a Swedish company which used modern machine-based methods to manufacture matchsticks using less labour. Wimco complained about the unfair labour practices of its local competitors and a tussle ensued in which almost everybody, from government officials to social activists, united in opposition to the foreign multinational. The government eventually imposed higher duties on the machines that Wimco imported for its capital-intensive production lines. The child labour continued. When it came to the crunch, people from across the political spectrum, including Gandhians, disliked foreign capital more than they disliked child labour.[20]

It is hard to make a good estimate of the extent of child labour in India because it is so difficult to define. The larger estimates of up to forty million children would include youngsters who help out in their parents' shops, or collect water in the morning for household use (often a very long walk).[21] But children who are at least indirectly employed by third parties, such as matchstick-makers, *bidi* cigarette-makers, brassware-polishers and middlemen in the carpet industry, probably number about ten million. Another way to estimate child labour is to look at school truancy, which again totals about forty million. Whichever number you eventually choose, it amounts to a lot of young lives.

Child illiteracy and child labour are very closely related. There is a widespread view that the problem will not disappear until poverty has first disappeared; in other words; it will sort itself out over time. More than a decade ago Myron Weiner wrote a devastating book, *The Child and the State in India*. He pointed out that the consensus among India's elites that child illiteracy and child labour were consequences not causes of poverty was the wrong way round. Most countries, for one reason or another, made education compulsory before they became developed economies. Weiner cited municipalities in Germany which made child education compulsory as early as 1524 under the influence of the Protestant zeal of Martin Luther, who believed all humans should have direct access to the Word of God. For the same reason, Massachusetts in 1647 made child attendance at school compulsory. Japan did the same in 1872 because it wanted to catch up with the west and education was deemed essential to nation-building. And the USSR wanted the opportunity to create a socialist 'new man', which it could achieve through indoctrination in its schools.[22] Much the same applies to China now, with its literacy rate of more than 90 per cent, compared to India's 65 per cent.

Weiner pointed out that India had on paper done all the right things, having enacted strict laws and incorporated high-sounding principles about child rights in the 1950 constitution. But when it came to implementing these laws, indifference reigned. The same point could be made about statutes outlawing the practice of dowry, untouchability and child marriage, all of which persist in India on gargantuan scales. As we have seen, some problems, such as dowry, are even getting worse. Weiner concluded that these laws were 'a kind of modern talisman intended to bring results by the magical power of words themselves'. Hundreds of years ago, foreign chroniclers of India (such as Alberuni and Fa Hsien) observed the tendency of Brahmins to prefer words to action, and sometimes to believe they were one and the same thing. Weiner also highlighted the traditional attitudes of the upper-caste elites, who might profess their support for equality of opportunity but in practice behave quite differently. Pratap Bhanu Mehta puts it succinctly: 'The state has internalised the message of the Bhagavad Gita – only intentions matter and not consequences.'[23] Hindu philosophy has produced some of the most sophisticated abstractions the world has known, but it has never produced a Martin Luther. Traditionally the lower castes were not permitted to read the classic Hindu texts. This tradition lingers in today's India. How else could one explain why a country which made education compulsory two generations ago should tolerate the daily absence of up to forty million children from its schools?

In the autumn of 2004 I visited India's 'carpet belt' districts in Uttar Pradesh. There are three districts around the holy town of Varanasi which together employ roughly 500,000 people and possess 175,000 handlooms, most of them at the cottage-industry level.[24] Tens of thousands of children are involved in the production of carpets. Naturally, the region has one of the lowest literacy rates in India. I was accompanied by Dipankar Gupta, the Delhi-based sociologist, who had recommended that I see a project commissioned by Ikea, the Swedish furniture chainstore, which buys carpets from the region. Ikea had requested that Unicef, the United Nations Children's Fund, manage the project. The Swedish company had examined and rejected an existing scheme – Rugmark – run by a collection of international companies. Any shopper in the west who buys a carpet with the Rugmark label is supposedly given a guarantee that it was not made with child labour. As I was to discover, the Rugmark guarantee is questionable. There are only a handful of Rugmark inspectors covering tens of thousands of villages. Like all cottage industries, carpet-making is highly decentralised and fragmented, so it is physically impossible for the inspectors to verify Rugmark's claims.

We drove down tiny dirt tracks to some of the most isolated villages in the area to observe local 'bridge schools', which give former child workers a year of intensive education before they are transferred to a mainstream school. Sitting under the shade of a capacious *neem* tree next to the village pond, the children were learning to count with the aid of carpet knots. At separate village classes, their mothers were being trained in better carpet-making methods (most of the fathers are working in the cities). Defenders of child labour in India's carpet industry use four arguments to justify its continuation. First, the children's parents are too poor to send them to school. Second, the education would be of no use to them since they could not put it into practice. Third, they work at home with their families, so the conditions are reasonable. Finally, children are essential to the intricate process of carpet-knotting, since they have nimble fingers. I had always believed the last one, but even that turns out to be false. Unicef calls it the 'nimble-finger myth'. In fact, the process of carpet-knotting requires considerable strength, so obviously adults are better suited to the task. 'Quality has improved since we moved to full adult labour,' said Fida Hussain, owner of Deluxe Carpets, which supplies Ikea.

As for Ikea, its investments are self-interested, which is why Unicef was convinced it would remain committed to the project. By supporting the move to full adult labour in carpet-making and by making it worthwhile for families to go along with the scheme, the company protects itself against possible consumer boycotts and adverse publicity in the west. Equally important, Ikea gets more value for its money because adults work at much higher rates of productivity than children.* 'So often human rights arguments are pitted against arguments of profitability in India and elsewhere,' said Dipankar Gupta, who carries out 'social audits' of foreign and domestic investments in India. 'If it is done right, it is usually more profitable to treat people well.'

The same argument could be applied on a much larger scale to the most distressing social problems that India continues to face. One of the reasons why it finds it so hard to develop a mass, labour-intensive manufacturing sector is because such a large

---

*Defenders of child labour in India deploy much the same logic as nineteenth-century plantation owners in the American South before the abolition of slavery. Free labour turned out to be much more productive than slave labour.

proportion of its rural adults are not educated to a minimum standard. Even for the most basic widget-making, the worker needs to be able to read simple instructions. Yet support for the highly inadequate status quo can be found in the most surprising quarters, for example among Gandhian groups and trade union members. Weiner gives an example of workers in India's large tea plantations, who are the most militant defenders of child labour because they want their children to inherit their jobs. Gandhian activists make similar arguments, believing that in many cases an early apprenticeship in traditional occupations, such as glass-making or carpet-making, will give the child a much more relevant skill in life than anything the formal education system could offer. There is some merit to some of these arguments, not least because India's government school system is so inadequate. But the notion that children should do what their parents do – and be denied, inadvertently or otherwise, the skills to make their own choice when they are old enough – is deeply conservative. At a much higher level of society, it provides an underpinning to the culture of nepotism that afflicts politics and administration. Essentially, it is about caste and the maintenance of hereditary occupations. Weiner calls it 'social reproduction': 'In short trade unionists, like most parents, employers, teachers and education officials, presume a social order that is guided by the principles of social reproduction.'[25]

The rest of the world could learn a lot from India, among which tolerance, the management of diversity and the rooting of democracy in a traditional society loom large. Most people who sample Indian food, music, dancing, literature, architecture and philosophy acquire a lifelong taste for all things Indian. If world trade were to be conducted purely in cultural products then India would have a thumping annual surplus. But India continues to lack in practice – if not in principle – the basic condition of genuine citizenship. Equal citizenship is enshrined in India's constitution; it is expounded by thousands of academics, journalists, activists and commentators; it is generally presumed to be a reality. But in practice India falls far short of the claims it makes. India's caste system and the traditional mentality of its upper castes are changing and may even be in long-term decline. But they have yet to disappear. As we have seen with the continuation of high illiteracy rates, the low status of women, and the economic valuation of lower-caste children, the persistence of certain traditional attitudes imposes a moral cost on Indian society. Male and female children ought to be seen as priceless. The continuation of such traditions also imposes an economic cost, which India can ill afford to pay.

CONCLUSION

HERS TO LOSE

India's huge opportunities and challenges in the twenty-first century

The only possible idea of India is a nation that is greater than the sum of its parts.

Shashi Tharoor, Indian author and Under Secretary-General
of the United Nations[1]

I was once offered a chance to ride through the streets of New Delhi on a white horse. To my subsequent regret, I turned it down. I and my family chose instead to arrive at my marriage ceremony in a fleet of white Ambassadors. The experience was unnerving. Priya had been convinced the entire wedding was heading for disaster since her parents had not got around to planning anything until a few days earlier. No Hindu priest would marry an Indian to a foreigner, she claimed. And none of my friends or relatives would have a clue what was going on. Nobody had told me what I was supposed to do during the two-hour ceremony – although I had been given a formal outfit of *kurta* pyjamas to wear. To add to the rising sense of panic, the car that was supposed to fetch Priya from the beauty parlour a couple of hours before the ceremony had failed to arrive: Priya had been forgotten. Armageddon, it seemed, could no longer be prevented.

But we were in India, not England. And what appears on the surface to be chaotic is often just how it should be. The wedding passed off beautifully, although it took me about ninety minutes to realise that there was method in the apparent madness that was going on around us. The Hindu priest had arrived. The lotus leaves were in place. The *ghee* for pouring on the fire was ready. And the knot that would bind us together was waiting to be tied. Sitting cross-legged in a small *mandap* – or house of flowers – we were one of only two still points in the kaleidoscope of colour. The other fixed point, which I occasionally used to check my bearings, was provided by my relatives, dressed in the sober wedding attire of Anglican England, vaguely wondering whether they were supposed to stand up and start singing. Their collective expression of awkward bemusement gradually dissolved into chatter and laughter as they realised nothing formal would be required of them. It was as good an illustration as any of the 'functioning anarchy' that J. K. Galbraith, US ambassador to New Delhi in the early 1960s, once said of India. In spite of all signs to the contrary, things came together perfectly. Priya, meanwhile, was feeling guilty at ever having doubted her parents.

Whenever events in India appear to be on the verge of falling apart, I often remind myself of our wedding and of Galbraith's very apt description of India. Occasionally I am also reminded of what I was once taught about the behaviour of bees. If you were to be transported inside a swarm, it would appear to be anarchic, with individual bees buzzing around in every different direction. But if you stood back and observed the swarm as a whole, it would be going in one direction.

In the last thirty years India has been through a nineteen-month spell of autocracy, it has lost two leaders of the Nehru–Gandhi family to assassination, it has faced separatist movements in Punjab, Kashmir, Assam and elsewhere, and it has switched from a closed economic regime to an open(ish) economy. It has moved from secular government to Hindu nationalist government and back again, it has gone from single-party rule to twenty-four-party rule, from anti-nuclear to nuclear, from undeclared border wars with Pakistan to a lengthy peace process. It has also moved from virtual bankruptcy to a lengthy boom. By any normal barometer, India appears to be highly unpredictable.

These are India's headlines of the last thirty years. But if you turn to the statistics buried deep in the inside pages you get a strikingly different impression. T. N. Ninan, one of the country's most respected editors, calls India the 'one per cent society'.[2] Whichever indicator you choose, whether it is economic or social, India is improving at a rate of roughly 1 per cent a year. For example, India's poverty rate is declining at about 1 per cent a year: in 1991 it was 35 per cent; by 2000 it was 26 per cent.[3] It has probably continued to decline at roughly the same rate since then. Or take India's literacy rate: in 1991 it was 52 per cent; by 2001 it was 65 per cent. Or life expectancy: in 1991 the average Indian would live until the age of fifty-eight; by 2001 that had risen to sixty-five years. Roughly the same congruence emerges from its international rankings. India's human development index, which is compiled by the United Nations Development Programme, went from 0.254 in 1970 to 0.602 in 2005, which translates into an annual improvement of about 1 per cent.

To judge by the living conditions of ordinary Indians and not by the drama of national events, the country is moving forward on a remarkably stable trajectory. Many friends of India wish the country would accelerate its rate of progress. An improvement of 1 per cent a year is fine if you already have a developed economy, but when almost 300 million people continue to live in absolute poverty, it is painfully slow. Unfortunately, though, India's fragmented political culture makes it very difficult for governments to take decisive action that would convert India into a 2 per cent society, like neighbouring China. Yet, on India's plus side it would take very large-scale disaster or war to halt or reverse its steady progress.

If intentions can be ascribed to nation states, you could say

India has given a higher priority to stability than it has to efficiency. In many ways the opposite could be said of China. Myron Weiner once said that India moved slowly because it was diverse. That also meant it was relatively stable. If something goes wrong in one part of the country, it does not necessarily spread to other areas as it would in a more homogeneous society, like China's. Recall the panicked reaction of China's ageing communist leadership in 1989 to the gathering of students in Beijing's Tiananmen Square in support of democracy. Fearing the protests would spread quickly into a national movement, they sent in the tanks. India faces a Tiananmen-style sit-down protest in one or other corner of the country for one reason or another every other week. Sometimes the police charge with their *lathis*, but bullets are very rare. 'India is like a lorry with twelve wheels,' wrote Weiner. 'If one or two puncture, it doesn't go into the ditch.'[4] To extend the analogy, China has fewer wheels so it can travel faster. But people far beyond China's borders worry about what would happen if a wheel came off.

What is it that keeps India stable? After independence, many foreign observers predicted the country would not last for long in its existing form. Because of its profound social, linguistic, religious and ethnic diversities, India would inevitably break up into separate nation states. One authoritative book from the early sixties, *India: The Most Dangerous Decades*, which dwelt on India's separatist threats, was very widely cited.[5] but India has not dissolved. Nor does it seem likely to. Another widespread expectation was that India would not remain a democracy for long. The assumption then, as now, was that democracy was not compatible with absolute poverty or with majority illiteracy. Again, this view has been belied by events. There are many reasons why these two expectations proved unfounded. Perhaps the most important reason why India has remained intact as a country is because it is a democracy: and perhaps the most important reason why India has remained a democracy is because it is so diverse. Far from endangering democracy, India's pluralism makes democracy essential.

A related but more insidious assumption is that China is growing faster than India because it is authoritarian. This view is held by some western and Asian commentators. I am certainly not alone in having ethical reservations about posing questions to which the only answer is dictatorship. But I also think the debate is misleading. India went through a period of autocracy under Indira Gandhi that turned out to be damaging to the country's social stability and to its economic prosperity.* The autocratic tendencies of Congress under Indira Gandhi strengthened the forces of regionalism in Indian politics and stoked separatist insurgencies on India's national borders that brought its national integrity into question. That India remains in one piece owes much to the fact that Gandhi restored the system of federal democracy, which has provided a peaceful outlet to most of the country's regional tendencies. As for India's plethora of insurgencies, only the Kashmiri struggle poses a serious threat to Indian nationhood, and it is partly sustained by a foreign power.

There is a better answer to those who argue that India suffers from a lack of autocracy: Pakistan. As Amartya Sen points out, India's economic growth rate has consistently outperformed that of Pakistan in the last two decades, achieving an average of 6 per cent compared to 3.5 per cent. For some of that period, Pakistan has had democracy, but even during periods of free elections the freedom of Pakistani citizens has been limited. As the joke goes, 'In Pakistan, freedom of expression is notably stronger than freedom after expression.'[6] Because of their ethnic and cultural similarities, Pakistan offers India a much better mirror than

---

*The Emergency was supported by intellectual trend-setters throughout the western world, including Robert McNamara, president of the World Bank and US Defense Secretary during the early stages of the Vietnam War, who believed a spell of autocracy would improve India's rate of investment by reducing populist democratic pressures to raise current spending.

China: 'The proximate comparison of India with a not-always democratic country must be with Pakistan, which somehow does not tend to be the focus of the rosy portrayals of the non-democratic alternative that India has missed,' said Sen.

The contrast between India and China is also selective. Although China has much better economic and social indicators than India, this arguably has little to do with their contrasting political systems. The Indian state of Kerala, which is as democratic as any other, has a life expectancy of seventy-four and a literacy rate over 90 per cent, compared to seventy years and 90 per cent for China. 'There is absolutely nothing to indicate that any of China's policies are inconsistent with greater democracy,' said Sen.[7] At a more important level, India challenges us to provide a clear definition of what we mean by development, which is usually taken to mean economic prosperity and little else. Should it not also mean giving people significant choices in how they express themselves and conduct their lives? If the answer is 'yes' then democracy should be seen as a development goal in itself. On this measure, India is ahead of China. Clearly India will have to find better ways of ensuring that its democracy delivers a fairer economic deal to its people. One way of achieving better governance would be for the Indian state to treat people as citizens with equal rights and not as supplicants on a scale graded according to social status. Viewed from this perspective, India is not democratic enough. As Arun Shourie, the Indian politician, points out: 'Governance is not golf: that we are a democracy does not entitle us to a handicap.'[8]

To understand why India's decision-making process is slower than China's, one should look at India's more deeply entrenched culture of pluralism. China is also diverse, but it has one script, one official language and very little religious division. India has eighteen official languages, several different scripts, and deep religious and caste divisions. The highly segmented nature of Indian society makes collective action much more difficult to carry out. Regardless of the political system, it would be difficult for Indian governments to take decisive action. A relatively homogeneous country like Norway that is scrupulously democratic has an efficient and decisive system of government, while dictatorships ruling over diverse tribal countries in Africa and elsewhere are chronically unable to impose consensus on their societies.[9] India's system of government is held back by ethnic division in society; it is much harder to build trust between ethnic groups than within them. This makes it far more difficult to undertake collective action. Academics call it the 'prisoner's dilemma'. I prefer the analogy that Indians themselves make about a bucket of crabs on the beach: whenever one crab tries to climb out of the bucket, the others pull it back down.

Some people dispute whether the term 'ethnic politics' is appropriate for India, because they do not agree that Indian castes or religious groups are ethnically distinct. The classical Sanskrit word for caste is *varna*, which can be translated as 'colour', perhaps giving an indication of the historical beginnings of caste division. One of the principal origins of caste was the gradual incorporation of indigenous Indian tribes into mainstream Indian society by sedentary communities. Each new tribe was allotted a place low down in the system. The battle – often between Hindu nationalists and Christian missionaries – to incorporate India's tribal groups into mainstream society continues today throughout the country.

What matters is what people perceive themselves to be. In many ways India's castes behave in a way that is much more similar to tribal or kinship groups than to economic classes. It is virtually impossible to tell which way Indians will vote only by knowing their socioeconomic status (you are more likely to vote your caste when you cast your vote). This is why so much of Indian politics continues to be absorbed by seemingly petty disputes over social dignity rather than concentrating on economic conditions ('It's the politics, stupid'). It is also why it is so hard in India to build a state that is blind to the identity of its citizens.

Most interactions between the individual and the state in India are governed by who you are and whom you know. Some people believe this will fade as India's middle class expands. As we saw in the last chapter, most middle-class Indians are employed in sectors that are subject to global competition, and they are increasingly likely to select their employees on the basis of merit rather than blood ties. India's middle class totals between just 200 million and 300 million people, as defined by international standards.[10] It is still hard for India's poor to gain entry to it.

The reforms of 1991 have benefited India. If carried out sequentially, further liberalisation would lead to higher growth rates and would bring greater benefits. But India's free market liberalisers cannot simply wish away the state. Nor should they want to. Without a more meritocratic and just state,* India's economy will suffer. To thrive, India's businesses need good infrastructure, a literate and healthy workforce, a sustainable environment and the promise of law and order. Very little of this can be accomplished by the private sector on its own. The division in India, and elsewhere, is too often between those who believe the state should dominate all aspects of life and those who believe it should play virtually no role beyond defence and law and order. As we shall see, it is in the interests of all people, rich or poor, right wing or left wing, for India to develop a more responsive and modern state.

In what follows we will look at four critical problems that India faces in the coming years and decades: first, the challenge of lifting 300 million people out of absolute poverty and of providing the remainder with a more secure standard of living; second, overcoming the dangers of rapid environmental degradation, which, at

---

*In addition to the fact that they restrict merit-based selection, there are questions about the justness of India's job reservations system for scheduled castes, tribes and other backward classes. According to India's Supreme Court, the 'creamy layers' – economically wealthy – among India's socially disadvantaged groups monopolise the public sector jobs quota.

the human level, is poisoning India's air and water supply and which at the global level will increasingly add to climate change; third, heading off the spectre of an HIV–Aids epidemic, which, if untackled, could derail India's upbeat economic projections; finally, protecting and strengthening India's system of liberal democracy, which, along with the talents of its people, is the most precious asset the country possesses. Then we will look at India's extraordinary potential to rise over the coming decades. But in order to exploit its opportunities fully, India will have to tackle its problems more directly. Overcoming them would tax the powers and resources of an efficient and forward-thinking state. In its present condition, there is a consderable question mark over India's state.

In 1900 the world's population was 1.6 billion. By 2050, India alone is projected to hit that figure, having overtaken China as the world's most populous nation by 2032. The various United Nations scenarios for India's population plateau range between 1.3 billion and 1.9 billion people.[11] There is a forecasting margin of error amounting to 600 million people. The more rapidly India can overcome poverty, the more likely it is that its population will stabilise nearer one billion than two billion people. Perhaps the key determinants of how quickly the nation will be able to eradicate mass poverty are whether it can establish a better economic climate for its farmers and create more jobs in manufacturing and services.

India lifted its agricultural yields drastically in the 1970s and 1980s. But in the last fifteen years its yield growth for cereals has tapered off. India does not necessarily require another generation of 'miracle' rice or wheat to achieve a second green revolution, although new seed technology would help.* At the moment the country's average yield per hectare is roughly half that of China.[12]

---

*India has experimented with genetically modified cotton with mixed results. There are proposals to permit GM mustard, sorghum and other crops.

To catch up with its neighbour, a series of long-overdue reforms must be implemented. But this is easier said than done. Rural land holdings must be consolidated by the creation of a market for voluntary land sales so that the average plot size can become large enough to permit mechanisation. Families who own just a hectare or two (90 per cent of India's farm holdings are of this size) cannot afford tractors or drip-irrigation technology. For some crops it makes sense for farmers to get together and create cooperative farms when there is a guaranteed market for their produce. But most Indian states make it compulsory for farmers to sell their produce to government-appointed middlemen who drive their buying prices down and their selling prices up and pocket much of the difference. India's farmers should be allowed to sell to whom they choose, irrespective of whether the buyer is foreign or domestic. Liberalising India's retail sector, which would bring investments into cold-storage facilities and new agribusinesses, would also stimulate more rapid change.

But the government must do more than abolish agricultural price controls if it wants to boost rural prosperity. The state must also play a more direct role. The most obvious deficiency is in India's dismal rural infrastructure, both physical and social. More all-weather roads must be built to link villages to towns, and India's primary and secondary education system has to be reformed to ensure that teachers turn up and do their jobs. The same applies to village health centres, which as often as not are dilapidated hulks stripped (by employees or local residents) of their equipment. Fewer than half of all Indian births are assisted by trained midwives or doctors, compared to 97 per cent in China.[13] The problem is neither money nor technology. It is the efficiency of government. In order to encourage farmers to grow other crops, New Delhi should overhaul its regressive system of food subsidies. As India grows richer, people are spending proportionately more on vegetables and proteins and less on basic cereals. But almost all of India's agricultural subsidies go to wheat and rice farmers.

Diversifying the public incentive system to encourage more horticulture, vegetable, fish and chicken farming, which have greater export potential, would give a large income boost to India's impoverished villagers. Wheat and rice are also heavily water-intensive, and India can ill afford to continue wasting the fickle offerings of its rain gods. Furthermore, crop diversification would employ more people: vegetable farming employs fifteen times more people per hectare than rice or wheat. The government should deliver reliable electricity and clean water to all its villages. Providing these resources free of charge to select categories of people (mostly rich farmers), makes it uneconomic to provide them to anyone else. If utilities are allowed to charge customers for what they use, there is an incentive to supply them. There must also be better incentives for farmers to collect rainwater. More than 70 per cent of India's rainfall runs off into the sea.[14] In the cities charging the poor for water would ensure that the poor would receive it. Giving it to them for free means they will continue to get either sewage or nothing. In practice, the poor pay private water suppliers a multiple of what it would cost the state to deliver.

The other half of India's poverty challenge is to create non-agricultural employment for many more people. India's workforce is expanding at roughly ten million people every year, but only about five million new jobs are created each year. Some new employment can be created by reforming agriculture, but not nearly enough. To stray into economic jargon for a moment, India's unreformed farming sector – as it exists now – has a zero or even a negative employment elasticity of growth.[15] This means that improvements to agricultural productivity entail less, not more, labour. India's service sector could take up some of the slack, particularly if the country can do more to boost its tourist industry, which remains surprisingly small considering the unparalleled wealth of things to see and experience in India. At just 2.5 million foreign visitors in 2005, India had fewer tourists than Dubai or

Singapore. Foreigners are put off by the country's unreliable transport links and its poor sanitation. Visiting the Taj Mahal is not as enthralling or romantic as it should be when you have to skirt around refuse dumps, and dodge beggars and stray dogs to get inside. Building up a tourism industry does not automatically require the 'Disneyfication' of your culture, as some fear. It is hard to believe that a stronger tourist sector that provided more formal jobs for the poor in transport, hotels, restaurants and other services would diminish the dignity of Indian culture. Indeed, higher revenues would help preserve some of the crumbling monuments.

However, there is no substitute for creating a larger and more labour-intensive manufacturing sector. This does not have to be polluting, because India possesses the technology and capital to develop in a cleaner fashion than countries that industrialised earlier. Nor does it have to be socially disruptive. Production, particularly in food processing and textiles, can take place in the small towns of provincial India, especially if the roads are paved and refrigeration is provided. We have already glimpsed India's aptitude in the garment and fashion sector, and the precision and value the country's entrepreneurs can add to auto-components and pharmaceuticals. But these cutting-edge sectors mostly employ graduates. The rest of India's labour force must be given better education and more vocational training if they are to become employable. The government must also remove the obstacles that inhibit investors, both domestic and foreign, from putting more money into the economy. Indian managers spend 15 per cent of their time dealing with government inspectors,[16] which is almost double that of China. Indian companies also spend far too much time filling in complicated tax forms and dealing with venal customs officers. Although New Delhi has taken steps to simplify its tax code, India still arguably has the most complicated tax system in the world.[17] In some parts of India *octroi* – a tax levied on the passage of goods from one state to another – costs more to administer than it generates. Corruption is the only possible explanation for why it has been kept in place.

Creating better infrastructure, particularly ports, roads, railway lines and electricity supply, is also indispensable for the development of manufacturing. The infrastructure projects themselves would significantly boost employment. India's government is stuck in chronic fiscal deficit. It needs all the capital it can get from domestic and foreign private sources to upgrade its infrastructure. New Delhi has pledged by 2009 to open up India's banking sector to full competition. Finance houses such as Citibank and Standard Chartered have already picked up significant business from the growing middle classes. Giving them and India's growing number of impressive and internationally competitive private banks better access to the poorly managed state-owned rural bank network would significantly boost the country's ability to translate savings into investment, which would generate more capital to invest in better infrastructure. New Delhi has also taken steps partially to open its insurance sector to foreign investors. Less than 10 per cent of the population has life insurance. The more people who can be insured, the more capital there is to invest. India has nothing to fear from further financial liberalisation.

Finally, as we saw in Chapters One and Two, India must reform its labour laws. This would not be anti-poor, as many have argued. If it is impossible to fire someone, you are much less likely to hire him in the first place. India has just ten million trade union members, of whom only 1.37 million are considered to be active in their unions.[18] But in the name of the poor the unions exercise a veto on reform of the very labour regulations that contribute to keeping most of India's 470-million-strong workforce locked out of the formal economy. India should acknowledge that on this issue the country's unions, like its business lobbies, are just another vested interest who speak for their members, not for the poor.

The second large challenge is to prevent wholesale environmental degradation. Understandably, Indians get irritable when western nations lecture them on protecting their forests or reducing carbon-dioxide emissions when the west is responsible for most of the world's environmental deterioration. India accounts for only 4 per cent of global carbon-dioxide emissions but has almost 17 per cent of the world's population.[19] Clearly on a per capita basis, the citizens of the US, Europe and other rich nations generate much more pollution and derive much greater benefit from doing so. But this situation is changing. Many of the richer nations are taking steps to promote energy efficiency and introduce cleaner fuels. India's share of the responsibility for global warming will escalate rapidly. No solution to climate change will be credible without the participation of India and China (led, of course, by the United States, the world's biggest polluter). The west, and particularly the US, should take a stronger lead in offering India and the rest of the developing world financial incentives to embark on a cleaner path of development. For its part, India must get over its resentment of western 'double standards' and acknowledge that Indians will be disproportionately harmed by the climate change which a majority of scientists are now predicting. India should not cut off its nose to spite its face.

Indians already face acute quality-of-life issues that are related to their environment. Fewer than 2 per cent of Indians own their own vehicles. (The comparable figure is 60 per cent for the United States.[20]) Yet India's cities are already clogged with traffic. In 2004, for the first time, more than a million private vehicles were sold in one year in India. That number will rise sharply. By 2030, India is projected to have 200 million vehicles, public and private, compared to 40 million in 2006.[21] Quite apart from urban air quality, or more mundane issues such as parking space, it is hard to imagine a road-building programme that could keep up with vehicle demand. An India with five times as many vehicles as today (and rising) is a vision of purgatory. There are many areas, such as telecoms (in which mobile phones are booming without the fixed-line service having improved much), where India has leapfrogged a stage of development by exploiting new technology. It could leapfrog the classic stage of traffic gridlock by planning now for cleaner and more efficient urban transport systems. Several projects, such as the Delhi Metro, point the way forward. Every Indian city needs a Delhi Metro, in spite of the high capital costs and subsidies that are involved in such mass-transit projects. Furthermore, India should upgrade its 63,000-kilometre rail network – the second most extensive in the world – which has the capacity to transport goods and people around the country in a much less polluting and more economically efficient way than roads. At the moment, the opposite is happening. Indian Railways overcharge freight users in order to subsidise passengers, and the high tariffs push freight on to the roads, which clogs them up. A similar problem exists in the power-generating sector. India's state power boards' high electricity charges make it difficult for small businesses to survive, since they have to buy their own highly polluting diesel generators.

The quality of air and water in India is declining as rapidly as the economy is improving (without being factored in as a cost). It is estimated that an eighth of the country's premature deaths are caused by air pollution.[22] Several hundred thousand children die every year from dirty water. Retreating to the past is not a solution, as some of India's environmental activists seem to believe. In the villages people die young of respiratory diseases because they lack electricity or access to gas. The climate and the topography of the village make it impractical to burn cow dung or wood outdoors, so they light their fire indoors, which gradually destroys their lungs. Only about half of India's village households have a power connection. Likewise, most water-borne diseases are caused by lack of modern sanitation. Even if it were technically possible to retreat to a prosperous rural idyll cut off from the modern world, it is too late because India simply has too many people. The lessons on electricity tariffs also apply to irrigation for India's farmers. As we have seen, only rich farmers can afford to pump water from the ground leaving everyone else with less water, and accelerating soil deterioration by increasing salinity levels. Deforestation is also a factor in soil erosion. In 1900 a third of India was covered by forest; now it is a sixth.[23] In order to encourage sustainable exploitation of resources, whether it is water, soil, forests or air, people must be made to pay for what they consume. Businesses that pollute should be fined or closed, which very rarely happens. Corrupt forest officials, who connive with illegal loggers and poachers, should be sacked, which they rarely are. And both water and power should be priced simply and fairly. Many Indians still believe both utilities should be provided for free or at a nominal cost. But somebody, somewhere, always pays.

Finally, India should develop a coherent energy strategy, for the sake of both its environment and its economy. Because of the demands of coalition politics, India's energy management is scattered across many different ministries – coal, steel, power, petroleum, hydroelectric and nuclear. Each has a different agenda that is often oblivious to those of the others. India needs one Ministry of Energy. Today the country imports 70 per cent of its oil, which is projected to rise to 90 per cent by 2020 unless significant new domestic oil fields can be discovered.[24] Politics makes it almost impossible to build large new dams for hydroelectric power, and India's reserves of coal are very high in ash content, which makes them a particularly dirty form of fossil fuel. As we have seen, the civil nuclear option is costly. But there are other sources of energy. India should move ahead with the controversial gas pipeline from Iran via Pakistan and explore other possible pipelines from Central Asia through Afghanistan and from Myanmar through Bangladesh. Gas is a relatively clean fuel. Others could also be developed. South Africa has demonstrated it is economically viable to 'gasify' dirty coal, but India is at least fifteen years behind in exploring the potential of what it could do if it gasified some of its reserves. As I have argued, India can reduce its demand for oil by modernising its national rail network and by building new-generation mass-transit systems. An India that repeats the mistakes of the west is both a horrific prospect and self-defeating. India has always believed it has much to teach the world. Perhaps the best lesson it could convey is that you do not have to ruin your natural surroundings or destroy the quality of life for future generations in order to lift your people out of poverty.

India's third challenge is to defeat the HIV–Aids epidemic. Many influential people in the country believe the threat has been exaggerated by the west and that they ought to focus on solving more long-standing problems like tuberculosis and malnutrition. In one sense they are right. Funding for HIV–Aids prevention and treatment should not come at the expense of efforts to provide basic healthcare to India's citizens. There should be no trade-off between the two. But unless India also tackles the Aids epidemic, its healthcare system could be rapidly overwhelmed. It is true that in 2005 fewer than 1 per cent of Indians had contracted HIV. But that amounts to 5.1 million people, making India the second-largest sufferer of HIV–Aids in the world after South Africa, which had 5.3 million infected people.[25] And the present is no guide to the future. One of the most terrifying features of the disease is the speed with which it spreads. In 1990 fewer than 1 per cent of South Africans had HIV; by 2005 that figure had shot up to 25 per cent. The epidemic has mutilated the economic prospects of entire tracts of Africa. America's National Intelligence Council estimates that unless India moves on to a war footing against the disease, it will have 25 million HIV-infected people by 2010, rising to 40 million by 2013 (which is only marginally less than the world's total HIV population in 2006).[26] Furthermore, most independent experts believe India's official statistics underestimate the true scale of the problem. Some states, such as Bihar, provide no data at all. Since there are millions of

Bihari men working in cities like New Delhi and Mumbai and then going home to their wives in the village once or twice a year, it is hard to believe the state is not suffering from the epidemic.

India must overcome a fundamental problem if it is to do better than sub-Saharan Africa in checking the spread of Aids: it must recognise the unprecedented nature of the threat. In 2005 Richard Feachem, head of the Global Fund to Fight Aids, Tuberculosis and Malaria, estimated that India already had the largest number of HIV-infected people in the world, in spite of New Delhi's statistics. India's response to this statement was not encouraging. In spite of its sensational news value, Feachem's estimate received very little publicity. Meanwhile, the Indian government quibbled with the small print. To some extent India's change of government in 2004 had brought a significant improvement in official attitudes to the disease. Unlike the BJP-led government it replaced, Manmohan Singh's administration was at least prepared to admit the scale of the problem and discuss sexual behaviour at public forums.*

But Singh's good intentions alone are not sufficient to inspire confidence that India is doing enough to head off the disease before it becomes a pandemic. For example, New Delhi rejected the advice of the country's Law Commission in 2005 to make homosexuality legal. The statute dates back to the 1880s, when British civil servants labelled homosexuality unnatural behaviour. In its legal treatment of homosexuals India remains in the same category as Iran and Saudia Arabia. It is also behind the times in its official attitudes towards contraception. Fewer than half of India's population has access to regular contraception, compared to more than 80 per cent in China.[27] This might owe something

---

*His Hindu nationalist predecessors had alternated between denial and prejudice. It is common in Hindu nationalist circles to hear people say that homosexuality is a western import and that Indian women have much higher moral values than foreign women. Apart from the xenophobic undertones, such language adds to the mystification of Aids as a disease that affects only those who deserve it.

to the enduring influence of Gandhi, who, unlike Nehru, abhorred contraception and preached abstinence instead. In India HIV is spread mostly by truck drivers and migrant workers, who can have sex with prostitutes for as little as twenty cents.[28] Then they go home and infect their wives. Such is the ignorance about condoms that one health worker reported a remarkable story to a colleague of mine. He demonstrated to prostitutes how the contraceptive should be used by placing it over his thumb. They took him literally and put condoms on their thumbs when they had sex. 'Can you beat it?' said the activist.[29] 'There's so much to do and look at the odds we are fighting.'

India's approach to Aids mirrors other glaring contradictions in its society. Indian drug companies have developed the world's most cost-effective anti-retroviral treatments by improving on the manufacturing processes of western-patented triple-therapy dosages. Cipla, based in Mumbai, has done more than any other company in the world to bring affordable Aids treatment to millions of sub-Saharan Africans. Yet India is treating only a tiny fraction of its own victims. As with so many problems in India, the country has the technology and the resources to tackle the problem, but it lacks a sense of urgency. A colleague once said to me: 'In Africa poverty is a tragedy; in India it is a scandal.'[30] By this he was not implying that Africans are less capable of reaching economic modernity than Indians, simply that India began life as a nation with better institutions and more intellectual capital than its counterparts in Africa. Having observed what has happened to Africa, India knows all about the human tragedy of Aids. It also knows the damage the disease can do to the economy in terms of crippling the workforce. The Bill and Melinda Gates Foundation has pumped a lot of money into India to assist in Aids treatment and prevention. In addition Bill Clinton, the former US President, has committed his presidential foundation to developing Aids-treatment drugs with Indian pharmaceutical companies and making them available to the poor in Africa, India and elsewhere. Clinton's advice to India should not be ignored. 'I want to be serious here and say that this is not something that you can take casually,' he said on a visit to Delhi in 2004. 'There is no time to waste and every day you delay you put India's economic future at risk. You have come too far and worked too hard for your future to choose any other course. But if you do not act now millions will die who do not need to die.'[31]

The fourth and final major challenge facing India is the need to protect and strengthen its liberal democracy. When India achieved independence many foreigners saw its diversity as a weakness. As we have seen, in some respects India's social divisions do impose a cost on the governance of the nation. But diversity is also India's greatest strength. Nowadays intellectual fashion has swung around to India's point of view. The remarkable project in Europe to build a continental union of many races, nationalities, religions and languages was born as an idea only a few years after India came into existence as a nation. It has taken many centuries of bloodshed and slaughter – the like of which India has never experienced – for Europe to reach this conclusion. India can teach Europe, South-east Asia and other parts of the world a great deal about how to keep a multinational, multi-ethnic entity together without imposing uniformity on its people or denying them basic freedoms. It can still live up to the dreams of Nehru and Gandhi and become a political beacon to the world. But in order to do so India must guard against a number of threats to its uncompleted project of constitutional liberalism. It must also complete that project.

The most coherent threat to India's liberal democracy is Hindu nationalism. The defeat of the BJP-led government in 2004 and the subsequent outbreak of bitter recrimination with the Hindu nationalist movement persuaded many people that saffron politics was on the decline. This may well prove to be true, but the BJP can still command almost a quarter of the national vote, which, with the exception of Congress (just over a quarter), is more than three times higher than any other party. The influence of the movement as a whole in society is arguably even greater. The *Sangh Parivar* controls India's largest trade union, its largest students' union and the largest network of daily and weekly publications in India.[32] The movement is attempting to repackage itself to fit in with a rapidly modernising India, so its image may change. But its basic aim – which is to downgrade the status of India's religious minorities, through peaceful or violent means – remains the same. There are concerns about the loyalties of Kashmiri Muslims that must be tackled, but attaching a stigma to 150 million Indians is not the solution. It is a recipe for permanent civil war. Readers will have noticed that I have had little positive to say about Hindu nationalism. Not only does it preach a violent and vengeful philosophy but it tarnishes by association all that is good and tolerant about Hinduism. If the BJP wishes to regain national office it should focus on combating corruption and modernising India's state. This would clearly differentiate it from Congress, which, apart from the royal touch, remains essentially a party of bureaucracy and patronage. In order to sell its message with any credibility the BJP would have to sever its ties with the RSS, which remains an unreconstructed enemy of liberalism and a threat to India's national identity. This currently seems unlikely. But unless the BJP does so, few will believe its claim to be reinventing itself as a moderate party of the centre-right.

India also needs to strengthen its system of parliamentary and local democracy. Preventing criminals from standing in elections would be a start.* But India must also find ways of raising the calibre of politicians in general. The quality of debate and scrutiny in India's Lok Sabha (parliament) is remarkably poor for a nation

---

*In 2003 India's Supreme Court made it compulsory for election candidates to publish their 'criminal antecedents', financial assets and educational qualifications. This boosted transparency but it did not result in a reduction of alleged criminals entering politics.

that has so many eloquent talkers and sharp intellects. The quality of Indian parliamentarians has declined markedly over the last generation, which has taken its toll on the quality of public reasoning. In the 1950s parliament met on average for between 120 and 138 days a year. The average today is between 70 and 80 days a year. This contrasts with the UK, where the House of Commons meets for 170 days a year, and the United States, where Congress meets for 150 days a year. Indian politicians often profess a passionate commitment to a subject or a cause and then do not bother to show up for the debate, the committee process or even the final vote. The Speaker of India's parliament frequently has to adjourn proceedings because MPs are unable to maintain discipline. India is a paradox: it has an impressive democracy that is peopled, for the most part, by unimpressive politicians. As Anil Ambani, one of India's most intelligent industrialists, who was elected to the upper chamber in 2004, wrote: 'It is time for India's VIPs to follow the people who get no pay for no work.'[33] Unfortunately Mr Ambani allowed himself to be sponsored for parliament by the Samajwadi Party – a party with a less than impeccable record for probity in office.

Finally, India could better protect its internal system of liberal democracy by improving relations with its immediate neighbours, none of which has been able to maintain democracy for long, and most of which are highly prone to instability. The most obvious external threat to India comes from Pakistan, assisted to some extent by China, although Beijing's support for Islamabad has moderated in recent years. At the time of writing, India was in the third year of its peace process with Pakistan, which showed signs of continuing. People far beyond the shores of the Indian subcontinent will be hoping that the process entrenches itself and becomes irreversible. India can foster this by shedding its deep-seated neurosis about its neighbour. Pakistan has many flaws, but India has yet fully to come to terms with its neighbour's existence. As the smaller and less secure nation, Pakistan is more volatile and more prone to initiating conflicts, whether by proxy, through terrorism, or by threatening wider conflagration by dropping hints about its nuclear weapons. India must adopt imaginative strategies to encourage a more moderate and less paranoid mindset in Islamabad. More generous and far-sighted statesmanship from New Delhi would help, particularly in addressing the aspirations of the Kashmiri people. Nobody except Pakistan expects or requires India to abandon its sovereignty over Kashmir. But we live in a changing world where new technology and economic integration are making borders less relevant. It is surely not beyond the intelligence and ingenuity of South Asia's diplomats to devise a fungible and blurred sovereignty for Kashmir that would be accepted by large majorities in both countries, as well as by Kashmiris themselves.

India also has a history of awkward relations with Bangladesh, which, in spite of the fact that it was created by India in 1971, is both fearful and resentful of its large neighbour. There are an estimated ten to fifteen million illegal Bangladeshi immigrants in India already, and many more will come if Bangladesh cannot achieve stable, long-term economic growth. India must take the largest share of the blame for the fact that trade is so anaemic within the South Asian Association for Regional Cooperation (which comprises India, Pakistan, Bangladesh, Nepal, Sri Lanka, the Maldives and Bhutan). Trade between the seven member countries amounts to less than 5 per cent of their overall trade flow. This is feeble. As by far the largest member country, nothing will change without India's lead. If it wishes to curb worrying signs of Islamic fundamentalism in Bangladesh and Pakistan, which will increasingly spill over into India, it must offer these countries an incentive to maintain social stability by giving their exporters generous access to India's vast domestic market. If India also wishes to curb the growing influence in the region of China, which maintains warm relations with Bangladesh, Pakistan and sometimes even Nepal, then it should try to treat its neighbours as partners, not as irritants.

Relations between India and Nepal have always been close, but, true to form, the former's diplomats can rarely resist the temptation to patronise their counterparts from the small Himalayan kingdom. Nepal is suffering from a decade-old Maoist rebellion. India has its own Maoist problem, with an estimated ten thousand guerrillas, or Naxalites, operating in the forests and remote areas between Bihar, which borders Nepal, and Andhra Pradesh in the south. This so-called 'red corridor' does not threaten India's national stability, but it destroys law and order in some of India's poorest states. India must tackle the domestic problem by providing a higher quality of governance. But foreign policy should also play a larger role. The Naxalites have strong links with Nepal's Maoists. Understandably, India does not want to show any signs of support for the 2005 Nepalese 'royal coup' that was launched by King Gyanendra, and which amounted to a public relations victory for the republican Maoists. But India can still help Nepal to defang its Maoist threat by assisting the restoration of democracy in the Hindu kingdom.

Most of this chapter has focused on the challenges India faces in the coming years if it is to continue to ascend the international rankings. They are Herculean. But equally, its advantages are colossal. India never lacks for scale. In spite of the pressures of population density, India's clearest advantage over China and other developing countries is its demographic profile. From 2010, China's dependency ratio – the proportion of the working-age population to the rest – will start to deteriorate. In contrast, India's dependency ratio will continue to improve until the 2040s.[34] In the next twenty years the proportion of dependants to workers will fall from 60 per cent of the population to 50 per cent. This will give India's economy a large 'demographic dividend'. It is commonplace to say a nation's future lies in its youth. But India's future also lies in its youthfulness. The higher the proportion of the population that is of working age, the higher the rate of savings in the economy. A higher savings rate boosts investment, which lifts economic growth in a virtuous circle that for India stretches almost as far as the eye can see. Already India's savings rate is improving – from about 18 per cent of gross domestic product in 1990 to 26 per cent in 2006. This is still well below China's savings rate of more than 40 per cent, but China's rate is falling, while India's is rising. India is also improving its economic efficiency. It has achieved between 6 and 8 per cent GDP growth with a savings rate of between a fifth and a quarter of national income. Growth in China has been comparatively expensive.

Furthermore, India has accomplished high growth without any of the tools of an autocratic state. No government in a democracy can impose compulsory saving on its population – as happened in much of East Asia – and hope to be re-elected. Equally, no government in a democracy is in a position to impose family planning, as China has done with its 'one-child' policy. India's growth potential is even more striking if you consider how much has been achieved with so little. It lacks the modern infrastructure projects that have helped propel China forward. It lacks foreign direct investment, which at $5 billion in 2005 was one-tenth the amount that China attracted. And it lacks universal literacy. Yet its economy is still growing rapidly. Imagine what India could achieve if it drastically improved its infrastructure or raised the quality of elementary education.

India also possesses institutional advantages that have convinced some people that the Indian tortoise will eventually overtake the Chinese hare. As India's economy develops, these 'soft' advantages, such as an independent judiciary and a free media, are likely to generate ever-greater returns. Many investors are deterred by the country's bureaucracy, but none fear that they would be subjected to the arbitrary controls on freedom of speech that Yahoo, Google and Rupert Murdoch's News Corporation have suffered (and to which they have reluctantly acquiesced) in

China. India can also draw on a deep well of intellectual capital. One in four business start-ups in Silicon Valley are launched by non-resident Indians. Almost half of America's annual H1B visas are awarded to Indians. More than a hundred multinational companies have research and development centres in India, compared to just thirty-three in China.[35]

None of these expectations of India's growing economic strengths can be taken for granted, which is why so much of this chapter has focused on the problems rather than the opportunities that confront the country in the coming years. India has in the past demonstrated a tendency to shoot itself in the foot. As the joke goes, 'India never misses an opportunity to miss an opportunity.' It is also suffering from a premature spirit of triumphalism, believing it is destined to achieve greatness in the twenty-first century without having to do very much to assist the process. Much of this self-confidence stems from the country's sheer weight of numbers. The nation's elites assess India purely in terms of its economic size, rather than comparing the standard of living of its people with those in other countries. Surpassing the overall size of Japan's economy is all very well (it is projected to happen during the 2020s on a dollar basis*), but Japan would still have only a tenth of India's population, and virtually nobody living in poverty. A nation should surely be judged by how it treats its people, not by how many people it has, or by how many nuclear weapons it has developed. Which brings us to one final challenge that India must overcome in the near future: the complacency of its privileged classes. The key to overcoming the first four problems lies in injecting a much greater sense of urgency into the mindsets of India's politico-bureaucratic elites. This will come only if India's electorate at large is more alert to the country's challenges and can transmit greater pressure through the ballot

---

*India is already very close to overtaking Japan's GDP by purchasing power parity – a measure of what you can buy if you convert dollars into the local currency.

box to reform the state. India is not on autopilot to greatness. But it would take an incompetent pilot to crash the plane. As Vijay Kelkar, one of India's wisest economists, has written: 'The twenty-first century is India's to lose.'[36]

I had just wrestled my way through the bustle and clamour of the crowded railway platform and was looking forward to a night of untroubled sleep. I had booked a berth in the first-class sleeper carriage, which in India still retains much of the feather-bedded comfort of the classical railway experience. It also shuts out the noise and the heat. I enjoy the little things, like adjusting the reading lamp or twiddling with the temperature controls. It provides a temporary break from the world outside. The Indian train journey is invariably soporific. There are few more comfortable sensations than fighting a losing battle with sleep as you watch India float past your window.

'What is your name?' asked a voice on the bunk opposite to mine. I turned towards the questioner and saw a young Sikh boy assessing me curiously. I answered his question. 'And which country are you from?' Again, I answered. 'I wrote a letter to the Queen once,' he said. 'She still hasn't replied.' He told me he had written to advise Her Majesty that she should visit India more often because lots of good things were happening here. He had also written a letter to President Bush, advising him to pull American forces out of Iraq. Again, he had received no reply. I asked him his age, which was ten, and where he went to school, which was in Allahabad. His father, who was not accompanying him, was a major in the army. His mother, who was on the bunk below (Indian first-class compartments always have four berths), then told him to leave the stranger alone and go to sleep. She switched off the main light. The young boy waited for a few minutes until he was sure his mother was asleep. Then he switched on his reading lamp and trained it on me. He caught me just as I was about to descend into the oblivion of a deep sleep. 'Tell me some interesting things,' said the cheerful voice. 'I have no plans to go to sleep tonight.'

I tried many different arguments to convince my young interrogator to turn off his light and go to sleep. But he managed somehow to brush aside all my pleadings, inducements, threats and protestations without enraging me. His persistence was too artless. 'I still don't understand why we can't have a conversation,' he said. So I resigned myself to his suggestion of a general knowledge test. I started with simple questions, which he brushed aside easily – the Prime Minister of India, then the Finance Minister, then India's biggest river, then the capital of Sri Lanka. 'I'm not completely stupid,' he said. So I moved on to the capitals of Europe, which he found a piece of cake, then the flora and fauna of India, about which he had far greater knowledge than I, then the presidents of America, and so on. After about an hour of swatting flies, he suddenly decided he wanted to scrutinise my career and educational background. Each of his questions was informed and refined by my previous answer. He was beginning to build my profile. It felt, in fact, like a criminal profile. Periodically he trained his lamp on me to check my energy was not flagging.

Finally, I struck a deal with my restless torturer. He would let me go to sleep if I gave him my mobile-phone number so that he could call me whenever he wanted to continue the conversation. We shook on it. But he had interpreted the deal far too literally. I do not know how long I had been asleep when my pillow started vibrating and brought me awake with a start. The phone underneath was ringing. 'I just wanted to check you didn't give me the wrong number,' said a familiar voice from the bunk opposite, speaking on his own previously undeclared mobile. I rebuked him sharply, only to regret it straight away. 'There's no time to lose,' he said, looking crestfallen. 'The train arrives in five hours. What shall we talk about?'

So our conversation resumed. Every hour or so the train would stop at one of north India's innumerable provincial towns. A couple of times we got down on to the platform to buy a cup of milky *chai masala* served in the disposable earthenware cups that are unique to India. I began to feel entertained by his unflagging curiosity and precocious intelligence. There cannot be many ten-year-olds in the world carrying around this amount of information in their heads. In spite of his utter disregard for my sleeping plans, he remained courteous to a fault. He was also wily. 'Would you like another of my biscuits?' he asked whenever my eyelids appeared to be wavering.

Eventually, having mined me for all the information he possibly could, he announced it was time to sleep. Dawn was already intruding. There was only about an hour of the journey left. 'We should really go to sleep now,' he said in a tone of mild admonition, gently wobbling his head in the way only Indians can. 'Tomorrow we can continue our conversation. Good night.' Within seconds he was asleep. But I was well past the point of no return. For some reason I found myself laughing. It began slowly, originating in the abdomen and rumbled its way silently upwards. It was that rare kind of laugh that spreads through the body and fills you – for the duration, at least – with a humorous optimism. Someone once said to me: 'Remember, India always wins.' India has a way of confounding you and still making you laugh about it. My chuckling did not subside until the train had reached Delhi.

NOTES

Introduction

1 <http://www.indiayogi.com/content/indsaints/mother.asp>.
2 Ramachandra Guha, 'Churchill's Indiaspeak', in *The Hindu* Sunday magazine, 5 June 2005.
3 André Malraux, *Tristes Tropiques*, cited in Pankaj Mishra, ed., *India in Mind,* (Vintage, New York, 2005), p. 172.
4 Amartya Sen, *The Argumentative Indian: Writings on Indian History, Culture and Identity* (Allen Lane, London, 2005), p. 152.
5 *Ibid.*, p. xiv.
6 This story was first told by Arun Shourie in his speech at the annual Dhirubhai Ambani Memorial Lecture in Mumbai, 2003. It has been confirmed to the author by Anil Ambani, Dhirubhai's younger son.
7 M. J. Akbar, *Nehru: The Making of India*, 3rd edn (Lotus Collection of Roli Books, New Delhi, 2005), p. 469.
8 Christophe Jaffrelot, *Dr Ambedkar and Untouchability: Analysing and Fighting Caste* (Permanent Black, New Delhi, 2005), p. 110.
9 Richard Lannoy, *The Speaking Tree: A Study of Indian Culture and Society*, 2nd edn (Oxford University Press, Oxford, 1971), p.138.
10 See Akbar, *Nehru*, p. 71.
11 *Ibid.*, p. 239.
12 *Ibid.*, p. 242.

Chapter 1 Global and Medieval

1 Pankaj Mishra, ed., *India in Mind* (Vintage, New York, 2005), p. 303.
2 Lloyd I. Rudolph and Susanne Hoeber Rudolph, *In Pursuit of*

Lakshmi: The Political Economy of the Indian State (Longman, New Delhi, 1998), p. 297.

3 Francine R. Frankel, *India's Political Economy, 1947–2004: The Gradual Revolution*, 2nd edn (Oxford University Press, New Delhi, 2005), p. 131.

4 *Lok Sabha Debates*, 19 February 1959, quoted in *ibid*.

5 *Congress Bulletin*, April–May 1969, quoted in *ibid*.

6 I am indebted for many of these points to Vijay Kelkar, who retired in 2004 as economic adviser to the Finance Minister, both in conversation and in his articles.

7 Uma Das Gupta, *Rabindranath Tagore: A Biography* (Oxford University Press, New Delhi, 2004), p. 32.

8 I am indebted to Omkar Goswami, head of CERG, a consultancy, and former chief economist of the Confederation of Indian Industry, for his studies on Indian agriculture and patterns of rural spending.

9 Tim Dyson, Robert Cassen and Leela Visaria, eds, *Twenty-first Century India: Population, Economy, Human Development and the Environment* (Oxford University Press, New Delhi, 2004), p. 168.

10 Gurcharan Das, *The Elephant Paradigm* (Penguin India, New Delhi, 2002).

11 See Rudolph and Rudolph *In Pursuit of Lakshmi*, p. 10, or consult any of the US National Intelligence Assessments of recent years.

12 See 2005 Human Development Report of UNDP.

13 CLSA, *The India Paradox*, Spring 2005.

14 *Made in India: The Next Big Manufacturing Story*, a McKinsey–CII report, October 2005.

15 Rakesh Mohan, 'Managing Metros', *Seminar*, January 2006.

16 *Ibid*.

17 See World Bank, *Poverty in India: The Challenge of Uttar Pradesh* (Washington, DC, 2003), p. 2.

Chapter 2 The Burra Sahibs

1 Filippo Osella and Caroline Osella in C. J. Fuller and Véronique Bénéï, eds, *The Everyday State & Society in Modern India* (Social Science Press, New Delhi, 2000), pp. 149–50.

2 Arun Shourie, *Governance and the Sclerosis That Has Set In* (Rupa & Co., New Delhi, 2004), pp. 3–7.

3 All of the following examples are drawn from the *Arthashastra*.

4 As explained by Thomas R. Trautmann, 'Foreword' to A. L. Basham, *The Wonder That Was India*, 3rd edn (Picador, New Delhi, 2004).

5 Philip Mason, 'Introduction', in *The Men Who Ruled India* (Rupa & Co., New Delhi, 1985).

6 *Ibid.*

7 Nirad C. Chaudhuri, 'Introduction', in *Autobiography of an Unknown Indian*.

8 Rudolph and Rudolph *In Pursuit of Lakshmi*, p. 61.

9 World Bank, *State Fiscal Reforms in India*, 2004, p. 21

10 Bimal Jalan, *The Future of India* (Viking, New Delhi, 2005), p. 27.

11 Pratap Bhanu Mehta, *The Burden of Democracy* (Penguin, New Delhi, 2003), p. 115.

12 Parth J. Shah and Naveen Mandava, *Law, Liberty & Livelihood: Making a Living on the Street* (Academic Foundation in association with the Centre for Civil Society, New Delhi, 2005), p. 28. They estimate the average bribe is 200 rupees a month.

13 *Ibid.*, p. 25.

14 See the UNDP's 2005 Human Development Report to compare country indices.

15 *Ibid.* India spends just 0.9 per cent of GDP on public health, compared to China's 2 per cent.

16 UNDP Development Report 2005.

17 To cite a few, see reports by India's Planning Commission, by the government's Centre for Vigilance on Corruption, the many writings by Jean Dréze, a noted economist, or the findings of the Centre for the Study of Developing Societes, a think tank in New Delhi.

18 Mehta, *The Burden of Democracy*, p. 104.

19 Rudolph and Rudolph, *In Pursuit of Lakshmi*, p. 89.

20 Jalan, *The Future of India*, pp. 107–8.

21 World Bank, *State Fiscal Reforms in India*, 2004, p. 11.

22 This is a detailed estimate provided by the National Institute for Public Finance, a government-sponsored think tank.

23 Sen, *The Argumentative Indian*, p. 206.

24 McKinsey Report on India, 2001.

25 A *smriti-sutra* (*Legal Commentaries*), cited in Basham, *The Wonder That Was India*, p. 115.

26 An estimate by ICICI Bank, India's largest private sector bank.

27 Craig Jeffrey and Jens Lerche in Fuller and Bénéï, eds, *The Everyday State & Society in Modern India*, p. 100.

28 Rudolph and Rudolph, *In Pursuit of Lakshmi*, p. 1.

Chapter 3 Battles of the Righteous

1 V. S. Naipaul, *India: A Million Mutinies Now* (Vintage, London, 1998), p. 517.

2 Lannoy, *Speaking Tree*, lists dozens of subtle differences in meaning of the word *dharma*, pp. 216–22.

3 Basham, *The Wonder That Was India*, p. 92.

4 *Ibid.*, pp. 143–4.

5 *Ibid.*, p. 67

6 *Ibid.*, p. 81.

7 Pradipta Chaudhury in *Seminar*, 549 (May 2005), p. 26.

8 I have taken all of these observations about Mahar village life from Neera Burra, 'Buddhism, Conversion and Identity' in M. N. Srinivas, ed., *Caste: Its Twentieth Century Avatar*, (Penguin India, New Delhi, 1996), pp. 155–69.

9 There are numerous and varying estimates of the average cost of elections in India. Probably the best research comes from Lok Satta, a Hyderabad-based body that monitors politics: <http://www.prajanet.org>.

10 Data from the Public Affairs Centre, a non-governmental think tank based in Bangalore, from its report: *Holding a Mirror to the New Lok Sabha*, by Dr Samuel Paul and Professor Vivekananda: <http://www.pacindia.org>.

11 Most of this data comes from the 2001 census but also from National Sample Surveys that look at the monthly nutritional intake of India's poor. Omkar Gosawami, who heads CERG, a consultancy in Delhi, provided me with most of the combined data.

12 *Ibid.*

13 Edward Luce, 'Beating Back the Brahmins', *Financial Times* magazine, 5 July 2003.

14 Myron Weiner in Ashutosh Varshney, ed., *The Indian Paradox* (Sage, New Delhi), p. 57.

15 From Lucia Michelutti, whose instructive essay 'We [Yadavs] Are a Caste of Politicians': Caste and Modern Politics in a North Indian

Town', appears in Dipankar Gupta, ed., *Caste in Question* (Sage, New Delhi, 2004), pp. 43–72.

16 From an intriguing essay by Anuja Agrawal, 'The Bedias are Rajputs: Caste Consciousness of a Marginal Community', in *ibid.*, pp. 221–45

17 National Human Rights Commission, *Report on the Prevention of Atrocities against Scheduled Castes*, 2004, p. 114.

18 *The Essential Writings of B. R. Ambedkar*, ed. Valerian Rodrigues (Oxford University Press, New Delhi, 2002), p. 267.

19 The term was coined by M. N. Srinivas, the 'father of Indian sociology'.

20 See Kanchan Chandra's superb book, *Why Ethnic Parties Succeed: Patronage and Ethnic Head Counts in India* (Cambridge University Press, Cambridge, 2004), p. 145.

21 *Ibid.*, p. 206.

22 Jean Dréze quoted in World Bank, *State Fiscal Reforms in India*, 2004, p. 8.

23 Quoted in *India Today*, 8 August 2005, p. 49.

24 The poll of fifteen thousand people nationwide was conducted by the Centre for the Study of Developing Societies for the IBN–CNN news channel.

Chapter 4 The Imaginary Horse

1 Quoted in Sen, *The Argumentative Indian*, p. 159.

2 Tupkary said some of the terms and ideas had been borrowed from Alvin Toffler, the American futurologist, whose books, including *The Third Wave* and *Future Shock*, were widely read in the 1970s and 1980s.

3 Readers interested in the Harappans have much from which to choose. They could start with Romila Thapar's *Early India*, A. Ghosh's *The City in Early Historical India*, F. Braudel's *A History of Early Civilisations* or Basham's *The Wonder That Was India*.

4 In interview with the author, 2004.

5 Natwar Jha and N. S. Rajaram, *The Deciphered Indus Script* (Aditya Prakashan, New Delhi, 2000).

6 Sen, *The Argumentative Indian*, p. 66.

7 Basham, *The Wonder That Was India*, p. 32.

8 Benedict Anderson, *Imagined Communities* (Verso, London, 1983) p. 15.

9 Christophe Jaffrelot, *The Hindu Nationalist Movement and Indian Politics, 1925 to the 1990s* (Hurst & Co, London, 1996).

10 All the Golwalkar quotes are taken from either *Bunch of Thoughts* or *We, or Our Nationhood Defined*.

11 For a detailed and instructive account of the RSS, see Walter K. Andersen and Shridhar D. Damle, *The Brotherhood in Saffron: The RSS and Hindu Revivalism* (Vistaar Publications, New Delhi, 1987).

12 Sen, *The Argumentative Indian*, p. 48.

13 To name a few, there are compendious reports by Amnesty International, Human Rights Watch, India's National Human Rights Commission, and India's Concerned Citizens' Tribunal. All of these reports reach much the same conclusions.

14 From the report *How Has the Gujarat Massacre Affected Minority Women? – The Survivors Speak*, contained in John Dayal, ed., *Gujarat 2002: Untold and Retold Stories of the Hindutva Lab* (Media House, Delhi, 2002), p. 289.

15 As quoted in an article by the author in the *Financial Times*, 15 April 2002.

16 Neena Vyas in *The Hindu*, 21 October 2002.

17 Amnesty International, Public Statement 183, 16 October 2002.

18 *Sify News*, 20 November 2004.

19 Swapan Dasgupta, 'Evangelical Hinduism', *Seminar*, January 2005.

Chapter 5 Long Live the Sycophants!

1 From Sonia Gandhi, *Rajiv* (Viking, New Delhi, 1992).

2 *Ibid.*

3 Quoted in Inder Malhotra's highly enjoyable *Dynasties of India and beyond* (HarperCollins, New Delhi, 2003), p.18.

4 Akbar, *Nehru*, pp. 24-6.

5 *Ibid.*, p. 23.

6 *Ibid.*, p. 42.

7 Katherine Franks, *Indira: The Life of Indira Nehru Gandhi* (HarperCollins, New Delhi, 2001), p. 399.

8 *Ibid.*

9 From Frankel, *India's Political Economy*, p. 679.

10 *Ibid.*, p. 203.

11 *Ibid.*, p. 222.

12 Cited in Yusuf Ahmed, *Sonia Gandhi: Triumph of Will* (Tara-India Research Press, New Delhi, 2005), p. 156.

13 A very apt description I borrow from Frankel, *India's Political Economy*, p. 685.

14 World Bank, *State Fiscal Reforms in India*, 2004, p. xxii.

15 Priya Basu, *India's Financial Sector Reforms, Recent Reforms, Future Challenges* (Macmillan India, New Delhi, 2005), p. 148,

16 'Introduction', in *ibid.*

17 Prime Minister's address to the nation, 24 June 2004.

18 This estimate come variously from the government, the promoters of the legislation and independent economists.

19 Swapan Dasgupta in *The Pioneer*, 14 August 2005.

20 Mehta, *The Burden of Democracy*, p. 88.

21 Ahmed, *Sonia Gandhi*, p. 95.

22 *Ibid.*, p. 245.

23 *Ibid.*, p. xxx.

24 Malhotra, *Dynasties of India and beyond*, p. 29.

25 At a press conference given by MKSS and Parivartan in New Delhi, August 2005.

26 Dyson, Cassen and Visaria, eds, *Twenty-first Century India*, p. 128.

Chapter 6 Many Crescents

1 Quoted in Akbar, *Nehru*, p. 6.

2 *Ibid.*, p. 17.

3 Francis Robinson, *Islam and Muslim History in South Asia* (Oxford University Press, New Delhi, 2000), p. 260.

4 The description provided by the school itself on its website: <http://www.darululoom-deoband.com>.

5 Akbar, *Nehru*, p. 380.

6 *Ibid.*, p. 318.

7 Rudolph and Rudolph, *In Pursuit of Lakshmi*, p. 70.

8 Robinson, *Islam and Muslim History*, p. 223.

9 Akbar, *Nehru*, p. 239.

10 *Ibid.*, p. 270.

11 Quoted in Robinson, *Islam and Muslim History*, p. 225.

12 Akbar, *Nehru*, p. 374.

13 There has been some controversy over whether the Maharajah signed the papers before or after Nehru airlifted troops to Kashmir, and whether he signed the papers under duress, with Indian historians and Pakistani historians naturally taking opposing views.

14 Stephen P. Cohen, *India: Emerging Power* (Oxford University Press, New Delhi, 2001), p. 224.

15 Stephen P. Cohen, *The Idea of Pakistan* (Oxford University Press, New Delhi, 2004), p. 243.

16 *Ibid.*, p. 249.

17 *Ibid.*, p. 58.

18 Census of India, 2001: *The First Report on Religion Data*.

19 Zarina Bhatty in Srinivas, ed., *Caste*, p. 246.

20 *Ibid.*, pp. 256-7.

21 Data from the Administrative Staff College of India (ASCI), Hyderabad.

22 Data from Educare, a Hyderabad-based non-governmental organisation that researches informal sector – or private – education.

Chapter 7 A Triangular Dance

1 I owe much of this insight into Gandhi to conversations with – and the thoughtful writings of – Ramachandra Guha, one of India's leading historians, who is currently writing a biography of Gandhi.

2 Quoted in the Washington-based Centre for Strategic and International Studies' 'US–India Relations: Convergence of Interests', *South Asia Monitor*, 84 (July 2005).

3 For a comprehensive and authoritative account of India's nuclear weapons programme, see George Perkovitch, *India's Nuclear Bomb: The Impact on Global Proliferation* (Oxford University Press, New Delhi, 1999), and Ashley Tellis, *India's Emerging Nuclear Posture: Between Recessed Deterrent and Ready Arsenal* (Rand, New Delhi, 2001).

4 Quoted in Cohen, *India: Emerging Power*, p. 257.

5 A phrase I borrowed from C. R. Mohan's *Crossing the Rubicon: The Shaping of India's New Foreign Policy* (Viking, New Delhi, 2003)

which provides a balanced assessment of India's post-non-align-ment foreign policy.

6 Cohen, *India: Emerging Power*, p. 86.

7 National Security Archives: <http://www.gwu.edu/~nsarchiv/news/20050629/>.

8 <http://www.rediff.com/news/2002/may/30war2.htm>.

9 <http://www.infopak.gov.pk/President_Addresses/presidential_addresses_index.htm>.

10 Farhan Bokhari and Edward Luce, *Financial Times*, 'We Want Peace, but with Honour – Musharraf', 28 May 2002.

11 James Kynge and Edward Luce, 'India and China Let Trade Take the Sting out of Tensions', *Financial Times*, 24 October 2003,

12 *Ibid.*

13 Quoted in Perkovitch, *India's Nuclear Bomb*, pp. 442–3.

14 Quoted in Richard McGregor and Edward Luce, 'A Share of Spoils: Beijing and New Delhi Get Mutual Benefits from Growing Trade', *Financial Times*, 24 February 2005.

15 Institute of Peace and Conflict Studes: <http://www.ipcs.org>.

16 *Ibid.*

17 From Ashley Tellis, *India as a New Global Power: An Action Agenda for the United States* (Carnegie Endowment, Washington, DC, 2005).

18 A phrase first used about India by the Bush administration in 2001 and reiterated ever since.

19 This quote comes from off-the-record briefings given by Ambassador Blackwill to a small group of foreign journalists. Since Blackwill is no longer in the Bush administration, I am taking the liberty of putting them on the record.

20 From Tellis, *India as a New Global Power*.

21 *Ibid.*

22 Strobe Talbott, *Engaging India: Diplomacy, Democracy and the Bomb* (Viking, New Delhi, 2005), p. 5.

23 Cohen, *India: Emerging Power*, p. 62.

24 From India's Ministry of External Affairs: <http://www.mea.gov.in/pressbriefing/2001/10/30pb01.htm>.

25 From another of Ambassador Blackwill's briefings to the foreign media in New Delhi.

26 *Ibid.*

27 Statistics derived from Nasscom, the Indian software body: most of

the remaining Indian software earnings come from the UK and Australia. <http://www.nasscom.org>.

28 From transcript of the Manmohan Singh interview conducted by Quentin Peel and Edward Luce that appeared in the *Financial Times*, 5 November 2004.

Chapter 8 New India, Old India

1 A term coined by Anderson in *Imagined Communities*.

2 Sen, *The Argumentative Indian*, p. 61.

3 Richard Eaton, *Essays on Islam and Indian History* (Oxford University Press, New Delhi, 2001), p. 108.

4 *Ibid.*, p. 105–6.

5 *Ibid.*, p. 124.

6 From Mishra, ed., *India In Mind*, p. 190.

7 From essay by J. Thavamangalam in Srinivas, ed., *Caste*, p. 269.

8 *Ibid.*, p. 280.

9 Quoted in Lannoy, *Speaking Tree*, p. 77.

10 Census, 2001.

11 Sen, *The Argumentative Indian*, pp. 225–6.

12 <http://www.hindu.com/thehindu/holnus/001200511270311.htm>.

13 *Sunday Brunch* magazine of *Hindustan Times*, 22 May 2005.

14 'Sex and the Single Woman', *India Today*, 26 September 2005, p. 43.

15 Dipankar Gupta, *Mistaken Modernity* (Harper Collins India, New Delhi, 2001), ch. 1.

16 Basham, *The Wonder That Was India*, p. 251.

17 Quoted in Lannoy, *Speaking Tree*, p. 330.

18 *Ibid.*, p. 306.

19 Basham, *The Wonder That Was India*, p. 262.

20 Myron Weiner, *The Child and the State in India* (Oxford University Press, New Delhi) pp. 23–7.

21 Estimates vary depending on the source. Main sources are government of India and Unicef.

22 Weiner, *The Child and the State*, pp. 127–178.

23 Mehta, *The Burden of Democracy*, p. 126.

24 Unicef estimates.

25 Weiner, *The Child and the State*, p. 201.

Conclusion: Hers to Lose

1 Shashi Tharoor, *India: Midnight to the Millennium* (Arcade, New York, 1997), p. 5.

2 'Weekend Ruminations', *Business Standard*, 11 September 2004.

3 There have been heated disputes about the degree to which poverty has been reduced since 1991. Ninan takes the largest estimate, which is the official figure used by the Indian government and the World Bank. Clearly India's Gini Coefficient – its measure of inequality – has risen since 1991, but that can be consistent with a sharply falling poverty ratio. Improvements in other figures, notably India's human development indicators, corroborate the poverty reduction data.

4 Weiner in Varshney, ed., *The Indian Paradox*, p. 36

5 By Selig Harrison (Princeton University Press, Princeton 1960).

6 Cohen, *The Idea of Pakistan*, p. 95.

7 Opening speech by Amartya Sen at a New Delhi conference in August 2003 on Sen's book *Development as Freedom*.

8 From a speech given by Arun Shourie in 2003 entitled 'The Fate of Reforms'.

9 I owe this and several other insights in this section to Pranab Bardhan, a political scientist at Berkeley University, whose comparative writings on India's political economy are always sharp and thought-provoking. Two of his articles are particularly instructive: 'Democracy and Distributive Politics in India' and 'Crouching Tiger, Lumbering Elephant: A China–India Comparison'. Both can be found on the Berkeley website: <www.berkeley.edu>.

10 The debate about the size of India's middle class is endless, with a huge variation in estimates. The most convincing data can be found at the National Council for Applied Economic Research, New Delhi.

11 Tim Dyson in Dyson, Cassen and Visaria, eds, *Twenty-first Century India*, p. 76.

12 From *Chindia: The Shape of Things to Come*, a report produced by CLSA, the French investment bank, in June 2005.

13 UNDP, Human Development Report, 2005.

14 From the Centre for Science and Environment, New Delhi.

15 Dyson, Cassen and Visaria, eds, *Twenty-first Century India*, p. 174.

16 *India's Investment Climate*, a joint World Bank–CII study, 2005.

17 This is a subjective judgement but it is shared, among others, by the World Bank; see above.

18 Vijay Kelkar, *India's Economic Future: Moving beyond State Capitalism*, the D. R. Gadgil Memorial Lecture, Mumbai, 26 October 2005, p. 50.

19 Estimate given in interview in December 2005 to the author by Dr Rajendra Pachauri, chairman of the United Nations' Inter-Governmental Panel on Climate Change, and head of the Energy Research Institute, New Delhi.

20 *Ibid.*

21 Dyson, Cassen and Visaria, eds, *Twenty-first Century India*, p. 190.

22 Pachauri interview.

23 TERI, *Looking Back to Think Ahead*, March 1998.

24 Estimates provided by India's Planning Commission.

25 Global Fund to Fight Aids, Tuberculosis and Malaria, Geneva.

26 Cited by Jo Johnson, 'Road to Ruin', *Financial Times*, 13 August 2005.

27 UNDP, Human Development Report, 2005.

28 Johnson, 'Road to Ruin'.

29 *Ibid.*

30 Martin Wolf, the *Financial Times*' main economics commentator and assistant editor, who worked extensively on India in the 1970s, when he was employed by the World Bank.

31 Quoted in Johnson, 'Road to Ruin'.

32 Cited in Christophe Jaffrelot, ed., *The Sangh Parivar: A Reader* (Oxford University Press, New Delhi, 2005), pp. 4–12.

33 Article by Anil Ambani in *Indian Express*, 4 September 2004.

34 Vijay Kelkar, *India's Growth on a Turnpike*, paper presented to the Australian National University, April 2004.

35 CLSA, *The Indian Paradox*, spring 2005.

36 Kelkar, *India's Growth on a Turnpike*.

GLOSSARY

Adivasi offical name for India's tribal groups – literally 'the ones who were already here'

aloo potato

Angrez English, often used to mean foreign

arti evening prayers

ashram monastery or retreat

badli casual labour

Bania merchant caste

Bhagavad Gita Hindu text interpolated in the Mahabharat, the longest epic.

bhakti medival anti-caste movements, usually devoted to one god.

Bharat ancient name for India

bhavan building.

bidi poor man's cigarette

bijli electricity

Brahmin the priestly caste

burqa complete veil worn by orthodox Muslim women

burra large

chai tea

Chamar an untouchable or Dalit caste, associated with scavenging

chamcha sycophant

chapatti flat north Indian bread

chappal sandals

charpoy a bed held together by woven jute

chawl working-class tenement

crore ten million

dal lentils

Dalit generic name given to untouchables, literally meaning 'broken to pieces' *dharma* multiple definitions, among which righteous, just and religious are most common

dharna a non-violent sit-down protest

dil heart

Doordarshan India's state television, literally meaning 'sight from afar'

fidayeen suicide terrorist

gau cow

ghar home

ghee clarified butter

goonda thug, political hatchetman

gopi cowgirl – associated with Krishna

Harijan Gandhi's name for untouchables, literally 'children of God'

Hindutva the project of Hindu nationalism, literally 'Hindu-ness'

janata public

jati sub-caste

jizya Islamic poll tax on unbelievers

kabbadi ancient Indian game, still popular today

karma past actions

Karwa Chauth Hindu festival in which a wife fasts for her husband's longevity

khadi homespun cotton

Khilafat 1920s movement to restore the Muslim Caliphate

Kshatriya warrior or military caste

kurta tunic

kutcha poor quality, literally 'raw'

lakh a hundred thousand

lathi bamboo stave used by police

linga phallic representation of Shiva

lok people

madrasa school for Muslim children

maidan public park

mandap ceremonial house of flowers, usually for weddings

mandir Hindu temple

masala spices

masjid mosque

maska to butter-up

mela fair

mithai sweetmeats

mofussil small town

mutt temple complex

namaste Hindi greeting

namaaz Muslim prayers

neem common tree in India with medicinal properties

nimbu lime

paan a leaf stuffed with betel nut and lime which is popular for chewing

panchayat local government

pani water

parivar family

peepul common tree

pracharak full-time Hindu nationalist volunteer

pucca good quality, literally 'cooked'

puja Hindu prayer

purana old

purdah a veil to conceal woman's face, literally 'curtain'

raj state

Rajput a warrior sub-caste

Rakhi Hindu festival where the sister ties a thread on her brother's wrist

roti flat bread

sabha assembly

sadak road

sadhu wandering ascetic

sahib foreign gentleman

salaam alekum Muslim greeting

salwar chameez loose-fitting trousers and tunic worn by women

samosa savoury fried pastry

sangh organisation

sanyasin a woman who renounces the material world

sari Indian women's garment

sarsanghchalak the most senior figure in the RSS Hindu nationalist group

shakha daily martial gathering of Hindu nationalists

shakti strength, feminine power

shala shelter

sherwani long formal tunic

stupa Buddhist temple

Sudra the lowest caste category (above untouchables)

swadeshi self-reliance

swaraj self-rule

swayamsevak volunteer

tandoor Indian barbecue

Upanishads collection of Hindu philosophical texts and commentaries

Vaishya merchant caste

varna the Sanskrit term for the four main castes (Brahmin, Kshatriya, Vaishya and Sudra)

vedas the earliest and most revered Hindu texts, originally preserved through oral recitation, of which the Rig-Veda is the most important

Yadav a lower caste associated with cow-herding

yatra procession

zamindar the name for the largest and most feudal landowners during the era of British rule

zindabad! long live! – used often at political rallies as a suffix to the name of the leader or the country (India, Pakistan, etc.)

INDEX